PROFESSIONAL
WORDPRESS® PLUGIN DEVELOPMENT

PROFESSIONAL

WordPress® Plugin Development

Brad Williams
Ozh Richard
Justin Tadlock

Wiley Publishing, Inc.

Professional WordPress® Plugin Development

Published by
Wiley Publishing, Inc.
10475 Crosspoint Boulevard
Indianapolis, IN 46256
www.wiley.com

Copyright © 2011 by Wiley Publishing, Inc., Indianapolis, Indiana

Published simultaneously in Canada

ISBN: 978-0-470-91622-3
ISBN: 978-1-118-07530-2 (ebk)
ISBN: 978-1-118-07532-6 (ebk)
ISBN: 978-1-118-07531-9 (ebk)

Manufactured in the United States of America

10 9 8 7 6 5 4 3 2 1

For general information on our other products and services please contact our Customer Care Department within the United States at (877) 762-2974, outside the United States at (317) 572-3993 or fax (317) 572-4002.

Wiley also publishes its books in a variety of electronic formats. Some content that appears in print may not be available in electronic books.

Library of Congress Control Number: 2011920897

To my Father, Robert "Basket Bob" Williams, for inspiring me to become the man I am today.

— BRAD WILLIAMS

To my wife Ariane for her support while I was escaping household chores, and to my kids Oscar and Cyrus who'll be WordPress hackers in 10 years.

— OZH RICHARD

To my family for allowing me to explore the online world as a career path and the WordPress community for inviting me in.

— JUSTIN TADLOCK

CREDITS

ABOUT THE AUTHORS

BRAD WILLIAMS is the CEO and co-founder of WebDevStudios.com. He is also a co-host on the SitePoint podcast and the co-author of *Professional WordPress*. Brad has been developing websites for more than 14 years, including the last 4 where he has focused on open-source technologies like WordPress. Brad has given presentations at various WordCamps across the country, is the organizer for the New Jersey and Philadelphia WordPress Meetups and WordCamp Philly. In 2010 Brad founded Pluginize.com, a company dedicated to building custom WordPress plugins.

OZH RICHARD is a web developer who started to use WordPress at version 1.0.1, published his first WordPress-powered website in May 2004, and released his first plugin three months later. He has since developed several popular plugins, won an Annual WordPress Plugin Competition, and is now an official judge. When not coding WordPress plugins or sharing tutorials, Ozh contributes to other Open Source projects such as YOURLS, a self-hosted URL shortener, or plays *Quake*. You can find Ozh online at http://ozh.org/.

JUSTIN TADLOCK is a Web developer and designer who coded his first Web page in 2003 at the age of 18, only months after getting his first computer. He found WordPress in 2005 and has been working with and contributing to the platform ever since. He has developed many popular WordPress plugins and themes while exploring several business paths using the open-source platform.

ACKNOWLEDGMENTS

THANK YOU to the love of my life, April, for your endless support, friendship, and continuing to put up with my nerdy ways. Thank you to my awesome nieces, Indiana Brooke and Austin Margaret. Thank you Carol Long for believing in this book idea and helping make it a reality. To Ozh and Justin, two amazing co-authors, your knowledge of WordPress is unmatched, and this book wouldn't have been what it is without you both. Thank you to the entire WordPress community for your support, friendships, motivation, and guidance. Thank you fizzypop for making WordCamp after parties the stuff of legend. Last but not least thank you to my ridiculous zoo: Lecter, Clarice, and Squeaks the Cat (aka Kitty Galore). Your smiling faces and wiggly butts always put a smile on my face.

— BRAD WILLIAMS

IT'S BEEN A LONG TIME in the WordPress community since I first started to dissect the few plugins that began to pop like daisies in 2004 and tried to understand how things worked. To all the coders who released the code that taught me the innards of WordPress, I can't express how much I owe you. To all the members of the WordPress community who don't write code but foster the creativity and water our community, thank you for your invaluable dedication. To Brad, who sent me that crazy proposal about a plugin book, I hope I'll cross the oceans one day to have a few beers with you. To Ronnie James Dio, Tom Araya, Bruce Dickinson, Blaze Bayley, Lemmy Kilmister, Dave Mustaine, Rob Zombie, Till Lindemann, and Mike Muir, whose gentle voices have lulled me and inspired me while I was writing late at night.

— OZH RICHARD

THE WORDPRESS COMMUNITY took me in as a lost kid who was trying to figure out life and presented me with opportunities that I'd never dreamed possible. A simple "thank you" is an understatement. To my plugin and theme users, you continue to inspire me and keep my skills sharp with your invaluable feedback and loyalty. To Brad, thank you for that oddly random email about writing a plugin book. To Ozh, thank you for coding all those cool plugins I learned from before becoming a developer myself. To Granny, thank you for allowing me to skip several dinners to work on this book. To my family and friends, thank you for supporting me and showing superhuman patience during hour-long conversations (i.e., crazed rants) about plugin development. Most importantly, to my father, who knows nothing about Web development but taught me everything about being successful and continues to teach me today.

— JUSTIN TADLOCK

CONTENTS

FOREWORD

STARTING OUT as a simple blogging system, over the last few years WordPress has morphed into a fully featured and widely used content management system. It offers individuals and companies world-wide a free and open-source alternative to closed-source and often very expensive systems.

When I say fully featured, that's really only true because of the ability to add any functionality needed in the form of a plugin. The core of WordPress is simple: You add in functionality with plugins as you need it. Developing plugins allows you to stand on the shoulders of a giant: You can showcase your specific area of expertise and help users benefit while not having to deal with parts of WordPress you don't care or know about.

I've written dozens of plugins, which together have been downloaded millions of times. Doing that has changed my life. It has helped me build out a business for myself, doing development and (SEO) consultancy work. This is in your outreach too!

I wish that when I started developing plugins for WordPress as a hobby, some five years back, this book had been around. It would have saved me countless hours of digging through code and half-finished documentation. I always ended up redoing pieces because I'd found yet another best practice or simply an easier way of doing things.

Although this book didn't exist yet, the authors of this book have always been a source of good information for me while developing my plugins. Each of them is an expert in his own right; together they are one of the best teams that could have been gathered to write this book.

WordPress makes it easy for people to have their say through words, sound, and visuals. For those who write code, WordPress allows you to express yourself in code. And it's simple. Anyone can write a WordPress plugin. With this guide in hand, you can write a plugin that is true to WordPress' original vision: Code is Poetry.

Happy coding!

JOOST DE VALK
Yoast.com

INTRODUCTION

DEAR READER, thank you for picking up this book! You have probably heard about WordPress already, the most popular self-hosted content management system (CMS) and blogging software in use today. WordPress powers literally millions of Web sites on the Internet, including high profile sites such as TechCrunch and CNN's blog. What makes WordPress so popular is that it's free, open source, and extendable beyond limits. Thanks to a powerful, architecturally sound, and easy-to-use plugin system, you can customize how WordPress works and extend its functionalities. There are already more than ten thousand plugins freely available in the official plugin repository, but they won't suit all your needs or client requests. That's where this book comes in handy!

As of this writing, we (Brad, Ozh, and Justin), have publicly released 50 plugins, which have been downloaded nearly one million times, and that's not counting private client work. This is a precious combined experience that we are going to leverage to teach you how to code your own plugins for WordPress by taking a hands-on approach with practical examples and real life situations you will encounter with your clients.

The primary reason we wanted to write this book is to create a preeminent resource for WordPress plugin developers. When creating plugins for WordPress, it can be a challenge to find the resources needed in a single place. Many of the online tutorials and guides are outdated and recommend incorrect methods for plugin development. This book is one of the most extensive collections of plugin development information to date and should be considered required reading for anyone wanting to explore WordPress plugin development from the ground up.

WHO THIS BOOK IS FOR

This book is for professional Web developers who want to make WordPress work exactly how they and their clients want. WordPress has already proven an exceptional platform for building any type of site from simple static pages to networks of full-featured communities. Learning how to code plugins will help you get the most out of WordPress and have a cost-effective approach to developing per-client features.

This book is also for the code freelancers who want to broaden their skill portfolio, understand the inner workings of WordPress functionality, and take on WordPress gigs. Since WordPress is the most popular software to code and power websites, it is crucial that you understand how things run under the hood and how you can make the engine work your way. Learning how to code plugins will be a priceless asset to add to your resume and business card.

Finally, this book is for hobbyist PHP programmers who want to tinker with how their WordPress blog works, discover the infinite potential of lean and flexible source code, and how they can interact with the flow of events. The beauty of open source is that it's easy to learn from and easy to give back in turn. This book will help you take your first step into a community that will welcome your creativity and contribution.

Simply put, this book is for anyone who wants to extend the way WordPress works, whether it is for fun or profit.

WHAT YOU NEED TO USE THIS BOOK

This book assumes you already have a Web server and WordPress running. For your convenience it is preferred that your Web server runs on your localhost, as it will be easier to modify plugin files as you read through the book, but an online server is also fine.

Code snippets written in PHP are the backbone of this book: You should be comfortable with reading and writing basic PHP code or referring to PHP's documentation to fill any gaps in knowledge about fundamental functions. Advanced PHP code tricks are explained, so you don't need to be a PHP expert.

You will need to have rudimentary HTML knowledge to fully understand all the code. A basic acquaintance with database and MySQL syntax will help with grasping advanced subjects. To make the most of the chapter dedicated to JavaScript and AJAX, comprehension of JavaScript code and jQuery syntax will be a plus.

WHAT THIS BOOK COVERS

As of this writing, WordPress 3.1 is around the corner and this book has been developed alongside this version. Following the best coding practices outlined in this book and using built-in APIs are keys to future-proof code that will not be deprecated when a newer version of WordPress is released. We believe that every code snippet in this book will still be accurate and up-to-date for several years, just as several plugins we coded many years ago are still completely functional today.

HOW THIS BOOK IS STRUCTURED

This book is, to date, one of the most powerful and comprehensive resources you can find about WordPress plugins. Advanced areas of the many WordPress APIs are covered, such as the Rewrite APIs, cron jobs, and Custom Post Types. This book is divided into three major parts. Reading the first three chapters (Introduction, Plugin Foundations, and Hooks) is required if you are taking your first steps in the wonders of WordPress plugins. Chapters 4 through 7 will cover most common topics in coding plugins, and understanding them will be useful when reading subsequent chapters. The remaining chapters cover advanced APIs and functions, can be read in any order, and will sometimes refer to other chapters for details on a particular function.

CONVENTIONS

To help you get the most from the text and keep track of what's happening, we've used a number of conventions throughout the book.

Boxes with a warning icon like this one hold important, not-to-be-forgotten information that is directly relevant to the surrounding text.

 The pencil icon indicates notes, tips, hints, tricks, and asides to the current discussion.

As for styles in the text:

➤ We *highlight* new terms and important words when we introduce them.

➤ We show keyboard strokes like this: Ctrl+A.

➤ We show file names, URLs, and code within the text like so: `persistence.properties`.

➤ We present code in two different ways:

```
We use a monofont type with no highlighting for most code examples.
We use bold to emphasize code that is particularly important in the
present context or to show changes from a previous code snippet.
```

SOURCE CODE

As you work through the examples in this book, you may choose either to type in all the code manually, or to use the source code files that accompany the book. All the source code used in this book is available for download at www.wrox.com. When at the site, simply locate the book's title (use the Search box or one of the title lists) and click the Download Code link on the book's detail page to obtain all the source code for the book. Code that is included on the Web site is highlighted by the following icon:

Available for download on Wrox.com

Listings include the filename in the title. If it is just a code snippet, you'll find the filename in a code note such as this:

Code snippet filename

 Because many books have similar titles, you may find it easiest to search by ISBN; this book's ISBN is 978-0-470-91622-3.

Once you download the code, just decompress it with your favorite compression tool. Alternately, you can go to the main Wrox code download page at www.wrox.com/dynamic/books/download .aspx to see the code available for this book and all other Wrox books.

ERRATA

We make every effort to ensure that there are no errors in the text or in the code. However, no one is perfect, and mistakes do occur. If you find an error in one of our books, like a spelling mistake or faulty piece of code, we would be very grateful for your feedback. By sending in errata, you may save another reader hours of frustration, and at the same time, you will be helping us provide even higher quality information.

To find the errata page for this book, go to www.wrox.com and locate the title using the Search box or one of the title lists. Then, on the book details page, click the Book Errata link. On this page, you can view all errata that has been submitted for this book and posted by Wrox editors. A complete book list, including links to each book's errata, is also available at www.wrox.com/misc-pages/ booklist.shtml.

If you don't spot "your" error on the Book Errata page, go to www.wrox.com/contact/ techsupport.shtml and complete the form there to send us the error you have found. We'll check the information and, if appropriate, post a message to the book's errata page and fix the problem in subsequent editions of the book.

P2P.WROX.COM

For author and peer discussion, join the P2P forums at p2p.wrox.com. The forums are a Web-based system for you to post messages relating to Wrox books and related technologies and interact with other readers and technology users. The forums offer a subscription feature to email you topics of interest of your choosing when new posts are made to the forums. Wrox authors, editors, other industry experts, and your fellow readers are present on these forums.

At p2p.wrox.com, you will find a number of different forums that will help you, not only as you read this book, but also as you develop your own applications. To join the forums, just follow these steps:

1. Go to p2p.wrox.com and click the Register link.

2. Read the terms of use and click Agree.

3. Complete the required information to join, as well as any optional information you wish to provide, and click Submit.

4. You will receive an email with information describing how to verify your account and complete the joining process.

You can read messages in the forums without joining P2P, but in order to post your own messages, you must join.

Once you join, you can post new messages and respond to messages other users post. You can read messages at any time on the Web. If you would like to have new messages from a particular forum emailed to you, click the Subscribe to this Forum icon by the forum name in the forum listing.

For more information about how to use the Wrox P2P, be sure to read the P2P FAQs for answers to questions about how the forum software works, as well as many common questions specific to P2P and Wrox books. To read the FAQs, click the FAQ link on any P2P page.

An Introduction to Plugins

WHAT'S IN THIS CHAPTER?

➤ Understanding a plugin

➤ Using available WordPress APIs

➤ Loading order of plugins

➤ Finding examples of popular plugins

➤ Determining the separation of plugin and theme functionality

➤ Managing and installing plugins

➤ Understanding types of WordPress plugins

WordPress is one of the most popular open source content management systems available today. One of the primary reasons WordPress is so popular is the ease with which you can customize WordPress through plugins. WordPress has an amazing framework in place giving plugin developers the tools needed to extend WordPress in any way imaginable.

Understanding how plugins work, and the tools available in WordPress, is critical knowledge when developing professional WordPress plugins.

WHAT IS A PLUGIN?

A plugin in WordPress is a PHP script that extends or alters the core functionality of WordPress. Quite simply plugins are files installed in WordPress to add a feature, or set of features, to WordPress. Plugins can range in complexity from a simple social networking plugin to an extremely elaborate e-commerce package. There is no limit to what a plugin can do in WordPress; because of this there is no shortage of plugins available for download.

How Plugins Interact with WordPress

WordPress features many different APIs for use in your plugin. Each API, or application programming interface, helps interact with WordPress in a different way. Following is a list of the main available APIs in WordPress and their function:

➤ **Plugin** — Provides a set of hooks that enable plugins access to specific parts of WordPress. WordPress contains two different types of hooks: Actions and Filters. The Action hook enables you to trigger custom plugin code at specific points during execution. For example, you can trigger a custom function to run after a user registers a user account in WordPress. The Filter hook to modifies text before adding or after retrieving from the database.

➤ **Widgets** — Create and manage widgets in your plugin. Widgets appear under the Appearance ⇨ Widgets screen and are available to add to any registered sidebar in your theme. The API enables multiple instances of the same widget to be used throughout your sidebars.

➤ **Shortcode** — Adds shortcode support to your plugin. A shortcode is a simple hook that enables you to call a PHP function by adding something such as [shortcode] to a post or page.

➤ **HTTP** — Sends HTTP requests from your plugin. This API retrieves content from an external URL or for submitting content to a URL. Currently you have five different ways to send an HTTP request. This API standardizes that process and tests each method prior to executing. Based on your server configuration, the API will use the appropriate method and make the request.

➤ **Settings** — Inserts settings or a settings section for your plugin. The primary advantage to using the Settings API is security. All settings data is scrubbed, so you do not need to worry about cross site request forgery (CSRF) and cross site scripting (XSS) attacks when saving plugin settings.

➤ **Options** — Stores and retrieves options in your plugin. This API features the capability to create new options, update existing options, delete options, and retrieve any option already defined.

➤ **Dashboard Widgets** — Creates admin dashboard widgets. Widgets automatically appear on the Dashboard of WordPress and contain all standard customization features including minimize, drag/drop, and screen options for hiding.

➤ **Rewrite** — Creates custom rewrite rules in your plugin. This API enables you to add static end-points (`/custom-page/`), structure tags (`%postname%`), and add additional feed links (`/feed/json/`).

➤ **Transients** — Creates temporary options (cached data) in your plugins. This API is similar to the Options API, but all options are saved with an expiration time.

➤ **Database** — Accesses the WordPress database. This includes creating, updating, deleting, and retrieving database records for use in your plugins.

WordPress also features pluggable functions. These functions enable you to override specific core functions in a plugin. For example, the `wp_mail()` function is a pluggable function. You can easily define this function in your plugin and send email using SMTP rather than the default method. All pluggable functions are defined in the `/wp-includes/pluggable.php` Core WordPress file.

You can use some predefined functions during specific plugin tasks, such as when a plugin is activated or deactivated and even when a plugin is uninstalled. Chapter 2, "Plugin Foundation," covers these functions in detail.

When Are Plugins Loaded?

Plugins are loaded early in the process when a WordPress powered web page is called. Figure 1-1 shows a diagram of the standard loading process when loading a page in WordPress:

Figure 1-1 illustrates the standard process when loading a page in WordPress. The flow changes slightly when loading an admin page. The differences are minor and primarily concern what theme is loaded: admin theme versus your web site theme.

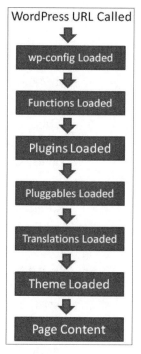

FIGURE 1-1

AVAILABLE PLUGINS

When researching available plugins you need to know where to find WordPress plugins. You can download plugins anywhere on the Internet, but this isn't always a good idea.

 As with any software, downloading plugins from an untrusted source could lead to malware injected and compromised plugin files. It's best to download plugins only from trusted web sites and official sources such as the official Plugin Directory.

Official Plugin Directory

The first place to start when researching available WordPress plugins is the official Plugin Directory at WordPress.org. The Plugin Directory is located at `http://wordpress.org/extend/plugins/`. With more than 10,000 plugins available and well over 100 million plugin downloads, it's easy to see the vital role plugins play in every WordPress web site. All plugins available in the Plugin Directory are 100% GPL and free to use for personal or commercial use.

Popular Plugin Examples

Take a look at the five most downloaded WordPress plugins available to get a sense of their diversity:

➤ **All in One SEO Pack** — Adds advanced search engine optimization functionality to WordPress. Features include custom meta data for all content, canonical URLs, custom post type support, and more!

    ➤ `http://wordpress.org/extend/plugins/all-in-one-seo-pack/`

➤ **Google XML Sitemaps** — Generates an XML sitemap of all content for submission to the popular search engines such as Google, Bing, and Ask.com.

    ➤ `http://wordpress.org/extend/plugins/google-sitemap-generator/`

➤ **Akismet** — A popular comment spam filter for WordPress. Checks all comments against the Akismet web service to verify whether the comment is spam.

    ➤ `http://wordpress.org/extend/plugins/akismet/`

➤ **NextGEN Gallery** — Adds advanced image gallery support to WordPress. You can easily create and manage image galleries and slideshows. Galleries can be embedded in posts or pages.

    ➤ `http://wordpress.org/extend/plugins/nextgen-gallery/`

➤ **Contact Form 7** — Adds a contact form to any post or page in WordPress. Supports multiple contact forms, Akismet spam filtering, and CAPTCHA.

    ➤ `http://wordpress.org/extend/plugins/contact-form-7/`

As you can see, the preceding plugins can handle any task. The features added by these plugins are universal and features that most web sites on the Internet should have.

Popular Plugin Tags

Now you will look at some popular tags for plugins. Plugin tags are just like blog post tags, simple keywords that describe a plugin in the Plugin Directory. This makes it easy to search for existing plugins by tag. Following are popular examples:

➤ **Twitter** — Everyone loves Twitter for micro-blogging and sharing links. You can find an abundance of Twitter-related plugins for WordPress.

    ➤ `http://wordpress.org/extend/plugins/tags/twitter`

➤ **Google** — With so many different services and APIs, Google is a popular plugin tag. Everything from Google ads to Google maps have been integrated into a WordPress plugin.

    ➤ `http://wordpress.org/extend/plugins/tags/google`

➤ **Widget** — Most plugins that include a widget also use the widget tag. This is great for viewing the many different types of widgets available for WordPress.

    ➤ `http://wordpress.org/extend/plugins/tags/widget`

Viewing popular plugin tags is a great way to get inspiration when developing new plugins for WordPress.

ADVANTAGES OF PLUGINS

WordPress offers many advantages to using plugins. You need to understand the advantages to building plugins to truly understand why you should build plugins. This can also help when determining the need for a specific plugin in WordPress.

Not Modifying Core

One of the main advantages to plugins is the ability to modify the behavior of WordPress without modifying any core files. Core files refer to any file that is a part of the default WordPress installation.

Hacking core files can make it difficult to update WordPress when a new version is released. If you made any modifications to a core file, that modification would be overwritten when the update occurs. Keeping WordPress up to date with the latest version is essential in keeping your web site secure.

Modifying core files can also lead to an unstable web site. Different areas of WordPress rely on other areas to function as expected. If you modify a core file and it no longer works as expected, it can cause instability and quite possibly break a completely unrelated feature in WordPress.

Why Reinvent the Wheel

Another advantage to building plugins is the structure that already exists for your plugin. Many of the common features have already been developed and are ready for use in your plugin. For example, you can take advantage of the built-in user roles in WordPress. Using the user roles you can easily restrict your code to execute only if a user is an administrator. Look at an example:

```php
<?php
if ( current_user_can( 'manage_options' ) ) {
  //any code entered here will only be executed IF
  //user is an administrator
}
?>
```

As you can see it's easy to verify a user has proper permissions prior to executing any code in your plugin. You learn about user accounts and roles in Chapter 8, "Users."

As another example, look at sending an email in WordPress. Sure you could create a new function in your plugin to send email, but why? WordPress has a handy function called wp_mail() for sending email. Look at an example:

```php
<?php
$email_to = 'you@example.com';
$email_subject = 'Plugin email example';
$email_message = 'How do you like my new plugin?';

wp_mail( $email_to, $email_subject, $email_message );
?>
```

As you can see sending an email in WordPress couldn't be easier. Unless your plugin needs some customized emailing functionality, you don't need to re-create this function from scratch. Using this function also ensures the widest adoption for sending emails from WordPress because you use the built-in function.

Using the available built-in features of WordPress can greatly reduce the time to develop a plugin. Another advantage to not reinventing the wheel is that this approach more often than not will allow for your plugins to work across a greater number of servers and setups, thereby maximizing compatibility. Don't reinvent the wheel with features that already exist in WordPress.

Separating Plugins and Themes

A plugin can take control of the rendering process; therefore, the plugin can become a "theme." Similarly a theme can have plugin functionality included. Because of this the difference between the two can sometimes become blurred, so why not just include your plugin code directly in a theme? This is a common question and one that can have a few different answers.

Should themes include plugin functionality? The short answer is no. The primary reason for this is because plugins are meant to add features and functionality to WordPress, regardless of the theme used. This creates a nice separation between your web site design and the functionality of your web site. The reason this separation is needed is so your theme is not directly tied to the functionality required. WordPress is built so that you can easily change your design, or theme, at any point with just a couple clicks. If all plugin functionality existed in your theme, and you switched themes, you will have lost all that functionality you required.

There is also a strong argument that certain features should be included in a theme. A common feature most themes include is breadcrumb navigation. This feature could certainly exist in a plugin, but being a navigation-centric feature it makes sense to include this in the theme. Search engine optimization features are also a common feature found in themes today.

Easy Updates

WordPress makes it easy to update a plugin to the latest version. Every plugin installed from the WordPress.org Plugin Directory alerts you when a new version of the plugin has been released. Updating the plugin is as simple as clicking the update notification listed just below the plugin details on the Plugin screen.

Plugins not installed from the Plugin Directory can also be updated using the auto-update functionality of WordPress. The plugin author must define where WordPress can download the latest version, and it will take care of the rest. If the plugin author doesn't define this location, you must manually update the plugin.

Keeping plugins updated is an important part in keeping your web site free from security vulnerabilities and bugs.

Easier to Share and Reuse

Plugins are easy to share with others. It's much easier to share a plugin than tell someone to modify specific lines of code in your theme or WordPress. Using plugins also makes it easy to use the same functionality across multiple sites. If you find a group of plugins that you like, you can easily install them on every WordPress web site you create.

Plugin Sandbox

When you activate a broken plugin in WordPress, it won't break your site. If the plugin triggers a fatal error, WordPress automatically deactivates the plugin before it has a chance to. This fail-safe feature makes it less risky when activating and testing out new plugins. Even if the plugin does cause a white screen of death (error message), you can easily rename the plugin folder, and WordPress deactivates the plugin. This makes it impossible for a rogue plugin to lock you out of your own site because of an error.

On the other hand, if you were to hack the WordPress core, you can most certainly cause fatal errors that will crash your web site. This can also include making unrecoverable damage to WordPress.

Plugin Community

A huge community is centered around plugin development, sharing knowledge and code, and creating wonderful plugins. Getting involved in the community is a great way to take your plugin development skills to the next level. Chapter 18, "The Developer Toolbox," covers many of these resources.

INSTALLING AND MANAGING PLUGINS

All plugin management in WordPress happens under the Plugins screen in the WordPress Dashboard, as shown in Figure 1-2.

The menu shown in Figure 1-2 is available only to administrators in WordPress, so nonadministrators cannot see this menu. If you use the Multisite feature of WordPress, the Plugins menu is hidden by default. You need to enable the menu under Network Admin ⇨ Settings.

FIGURE 1-2

Installing a Plugin

WordPress features three different methods for installing a new plugin. Your server setup dictates which method is the best to use.

The first method uses the built-in auto installer. This method enables you to search the Plugin Directory on WordPress.org directly from the admin dashboard of your WordPress web site. After you find a plugin to install, simply click the Install link, and the plugin automatically downloads and installs.

The second method uses the zip uploader. Zipped plugin files can be uploaded, extracted, and installed by WordPress. To use this method click the Upload link at the top of the Install Plugins page. Click the Browser button and select the plugin zip file you want to install. After you select the plugin, click the Install Now button, as shown in Figure 1-3.

The third and final method to install a plugin in WordPress uses File Transfer Protocol (FTP). Using FTP is simply connecting to your web server using an FTP client and manually uploading the plugin to your WordPress installation. To use this method upload the uncompressed plugin folder or file to the `wp-content/plugins` directory on your web server.

FIGURE 1-3

Managing Plugins

After you install a plugin in WordPress, you can manage it, along with all other plugins, under the Plugins ➪ Plugins screen. Here you can find a list of all plugins, active or not, available in your WordPress installation. You can easily activate, deactivate, edit, update, and delete plugins from this screen.

The Plugin screen also features bulk actions for activating, deactivating, updating, and deleting plugins. Check all the plugins you want to manage and then select the appropriate bulk action from the drop-down menu. This process makes managing multiple plugins a breeze!

Editing Plugins

WordPress features a built-in plugin editor under the Plugins ➪ Editor screen. The plugin editor enables you to view and edit the source code of any plugin installed in WordPress. Keep in mind you can only edit the source code if the plugin file is writeable by the web server, otherwise you can only view the code.

To use the editor, select the plugin from the drop-down menu on the top-left portion of the Edit Plugins page. The editor lists all files associated with the selected plugin. There is also a documentation lookup feature making it easy to research a specific function's purpose in the plugin you are reviewing.

 A word of caution when using the built-in plugin editor: A browser doesn't have an Undo button. There is also no code revision history, so one bad code edit can crash your entire site with no way to revert the changes back. It's best to use the code editor for reference only and never use it to edit your plugin files.

Plugin Directories

A lesser known fact is WordPress actually features two plugin directories. The primary plugin directory is located under `wp-content/plugins` in a standard WordPress installation. The second, lesser known, plugin directory is located under `wp-content/mu-plugins`. The `mu-plugins` directory, which stands for Must-Use, is not auto-created by WordPress, so it must be manually created to be used.

The primary difference between the two is the `mu-plugins` directory is for plugins that are always executed. This means any plugin included in this directory will automatically be loaded in WordPress and across all sites in the network if you run Multi-site.

> *The `mu-plugins` directory will not read plugins in a subfolder, so all plugins much be individual files or must include additional files that exist in a subdirectory. Any plugin files in a subfolder will be ignored unless included in the primary plugin file.*

Types of Plugins

WordPress features a few different types and statuses for plugins, as shown in Figure 1-4. You need to understand the difference when administering and creating plugins for WordPress.

FIGURE 1-4

➤ **Active** — Plugin is active and running in WordPress.

➤ **Inactive** — Plugin is installed but not active. No code from the plugin is executed.

➤ **Must-Use** — All plugins installed in the `wp-content/mu-plugins` directory. All Must-Use, or MU, plugins are loaded automatically. The only way to deactivate an MU plugin is to remove it completely from the directory.

➤ **Drop-ins** — Core functionality of WordPress can be replaced by Drop-in plugins. These plugins are a specifically named PHP files located in the `wp-content` directory. If WordPress detects one of these files, it will be auto-loaded and listed under the Drop-in filter on the Plugin screen. Currently ten Drop-in plugins are available:

    ➤ `advanced-cache.php` — Advanced caching plugin

    ➤ `db.php` — Custom database class

    ➤ `db-error.php` — Custom database error message

    ➤ `install.php` — Custom installation script

    ➤ `maintenance.php` — Custom maintenance message

    ➤ `object-cache.php` — External object cache

    ➤ `sunrise.php` — Advanced domain mapping

    ➤ `blog-deleted.php` — Custom blog deleted message

    ➤ `blog-inactive.php` — Custom blog inactive message

    ➤ `blog-suspended.php` — Custom blog suspended message

The last four drop-in plugins are specific to the WordPress Multisite feature. A standard WordPress installation will have no use for these plugins.

When developing a new plugin, determine what type of plugin you want to create before you start the development process. Most plugins will be standard WordPress plugins, but occasionally you might need to create a Must-Use or Drop-in specific plugin.

Testing Plugin Functionality

On occasion you may want to test some plugin functionality without actually creating a plugin to do so. Many developers will place code directly in the wp-config.php file to do so. This is a bad technique and should not be used because when the config file is parsed and loaded, WordPress is not wholly instantiated yet.

Instead of hacking wp-config.php, make a test.php file with the following code snippet and place it in your WordPress root directory:

```php
<?php
// Load the WordPress Environment
// define( 'WP_DEBUG', true ); /* uncomment for debug mode */
require('./wp-load.php');
// require_once ('./wp-admin/admin.php'); /* uncomment for is_admin() */
?>
<pre>
<?php

/* test stuff here */
var_dump( is_admin() );

?>
</pre>
```

Code snippet test.php

This is a quick way to load all of the required WordPress functions to test plugin functionality without actually creating a plugin. As you can see wp-load.php is included at the beginning of the file. You can also include wp-admin/admin.php if you want to test admin side functionality. Once you have included the required WordPress core files, you want test any code that would otherwise exist reside in your plugin. Don't forget to remove your test.php file when you are done testing.

SUMMARY

In this chapter you learned what about plugins and how they can interact with WordPress using the available APIs. The major advantages to using plugins and why plugin functionality shouldn't always be included in a theme was discussed. Installing and managing plugins in the WordPress admin dashboard was covered.

Now that you understand how plugins work in WordPress, it's time to create the plugin foundation!

Plugin Foundation

WHAT'S IN THIS CHAPTER?

➤ Creating a solid plugin foundation

➤ Determining directory and file paths

➤ Using Activate and Deactivate functions

➤ Understanding available plugin uninstall methods

➤ Managing sanity practices and coding standards

➤ Understanding proper code documentation

➤ Using plugin development checklists

When developing a plugin in WordPress, it's essential to start with a solid plugin foundation. Starting with a good foundation can eliminate many headaches as you develop your new plugin. The techniques discussed in this chapter will be used throughout this book as a good example of what to do.

CREATING A PLUGIN FILE

A plugin in WordPress can be a single PHP file or a group of files inside a folder. You need to consider many things when creating a new plugin in WordPress such as the plugin name and proper folder usage.

Naming Your Plugin

When choosing a name for your plugin, it's good practice to consider a name based on what your plugin actually does. For example, if you create an SEO-focused plugin, you wouldn't want to name it Bob's Plugin. Your audience would have no idea what your plugin actually does based on the plugin name. Your plugin name should be unique to your plugin and should also be descriptive of your plugin's purpose.

It's also a good idea to search the Plugin Directory on WordPress.org (http://wordpress.org/extend/plugins/) for similar plugins to avoid confusion. If you decide to name your plugin SEO Gold, and a plugin named SEO Silver already exists, there might be some confusion on whether your plugin is new or just a newer version of an old plugin. You don't want the first impression of your plugin to be met with confusion. Chapter 17, "Marketing Your Plugins," covers this in more detail.

Using a Folder

It's highly recommended to store all your plugin files inside a folder within the plugins directory in WordPress. All plugins downloaded from the WordPress.org Plugin Directory are automatically structured in subfolders. This enables your plugin to easily contain multiple files and any other items you want to include, such as images. You can also include subfolders to help organize your plugin files better. The folder name should be the same as the main plugin filename. You shouldn't include any spaces or underscores in the folder name; instead use hyphens if needed. Subfolders and the hierarchical directory structure of the files are discussed further in the "Sanity Practices" section of this chapter.

SANITY PRACTICES

Following a common set of sanity practices is a best practice for developing plugins in WordPress. The practices described in this section should be strictly followed for any plugin you develop. This can help eliminate many common errors in WordPress. These practices can also make the organization of your plugins much cleaner.

Prefix Everything

When building a custom plugin, it's essential that you prefix everything with a unique prefix. This means all plugins files, function names, variable names, and everything included with your plugin. Why? Simple, one of the most common errors in plugins is using all too common names for function and variables. For example, if you have a function named `update_options()` and the user installs another plugin with the same function name, the website will break because you can't have two functions with the same name in PHP.

A good rule of thumb is to prefix everything with your plugin initials and your own initials. For instance if your name is Michael Myers and your plugin is named Halloween Revenge, you would prefix the function as `mm_hr_update_options()`. There is a strong chance no other plugin in the world exists with the same function name; therefore there is little risk of having conflicts with other plugins.

This is also a good rule for variable names. Don't use general names when creating variables. For instance, say your plugin creates and uses a variable called `$post`. That could cause unexpected results because $post is a global variable in WordPress containing the post data. If your plugin overwrites the data in $post and something else in WordPress expects the post data to still exist, you might have a serious problem. Instead you can use the same prefix method previously described and name your variable $mm_hr_post. This is a unique variable name most likely not used in any other plugin.

This book prefixes everything with boj_ (a mashup of the Authors' initials) and myplugin_ (assuming the fictitious plugin is named My Plugin) like so: boj_myplugin_function_name().

File Organization

Keeping your plugin files organized is a key step in producing a professional plugin. Generally speaking, you should have only two files in your plugin folder: the primary plugin PHP file and your uninstall.php file. For organizational reasons, store all other plugin files in a subdirectory.

It is also recommended you split your plugin into several smaller files. One primary reason for doing so is for performance reasons. For instance, you should group all admin interface functions in a separate file. This allows you to conditionally include the admin code only when the user is viewing the admin side of WordPress:

```php
<?php
if ( is_admin() ) {
    // we're in wp-admin
    require_once( dirname( __FILE__ ).'/includes/admin.php' );
}
?>
```

The preceding example uses the is_admin() conditional statement to verify the user is in the admin dashboard of WordPress. If so your plugin should include and process the /includes/admin.php file for your plugin.

Folder Structure

Another important step to a professional plugin is maintaining a clean folder structure, which pertains to keeping all similar files together. For example, if your plugin requires JavaScript files, create a /js folder and store all the JavaScript files in this directory. If you have custom style sheet files, create a /css folder to store all your CSS files. Keep all images stored in a /images folder.

Now look at a standard folder structure for a plugin:

➤ /unique-plugin-name — (no spaces or special characters)

    ➤ unique-plugin-name.php — Primary plugin PHP file

    ➤ uninstall.php — The uninstall file for your plugin

    ➤ /js — Folder for JavaScript files

    ➤ /css — Folder for stylesheet files

    ➤ /includes — Folder for other PHP includes

    ➤ /images — Folder for plugin images

As you can see, keeping your files organized using a clean folder structure can make it much easier to track the flow of your plugin over time. It can also make it much easier for other plugin developers to follow your logic when they view your plugin's source code.

HEADER REQUIREMENTS

The plugin header is the only requirement for a plugin to function in WordPress. The plugin header is a PHP comment block located at the top of your primary plugin PHP file. This comment block tells WordPress that this is a valid WordPress plugin.

Creating the Header

Following is an example of a plugin header:

```php
<?php
/*
Plugin Name: My Plugin
Plugin URI: http://example.com/wordpress-plugins/my-plugin
Description: A brief description of my plugin
Version: 1.0
Author: Brad Williams
Author URI: http://example.com
License: GPLv2
*/
?>
```

Code snippet header-example.php

As you can see, the plugin header is straightforward. The only required line for WordPress to recognize your plugin is the plugin name, but it's good practice to fill in the entire header as shown.

The Plugin URI is a direct link to your plugin detail web page. The description is a short description of your plugin, which displays on the Plugin screen in WordPress. The version number is the current version of the plugin. WordPress uses the version number set here to check for new plugin updates at WordPress.org. The next two lines are the Author and Author URI. The Author is listed on the Plugin screen with a link to the Author URI set here. The final line is the software license the plugin is released under.

Figure 2-1 shows how your plugin header is rendered in WordPress.

☐ **My Plugin**	A brief description of my plugin
Activate	Edit	Delete	Version 1.0	By Brad Williams	Visit plugin site

FIGURE 2-1

The plugin Author's name, Brad Williams in this case, will link directly to the Author URI. The "Visit plugin site" text will link to the Plugin URI as defined in your plugin header. As you can see, both of these links can help users of your plugin find additional information about you and your plugin.

Plugin License

Below the plugin header comment block, it's a good idea to include the license for your plugin. This is not a requirement for your plugin to function, but anytime you release code to the public, it's a good idea to include a license with that code. This gives your users clear answers in how your plugin is licensed and how they can use your code. Chapter 17, "Marketing Your Plugins," covers this topic.

WordPress is licensed under the GNU General Public License (GPL) software license and as such any plugin distributed for WordPress should be compatible with the GPL. Following is an example of a standard GPL license comment block:

```php
<?php
/*  Copyright YEAR  PLUGIN_AUTHOR_NAME  (email : PLUGIN AUTHOR EMAIL)

    This program is free software; you can redistribute it and/or modify
    it under the terms of the GNU General Public License as published by
    the Free Software Foundation; either version 2 of the License, or
    (at your option) any later version.

    This program is distributed in the hope that it will be useful,
    but WITHOUT ANY WARRANTY; without even the implied warranty of
    MERCHANTABILITY or FITNESS FOR A PARTICULAR PURPOSE.  See the
    GNU General Public License for more details.

    You should have received a copy of the GNU General Public License
    along with this program; if not, write to the Free Software
    Foundation, Inc., 51 Franklin St, Fifth Floor, Boston, MA  02110-1301  USA
*/
?>
```

Code snippet license-example.php

Simply fill out the year, plugin author name, and email in the preceding license code. Now place the license code just below your plugin header. By including this software license, your plugin will be licensed under the GPL.

DETERMINING PATHS

Often you need to determine file and folder paths within your plugins. For example, you might have an image in your plugin folder that you want to display. Generally speaking, it isn't a good idea to hardcode a directory path in a plugin. WordPress can be configured to run in a million different ways, so assuming you know the proper directory paths is a mistake. This section looks at the proper way to determine file and folder paths in your WordPress plugin.

Plugin Paths

A common task in any plugin is referencing files and folders in your WordPress installation. You can reference files in your code in two ways: using the local server path or by using a standard URL.

Think of the local server path as nothing more than the directory path on a computer. The local server path is generally used whenever you need to include something that is local on your server. A URL is typically used to link to something external to your server, but that doesn't mean you can't link to images and such using the URL path.

WordPress features the ability to move the wp-content directory to a different location. Because of this you shouldn't hardcode directory paths in WordPress, but rather use the available functions to determine the correct path.

Local Paths

Here's one common question in plugin development: What is the proper way to determine the local path to your plugin files? To determine the local path to your plugin, you need to use the plugin_dir_path() function. The plugin_dir_path() function extracts the physical location relative to the plugins directory from its filename.

```php
<?php plugin_dir_path( $file ); ?>
```

Parameters:

➤ $file - (string) (required) — The filename of a plugin

Now look at an example on how to determine the local path to your plugin folder:

```php
<?php
echo plugin_dir_path( __FILE__ );
?>
```

You can see you pass the __FILE__ PHP constant to the plugin_dir_path() function. This produces the full local server path to your plugin directory:

```
/public_html/wp-content/plugins/my-custom-plugin/
```

What if you need to get the local path to a file in a subdirectory inside your plugin directory? You can also use the plugin_dir_path() function along with the subdirectory and files you want to reference:

```php
<?php
echo plugin_dir_path( __FILE__ ) .'js/scripts.js';
?>
```

This code would produce the following results:

```
/public_html/wp-content/plugins/my-custom-plugin/js/scripts.js
```

As you can see, this function will be instrumental in developing a solid WordPress plugin. Using the proper methods to access your plugin files and directories can ensure maximum compatibility with all WordPress installations, regardless of how custom it is.

URL Paths

Functions are also available to help determine URLs in WordPress. Following is a list of those functions:

- ➤ `plugins_url()` — Full plugins directory URL (for example, `http://example.com/wp-content/plugins`)

- ➤ `includes_url()` — Full includes directory URL (for example, `http://example.com/wp-includes`)

- ➤ `content_url()` — Full content directory URL (for example, `http://example.com/wp-content`)

- ➤ `admin_url()` — Full admin URL (for example, `http://example.com/wp-admin/`)

- ➤ `site_url()` — Site URL for the current site (for example, `http://example.com`)

- ➤ `home_url()` — Home URL for the current site (for example, `http://example.com`)

The `site_url()` and `home_url()` functions are similar and can lead to confusion in how they work. The `site_url()` function retrieves the value as set in the wp_options table value for siteurl in your database. This is the URL to the WordPress core files. If your core files exist in a subdirectory /wordpress on your web server, the value would be `http://example.com/wordpress`.

The `home_url()` function retrieves the value for home in the wp_options table. This is the address you want people to visit to view your WordPress web site. If your WordPress core files exist in /wordpress, but you want your web site URL to be `http://example.com` the home value should be `http://example.com`.

The `plugins_url()` function will be one of your best friends when building plugins in WordPress. This function can help you easily determine the full URL to any file within your plugin directory.

```php
<?php plugins_url( $path, $plugin ); ?>
```

Parameters:

- ➤ `$path` - (string) (optional) — Path relative to the plugins URL

- ➤ `$plugin` - (string) (optional) — Plugin file that you want to be relative (that is, pass in `__FILE__`)

For example, say you want to reference an image file to use as an icon in your plugin. You could easily accomplish this using the following example:

```php
<?php
echo '<img src="' .plugins_url( 'images/icon.png' , __FILE__ ). '">';
?>
```

The first parameter value you pass to the function is the relative path to the image file you want to include. The second parameter is the plugin file that you want to be relative, which in this case you can simply send in the PHP constant __FILE__. The preceding code would generate the HTML img tag as follows:

```
<img src="http://example.com/wp-content/plugins/my-custom-plugin/images/icon.png">
```

Following are some of the advantages to using the plugins_url() function to determine plugin URLs:

➤ Supports the mu-plugins plugin directory.

➤ Auto detects SSL, so if SSL is enabled in WordPress, the URL returned would contain https.

➤ Uses the WP_PLUGIN_URL constant, meaning it can detect the location of the plugin even if the user has moved it to a custom location.

➤ Supports Multisite using the WPMU_PLUGIN_URL constant.

ACTIVATE/DEACTIVATE FUNCTIONS

WordPress features some common functions you can use in all plugins that you develop. This section covers the activate and deactivate functions.

Plugin Activation Function

The plugin activation function is triggered when, you guessed it, a plugin is activated in WordPress. This function is called register_activation_hook(). Using this function is a great way to set some default options for your plugin. It can also verify that the version of WordPress is compatible with your plugin. The function accepts two parameters as shown here:

```
<?php register_activation_hook( $file, $function ); ?>
```

Parameters:

➤ $file - (string) (required) — Path to the primary plugin file

➤ $function - (string) (required) — The function to be executed when the plugin is activated

Now look at an example of this function in action:

```
<?php
register_activation_hook( __FILE__, 'boj_myplugin_install' );

function boj_myplugin_install() {
    //do cool activation stuff
}
?>
```

The first parameter you send the function is the path to your file, using the __FILE__ constant. This is a PHP constant that always contains the absolute path to the file it is called from. The second parameter is the unique function you want to call when your plugin is activated.

Now that you understand how the `register_activation_hook()` function works, look at a real-world example. Following is an example of how you can easily verify the version of WordPress is compatible with your plugin.

```php
<?php
register_activation_hook( __FILE__, 'boj_install' );

function boj_install() {
    If ( version_compare( get_bloginfo( 'version' ), '3.1', '<' ) ) {
        deactivate_plugins( basename( __FILE__ ) ); // Deactivate our plugin
    }
}
?>
```

Code snippet version-requirement.php

Your install function `boj_install()` uses the `get_bloginfo()` function to retrieve the current version of WordPress the user runs. Next you use the PHP function `version_compare()` to verify the installed version of WordPress is at least 3.1. If the WordPress version is older than 3.1, deactivate your plugin using the `deactivate_plugins()` function.

Create Default Settings on Activate

Another common plugin activation technique is to set some default settings when your plugin is activated. Imagine your plugin has an entire page worth of options available. Chances are some of those options need to be defined for your plugin to work properly. Rather than forcing the user to visit your settings page and set those options, you can automatically set default options when the plugin is activated.

```php
<?php
register_activation_hook( __FILE__, 'boj_install' );

function boj_install() {
    $boj_myplugin_options = array(
        'view' => 'grid',
        'food' => 'bacon',
        'mode' => 'zombie'
    );
    update_option( 'boj_myplugin_options', $boj_myplugin_options );
}
?>
```

The preceding code example creates an array of default options and stores them in WordPress when your plugin is activated. Chapter 7, "Plugin Settings," covers creating and saving options in WordPress in more detail.

Plugin Deactivation Function

Just as there is an activation function, there is also a deactivation function. This is called the `register_deactivation_hook()` function. This function is triggered when your plugin is deactivated in the WordPress Plugins screen. This function accepts the same two parameters as the previous activation function.

```php
<?php register_ deactivation_hook( $file, $function ); ?>
```

Parameters:

➤ $file - (string) (required) — Path to the primary plugin file

➤ $function - (string) (required) — The function to be executed when the plugin is activated

Now look at an example of the deactivation function in action:

```php
<?php
register_deactivation_hook( __FILE__, 'boj_myplugin_uninstall' );

function boj_myplugin_uninstall() {
    //do something
}
?>
```

The preceding example would execute your `boj_myplugin_uninstall()` function when your plugin is deactivated in WordPress.

Deactivate Is Not Uninstall

When dealing with the deactivation function, you shouldn't include uninstall functionality when a plugin is deactivated. Imagine if you accidentally deactivate a plugin and upon reactivation you realize all your settings for that plugin have been deleted. Also, remember the WordPress automatic update feature deactivates all plugins prior to installing the new version of WordPress.

UNINSTALL METHODS

Adding an uninstall feature to your plugin is an easy way to remove any data that your plugin added to WordPress. This should be a required step to any plugin you develop. It doesn't take much work but can make the users of your plugin confident that they can remove your plugin completely whenever they chose to.

Why Uninstall Is Necessary

Think of your plugin as a piece of software installed on your computer. You expect that piece of software to have an easy way to uninstall it from your computer. You also expect the uninstaller to remove any trace of that software from your computer. A plugin in WordPress is no different; it's essentially a piece of software installed in WordPress. If users want to uninstall your plugin, you should provide the necessary uninstall functionality to remove all traces of the plugin from their WordPress site.

A good rule of thumb is to be considerate of your plugin user's data. For example if your plugin creates events as a custom post type, chances are the user does not want all of their events deleted if they uninstall your plugin. In that case you might want to ask the user if they want to delete all plugin data or not.

WordPress provides two different methods for uninstalling a plugin: the uninstall.php file and the uninstall hook.

Uninstall.php

The first method is the uninstall.php file. This is typically the preferred method because it keeps all your uninstall code in a separate file. To use this method, create an uninstall.php file and place it in the root directory of your plugin. If this file exists WordPress executes its contents when the plugin is deleted from the WordPress Plugins screen page. Now look at an example using the uninstall.php file:

```php
<?php
// If uninstall not called from WordPress exit
if( !defined( 'WP_UNINSTALL_PLUGIN' ) )
    exit ();

// Delete option from options table
delete_option( 'boj_myplugin_options' );

//remove any additional options and custom tables
?>
```

The first thing you want to do is verify that WordPress is actually calling the uninstall.php file. Do this by verifying the WP_UNINSTALL_PLUGIN constant is defined. If it is not, immediately exit the script. This is a security measure to ensure this file is not executed except during the uninstall process of your plugin.

After you have verified this is a valid uninstall call, you can delete your plugin options from the database. The goal of a plugin uninstall script is to remove any trace of the plugin from the WordPress database. This includes deleting all options and dropping any custom tables that may have been created. You don't need to worry about deleting the actual plugin files or directories in this function. WordPress will do that for you once your uninstall script runs.

Uninstall Hook

The second uninstall method available is the uninstall hook. If you delete a plugin in WordPress and uninstall.php does not exist, WordPress executes the uninstall hook (if it exists).

```php
<?php register_uninstall_hook( $file, $function ); ?>
```

Parameters:

➤ $file - (string) (required) — Path to the primary plugin file

➤ $function - (string) (required) — The function to be executed when the plugin is uninstalled

Now look at an example of the uninstall function in action:

```php
<?php
register_activation_hook( __FILE__, 'boj_myplugin_activate' );

function boj_myplugin_activate() {

    //register the uninstall function
    register_uninstall_hook( __FILE__, 'boj_myplugin_uninstaller' );

}

function boj_myplugin_uninstaller() {

    //delete any options, tables, etc the plugin created
    delete_option( 'boj_myplugin_options' );

}
?>
```

As you can see, the `register_uninstall_hook()` should be called on activation and not on every plugin load. To do this you'll include the uninstall hook when the plugin is activated using the `register_activation_hook()`. Next call the uninstall function. Again pass the `__FILE__` constant as the first parameter. The second parameter is your uninstall function that you want to execute.

Inside your `boj_myplugin_uninstaller()` function is where all uninstall procedures take place. Remember if the uninstall.php file exists in your plugins root folder, the uninstall hook won't actually execute.

 It's important to note you cannot use a class method as a callback for the uninstall hook. The reason is the uninstall hook would store a reference to `$this` in the database, which would be unique to that page load.

As suggested in this section, there are many pitfalls to using the uninstall hook. It's a much cleaner, and easier, process to use the uninstall.php method described earlier for removing plugin settings and options when a plugin is deleted in WordPress.

CODING STANDARDS

WordPress maintains a set of coding standards for all core code. This helps keep the code style consistent and clean throughout WordPress so it is easy to read. It's recommended to follow these coding standards when writing plugins for WordPress. This helps keep the consistency of the core code within your plugin.

You can view the official WordPress coding standards at `http://codex.wordpress.org/WordPress_Coding_Standards`.

Document Your Code

One of the most obvious, yet commonly skipped steps, is code commenting. Commenting your plugin's source code is a quick and easy way to document exactly how your plugin works. There are many benefits to commenting your code. The major benefit to code commenting is to explain what your code actually does, in plain English.

Imagine writing an extremely complex plugin without a single comment. If you don't review the code for months and then return to it, you might have a hard time understanding what your code actually does. Now imagine other developers are reviewing your code; without comments it could take them a much longer time to follow your code logic and understand how your plugin functions. Comments are beneficial to everyone involved, so for everyone's sanity, always comment your code!

Nearly all functions in WordPress core contain inline documentation in PHPDoc form. PHPDoc is a standardized method of describing a function's usage in PHP comment form. Following is a basic example of a PHPDoc formatted function comment:

```php
<?php
/**
 * Short description
 *
 * Longer more detailed description
 *
 * @param    type    $varname1    Description
 * @param    type    $varname2    Description
 * @return   type    Description
 */
function boj_super_function( $varname1, $varname2 ) {
    //do function stuff
}
?>
```

As you can see, the preceding PHPDoc comment helps to describe the function directly below the comment block. If I'm a developer looking over your plugin's code, I can quickly determine exactly how your function works, what parameters it accepts, and what I can expect returned without even reading your function's code. These comments are also used by more visual tools such as PHPDocumentor and PHPXref.

Naming Variables, Functions, and Files

Variable and function names should always be written in lowercase. Words should also be separated using underscores. Following is an example showing the proper way to name a function and variable:

```php
<?php
function boj_myplugin_function_name ( $boj_myplugin_variable ) {
    //do something
}
?>
```

Files should also be named using only lowercase letters; however, filenames should use hyphens to separate words and not underscores. For example you might name your plugin: boj-plugin-name.php.

Single and Double Quotes

PHP enables you to define strings using single or double quotes. In WordPress it's recommended to use single quotes whenever possible. One of the benefits of using single quotes is you rarely need to escape HTML quotes in a string. Following is an example showing how to echo a link using the single quote method:

```php
<?php
echo '<a href="http://example.com/">Visit Example.com</a>';
?>
```

You can also use the double quote method when concatenating a string in PHP. For example, look at a simple way to insert a variable for your website URL:

```php
<?php
$boj_myplugin_website = 'http://example.com/';
echo "<a href='$boj_myplugin_website'>Visit Example.com</a>";?>
```

Set the `$boj_myplugin_website` variable to the URL you want to include in your HTML link. Then concatenate the string to include the web site URL in your echo statement.

Indentation

Indentation should always reflect the logical structure of the code. This means using real tabs, and not spaces, when indenting your code. As an example look at a poorly indented `if` statement:

```php
if ( condition ) {
echo 'Yes';
} elseif ( condition2 ) {
echo 'No';
}
```

The preceding code logic is hard to follow because no indentation reflects the logical structure of the `if` statement. Now look at the same code sample using proper indentation:

```php
<?php
if ( condition ) {
    echo 'Yes';
} elseif ( condition2 ) {
    echo 'No';
}
?>
```

Notice how using proper indentation makes reading the logic of the preceding `if` statement much easier to follow. You can easily skim this code and understand the outcome of the statement. This is why proper indentation is a must with any code you write.

Brace Style

Braces should always be used for multiline blocks of code. The brace should be positioned on the same line as the conditional statement you are checking. Look at an example using the proper bracing technique:

```php
<?php
if ( condition ) {
    action1();
    action2();
} elseif ( condition2 || condition3 ) {
    action3();
    action4();
} else {
    defaultaction();
}
?>
```

If you have an extremely long block of code, it's a good idea to put a short comment at the ending brace to help determine at a glance what that ending brace actually ends:

```php
<?php
if ( condition ) {
    action1();
    action2();
} elseif ( condition2 || condition3 ) {
    action3();
    action4();
} else {
    defaultaction();
} //end of condition check
?>
```

Space Usage

Spaces should always be used after commas and on both sides of logical and assignment operators. Now look at a few different examples using the proper spacing methods:

```php
<?php
if ( $foo == 34 ) {
    //do something
}

foreach ( $foo as $bar ) {
    //do something
}

$foo = array( 34, 16, 8 );

function super_function( $param1 = 'foo', $param2 = 'bar' ) {
    //do something
}
?>
```

Notice the spacing technique for each statement. This makes reading and following your code logic much easier because the code examples are clean and consistent throughout.

Shorthand PHP

You shouldn't use the shorthand PHP tags (`<?` `?>`) in your code. The reason for this is that shorthand PHP tags must be enabled on your server before they will function. Many hosting configurations have this feature disabled by default, which means your plugin would immediately break when activated in WordPress. Instead, you should wrap your PHP code in standard tags: `<?php ?>`

SQL Statements

When making database calls in WordPress you may need to write custom SQL statements to query the proper data from the database. SQL statements can be broke into multiple lines if the complexity of the statement warrants it. Even though SQL is not case-sensitive, it's good practice to capitalize the SQL commands in the statement.

```
SELECT username FROM table1 WHERE status = 'active'
```

Chapter 6, "Plugin Security," discusses the proper way to use SQL statements in WordPress.

PLUGIN DEVELOPMENT CHECKLIST

When developing a new plugin in WordPress, you need to remember many things to create a proper plugin foundation. Following is a checklist to help with the process. Following this checklist you can be confident you have a proper plugin foundation for your new plugin:

➤ Determine a unique and descriptive plugin name.

  ➤ Is the name descriptive of your plugin's function?

  ➤ Have you verified the plugin doesn't exist in the Plugin Directory?

➤ Set a unique plugin prefix.

  ➤ Is the prefix unique enough to avoid conflicts?

➤ Create your plugin folder structure.

  ➤ Will your plugin need a PHP directory?

  ➤ Will your plugin need a JavaScript directory?

  ➤ Will your plugin need a CSS directory?

  ➤ Will your plugin need an images directory?

➤ Create your default plugin files.

  ➤ Create your primary file named the same as your plugin folder.

  ➤ Create the uninstall.php file for your uninstall procedures.

➤ Create your plugin's header code.

   ➤ Set your plugin name as you want it displayed.

   ➤ Add a detailed description about your plugin's purpose.

   ➤ Set the proper version for your plugin.

   ➤ Verify both Plugin URI and Author URI values are set.

➤ Include a license for your plugin.

   ➤ Place the license code directly below your plugin header.

➤ Create your plugin's activation function.

   ➤ Does your plugin require a specific version of WordPress or higher to function?

   ➤ Does your plugin require default options to be set when activated?

➤ Create your plugin's deactivation function.

   ➤ Does your plugin require something to happen when it is deactivated?

➤ Create your plugin's uninstall script.

   ➤ Create an uninstall.php file

   ➤ Include uninstall scripts in the file

➤ File references.

   ➤ Use the proper directory constants and functions to determine paths within WordPress and your plugin.

SUMMARY

This chapter discussed creating a proper foundation when developing plugins for WordPress. Following these techniques is essential in creating plugins that work across all types of WordPress setups. Keeping your code properly documented is also an important step in detailing how your code functions and why. This can save time in the future when revisiting your code for updates. It can also help other developers understand your code logic.

3

Hooks

WHAT'S IN THIS CHAPTER?

➤ Creating actions for action hooks

➤ Creating filters for filter hooks

➤ Using hooks within a PHP class

➤ Adding custom hooks to plugins

➤ Finding hooks within WordPress

Hooks are the backbone of WordPress. They enable plugin developers to "hook" into the WordPress workflow to change how it works without directly modifying the core code. This enables users to easily upgrade to newer versions of WordPress without losing modifications.

If a developer modified the core code, those edits would be lost the next time WordPress was updated. The update would overwrite all those changes. Using hooks enables you to develop plugins in separate folders apart from the core, keeping the plugin code safe from updates.

Without hooks, plugins would have no way to modify how WordPress works. The hooks system you learn about in this chapter is used throughout the book and is something you will use in nearly every plugin you create. After you learn how to use hooks, you will understand exactly why WordPress is such a powerful platform and has thousands of plugins built for its millions of users.

WordPress has two primary types of hooks: action hooks and filter hooks. The former enables you to execute a function at a certain point, and the latter enables you to manipulate the output passed through the hook.

Hooks aren't just for plugins. WordPress uses hooks internally. If you browse through the core source code, you can see many examples of how WordPress uses its own system to hook into itself.

ACTIONS

Action hooks enable you to fire a function at specific points in the WordPress loading process or when an event occurs. For example, you might want a function to execute when WordPress first loads a page or when a blog post is saved.

You need to understand the `do_action()` function. When hooking into WordPress, your plugin won't call this function directly; however, your plugin will almost always use it indirectly.

```php
<?php
do_action( $tag, $arg = '' );
?>
```

➤   `$tag` — The name of the action hook.

➤   `$arg` — Value(s) passed to registered actions. It looks like a single parameter, but this isn't always the case. Action hooks have the option to pass any number of parameters or no parameters at all. You need to check the WordPress source code for specific hooks because the number of parameters changes on a per-hook basis.

Following is an example of what an action hook would look like with multiple parameters.

```php
<?php
do_action( $tag, $arg_1, $arg_2, $arg_3 );
?>
```

Now take a look at a WordPress action hook called `wp_head` and how it appears in WordPress. This hook is fired within the `<head>` area on the front end of the site. WordPress and plugins usually use this hook to add meta information, style sheets, and scripts.

```php
<?php
do_action( 'wp_head' );
?>
```

When this code fires in WordPress, it looks for any actions registered for the `wp_head` action hook. It then executes them in the order specified. As you can see, it has a name of `wp_head` but passes no extra parameters. This is often the case with action hooks.

Following is an example of an action hook that has two extra parameters.

```php
<?php
 do_action('save_post', $post_ID, $post);
?>
```

Here, you can see that the hook name is `save_post` and the parameters it passes are `$post_ID` and `$post`.

What Is an Action?

An action is technically a PHP function. For a function to be considered an action, it would need to be registered for an action hook. In the previous section, you can see what action hooks are, but for action hooks to serve any purpose, they need to have an action registered for them.

That's where plugins come in. You develop custom functions (actions) that perform a specific task when the action hook is fired. To do this, you would use the `add_action()` function.

```php
<?php
add_action( $tag, $function, $priority, $accepted_args );
?>
```

➤ `$tag` — The name of the action hook your function executes on.

➤ `$function` — The name of your function that WordPress calls.

➤ `$priority` — An integer that represents the order in which the action is fired. When no value is given, it defaults to 10. The lower the number, the earlier the function will be called. The higher the number, the later it will be called.

➤ `$accepted_args` — The number of parameters the action hook will pass to your function. By default, it passes only one parameter.

Action hooks aren't limited to a single action. Your plugin can add multiple functions to an action hook. Other plugins, and even WordPress core, often add functions to the same hook.

Now it's time for you to put action hooks to use. One common action hook is `wp_footer`. It is fired on the front end of the site by the user's WordPress theme. Generally, it is fired just before the closing `</body>` tag in the HTML. In this example, you're going to register an action for the `wp_footer` hook that adds a custom message to the footer.

Available for download on Wrox.com

```php
<?php

add_action( 'wp_footer', 'boj_example_footer_message', 100 );

function boj_example_footer_message() {

    echo 'This site is built using <a href="http://wordpress.org"
    title="WordPress publishing platform">WordPress</a>.';

}

?>
```

Code snippet boj-example-footer-message.php

Take a closer look at how you used `add_action()` from the preceding code.

```php
<?php
add_action( 'wp_footer', 'boj_example_footer_message', 100 );
?>
```

The first parameter is the name of the hook (`wp_footer`). The second parameter is a callback to your custom function (`boj_example_footer_message`). The third parameter is the priority (`100`). Your function will likely be executed much later than other functions hooked to `wp_footer` because of its priority of `100`. If this number were changed to `1`, it would be called earlier.

 It should be noted that hooks might be fired more than once in the WordPress flow for various reasons. Any actions added to these hooks will execute each time the hook is fired.

Action Hook Functions

You've now learned how the two most basic action hook functions work: `do_action()` and `add_action()`. WordPress also has other functions for working with action hooks that can be useful in your plugins.

do_action_ref_array

The `do_action_ref_array()` function works the same way as `do_action()` works, with a difference in how the arguments are passed. Rather than passing multiple, optional values as additional parameters, it passes an array of arguments. The array of arguments is also a required parameter. The purpose of the function is to pass an object by reference to actions added to a specific hook. This means the action can change the object itself without returning it.

```php
<?php
do_action_ref_array( $tag, $args );
?>
```

➤ `$tag` — The name of the action hook.

➤ `$args` — An array of arguments passed to actions registered for the hook. Generally, this would be an object that actions can change.

Now take a look at a specific instance of how WordPress calls `do_action_ref_array()`. The following code shows the `pre_get_posts` action hook. WordPress executes this hook before loading posts from the database, enabling plugins to change how posts are queried.

```php
<?php
do_action_ref_array( 'pre_get_posts', array( &$this ) );
?>
```

You can see that the pre_get_posts is the hook name, which is the first parameter. The second parameter in this case is an array of query arguments for pulling posts from the database. This hook enables you to execute code based on that array of arguments.

Suppose you wanted to randomly order posts on the blog home page rather than have the default ordering by the post date. You would register an action on this hook and change the order.

Available for download on Wrox.com

```php
<?php

add_action( 'pre_get_posts', 'boj_randomly_order_blog_posts' );

function boj_randomly_order_blog_posts( $query ) {

    if ( $query->is_home && empty( $query->query_vars['suppress_filters'] ) )
        $query->set( 'orderby', 'rand' );
}

?>
```

Code snippet boj-random-blog-posts.php

remove_action

remove_action() enables you to remove an action that has previously been added to a hook. Typically, you would remove actions that WordPress adds by default. To remove an action, the action must have already been added using the add_action() function. If your code runs before the action is registered, the action will not be removed from the hook.

The function returns true when the action was successfully removed and false when the action could not be removed.

```php
<?php
remove_action( $tag, $function_to_remove, $priority, $accepted_args );
?>
```

➤ $tag — The name of the action hook the action you want to remove is hooked to.

➤ $function_to_remove — The name of the function that has been added to the hook.

➤ $priority — The priority given in the add_action() function. This defaults to a value of 10.

➤ $accepted_args — The number of accepted arguments the action accepts. This defaults to a value of 1.

To successfully remove an action from a hook, the $tag, $function_to_remove, and $priority parameters must exactly match the parameters used in do_action(). Otherwise, the action will not be removed and remove_action() will return false.

Let's take a look at one of WordPress' default actions called rel_canonical. This action adds a canonical link between the opening <head> and closing </head> element on the site's front end.

```php
<?php
add_action( 'wp_head', 'rel_canonical' );
?>
```

To remove this action, you must use the `remove_action()` function in your plugin. You need to define the `$tag` and `$function_to_remove` parameters. In this case, you don't need to add the `$priority` parameter because no priority was explicitly given in the action previously defined.

```php
<?php
remove_action( 'wp_head', 'rel_canonical' );
?>
```

It is possible to remove any action added by WordPress, a plugin, or a theme within your plugin. Generally, you remove actions within WordPress. Many of its default actions are defined in the `wp-includes/default-filters.php` file. Browsing this file can give you a general overview of how WordPress uses action hooks.

remove_all_actions

In some plugins, you may find it necessary to remove all actions for a given tag or all actions for a given tag and priority. The `remove_all_actions()` function enables you to do this with a single line of code instead of multiple uses of the `remove_action()` function.

```php
<?php
remove_all_actions( $tag, $priority );
?>
```

➤ `$tag` — The name of the action hook that you want to remove all actions on.

➤ `$priority` — The priority of the actions to remove. This parameter is optional and defaults to `false`. If you set this parameter, only actions with this specific priority will be removed.

In this next example, you remove all actions, regardless of priority, from the `wp_head` action hook.

```php
<?php
remove_all_actions( 'wp_head' );
?>
```

If you want to remove only actions with a specific priority, you would give a value for the second parameter of `$priority`. To remove all actions with a priority of `1` for the `wp_head` hook use the following code.

```php
<?php
remove_all_actions( 'wp_head', 1 );
?>
```

You should be careful when using this function. Other plugins and themes may add actions that you are unaware of. Using this may break functionality that your plugin users are expecting to work. It's usually better to be as specific as possible with your code. In most cases, you should use the `remove_action()` function instead.

has_action

Sometimes, you may find it necessary to check if a hook has any actions or if a specific action has been added to a hook before executing code. The `has_action()` function is a conditional function that gives you the ability to check both these cases.

```php
<?php
has_action( $tag, $function_to_check );
?>
```

➤ `$tag` — The name of the action hook you want to check for actions registered to it.

➤ `$function_to_check` — The name of a function to check if it has been added to the hook. This parameter is optional and defaults to a value of `false`.

The return value for `has_action()` varies between a Boolean value and an integer. If `$function_to_check` is not set, the function returns `true` if actions are added to the hook or `false` if no actions are added to the hook. If `$function_to_check` is set and the function has been added to the hook, the priority (integer) of the action will be returned. Otherwise, a value of `false` will be returned.

In the next example, you display a message based on whether the `wp_footer` action hook has any action registered for it.

```php
<?php

if ( has_action( 'wp_footer' ) )
    echo '<p>An action has been registered for the footer.</p>';

else
    echo '<p>An action hasn\'t been registered for the footer.</p>';

?>
```

Now look at an action WordPress core adds to `wp_footer`. The `wp_print_footer_scripts()` is registered for this hook by default.

```php
<?php
add_action( 'wp_footer', 'wp_print_footer_scripts' );
?>
```

If you want to display a message if that particular action were registered for the hook, you would use the following code.

```php
<?php

if ( has_action( 'wp_footer', 'wp_print_footer_scripts' ) )
    echo '<p>The wp_print_footer_scripts is registered for wp_footer.</p>';

?>
```

did_action

The `did_action()` function enables your plugin to check if an action hook has already been executed or to count the number of times one has been executed. This also means that some action hooks are fired multiple times during a single page load.

```php
<?php
did_action( $tag );
?>
```

➤ `$tag` — Name of the action hook to check.

The function returns the number of times the hook has been fired or `false` if it hasn't been fired. The most common use case of the function is to check if an action hook has already been fired and execute code based on the return value of `did_action()`.

In the next example, you define a PHP constant if the `plugins_loaded` action hook has already fired.

```php
<?php

if ( did_action( 'plugins_loaded' ) )
    define( 'BOJ_MYPLUGIN_READY', true );

?>
```

register_activation_hook and register_deactivation_hook

WordPress has two functions for registering action hooks for the activation and deactivation of individual plugins. Although these are technically functions to create custom hooks, both functions are covered in Chapter 2, "Plugin Foundation," in complete detail.

Commonly Used Action Hooks

WordPress has many action hooks, but some of them are used more often than others. Knowing what these hooks are can help you lay down the groundwork for your plugins.

plugins_loaded

For plugin developers, the `plugins_loaded` action hook is probably the most important hook. It is fired after most of the WordPress files are loaded but before the pluggable functions and WordPress starts executing anything. In most plugins, no other code should be run until this hook is fired. `plugins_loaded` is executed when all the user's activated plugins have been loaded by WordPress. It is also the earliest hook plugin developers can use in the loading process.

A WordPress plugin should do its setup on this hook. Other actions should also be added within the callback function used on this hook.

In the following example, you use the `boj_example_footer_message` action you created in the previous section. Rather than calling it separately, add it to your setup action, which is hooked to `plugins_loaded`.

```php
<?php

add_action( 'plugins_loaded', 'boj_footer_message_plugin_setup' );

function boj_footer_message_plugin_setup() {

    /* Add the footer message action. */
    add_action( 'wp_footer', 'boj_example_footer_message', 100 );

}

function boj_example_footer_message() {

    echo 'This site is built using <a href="http://wordpress.org"
    title="WordPress publishing platform">WordPress</a>.';

}

?>
```

 It is good practice to create a setup function and hook it to `plugins_loaded`. *By doing this, you can ensure that you don't inadvertently trigger any errors from a specific WordPress function not being loaded.*

init

The `init` hook is fired after most of WordPress is set up. WordPress also adds a lot of internal functionality to this hook such as the registration of post types and taxonomies and the initialization of the default widgets.

Because nearly everything in WordPress is ready at this point, your plugin will probably use this hook for anything it needs to do when all the information from WordPress is available.

In the following example, you add the ability for users to write an excerpt for pages. You would do this on `init` because the "page" post type is created at this point using the `add_post_type_support()` function (see Chapter 11, "Extending Posts").

```php
<?php

add_action( 'init', 'boj_add_excerpts_to_pages' );

function boj_add_excerpts_to_pages() {

    add_post_type_support( 'page', array( 'excerpt' ) );

}

?>
```

admin_menu

The `admin_menu` hook is called only when an administration page loads. Whenever your plugin works directly in the admin, you would use this hook to execute your code.

The next example adds a sub-menu item labeled BOJ Settings to the Settings menu in the WordPress admin (for more on this, see Chapter 7, "Plugin Settings").

```php
<?php

add_action( 'admin_menu', 'boj_admin_settings_page' );

function boj_admin_settings_page() {

    add_options_page(
        'BOJ Settings',
        'BOJ Settings',
        'manage_options',
        'boj_admin_settings',
        'boj_admin_settings_page'
    );

}

?>
```

template_redirect

The `template_redirect` action hook is important because it's the point where WordPress knows which page a user is viewing. It is executed just before the theme template is chosen for the particular page view. It is fired only on the front end of the site and not in the administration area. This is a good hook to use when you need to load code only for specific page views.

In the next example, you load a style sheet file only for a singular post view.

```php
<?php

add_action( 'template_redirect', 'boj_singular_post_css' );

function boj_singular_post_css() {

    if ( is_singular( 'post' ) ) {
        wp_enqueue_style(
            'boj-singular-post',
            'boj-example.css',
            false,
            0.1,
            'screen'
        );
    }

}

?>
```

wp_head

On the front end of the site, WordPress themes call the `wp_head()` function, which fires the `wp_head` hook. Plugins use this hook to add HTML between the opening `<head>` tag and its closing `</head>`.

In the following example, you add a meta description on the front page of the site using the site's description.

```php
<?php

add_action( 'wp_head', 'boj_front_page_meta_description' );

function boj_front_page_meta_description() {

    /* Get the site description. */
    $description = esc_attr( get_bloginfo( 'description' ) );

    /* If a description is set, display the meta element. */
    if ( !empty( $description ) )
        echo '<meta name="description" content="' . $description . '" />';
}

?>
```

 Many plugins incorrectly use the `wp_head` *action hook to add JavaScript to the header when they should be using the* `wp_enqueue_script()` *function (see Chapter 12, "JavaScript and AJAX"). The only time JavaScript should be added to this hook is when it's not located in a separate JavaScript file.*

FILTERS

Filter hooks are much different than action hooks. They enable you to manipulate the output of code. Whereas action hooks enable you to insert code, filter hooks enable you to overwrite code that WordPress passes through the hook. Your function would "filter" the output.

To grasp the concept of filter hooks, you must first understand how the `apply_filters()` WordPress function works.

```php
<?php
apply_filters( $tag, $value );
?>
```

➤   `$tag` — The name of the filter hook.

➤   `$value` — The parameter passed to any filters added to the hook. The function can also take in any number of extra `$value` parameters to pass to filters.

It is important to note here that `$value` must be returned back to WordPress when writing a filter.

Here is an example of a filter hook from the core WordPress code.

```php
<?php
apply_filters( 'template_include', $template );
?>
```

In this example, `template_include` is name of the filter hook. `$template` is a file name that can be changed through filters registered for the filter hook.

What Is a Filter?

A filter is a function registered for a filter hook. The function itself would take in at least a single parameter and return that parameter after executing its code. Without a filter, filter hooks don't do anything. They exist so that plugin developers can change different variables. This can be anything from a simple text string to a multidimensional array.

When a filter hook is called by the `apply_filters()` function, any filters registered for the hook are executed. To add a filter, use the `add_filter()` function.

```php
<?php
add_filter( $tag, $function, $priority, $accepted_args );
?>
```

➤ `$tag` — The name of the hook you want to register your filter for.

➤ `$function` — The function name of the filter that you create to manipulate the output.

➤ `$priority` — An integer that represents in what order your filter should be applied. If no value is added, it defaults to `10`.

➤ `$accepted_args` — The number of parameters your filter function can accept. By default this is `1`. Your function must accept at least one parameter, which will be returned.

You can add multiple filters to the same filter hook. Other plugins and WordPress can also add filters to the hook. Filter hooks aren't limited to a single filter. It is important to note this because each filter must always return a value for use by the other filters. If your function doesn't return a value, you risk breaking the functionality of both WordPress and other plugins.

Now look at the `wp_title` filter hook in WordPress, which is a filter hook responsible for the `<title>` element on a page.

```php
<?php
apply_filters( 'wp_title', $title, $sep, $seplocation );
?>
```

➤ `wp_title` — The name of the hook.

➤ `$title` — A string and the value that you want to filter and return back to WordPress.

➤ `$sep` — A string that tells you what the separator should be between elements in the `<title>` element.

➤ `$seplocation` — The location of the separator. In the next example, you don't use it.

You're now going to write a function that filters the output of `$title` by appending the site's name to the end of page title.

```php
<?php

add_filter( 'wp_title', 'boj_add_site_name_to_title', 10, 2 );

function boj_add_site_name_to_title( $title, $sep ) {

    /* Get the site name. */
    $name = get_bloginfo( 'name' );

    /* Append the name to the $title variable. */
    $title .= $sep . ' ' . $name;

    /* Return the title. */
    return $title;
}

?>
```

Take a look at the line telling WordPress to add a filter to `wp_title`.

```php
<?php
add_filter( 'wp_title', 'boj_add_site_name_to_title', 10, 2 );
?>
```

It says that you want to add a filter named `boj_add_site_name_title_title` to the `wp_title` filter hook. You set a priority of `10` and tell your filter to accept two parameters.

The `boj_add_site_name_to_title()` function manipulates the `$title` parameter and returns it back to WordPress. The `$sep` parameter can be used within the function but is not returned.

Filter Hook Functions

Aside from the `apply_filters()` and `add_filter()` functions covered in the previous sections of this chapter, WordPress has several other functions for working with filter hooks.

apply_filters_ref_array

The `apply_filters_ref_array()` function works nearly the same as `apply_filters()`. One major difference is what parameters are passed. Rather than accepting multiple values, it accepts an array of arguments. Both parameters are required. It is also important to note that the `$args` parameter should be passed by reference rather than value.

```php
<?php
apply_filters_ref_array( $tag, $args );
?>
```

➤   `$tag` — The name of the filter hook.

➤   `$args` — An array of arguments to pass to filters registered for the hook.

Suppose you have a complex database query that you need to perform to load posts for the front page of the site that normal WordPress functions don't enable. WordPress has a filter hook called `posts_results` that enables you to change this. Here's what it looks like in the WordPress core code.

```php
<?php
$this->posts = apply_filters_ref_array(
    'posts_results', array( $this->posts, &$this )
);
?>
```

This filter hook passes an array of post objects to any filters registered for it. Using the following example, you completely overwrite this array of post objects and replace it with a custom set. By default, WordPress queries posts of the `post` post type. You change this to list posts of the `page` post type on the site home page.

The code example uses the `wpdb` class, which is covered in more detail in Chapter 6, "Plugin Security."

```php
<?php

add_filter( 'posts_results', 'boj_custom_home_page_posts' );

function boj_custom_home_page_posts( $results ) {
    global $wpdb, $wp_query;

    /* Check if viewing the home page. */
    if ( is_home() ) {

        /* Posts per page. */
        $per_page = get_option( 'posts_per_page' );

        /* Get the current page. */
        $paged = get_query_var( 'paged' );

        /* Set the $page variable. */
        $page = ( ( 0 == $paged || 1 == $paged ) ? 1 : absint( $paged ) );

        /* Set the number of posts to offset. */
        $offset = ( $page - 1 ) * $per_page . ', ';

        /* Set the limit by the $offset and number of posts to show. */
        $limits = 'LIMIT '. $offset . $per_page;

        /* Get results from the database. */
        $results = $wpdb->get_results( "
            SELECT SQL_CALC_FOUND_ROWS $wpdb->posts.*
            FROM $wpdb->posts
            WHERE 1=1
            AND post_type = 'page'
            AND post_status = 'publish'
```

```
            ORDER BY post_title ASC
            $limits
        " );
    }

    return $results;
}

?>
```

Code snippet boj-custom-home-page.php

remove_filter

The `remove_filter()` function enables plugins to remove filters that have been previously registered for a filter hook. To successfully remove a filter, this function must be called after a filter has been registered using the `add_filter()` function.

```php
<?php
remove_filter( $tag, $function_to_remove, $priority, $accepted_args );
?>
```

➤   `$tag` — The name of the filter hook to remove a filter from.

➤   `$function_to_remove` — The function to remove from the filter hook.

➤   `$priority` — The priority previously used in `add_filter()` to register the filter. This parameter defaults to `10`.

➤   `$accepted_args` — The number of accepted arguments previously declared in the `add_filter()` called to register the filter. This parameter defaults to `1`.

The function returns `true` when the filter is successfully removed and returns `false` when the removal is unsuccessful. The `$tag`, `$function_to_remove`, and `$priority` parameters must also match the parameters set with `add_filter()` exactly. Otherwise, the filter will not be removed.

Now look at WordPress' default filters defined in `wp-includes/default-filters.php`. One interesting filter is a function called `wpautop()`, which converts double line breaks into HTML paragraphs. It is executed on several hooks in the core code. Here's how one instance of it looks in the core WordPress code.

```php
<?php
add_filter( 'the_content', 'wpautop' );
?>
```

This applies the `wpautop()` filter to a post's content, converting each double line break of the post into a paragraph. You may have a client project that requires that specific language and formatting rules be followed. For example, the client may not want their content to have paragraphs automatically formatted. You would use the `remove_filter()` function to remove the filter from the `the_content` hook.

```php
<?php

remove_filter( 'the_content', 'wpautop' );

?>
```

In the previous code, you had to define the $tag and $function_to_remove parameters to ensure that the correct filter was removed from the correct hook. Since the original action defined no priority and the default is 10, you didn't have to define the $priority parameter.

remove_all_filters

In some plugins, you may need to remove all filters from a specific filter hook or remove filters with a particular priority from a filter hook. The remove_all_filters() function enables you to do this with a single line of code.

```php
<?php
remove_all_filters( $tag, $priority );
?>
```

➤ $tag — Name of the filter hook to remove all filters from.

➤ $priority — Priority of the filters to remove from the filter hook. This parameter is optional. If not set, all filters will be removed from the hook.

Suppose you want to remove all default formatting such as auto-paragraphs and the conversion of certain characters to their character entity equivalents for post content. WordPress adds several filters to the the_content filter hook that handles this automatically. To remove all these filters, use the remove_all_filters() with a single parameter with a value of the_content.

```php
<?php
remove_all_filters( 'the_content' );
?>
```

If you want to remove only filters with a specific priority, you need to set the second parameter. In the next example, you remove filters for the_content with the priority of 11.

```php
<?php
remove_all_filters( 'the_content', 11 );
?>
```

has_filter

The has_filter() function enables plugins to check if any filters have been registered for a filter hook or if a specific filter has been registered for the hook.

```php
<?php
has_filter( $tag, $function_to_check );
?>
```

➤ `$tag` — Name of the filter hook to check whether it has any registered filters.

➤ `$function_to_check` — A specific function to check against the filter. This parameter is optional.

The function returns `false` if no filter is found for the given hook. It returns `true` if a filter is found. However, if the `$function_to_check` parameter is set, it returns the priority of the filter.

Using the following code, you can check if a filter has been added to `the_content`. The code prints a message based on the return value of `has_filter()`.

```php
<?php

if ( has_filter( 'the_content' ) )
    echo 'The content filter hook has at least one filter.';

else
    echo 'The content filter hook has no filters.';

?>
```

If you want to check for a specific filter registered for a filter hook, you need to use the `$function_to_check` parameter. Suppose you want to check if the WordPress auto-paragraph functionality was applied to the post content. With the following code, you can print a message if this is true.

```php
<?php

if ( has_filter( 'the_content', 'wpautop' ) )
    echo 'Paragraphs are automatically formatted for the content.';

?>
```

current_filter

The `current_filter()` function returns the name of the filter hook currently executed. However, it doesn't just work with filter hooks; it applies to action hooks as well, so it returns the name of the current action or filter hook. This function is especially useful if you use a single function for multiple hooks but need the function to execute differently depending on the hook currently firing.

Suppose you have a client that needs to remove specific words from post titles and post content. The client wants to allow some words in the post title, but the allowed set of words is slightly different for the post content. You can use a single function to filter both `the_content` and `the_title` while using the `current_filter()` function to set the words based on which hook is currently executed.

Using the following code, you can set an array of unwanted words depending on the case and replace them with "Whoops!" in the text.

Available for
download on
Wrox.com

```php
<?php

add_filter( 'the_content', 'boj_replace_unwanted_words' );
add_filter( 'the_title', 'boj_replace_unwanted_words' );

function boj_replace_unwanted_words( $text ) {
```

```
    /* If the_content is the filter hook, set its unwanted words. */
    if ( 'the_content' == current_filter() )
        $words = array( 'profanity', 'curse', 'devil' );

    /* If the_title is the filter hook, set its unwanted words. */
    elseif ( 'the_title' == current_filter() )
        $words = array( 'profanity', 'curse' );

    /* Replace unwanted words with "Whoops!" */
    $text = str_replace( $words, 'Whoops!', $text );

    /* Return the formatted text. */
    return $text;
}

?>
```

Code snippet boj-replace-unwanted-words.php

Quick Return Functions

Often, you'll need to write a function that returns a common value to a filter hook such as `true`, `false`, or an empty array. You might even be tempted to use PHP's `create_function()` function to quickly return a value.

WordPress has several functions for handling scenarios such as this. With the next example code, you disable the user contact methods, which are a list of `<input>` boxes on individual user edit screens in the WordPress admin. To disable these boxes, you would need to return an empty array. Normally, you'd have to add the filter hook call and code the function.

```
<?php

add_filter( 'user_contactmethods', 'boj_return_empty_array' );

function boj_return_empty_array() {
    return array();
}

?>
```

Writing the code for that isn't so bad if doing it once or twice. However, it almost seems silly to have to write an entire function to return an empty array. WordPress makes this much easier. Because you're simply disabling these boxes, you can use WordPress's `__return_empty_array()` function as a filter for quickly returning an empty array, replacing the previous code snippet with the following.

```
<?php

add_filter( 'user_contactmethods', '__return_empty_array' );

?>
```

Using __return_empty_array is important here. WordPress will expect the value returned to be an array, so returning something other than an array would result in a PHP error.

The WordPress functions for quickly returning values can come in handy when developing plugins. It's always important to check the core code to see what value is expected after filters have been applied. Each scenario will call for a specific return value type:

➤ __return_false — Returns the Boolean value of false.

➤ __return_true — Returns the Boolean value of true.

➤ __return_empty_array — Returns an empty PHP array.

➤ __return_zero — Returns the integer 0.

These are simply a few functions WordPress makes available for use within plugins. If you find yourself writing one-line functions just to return a single value to a filter hook, you have the option of creating your own functions for handling this if the previous list of functions doesn't cover your use case.

Commonly Used Filter Hooks

WordPress has hundreds of filter hooks for use by plugin developers. Narrowing these down to a small list of some commonly used hooks doesn't come close to accurately representing what a plugin can accomplish by using the hook system. In this section, you learn how to use some of the more common filter hooks that plugin developers use in their plugins.

the_content

If there's one filter hook that plugin authors use more than any other, it is the_content. Without content, a site would be essentially useless. It is the most important thing displayed on the site, and plugins use this hook to add many features to a site.

The the_content hook passes a post's content to any filters registered for it. Filters then manipulate the content, usually for extra formatting or to append additional information about the post.

With the next code example, you append a list of related posts by post category to the_content for a reader to see when viewing a single post.

Available for
download on
Wrox.com

```php
<?php

add_filter( 'the_content', 'boj_add_related_posts_to_content' );

function boj_add_related_posts_to_content( $content ) {

    /* If not viewing a singular post, just return the content. */
    if ( !is_singular( 'post' ) )
        return $content;

    /* Get the categories of current post. */
    $terms = get_the_terms( get_the_ID(), 'category' );

    /* Loop through the categories and put their IDs in an array. */
```

```php
        $categories = array();
        foreach ( $terms as $term )
            $categories[] = $term->term_id;

        /* Query posts with the same categories from the database. */
        $loop = new WP_Query(
            array(
                'cat__in' => $categories,
                'posts_per_page' => 5,
                'post__not_in' => array( get_the_ID() ),
                'orderby' => 'rand'
            )
        );

        /* Check if any related posts exist. */
        if ( $loop->have_posts() ) {

            /* Open the unordered list. */
            $content .= '<ul class="related-posts">';

            while ( $loop->have_posts() ) {
                $loop->the_post();

                /* Add the post title with a link to the post. */
                $content .= the_title(
                    '<li><a href="' . get_permalink() . '">',
                    '</a></li>',
                    false
                );
            }

            /* Close the unordered list. */
            $content .= '</ul>';

            /* Reset the query. */
            wp_reset_query();
        }

        /* Return the content. */
        return $content;
}

?>
```

Code snippet boj-related-posts.php

the_title

Post titles are almost as important as the post content, which makes the_title a popular filter hook for use. You can use this hook to add information or overwrite completely.

One useful filter to use for the_title is a function to strip HTML tags from it. Users sometimes add tags here that can mess up the formatting of the title on output. Using the following code, you can strip all tags a user might use when writing a post title.

```php
<?php

add_filter( 'the_title', 'boj_strip_tags_from_titles' );

function boj_strip_tags_from_titles( $title ) {

    $title = strip_tags( $title );

    return $title;
}

?>
```

comment_text

The `comment_text` hook is often a useful filter hook because comments typically play a large role for blogs and other types of sites.

With the next code example, you check if a comment was made by a registered user on the site. If the user is registered, you can append a paragraph that prints the user's role for the site (see Chapter 8, "Users").

```php
<?php

add_filter( 'comment_text', 'boj_add_role_to_comment_text' );

function boj_add_role_to_comment_text( $text ) {
    global $comment;

    /* Check if comment was made by a registered user. */
    if ( $comment->user_id > 0 ) {

        /* Create new user object. */
        $user = new WP_User( $comment->user_id );

        /* If user has a role, add it to the comment text. */
        if ( is_array( $user->roles ) )
            $text .= '<p>User Role: ' . $user->roles[0] . '</p>';
    }

    return $text;
}

?>
```

template_include

`template_include` is a sort of catchall filter hook for many other, more specific filter hooks.

- ➤ `front_page_template`
- ➤ `home_template`
- ➤ `single_template`

- ➤ page_template

- ➤ attachment_template

- ➤ archive_template

- ➤ category_template

- ➤ tag_template

- ➤ author_template

- ➤ date_template

- ➤ archive_template

- ➤ search_template

- ➤ 404_template

- ➤ index_template

It is used after the theme template file for the current page has been chosen. WordPress chooses a template based on the page currently viewed by a reader. You can add a filter for each of the individual filter hooks or filter them all at the end with the template_include hook.

Suppose you wanted to build a custom template hierarchy to allow themes to use templates based on your plugin's criteria instead of the normal WordPress template hierarchy. The template_include and the other hooks in the previous list enable you to do this.

Using the next example code, you check if a template exists for single posts by category. By default, WordPress looks for a single.php file first and then falls back to index.php if it doesn't exist. Your function looks for a file called single-category-$slug.php ($slug is the category slug), so if a user has a category with the slug of "art" and a template named single-category-art.php in their theme, this file will be used in lieu of single.php.

```php
<?php

add_filter( 'single_template', 'boj_single_template' );

function boj_single_template( $template ) {
    global $wp_query;

    /* Check if viewing a singular post. */
    if ( is_singular( 'post' ) ) {
        /* Get the post ID. */
        $post_id = $wp_query->get_queried_object_id();

        /* Get the post categories. */
        $terms = get_the_terms( $post_id, 'category' );

        /* Loop through the categories, adding slugs as part of the file name. */
        $templates = array();
        foreach ( $terms as $term )
            $templates[] = "single-category-{$term->slug}.php";
```

```
        /* Check if the template exists. */
        $locate = locate_template( $templates );

        /* If a template was found, make it the new template. */
        if ( !empty( $locate ) )
            $template = $locate;
    }

    /* Return the template file name. */
    return $template;
}

?>
```

Code snippet boj-single-template.php

USING HOOKS FROM WITHIN A CLASS

Throughout this chapter, you've seen many examples of using action and filter hooks with PHP functions. When adding a method of a class as an action or filter, the format of the calls to add_action() and add_filter() is slightly different.

In general, plugins most often use functions as actions and filters rather than class methods. However, there will be cases in which using a class will be beneficial to your plugin, and you will need to know how to register methods for hooks from within the class.

Take a look at a basic function registered for an action hook, which was covered in detail in the section on actions earlier in the chapter.

```
<?php
add_action( $tag, $function_to_add );
?>
```

When using a method such as $function_to_add from within a class, you must change $function_to_add to an array with &$this as the first argument and the method name as the second argument.

```
<?php
add_action( $tag, array( &$this, $method_to_add ) );
?>
```

The same is true for filter hooks as well. A function added to a filter hook would normally look like this:

```
<?php
add_filter( $tag, $function_to_add );
?>
```

When using a class method as a filter, you must also change the $function_to_add parameter.

```
<?php
add_filter( $tag, array( &$this, $method_to_add ) );
?>
```

In the following example, you build a class that has a constructor method, a method used as an action, and a method used as a filter. The `add_filters()` method checks if the reader is currently viewing a singular post view. If true, the `content()` method appends the last modified date of the post to the post content.

```php
<?php

class BOJ_My_Plugin_Loader {

    /* Constructor method for the class. */
    function BOJ_My_Plugin_Loader() {

        /* Add the 'singular_check' method to the 'template_redirect' hook. */
        add_action( 'template_redirect', array( &$this, 'singular_check' ) );
    }

    /* Method used as an action. */
    function singular_check() {

        /* If viewing a singular post, filter the content. */
        if ( is_singular() )
            add_filter( 'the_content', array( &$this, 'content' ) );
    }

    /* Method used as a filter. */
    function content( $content ) {

        /* Get the date the post was last modified. */
        $date = get_the_modified_time( get_option( 'date_format' ) );

        /* Append the post modified date to the content. */
        $content .= '<p>Post last modified: ' . $date . '</p>';

        /* Return the content. */
        return $content;
    }
}

$boj_myplugin_loader = new BOJ_My_Plugin_Loader();

?>
```

Code snippet boj-class-hooks.php

CREATING CUSTOM HOOKS

Not only can plugins take advantage of the core code's built-in hooks, but they can also create custom hooks for use by other plugins and themes. Doing so can be especially beneficial with code when it's okay to change the output of that code.

Your plugin would use one of four available functions for creating custom action hooks.

➤ `do_action()`

➤ `do_action_ref_array()`

➤ `apply_filters()`

➤ `apply_filters_ref_array()`

You would use the first two functions for creating custom action hooks and the next two functions for creating custom filter hooks.

Benefits of Creating Custom Hooks

Custom hooks make your plugin more flexible, allow it to be extended by others, and gives you the ability to hook into the execution of various processes throughout your plugin within the plugin itself.

Using custom hooks also keep users from editing your work directly. The importance of this is that when you provide an update for the plugin, users won't lose any modifications they've made.

Custom Action Hook Example

In this custom action hook example, you create a plugin setup function. The function defines a constant that can be altered. Other plugins may also execute any code they want on the hook. You provide it so that they have an opportunity to run code at that point.

```php
<?php

add_action( 'plugins_loaded', 'boj_myplugin_setup' );

function boj_myplugin_setup() {

    /* Allow actions to fire before anything else. */
    do_action( 'boj_myplugin_setup_pre' );

    /* Check if the root slug is defined. */
    if ( !defined( 'BOJ_MYPLUGIN_ROOT_SLUG' ) )
        define( 'BOJ_MYPLUGIN_ROOT_SLUG', 'articles' );
}

?>
```

Other plugins or themes may hook into `boj_myplugin_setup_pre` and execute any function. Suppose you want to change the `BOJ_MYPLUGIN_ROOT_SLUG` constant from "articles" to "papers." You can create a custom action to add to the hook.

```php
<?php

add_action( 'boj_myplugin_setup_pre', 'boj_define_myplugin_constants' );

function boj_define_myplugin_constants() {

    define( 'BOJ_MYPLUGIN_ROOT_SLUG', 'papers' );
}

?>
```

Custom Filter Hook Example

Suppose you have a function that displays a list of posts given a specific set of arguments. You may want to grant others the ability to filter the arguments and filter the final output.

In this example, you write a function that lists the top 10 posts by the number of comments a post has received. The function enables users to filter the arguments for grabbing the posts from the database and enables them to filter the final HTML output of the list.

```php
<?php

function boj_posts_by_comments() {

    /* Default arguments. */
    $args = array(
        'post_type' => 'post',
        'posts_per_page' => 10,
        'order' => 'DESC',
        'orderby' => 'comment_count'
    );

    /* Apply filters to the arguments. */
    $args = apply_filters( 'boj_posts_by_comments_args', $args );

    /* Set up the output variable. */
    $out = '';

    /* Query posts from the database by the given arguments. */
    $loop = new WP_Query( $args );

    /* Check if posts are found. */
    if ( $loop->have_posts() ) {

        /* Open the unordered list. */
        $out .= '<ul class="posts-by-comments">';

        /* Loop through the posts. */
        while ( $loop->have_posts() ) {

            $loop->the_post();

            /* Add the post title to the list. */
            $out .= the_title( '<li>', '</li>', false );
        }

        /* Close the unordered list. */
        $out .= '</ul>';
    }

    /* Apply filters to the final output. */
    $out = apply_filters( 'boj_posts_by_comments', $out );
```

```
        /* Display the HTML. */
        echo $out;
    }

?>
```

To filter the arguments, add a filter to `boj_posts_by_comments_args`. Suppose you want to change the default number of `10` posts to `15`. You add a custom filter for this.

```php
<?php

add_filter( 'boj_posts_by_comments_args', 'boj_change_posts_by_comments_args' );

function boj_change_posts_by_comments_args( $args ) {

    /* Change the value of the posts_per_page array key. */
    $args['posts_per_page'] = 15;

    /* Return the $args parameter. */
    return $args;
}

?>
```

To filter the final HTML output, add a filter to `boj_posts_by_comments`. Suppose you want to change the unordered list to an ordered list with a custom filter.

```php
<?php

add_filter( 'boj_posts_by_comments', 'boj_change_posts_by_comments' );

function boj_change_posts_by_comments( $out ) {

    /* Change the opening <ul> to an <ol>. */
    $out = str_replace( '<ul ', '<ol ', $out );

    /* Change the closing </ul> to an </ol>. */
    $out = str_replace( '</ul>', '</ol>', $out );

    /* Return the filtered HTML. */
    return $out;
}

?>
```

HOW TO FIND HOOKS

It would be nearly impossible to give a complete list of all the available hooks in WordPress. In earlier sections of this chapter, you learned about some of the more common action and filter hooks, but these sections cover only a small sampling of what WordPress has to offer.

New hooks are always added with new versions of WordPress. Keeping track of changes in the core code from version to version can help you stay on top of new hooks that you can use within your plugins.

Searching for Hooks in the Core Code

As a plugin developer, you should become familiar with the core WordPress code. Looking for hooks is a great way to start familiarizing yourself with how WordPress works. There's no better process for understanding how PHP code works than actually looking at the code and following each statement made within the code.

An easy way to search for hooks is to open a file from the wordpress folder in your preferred text editor and run a text search for one of four function names.

➤   do_action

➤   do_action_ref_array

➤   apply_filters

➤   apply_filters_ref_array

Those are the functions you learned to use earlier in the chapter. Each function creates a hook, so by searching for one of those strings, you can find new hooks in WordPress.

Variable Hooks

When searching for hooks throughout the core WordPress code, you will come across what's known as "variable hooks." Normally, hook names are a static string of text. However, variable hook names change based on a specific variable.

A good example of this is the load-$pagenow action hook. The $pagenow variable changes depending on the WordPress admin page currently viewed. The hook looks like the following in the core code.

```php
<?php
do_action( "load-$pagenow" );
?>
```

The $pagenow variable will become the page name being viewed. For example, the hook for the new post page in the admin would be load-post-new.php and the hook on the edit posts screen would be load-post.php. This enables plugins to run code only for specific page views in the admin.

WordPress has several action and filter hooks with variables as part of the hook name. Generally, these hook names change to provide context to plugin developers so that they can execute code only when specific circumstances are met. It is important to keep this in mind when searching for just the right hook to use in your plugin.

Hook Reference Lists

Although searching for hooks within the core code can be beneficial to your learning experience, sometimes you may find it easier to access some of the publicly available reference lists on the Web. These lists can sometimes save you time and may also have descriptions about the hook.

WordPress has both an official action and filter hook reference list in its Codex.

➤ `http://codex.wordpress.org/Plugin_API/Action_Reference`

➤ `http://codex.wordpress.org/Plugin_API/Filter_Reference`

Chapter 18, "The Developer Toolbox," covers more materials and tools to help plugin developers.

SUMMARY

Hooks are the most important aspect of building plugins for WordPress. Each time you start a new plugin project, you hook your plugin's functions into the WordPress action and filter hooks. You can use everything you learned throughout this chapter in the following chapters of the book because hooks play such an integral part in plugin development.

Now that you can fully grasp how hooks work, it's time to start building plugins.

Integrating in WordPress

WHAT'S IN THIS CHAPTER?

➤ Creating menus and submenus

➤ Creating widgets and dashboard widgets

➤ Defining meta boxes for content

➤ Designing and styling your plugin

Integrating your plugin in WordPress is a critical step in building a professional plugin. WordPress features many different ways to integrate your plugin including adding top-level and submenu items, creating widgets and dashboard widgets, and adding meta boxes to your content screens.

In this chapter you learn how to properly integrate your plugin into the various areas of WordPress. You also learn the proper design and styles available that your plugins can take advantage of to provide your users with a consistent user-interface experience.

ADDING MENUS AND SUBMENUS

Many plugins you create need some type of menu item, which generally links to your plugin's settings page where the user can configure your plugin options. WordPress features two methods for adding a plugin menu: a top-level menu or a submenu item.

Creating a Top-Level Menu

The first menu method for your plugin to explore in WordPress is a new top-level menu, which is added to the admin dashboard menu list. For example, Settings is a top-level menu. A top-level menu is common practice for any plugin that needs multiple option pages. To register a top-level menu, you use the `add_menu_page()` function.

```php
<?php add_menu_page( page_title, menu_title, capability, menu_slug, function,
        icon_url, position ); ?>
```

The `add_menu_page()` function accepts the following parameters:

➤ `page_title` — The title of the page as shown in the `<title>` tags

➤ `menu_title` — The name of your menu displayed on the dashboard

➤ `capability` — Minimum capability required to view the menu

➤ `menu_slug` — Slug name to refer to the menu; should be a unique name

➤ `function`: Function to be called to display the page content for the item

➤ `icon_url` — URL to a custom image to use as the Menu icon

➤ `position` — Location in the menu order where it should appear

Now create a new menu for your plugin to see the menu process in action. Use the `admin_menu` action hook to trigger your menu code. This is the appropriate hook to use whenever you create menus and submenus in your plugins.

```php
<?php
add_action( 'admin_menu', 'boj_menuexample_create_menu' );

function boj_menuexample_create_menu() {

    //create custom top-level menu
    add_menu_page( 'My Plugin Settings Page', 'Menu Example Settings',
        'manage_options', __FILE__, 'boj_menuexample_settings_page',
        plugins_url( '/images/wp-icon.png', __FILE__ ) );

}

?>
```

As you can see, the `admin_menu` action hook calls your custom `boj_menuexample_create_menu()` function. Next you need to call the `add_menu_page()` function to register the custom menu in WordPress. Set the name of your menu to Menu Example Settings, which requires that the user has `manage_options` capabilities (that is, is an administrator), and even set a custom icon located in the `/images` folder of your plugin, as shown in Figure 4-1.

FIGURE 4-1

Menus are a common feature in WordPress plugins and are generally expected by the user. It's a good idea to mention where your plugin settings can be found in the plugin description and documentation.

Adding a Submenu

Now that you have a new top-level menu created, create some submenus for it, which are menu items listed below your top-level menu. For example, Settings is a top-level menu whereas General, listed below Settings, is a submenu of the Settings menu. To register a submenu, use the add_submenu_page() function.

```php
<?php add_submenu_page( parent_slug, page_title, menu_title, capability,
        menu_slug, function ); ?>
```

The add_submenu_page() function accepts the following parameters:

➤   parent_slug: Slug name for the parent menu (menu_slug previously defined)

➤   page_title: The title of the page as shown in the <title> tags

➤   menu_title: The name of your submenu displayed on the dashboard

➤   capability: Minimum capability required to view the submenu

➤   menu_slug: Slug name to refer to the submenu; should be a unique name

➤   function: Function to be called to display the page content for the item

Now that you know how submenus are defined, you can add one to your custom top-level menu:

Available for download on Wrox.com

```php
<?php
add_action( 'admin_menu', 'boj_menuexample_create_menu' );

function boj_menuexample_create_menu() {

    //create custom top-level menu
    add_menu_page( 'My Plugin Settings Page', 'Menu Example Settings',
        'manage_options', __FILE__, 'boj_menuexample_settings_page',
        plugins_url( '/images/wp-icon.png', __FILE__ ) );

    //create submenu items
    add_submenu_page( __FILE__, 'About My Plugin', 'About', 'manage_options',
        __FILE__.'_about', boj_menuexample_about_page );
    add_submenu_page( __FILE__, 'Help with My Plugin', 'Help', 'manage_options',
        __FILE__.'_help', boj_menuexample_help_page );
    add_submenu_page( __FILE__, 'Uninstall My Plugin', 'Uninstall', 'manage_
options',
        __FILE__.'_uninstall', boj_menuexample_uninstall_page );

}
?>
```

Code snippet boj-custom-menu-plugin.php

The preceding code creates three submenus for your custom top-level menu: About, Help, and Uninstall, as shown in Figure 4-2. Each of these submenu items link to a different custom function that can contain any code you want to use for that submenu page.

Adding a Menu Item to an Existing Menu

If your plugin requires only a single options page, you do not need to create a custom top-level menu. Instead you can simply add a submenu to an existing menu, such as the Settings menu.

WordPress features many different functions to add submenus to the existing default menus in WordPress. One of these functions is the `add_options_page()` function. Now explore how the `add_options_page()` function works to add a submenu item to the Settings menu.

```php
<?php add_options_page( page_title, menu_title, capability, menu_slug, function);?>
```

FIGURE 4-2

The `add_options_page()` function accepts the following parameters:

➤ `page_title` — The title of the page as shown in the `<title>` tags

➤ `menu_title` — The name of your submenu displayed on the dashboard

➤ `capability` — Minimum capability required to view the submenu

➤ `menu_slug` — Slug name to refer to the submenu; should be a unique name

➤ `function` — Function to be called to display the page content for the item

Now add a submenu item to the Settings menu:

Available for download on Wrox.com

```php
<?php
add_action( 'admin_menu', 'boj_menuexample_create_menu' );

function boj_menuexample_create_menu() {

    //create a submenu under Settings
    add_options_page( 'My Plugin Settings Page', 'Menu Example Settings',
        'manage_options', __FILE__, 'boj_menuexample_settings_page' );

}
?>
```

Code snippet boj-options-page-plugin.php

The preceding code adds a submenu labeled Menu Example Settings under the Settings menu, as shown in Figure 4-3. Set the page title to My Plugin Settings Page, set the capability to `manage_options` so that only administrators can view it, and set the function `boj_menuexample_settings_page()` to be called when the submenu is clicked.

Following is a list of all available submenu functions in WordPress.

➤ `add_dashboard_page` — Adds a submenu to the Dashboard menu

➤ `add_posts_page` — Adds a submenu to the Posts menu

➤ `add_media_page` — Adds a submenu to the Media menu

➤ `add_links_page` — Adds a submenu to the Links menu

➤ `add_pages_page` — Adds a submenu to the Pages menu

➤ `add_comments_page` — Adds a submenu to the Comments page

➤ `add_theme_page` — Adds a submenu to the Appearance menu

➤ `add_plugins_page` — Adds a submenu to the Plugins menu

➤ `add_users_page` — Adds a submenu to the Users menu

➤ `add_management_page` — Adds a submenu to the Tools menu

➤ `add_options_page` — Adds a submenu to the Settings menu

To use any of these functions, simply swap out the function name in the code shown earlier.

FIGURE 4-3

 If your plugin requires only a single options page, it's best to add it as a submenu to an existing menu. If you require more than one, create a custom top-level menu.

CREATING WIDGETS

Widgets are a great way to give the users of your plugin an easy method to display your plugin information or data. WordPress features a Widgets API for creating and interacting with widgets. In this section you explore how to create widgets, add and save widget options, and display plugin information in the widget.

Creating a Widget

You create all widgets in WordPress using the `WP_Widget` class. To understand how the widget class works, it's helpful to look at an overview of the class:

```php
<?php
class My_Widget extends WP_Widget {

    function My_Widget() {
        // processes the widget
    }

    function form($instance) {
```

```
        // displays the widget form in the admin dashboard
    }

    function update($new_instance, $old_instance) {
        // process widget options to save
    }

    function widget($args, $instance) {
        // displays the widget
    }

}
?>
```

As you can see, the `WP_Widget` class features multiple functions for your widget, each with a specific purpose.

Now it's time to create a widget for your plugin. For this first widget, you create a simple text-based widget to save and display your favorite movie and song. It is a simple example that demonstrates how to save text data in a WordPress widget.

To start you use the `widgets_init` action hook. This hook is triggered after the default widgets have been registered in WordPress.

```
<?php
// use widgets_init action hook to execute custom function
add_action( 'widgets_init', 'boj_widgetexample_register_widgets' );

 //register our widget
function boj_widgetexample_register_widgets() {
    register_widget( 'boj_widgetexample_widget_my_info' );
}
?>
```

The `widgets_init` hook triggers the custom function to register your widget, in this case `boj_widgetexample_register_widgets()`. Next you use the `register_widget()` function to register your new widget; in this example you register the class name as `boj_widgetexample_widget_my_info()`. This function accepts one parameter, and that is the class name that will extend `WP_Widget`. The widget class name can be anything, but it must be unique and should always be descriptive of your widget. You can also register as many widgets as needed using this function.

Now that you've registered your widget, it's time to set up the widget class.

```
<?php
//boj_widgetexample_widget_my_info class
class boj_widgetexample_widget_my_info extends WP_Widget {
?>
```

You need to extend the `WP_Widget` class by creating a new class with the unique name you defined when you registered your widget. Now that you've defined the class, it's time to start building the widget.

```php
<?php
    //process the new widget
    function boj_widgetexample_widget_my_info() {
        $widget_ops = array(
            'classname' => 'boj_widgetexample_widget_class',
            'description' => 'Display a user\'s favorite movie and song.'
        );
        $this->WP_Widget( 'boj_widgetexample_widget_my_info', 'My Info Widget',
            $widget_ops );
    }
?>
```

First, make a new array to store your widget options called $widget_ops. This array can hold the classname and description options. The classname option is the class name added to the <li> element of the widget. Sidebars, by default, display all widgets in an unordered list. Each individual widget is a list item in that list, so by adding a custom classname and ID, you can easily create custom styles and designs for your widget. The description displays under the widget on the Appearance ➪ Widgets screen and is used to describe your widgets function.

After building your options array, you then pass those values to WP_Widget. The first value you pass is the ID for the list item of your widget, in this case boj_widgetexample_widget_my_info(). The second value to pass is the widget name displayed in the Widgets screen. The widget name should be a short and sweet name describing your widget. The final value to pass is your array of options you set earlier.

Next you need to create your widgets settings form. This widget accepts three values: Title, Favorite movie, and Favorite song.

```php
<?php
    //build the widget settings form
    function form($instance) {
        $defaults = array( 'title' => 'My Info', 'movie' => '', 'song' => '' );
        $instance = wp_parse_args( (array) $instance, $defaults );
        $title = $instance['title'];
        $movie = $instance['movie'];
        $song = $instance['song'];
        ?>
        <p>Title: <input class="widefat" name="
            <?php echo $this->get_field_name( 'title' ); ?>"  type="text"
            value="<?php echo esc_attr( $title ); ?>" /></p>
        <p>Favorite Movie: <input class="widefat" name="
            <?php echo $this->get_field_name( 'movie' ); ?>"  type="text"
            value="<?php echo esc_attr( $movie ); ?>" /></p>
        <p>Favorite Song: <textarea class="widefat" name="
            <?php echo $this->get_field_name( 'song' ); ?>" / >
            <?php echo esc_attr( $song ); ?></textarea></p>
        <?php
    }
?>
```

First, you create a $defaults variable to set the default values of each option. In this example, you set only the default title to My Info. Next pull in the instance values; that is, the widget settings that have been saved. If this is a new widget and was just added to a sidebar, there won't be any settings saved, so this value will be empty.

The final part to your widget settings is to display the form elements for entering the widget information. Use a standard HTML input text field for all three of your fields: title, movie, and song. You'll notice you don't need to include the <form> tags or submit button; the widget class handles that for you. Also notice you use the esc_attr() function to escape the saved value prior to displaying it in the field.

Now it's time to save your widget settings using the update function of the widget class.

```php
<?php
    //save the widget settings
    function update($new_instance, $old_instance) {
        $instance = $old_instance;
        $instance['title'] = strip_tags( $new_instance['title'] );
        $instance['movie'] = strip_tags( $new_instance['movie'] );
        $instance['song'] = strip_tags( $new_instance['song'] );

        return $instance;
    }
?>
```

As you can see, the widget class handles all the saving for you. You simply pass in the $new_instance values for each of your widget settings. Always be sure to sanitize any user-entered data, in this case using the strip_tags() PHP function.

The final piece to the widget puzzle is displaying your widget in the sidebar. To do this you use the widget function of the widget class.

```php
<?php
    //display the widget
    function widget($args, $instance) {
        extract($args);

        echo $before_widget;
        $title = apply_filters( 'widget_title', $instance['title'] );
        $movie = empty( $instance['movie'] ) ? ' ' : $instance['movie'];
        $song = empty( $instance['song'] ) ? ' ' : $instance['song'];

        if ( !empty( $title ) ) { echo $before_title . $title . $after_title; };
        echo '<p>Fav Movie: ' . $movie . '</p>';
        echo '<p>Fav Song: ' . $song . '</p>';
        echo $after_widget;
    }
?>
```

The first step is to extract the $args parameter. This variable holds global theme values such as $before_widget and $after_widget. These values can be defined when a sidebar is registered and can be used to customize the code that wraps your widget, such as adding a custom <div> tag.

Next you set the $title variable for the title of your widget. You need to apply the widget_title filter hook to the title. This enables other developers to modify the display of the widget title if needed. To set the $movie and $song variables, use a PHP ternary operator. In plain English this line breaks down as follows: If $movie is empty, set it to ' ', if it's not empty set it to $instance['movie'].

Now that you've defined all your widget setting variables and populated their values, it's time to display them. First, display the $title variable. It's always important to wrap this value with the $before_title and $after_title variables. These global variables can also be set by developers when registering a sidebar. After displaying the $title value, display the favorite movie and song values. Finally, remember to end your widget display with the $after_widget global value.

Congratulations! You just created a WordPress widget! Now you can add your newly created widget and fill in the widget settings, as shown in Figure 4-4.

Your new widget then displays in your sidebar, as shown in Figure 4-5.

Now review the full widget code that's put together:

FIGURE 4-4

FIGURE 4-5

Available for download on Wrox.com

```php
<?php
/*
Plugin Name: Widget Example Plugin
Plugin URI: http://example.com/wordpress-plugins/my-plugin
Description: A plugin to create widgets in WordPress
Version: 1.0
Author: Brad Williams
Author URI: http://wrox.com
License: GPLv2
*/

// use widgets_init action hook to execute custom function
add_action( 'widgets_init', 'boj_widgetexample_register_widgets' );

 //register our widget
function boj_widgetexample_register_widgets() {
    register_widget( 'boj_widgetexample_widget_my_info' );
}

//boj_widget_my_info class
class boj_widgetexample_widget_my_info extends WP_Widget {

    //process the new widget
    function boj_widgetexample_widget_my_info() {
        $widget_ops = array(
            'classname' => 'boj_widgetexample_widget_class',
            'description' => 'Display a user\'s favorite movie and song.'
            );
        $this->WP_Widget( 'boj_widgetexample_widget_my_info', 'My Info Widget',
            $widget_ops );
    }

    //build the widget settings form
```

```php
function form($instance) {
    $defaults = array( 'title' => 'My Info', 'movie' => '', 'song' => '' );
    $instance = wp_parse_args( (array) $instance, $defaults );
    $title = $instance['title'];
    $movie = $instance['movie'];
    $song = $instance['song'];
    ?>
        <p>Title: <input class="widefat" name="
            <?php echo $this->get_field_name( 'title' ); ?>"
            type="text" value="<?php echo esc_attr( $title ); ?>" /></p>
        <p>Favorite Movie: <input class="widefat" name="
            <?php echo $this->get_field_name( 'movie' ); ?>"
            type="text" value="<?php echo esc_attr( $movie ); ?>" /></p>
        <p>Favorite Song: <textarea class="widefat" name="
            <?php echo $this->get_field_name( 'song' ); ?>" / >
            <?php echo esc_attr( $song ); ?></textarea></p>
    <?php
}

//save the widget settings
function update($new_instance, $old_instance) {
    $instance = $old_instance;
    $instance['title'] = strip_tags( $new_instance['title'] );
    $instance['movie'] = strip_tags( $new_instance['movie'] );
    $instance['song'] = strip_tags( $new_instance['song'] );

    return $instance;
}

//display the widget
function widget($args, $instance) {
    extract($args);

    echo $before_widget;
    $title = apply_filters( 'widget_title', $instance['title'] );
    $movie = empty( $instance['movie'] ) ? ' ' : $instance['movie'];
    $song = empty( $instance['song'] ) ? ' ' : $instance['song'];

    if ( !empty( $title ) ) { echo $before_title . $title . $after_title; };
    echo '<p>Fav Movie: ' . $movie . '</p>';
    echo '<p>Fav Song: ' . $song . '</p>';
    echo $after_widget;
}
}
?>
```

Code snippet boj-widget-plugin.php

Advanced Widget

Now that you have a solid understanding of how widgets work, you can create a more advanced widget. In this example, you create a widget that retrieves an RSS feed and displays its results. You also use different types of form elements for your widget options. First, you need to register your new widget.

```php
<?php
// use widgets_init action hook to execute custom function
add_action( 'widgets_init', 'boj_awe_register_widgets' );

//register our widget
function boj_awe_register_widgets() {
    register_widget( 'boj_awe_widget' );
}
?>
```

Register your new widget as `boj_awe_widget`. Now that your widget is registered, it's time to extend the `WP_Widget` class for your new widget.

```php
<?php
//boj_widget_my_info class
class boj_awe_widget extends WP_Widget {

    //process the new widget
    function boj_awe_widget() {

        $widget_ops = array(
        'classname' => 'boj_awe_widget_class',
        'description' => 'Display an RSS feed with options.'
        );

        $this->WP_Widget( 'boj_awe_widget', 'Advanced RSS Widget', $widget_ops );
    }
?>
```

As before, you set the class name and description of your new widget. In this example, the new widget title is set to Advanced RSS Widget. Next create the widget options.

```php
<?php
    //build the widget settings form
    function form($instance) {
        $defaults = array(
            'title' => 'RSS Feed',
            'rss_feed' => 'http://strangework.com/feed',
            'rss_items' => '2'
        );
        $instance = wp_parse_args( (array) $instance, $defaults );
        $title = $instance['title'];
        $rss_feed = $instance['rss_feed'];
        $rss_items = $instance['rss_items'];
        $rss_date = $instance['rss_date'];
        $rss_summary = $instance['rss_summary'];
        ?>
            <p>Title: <input class="widefat" name="
                <?php echo $this->get_field_name( 'title' ); ?>"
```

```php
            type="text" value="<?php echo esc_attr( $title ); ?>" /></p>
        <p>RSS Feed: <input class="widefat" name="
            <?php echo $this->get_field_name( 'rss_feed' ); ?>"
            type="text" value="<?php echo esc_attr( $rss_feed ); ?>" /></p>
        <p>Items to Display:
        <select name="<?php echo $this->get_field_name( 'rss_items' ); ?>">
            <option value="1" <?php selected( $rss_items, 1 ); ?>>1</option>
            < option value="2" <?php selected( $rss_items, 2 ); ?>>2</option>
            < option value="3" <?php selected( $rss_items, 3 ); ?>>3</option>
            < option value="4" <?php selected( $rss_items, 4 ); ?>>4</option>
            < option value="5" <?php selected( $rss_items, 5 ); ?>>5</option>
        </select>
        </p>
        <p>Show Date?: <input name="
            <?php echo $this->get_field_name( 'rss_date' ); ?>"
            type="checkbox" <?php checked( $rss_date, 'on' ); ?> /></p>
        <p>Show Summary?: <input name="
            <?php echo $this->get_field_name( 'rss_summary' ); ?>"
            type="checkbox" <?php checked( $rss_summary, 'on' ); ?> /></p>
    <?php
    }
?>
```

This widget features five options enabling the user to set the title, RSS feed, items to display, and whether a date and summary of each post will be displayed. The title and RSS feed options are standard text fields.

The items to display option is an HTML select list. Notice the use of the `selected()` function, which is an extremely useful tool for comparing two values in a select field to determine if that option is selected. If the option value compared is the option that is saved, WordPress adds `selected='selected'` value to the option field, which makes it the selected option.

The show date and show summary options are both check box form fields. Here you use the `checked()` WordPress function. This function works just like the `selected()` function in that it compares two values and determines if they are identical, but the difference is the `checked()` function outputs `checked='checked'`, which makes the option checked.

Now that your widget form is set up, it's time to save your widget options.

```php
<?php
    //save the widget settings
    function update($new_instance, $old_instance) {
        $instance = $old_instance;
        $instance['title'] = strip_tags( $new_instance['title'] );
        $instance['rss_feed'] = strip_tags( $new_instance['rss_feed'] );
        $instance['rss_items'] = strip_tags( $new_instance['rss_items'] );
        $instance['rss_date'] = strip_tags( $new_instance['rss_date'] );
        $instance['rss_summary'] = strip_tags( $new_instance['rss_summary'] );

        return $instance;
    }
?>
```

As always make sure you sanitize the widget option values using the proper sanitizing function, in this case `strip_tags()`. Now that the widget options are saved, it's time to display the widget based on the set options.

```php
<?php
    //display the widget
    function widget($args, $instance) {
        extract($args);

        echo $before_widget;

        //load the widget settings
        $title = apply_filters( 'widget_title', $instance['title'] );
        $rss_feed = empty( $instance['rss_feed'] ) ? '' : $instance['rss_feed'];
        $rss_items = empty( $instance['rss_items'] ) ? 2 : $instance['rss_items'];
        $rss_date = empty( $instance['rss_date'] ) ? 0 : 1;
        $rss_summary = empty( $instance['rss_summary'] ) ? 0 : 1;

        if ( !empty( $title ) ) { echo $before_title . $title . $after_title; };

            if ( $rss_feed ) {
                //display the RSS feed
                wp_widget_rss_output( array(
                    'url' => $rss_feed,
                    'title' => $title,
                    'items' => $rss_items,
                    'show_summary' => $rss_summary,
                    'show_author' => 0,
                    'show_date' => $rss_date
                ) );
            }

        echo $after_widget;
    }
?>
```

First, you need to load all the widget options to determine how the RSS feed should display. The defaults for each option are set using a ternary operator. For example, if the RSS date option is checked by the user, the `$rss_date` variable will be set to `1`; if not it will be set to `0`.

You have just created an advanced RSS widget in WordPress! This widget is a great example of how to create and set different types of options and use them appropriately in your widget's display. Now look at the full source code for the widget.

```php
<?php
/*
Plugin Name: Advanced Widget Example Plugin
Plugin URI: http://example.com/wordpress-plugins/my-plugin
Description: A plugin to create widgets in WordPress
Version: 1.0
Author: Brad Williams
Author URI: http://wrox.com
License: GPLv2
```

```
*/

// use widgets_init action hook to execute custom function
add_action( 'widgets_init', 'boj_awe_register_widgets' );

//register our widget
function boj_awe_register_widgets() {
    register_widget( 'boj_awe_widget' );
}

//boj_widget_my_info class
class boj_awe_widget extends WP_Widget {

    //process the new widget
    function boj_awe_widget() {

        $widget_ops = array(
            'classname' => 'boj_awe_widget_class',
            'description' => 'Display an RSS feed with options.'
            );

        $this->WP_Widget( 'boj_awe_widget', 'Advanced RSS Widget', $widget_ops );
    }

     //build the widget settings form
    function form($instance) {
        $defaults = array(
            'title' => 'RSS Feed',
            'rss_feed' => 'http://strangework.com/feed',
            'rss_items' => '2'
        );
        $instance = wp_parse_args( (array) $instance, $defaults );
        $title = $instance['title'];
        $rss_feed = $instance['rss_feed'];
        $rss_items = $instance['rss_items'];
        $rss_date = $instance['rss_date'];
        $rss_summary = $instance['rss_summary'];
        ?>
            <p>Title: <input class="widefat" name="
                <?php echo $this->get_field_name( 'title' ); ?>"
                type="text" value="<?php echo esc_attr( $title ); ?>" /></p>
            <p>RSS Feed: <input class="widefat" name="
                <?php echo $this->get_field_name( 'rss_feed' ); ?>"
                type="text" value="<?php echo esc_attr( $rss_feed ); ?>" /></p>
            <p>Items to Display:
                <select name="<?php echo $this->get_field_name( 'rss_items' ); ?>">
                    <option value="1" <?php selected( $rss_items, 1 ); ?>>1</option>
                    <option value="2" <?php selected( $rss_items, 2 ); ?>>2</option>
                    <option value="3" <?php selected( $rss_items, 3 ); ?>>3</option>
                    <option value="4" <?php selected( $rss_items, 4 ); ?>>4</option>
                    <option value="5" <?php selected( $rss_items, 5 ); ?>>5</option>
                </select>
            </p>
            <p>Show Date?: <input name="
```

```php
            <?php echo $this->get_field_name( 'rss_date' ); ?>"
                type="checkbox" <?php checked( $rss_date, 'on' ); ?> /></p>
            <p>Show Summary?: <input name="
                <?php echo $this->get_field_name( 'rss_summary' ); ?>"
                type="checkbox" <?php checked( $rss_summary, 'on' ); ?> /></p>
        <?php
    }

    //save the widget settings
    function update($new_instance, $old_instance) {
        $instance = $old_instance;
        $instance['title'] = strip_tags( $new_instance['title'] );
        $instance['rss_feed'] = strip_tags( $new_instance['rss_feed'] );
        $instance['rss_items'] = strip_tags( $new_instance['rss_items'] );
        $instance['rss_date'] = strip_tags( $new_instance['rss_date'] );
        $instance['rss_summary'] = strip_tags( $new_instance['rss_summary'] );

        return $instance;
    }

    //display the widget
    function widget($args, $instance) {
        extract($args);

        echo $before_widget;

        //load the widget settings
        $title = apply_filters( 'widget_title', $instance['title'] );
        $rss_feed = empty( $instance['rss_feed'] ) ? '' : $instance['rss_feed'];
        $rss_items = empty( $instance['rss_items'] ) ? 2 : $instance['rss_items'];
        $rss_date = empty( $instance['rss_date'] ) ? 0 : 1;
        $rss_summary = empty( $instance['rss_summary'] ) ? 0 : 1;

        if ( !empty( $title ) ) { echo $before_title . $title . $after_title; };

        if ( $rss_feed ) {
            //display the RSS feed
            wp_widget_rss_output( array(
                'url' => $rss_feed,
                'title' => $title,
                'items' => $rss_items,
                'show_summary' => $rss_summary,
                'show_author' => 0,
                'show_date' => $rss_date
            ) );
        }

        echo $after_widget;
    }
}
?>
```

Code snippet boj-advanced-rss-widget.php

Creating Dashboard Widgets

WordPress also features a dashboard widget API. You can use this API to create custom widgets on the WordPress dashboard screen.

To create your dashboard widget, you use the `wp_add_dashboard_widget()` function. Here's how to use this function to create a dashboard widget:

```php
<?php wp_add_dashboard_widget( widget_id, widget_name, callback,
    control_callback ); ?>
```

The `wp_add_dashboard_widget()` function accepts the following parameters:

➤ `widget_id` — The CSS ID added to the widget DIV element

➤ `widget_name` — The name of your widget displayed in its heading

➤ `callback` — Function to be called to display your widget

➤ `control_callback` — Function to be called to handle for elements and submission

Following are some different examples. First, you create a simple dashboard widget that displays a piece of content to the user.

To create a dashboard widget, use the `wp_dashboard_setup` action hook. This hook is executed directly after the default dashboard widgets have been initialized, but prior to them being displayed.

```php
<?php
add_action( 'wp_dashboard_setup', 'boj_dashboard_example_widgets' );

function boj_dashboard_example_widgets() {

    //create a custom dashboard widget
    wp_add_dashboard_widget( 'dashboard_custom_feed',
        'My Plugin Information', 'boj_dashboard_example_display' );

}
?>
```

The `wp_dashboard_setup` hook can call your custom `boj_dashboard_example_widgets()` function. Next use the `wp_add_dashboard_widget()` function to register your new dashboard widget. Set the widget title to My Plugin Information, and call the custom function `boj_dashboard_example_display()`. Now that your dashboard widget is registered, you need to set up the custom function to display a message to your users.

```php
<?php
function boj_dashboard_example_display()
{
    echo '<p>Please contact support@example.com to report bugs.</p>';
}
?>
```

You now have a custom dashboard widget with a simple message displayed to your users, as shown in Figure 4-6. The Dashboard Widget API automatically makes your widget draggable, collapsible, and even adds your widget to the Screen Options tab so that users can easily hide it if they choose.

FIGURE 4-6

Now review the widget code in its entirety:

Available for
download on
Wrox.com

```php
<?php
/*
Plugin Name: Dashboard Widget Example Plugin
Plugin URI: http://example.com/wordpress-plugins/my-plugin
Description: A plugin to create dashboard widgets in WordPress
Version: 1.0
Author: Brad Williams
Author URI: http://wrox.com
License: GPLv2
*/

add_action( 'wp_dashboard_setup', 'boj_dashboard_example_widgets' );

function boj_dashboard_example_widgets() {

    //create a custom dashboard widget
    wp_add_dashboard_widget( 'dashboard_custom_feed',
        'My Plugin Information', 'boj_dashboard_example_display' );

}

function boj_dashboard_example_display()
{
    echo '<p>Please contact support@example.com to report bugs.</p>';
}
?>
```

Code snippet boj-dashboard-widget.php

Creating a Dashboard Widget with Options

Now that you understand dashboard widgets, you can create a more advanced widget that stores an option value. Dashboard widgets can store options, making them easily customizable by the user. If a dashboard widget has any options, you see a Configure link display when you hover over the widget title.

The dashboard widget in this example enables you to set a custom RSS feed URL and display the contents of that feed.

```php
<?php
add_action( 'wp_dashboard_setup', 'boj_dashboard_example_widgets' );

function boj_dashboard_example_widgets() {
```

```
//create a custom dashboard widget
wp_add_dashboard_widget( 'dashboard_custom_feed',
    'My Plugin Information', 'boj_dashboard_example_display',
    'boj_dashboard_example_setup' );

}
?>
```

Notice the `wp_add_dashboard_widget()` function has the fourth parameter set, in this example `boj_dashboard_example_setup()`, which is the control callback. This is the function that displays your widget setting field and saves the data entered as an option for your widget. Next you need to create the `boj_dashboard_example_display()` function to display the custom RSS feed in your widget.

```
<?php
function boj_dashboard_example_display()
{
    //load our widget option
    $boj_option = get_option( 'boj_dashboard_widget_rss ');

    //if option is empty set a default
    $boj_rss_feed = ( $boj_option ) ? $boj_option : 'http://wordpress.org/news/feed/';

    //retrieve the RSS feed and display it
    echo '<div class="rss-widget">';

    wp_widget_rss_output( array(
        'url' => $boj_rss_feed,
        'title' => 'RSS Feed News',
        'items' => 2,
        'show_summary' => 1,
        'show_author' => 0,
        'show_date' => 1
    ) );

    echo '</div>';
}
?>
```

The first two lines load the RSS feed saved as an option in the widget. Chapter 7, "Plugin Settings," covers plugin settings and options in more detail. Next the widget uses the `wp_widget_rss_output()` function to retrieve the RSS feed and display it. This handy little function is great for retrieving and displaying RSS feeds in WordPress. The widget defines the RSS URL, sets the title to RSS Feed News, sets the number of posts to show to 2, and includes a few other options.

Now that you have the widget display, you need to create the control callback function `boj_dashboard_example_setup()`. This function adds the form field to your widget and can also save the value entered by the user.

```php
<?php
function boj_dashboard_example_setup() {

    //check if option is set before saving
    if ( isset( $_POST['boj_rss_feed'] ) ) {
        //retrieve the option value from the form
        $boj_rss_feed = esc_url_raw( $_POST['boj_rss_feed'] );

        //save the value as an option
        update_option( 'boj_dashboard_widget_rss', $boj_rss_feed );
    }

    //load the saved feed if it exists
    $boj_rss_feed = get_option( 'boj_dashboard_widget_rss ');

    ?>
    <label for="feed">
        RSS Feed URL: <input type="text" name="boj_rss_feed" id="boj_rss_feed"
            value="<?php echo esc_url( $boj_rss_feed ); ?>" size="50" />
    </label>
    <?php
}
?>
```

The first task the function handles is saving the widget option. You should always check to verify the POST value exists prior to saving it using the `isset()` PHP function. Next you set the value of `$_POST['boj_rss_feed']` to the `$boj_rss_feed` variable. Notice how the POST value is escaped using `esc_url_raw()`. This verifies the value is a properly formatted URL and free from any illegal characters prior to saving the data. Finally, the widget option is saved using `update_option()`.

Now that the widget option is saved, you need to display the widget form field so that your users can enter in the RSS feed URL they want displayed. First, retrieve the widget option from the database if it exists, so you can display it in the form field. Next create a simple text input named `boj_rss_feed`. Notice the value is set to `$boj_rss_feed`, which is storing the RSS feed URL value entered by the user.

You now have a custom dashboard widget that stores a custom RSS feed URL and displays the latest two posts to the user, as shown in Figure 4-7!

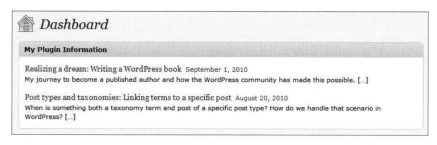

FIGURE 4-7

Now look at the full source for the custom RSS feed dashboard widget:

```php
<?php
/*
Plugin Name: RSS Dashboard Widget Example Plugin
Plugin URI: http://example.com/wordpress-plugins/my-plugin
Description: A plugin to create dashboard widgets in WordPress
Version: 1.0
Author: Brad Williams
Author URI: http://wrox.com
License: GPLv2
*/

add_action( 'wp_dashboard_setup', 'boj_dashboard_example_widgets' );

function boj_dashboard_example_widgets() {

    //create a custom dashboard widget
    wp_add_dashboard_widget( 'dashboard_custom_feed', 'My Plugin Information',
                'boj_dashboard_example_display', 'boj_dashboard_example_setup' );

}

function boj_dashboard_example_setup() {

    //check if option is set before saving
    if ( isset( $_POST['boj_rss_feed'] ) ) {
        //retrieve the option value from the form
        $boj_rss_feed = esc_url_raw( $_POST['boj_rss_feed'] );

        //save the value as an option
        update_option( 'boj_dashboard_widget_rss', $boj_rss_feed );
    }

     //load the saved feed if it exists
    $boj_rss_feed = get_option( 'boj_dashboard_widget_rss ' );

    ?>
    <label for="feed">
        RSS Feed URL: <input type="text" name="boj_rss_feed" id="boj_rss_feed"
            value="<?php echo esc_url( $boj_rss_feed ); ?>" size="50" />
    </label>
    <?php
}

function boj_dashboard_example_display()
{
    //load our widget option
    $boj_option = get_option( 'boj_dashboard_widget_rss ' );

    //if option is empty set a default
    $boj_rss_feed = ( $boj_option ) ? $boj_option : 'http://wordpress.org/news/feed/';

    //retrieve the RSS feed and display it
```

```
echo '<div class="rss-widget">';

wp_widget_rss_output( array(
    'url' => $boj_rss_feed,
    'title' => 'RSS Feed News',
    'items' => 2,
    'show_summary' => 1,
    'show_author' => 0,
    'show_date' => 1
) );

echo '</div>';
}
?>
```

Code snippet boj-rss-dashboard-widget.php

 Dashboard widgets are a great way to get important information in front of your users. The majority of WordPress users log directly into the admin dashboard, so what better way to feature important information about your plugin?

META BOXES

WordPress features multiple sections, or meta boxes, on the post, page, and link manager screens. These meta boxes enable you to easily add additional data to your content. For example, the Post Tags meta box enables you set tags for your post.

Adding a Custom Meta Box

To create a custom meta box in WordPress, you use the `add_meta_box()` function. This function enables you to define all aspects of your meta box. Following is how this function is used:

```php
<?php add_meta_box( id, title, callback, page, context, priority,
        callback_args ); ?>
```

The `add_meta_box()` function accepts the following parameters:

- ➤ `id` — The CSS ID added to the DIV element that wraps your meta box
- ➤ `title` — The name of your meta box displayed in its heading
- ➤ `callback` — Function to be called to display your meta box
- ➤ `page` — The screen where your meta box should show
- ➤ `context` — The part of the page where the meta box should be shown
- ➤ `priority` — The priority in which your meta box should be shown
- ➤ `callback_args` — Arguments to pass into your callback function

Now you can build a custom meta box for the post screen.

```php
<?php
add_action( 'add_meta_boxes', 'boj_mbe_create' );

function boj_mbe_create() {

    add_meta_box( 'boj-meta', 'My Custom Meta Box', 'boj_mbe_function', 'post',
        'normal', 'high' );

}

function boj_mbe_function() {

    echo 'Welcome to my meta box!';

}
?>
```

In this example, you create a meta box on the post screen. You use the `add_meta_boxes` action hook to trigger your `boj_mbe_create()` function to add a new meta box. The meta box title is set to My Custom Meta Box; it calls the `boj_mbe_function()` for display. Also notice you set the context parameter to `normal` and the priority to `high`. This displays your meta box directly below the visual editor on your post screen, as shown in Figure 4-8.

 You can add a custom meta box to any custom post type in WordPress by simply setting the page parameter to the name of your custom post type.

Saving Meta Box Data

The real power of meta boxes is saving data to a post, page, or any type of content in WordPress. Any data saved against your content is called metadata. In the WordPress edit screens, the meta box for custom fields exists by default. Custom fields are just a quick way to save metadata against your content. Chapter 11, "Extending Posts," covers metadata in more detail, but you need understand the concept to save data in your meta box.

In this example, you create a meta box on the post screen to save two fields of data against your post.

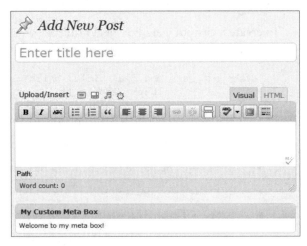

FIGURE 4-8

```php
<?php
add_action( 'add_meta_boxes', 'boj_mbe_create' );

function boj_mbe_create() {

    //create a custom meta box
    add_meta_box( 'boj-meta', 'My Custom Meta Box', 'boj_mbe_function', 'post',
        'normal', 'high' );


}
?>
```

You need to initialize and create your meta box just as you did before. Now create the function to display the form fields.

```php
<?php
function boj_mbe_function( $post ) {

    //retrieve the metadata values if they exist
    $boj_mbe_name = get_post_meta( $post->ID, '_boj_mbe_name', true );
    $boj_mbe_costume = get_post_meta( $post->ID, '_boj_mbe_costume', true );

    echo 'Please fill out the information below';
    ?>
    <p>Name: <input type="text" name="boj_mbe_name" value="
        <?php echo esc_attr( $boj_mbe_name ); ?>" /></p>
    <p>Costume:
    <select name="boj_mbe_costume">
        <option value="vampire" <?php selected( $boj_mbe_costume, 'vampire' ); ?>>
            Vampire
        </option>
        <option value="zombie" <?php selected( $boj_mbe_costume, 'zombie' ); ?>>
            Zombie
        </option>
        <option value="smurf" <?php selected( $boj_mbe_costume, 'smurf' ); ?>>
            Smurf
        </option>
    </select>
    </p>
    <?php

}
?>
```

The first thing you should notice is the $post object passed as a parameter to your custom function. This gives you access to all the post data available in the object, in this case the post ID, to use in your meta box.

Now you need to retrieve the two metadata values from WordPress if they exist. To do this use the get_post_meta() function. This function accepts three parameters.

➤ `post_id` — The ID of the post you want to load metadata from

➤ `key` — The unique name of the metadata field you want to load

➤ `single` — Whether to return the string as an array (`false`) or a single string (`true`)

If you create a new post, the two metadata values would not exist because they haven't been created yet. Next in the code, the two form fields display. The first is a text field for a name. Notice the value of the text field is set to `$boj_mbe_name`, the variable that stores the metadata value you retrieve, and is escaped using the `esc_attr()` function for security.

The second field in the form is an HTML `<select>` form field. This field has three options to choose as your costume: Vampire, Zombie, or Smurf. In the example, you use the `selected()` function to determine if the item is selected. The meta box form is now complete, and as you can see there is no need to add a Submit button or form tags. Using use the `save_post` action hook, the values are passed to your `boj_mbe_save_meta()` function as shown here.

```php
<?php

//hook to save the meta box data
add_action( 'save_post', 'boj_mbe_save_meta' );

function boj_mbe_save_meta( $post_id ) {

    //verify the metadata is set
    if ( isset( $_POST['boj_mbe_name'] ) ) {

        //save the metadata
        update_post_meta( $post_id, '_boj_mbe_name',
            strip_tags( $_POST['boj_mbe_name'] ) );
        update_post_meta( $post_id, '_boj_mbe_costume',
            strip_tags( $_POST['boj_mbe_costume'] ) );

    }

}
?>
```

First use the `add_action()` function to trigger the `save_post` action hook, which will call your `boj_mbe_save_meta()` function when a post is saved. This function saves the data entered by the user in your meta box. Notice you pass the `$post_id` variable to your function as a parameter. The post ID is used when saving your metadata. It's always a good idea to verify the form field you want to work with is set prior to doing so, as shown using the `isset()` PHP function. Finally, the `update_post_meta()` function adds or updates the post meta entered in your meta box. This function accepts four parameters.

➤ `post_id` — The ID of the post you want to save metadata to

➤ `meta_key` — The unique name of the metadata field you want to save

➤ `meta_value` — The value of the metadata field to save

➤ `prev_value` — The old value of the metadata field, which differentiates between multiple fields with the same name

In this example you use only the first three parameters because the fourth is optional. You set the post ID, name of the metadata field, and the value entered in your custom meta box. The form values are sanitized using the `strip_tags()` function.

> *If your metadata name starts with an underscore, it does not display in the default custom fields meta box in WordPress. This can help eliminate confusion by the user when entering metadata.*

You have just successfully created a custom meta box that stores data in WordPress! Now review the full code for your plugin.

Available for download on Wrox.com

```php
<?php
/*
Plugin Name: Meta Box Example Plugin
Plugin URI: http://example.com/wordpress-plugins/my-plugin
Description: A plugin to create meta boxes in WordPress
Version: 1.0
Author: Brad Williams
Author URI: http://wrox.com
License: GPLv2
*/

add_action( 'add_meta_box', 'boj_mbe_create' );

function boj_mbe_create() {

    //create a custom meta box
    add_meta_box( 'boj-meta', 'My Custom Meta Box', 'boj_mbe_function',
                'post', 'normal', 'high' );


}

function boj_mbe_function( $post ) {

    //retrieve the metadata values if they exist
    $boj_mbe_name = get_post_meta( $post->ID, '_boj_mbe_name', true );
    $boj_mbe_costume = get_post_meta( $post->ID, '_boj_mbe_costume', true );

    echo 'Please fill out the information below';
    ?>
    <p>Name: <input type="text" name="boj_mbe_name" value="
            <?php echo esc_attr( $boj_mbe_name ); ?>" /></p>
    <p>Costume:
    <select name="boj_mbe_costume">
        <option value="vampire" <?php selected( $boj_mbe_costume, 'vampire' ); ?>>
            Vampire
        </ option>
        <option value="zombie" <?php selected( $boj_mbe_costume, 'zombie' ); ?>>
            Zombie
        </option>
```

```php
            <option value="smurf" <?php selected( $boj_mbe_costume, 'smurf' ); ?>>
                Smurf
            </option>
        </ select>
        </p>
            <?php
}

//hook to save the meta box data
add_action( 'save_post', 'boj_mbe_save_meta' );

function boj_mbe_save_meta( $post_id ) {

    //verify the metadata is set
    if ( isset( $_POST['boj_mbe_name'] ) ) {

        //save the metadata
        update_post_meta( $post_id, '_boj_mbe_name',
                        strip_tags( $_POST['boj_mbe_name'] ) );
        update_post_meta( $post_id, '_boj_mbe_costume',
                        strip_tags( $_POST['boj_mbe_costume'] ) );

    }

}
?>
```

Code snippet boj-meta-box.php

Advanced Meta Box

Now that you understand how meta boxes work, you can build a more complex one. In this example, you create a custom meta box that enables the user to select an image from the WordPress Media Library and save the URL in the meta box.

First, you use the add_meta_boxes action hook as before to execute the custom function to create your meta box.

```php
<?php
add_action( 'add_meta_boxes', 'boj_mbe_image_create' );

function boj_mbe_image_create() {

    //create a custom meta box
    add_meta_box( 'boj-image-meta', 'Set Image', 'boj_mbe_image_function',
        'post', 'normal', 'high' );

}
?>
```

Using the add_meta_box() function, you can define the settings for your custom meta box. In this case the meta box is named Set Image and calls the custom boj_mbe_image_function() function.

Now that the meta box has been created, you need to create the function to display meta box content.

```php
<?php
function boj_mbe_image_function( $post ) {

    //retrieve the metadata value if it exists
    $boj_mbe_image = get_post_meta( $post->ID, '_boj_mbe_image', true );
    ?>
    Image <input id="boj_mbe_image" type="text" size="75"
        name="boj_mbe_image" value="<?php echo esc_url( $boj_mbe_image ); ?>" />
    <input id="upload_image_button" type="button"
        value="Media Library Image" class="button-secondary"  />
    <br /> Enter an image URL or use an image from the Media Library
    <?php

}
?>
```

The first step is to load the metadata value if it exists to the $boj_mbe_image variable. If this meta value has not been saved, it will be empty. Next display the text form field to enter and display the image URL. You also create a button that enables the user to select an image from the Media Library, as shown in Figure 4-9.

FIGURE 4-9

Now call the save_post action hook to execute your custom boj_mbe_image_save_meta() function to save the meta box data.

```php
<?php

//hook to save the meta box data
add_action( 'save_post', 'boj_mbe_image_save_meta' );

function boj_mbe_image_save_meta( $post_id ) {

    //verify the metadata is set
    if ( isset( $_POST['boj_mbe_image'] ) ) {

        //save the metadata
        update_post_meta( $post_id, '_boj_mbe_image',
            esc_url_raw( $_POST['boj_mbe_image'] ) );

    }

}
?>
```

It's a good practice to verify the form field is set prior to retrieving the form field value. If the field is set, your function can use the `update_post_meta()` function to save the metadata to the post. Notice you're using the `esc_url_raw()` function to sanitize the URL. This can eliminate invalid characters, remove dangerous characters, and verify the URL has a proper protocol set (http, https, ftp, and so on).

Up to this point this is a fairly standard meta box plugin. Now is where the fun begins! To prompt for the Media Library overlay, you need to use some JavaScript. Create a new file named `boj-meta-image.js`. This file can contain the JavaScript code that inserts the image URL into your meta box text field when selected from the Media Library. Now review the code.

```javascript
jQuery(document).ready(function($) {

    var formfield = null;

    $('#upload_image_button').click(function() {
        $('html').addClass('Image');
        formfield = $('#boj_mbe_image').attr('name');
        tb_show('', 'media-upload.php?type=image&TB_iframe=true');
        return false;
    });


    // user inserts file into post.
    //only run custom if user started process using the above process
    // window.send_to_editor(html) is how wp normally handle the received data

    window.original_send_to_editor = window.send_to_editor;
    window.send_to_editor = function(html){
        var fileurl;

        if (formfield != null) {
            fileurl = $('img',html).attr('src');

            $('#boj_mbe_image').val(fileurl);

            tb_remove();

            $('html').removeClass('Image');
            formfield = null;
        } else {
            window.original_send_to_editor(html);
        }
    };

});
```

Remember this is JavaScript code and cannot be surrounded by `<?php ?>` tags. First, the code opens the Media overlay when the `upload_image_button` is clicked, which is the name of the Submit button in your meta box. The second part of the code takes the image URL and inserts it into the image URL text field in your form, named `boj_mbe_image`.

Now that the JavaScript file is in place, you need to call this file from your plugin.

```php
<?php
//script actions with page detection
add_action('admin_print_scripts-post.php', 'boj_mbe_image_admin_scripts');
add_action('admin_print_scripts-post-new.php', 'boj_mbe_image_admin_scripts');

function boj_mbe_image_admin_scripts() {

    wp_enqueue_script( 'boj-image-upload',
        plugins_url( '/boj-meta-box/boj-meta-image.js' ),
        array( 'jquery','media-upload','thickbox' )
    );

}
?>
```

Use the `admin_print_scripts` action hook to execute the custom function for including your JavaScript file. Notice how the action hook has `-post.php` and `-post-new.php` appended to the hook name. This is called page detection, so the hook calls only the custom `boj_mbe_image_admin_scripts()` function when the user is on the `post.php` or `post-new.php` pages in WordPress.

To insert your JavaScript fill to the header of the page, use the `wp_enqueue_script()` function. This is the proper way to include JavaScript files in the header of WordPress, which Chapter 12, "JavaScript and Ajax," covers in more detail.

The final step is to add the `thickbox` style using the `wp_enqueue_styles()` function.

```php
<?php

//style actions with page detection
add_action('admin_print_styles-post.php', 'boj_mbe_image_admin_styles');
add_action('admin_print_styles-post-new.php', 'boj_mbe_image_admin_styles');

function boj_mbe_image_admin_styles() {
    wp_enqueue_style( 'thickbox' );
}
?>
```

This includes the `thickbox` style in the header of the page.

To set an image in your meta box, just click the Media Library Image button. Next select an image from the Media Library, and click the Insert into Post button. This inserts the image URL into your meta box form field. This happens only if the user clicks the Media Library Image button in your meta box.

Now review the full plugin code.

BOJ-META-BOX-IMAGE.PHP

```php
<?php
/*
Plugin Name: Meta Box Media Library Image Example
Plugin URI: http://example.com/wordpress-plugins/my-plugin
Description: Adds the ability to select an image from the media library
Version: 1.0
```

```php
Author: Brad Williams
Author URI: http://wrox.com
License: GPLv2
*/

add_action( 'admin_init', 'boj_mbe_image_create' );

function boj_mbe_image_create() {

    //create a custom meta box
    add_meta_box( 'boj-image-meta', 'Set Image', 'boj_mbe_image_function', 'post',
        'normal', 'high' );

}

function boj_mbe_image_function( $post ) {

    //retrieve the metadata value if it exists
    $boj_mbe_image = get_post_meta( $post->ID, '_boj_mbe_image', true );
    ?>
    Image <input id="boj_mbe_image" type="text" size="75" name="boj_mbe_image"
        value="<?php echo esc_url( $boj_mbe_image ); ?>" />
            <input id="upload_image_button" type="button"
                value="Media Library Image" class="button-secondary"  />
      <p>Enter an image URL or use an image from the Media Library</p>
      <?php
}

//script actions with page detection
add_action('admin_print_scripts-post.php', 'boj_mbe_image_admin_scripts');
add_action('admin_print_scripts-post-new.php', 'boj_mbe_image_admin_scripts');

function boj_mbe_image_admin_scripts() {
    wp_enqueue_script( 'boj-image-upload',
        plugins_url( '/boj-meta-box/boj-meta-image.js' ),
        array( 'jquery','media-upload','thickbox' ) );
}

//style actions with page detection
add_action('admin_print_styles-post.php', 'boj_mbe_image_admin_styles');
add_action('admin_print_styles-post-new.php', 'boj_mbe_image_admin_styles');

function boj_mbe_image_admin_styles() {
    wp_enqueue_style( 'thickbox' );
}


//hook to save the meta box data
add_action( 'save_post', 'boj_mbe_image_save_meta' );


function boj_mbe_image_save_meta( $post_id ) {

    //verify the metadata is set
```

```php
                  if ( isset( $_POST['boj_mbe_image'] ) ) {

                      //save the metadata
                      update_post_meta( $post_id, '_boj_mbe_image',
                          esc_url( $_POST['boj_mbe_image'] ) );

                  }

      }
      ?>
```

Code snippet boj-meta-box-image.zip

BOJ-META-IMAGE.JS

```javascript
jQuery(document).ready(function($) {

    var formfield = null;

    $('#upload_image_button').click(function() {
        $('html').addClass('Image');
        formfield = $('#boj_mbe_image').attr('name');
        tb_show('', 'media-upload.php?type=image&TB_iframe=true');
        return false;
    });


    // user inserts file into post.
    // only run custom if user started process using the above process
    // window.send_to_editor(html) is how wp normally handle the received data

    window.original_send_to_editor = window.send_to_editor;
    window.send_to_editor = function(html){
        var fileurl;

        if (formfield != null) {
            fileurl = $('img',html).attr('src');

            $('#boj_mbe_image').val(fileurl);

            tb_remove();

            $('html').removeClass('Image');
            formfield = null;
        } else {
            window.original_send_to_editor(html);
        }
    };

});
```

Code snippet boj-meta-box-image.zip

KEEPING IT CONSISTENT

They say consistency is one of the principles of good UI design. Creating a plugin for WordPress is no different, and it's a best practice to make your plugin match the WordPress user interface as closely as possible. This helps keep the interface consistent for end users and can make your plugin more professional by providing a solid user experience from the start.

WordPress features many different styles that you can easily use in your plugin. In this section you learn how to use the styling available in WordPress for your plugins. To demonstrate, create a simple plugin with a settings page:

```php
<?php
add_action( 'admin_menu', 'boj_styling_create_menu' );

function boj_styling_create_menu() {

    //create custom top-level menu
    add_menu_page( 'My Plugin Settings', 'Plugin Styling',
        'manage_options', __FILE__, 'boj_styling_settings' );

}
?>
```

Throughout this section you modify the `boj_styling_settings()` function.

Using the WordPress UI

The most important part of using the WordPress styles is to wrap your plugin in the class `wrap div`.

```
<div class="wrap">
    Plugin Page
</div>
```

This class sets the stage for all admin styling.

Headings

WordPress has custom styles available for all heading tags. Now look at how those heading tags display:

```php
<?php
function boj_styling_settings() {
    ?>
    <div class="wrap">
        <h2>My Plugin</h2>
        <h3>My Plugin</h3>
        <h4>My Plugin</h4>
        <h5>My Plugin</h5>
        <h6>My Plugin</h6>
    </div>
    <?php
}
?>
```

Each heading is slightly smaller than the previous, as shown in Figure 4-10. Notice there is no `<h1>` tag defined. The `<h1>` tag is reserved for the name of your website displayed at the top of the admin dashboard. Because of this you should always use the `<h2>` tag for your primary heading.

Icons

WordPress features many different icons for each section head. These icons are also available for use in your plugins. For example, the dashboard header icon is a house icon.

FIGURE 4-10

```
<div id="icon-index" class="icon32"></div>
<div id="icon-edit" class="icon32"></div>
<div id="icon-upload" class="icon32"></div>
<div id="icon-link-manager" class="icon32"></div>
<div id="icon-edit-pages" class="icon32"></div>
<div id="icon-edit-comments" class="icon32"></div>
<div id="icon-themes" class="icon32"></div>
<div id="icon-plugins" class="icon32"></div>
<div id="icon-users" class="icon32"></div>
<div id="icon-tools" class="icon32"></div>
<div id="icon-options-general" class="icon32"></div>
```

These divs generate the icons shown in Figure 4-11.

Rather than hardcoding these values, WordPress features a function to generate the icon divs called `screen_icon()`. This function accepts one parameter, and that is the screen icon you want to load.

FIGURE 4-11

Now modify your `boj_styling_settings()` function to display an icon and header.

```php
<?php
function boj_styling_settings() {
    ?>
    <div class="wrap">
        <?php screen_icon( 'plugins' ); ?>
        <h2>My Plugin</h2>
    </div>
    <?php
}
?>
```

Now your plugin has a clean header and uses the Plug icon.

Messages

When an action occurs in your plugin, such as saving settings, it's important to display a message to the user verifying whether the update was successful. WordPress features some different styles for displaying these messages.

```php
<?php
function boj_styling_settings() {
    ?>
    <div class="wrap">
        <h2>My Plugin</h2>
        <div id="message" class="updated">Settings saved successfully</div>
        <div id="message" class="error">Error saving settings</div>
    </div>
    <?php
}
?>
```

These styles will generate the messages shown in Figure 4-12.

Buttons

When adding buttons to your form, you can take advantage of multiple classes. The first two you use are the `button-primary` and `button-secondary` classes. These classes style your buttons to match the WordPress UI.

FIGURE 4-12

```html
<p>
<input type="submit" name="Save" value="Save Options" />
<input type="submit" name="Save" value="Save Options" class="button-primary" />
</p><p>
<input type="submit" name="Secondary" value="Secondary Button" />
<input type="submit" name="Secondary" value="Secondary Button"
    class="button-secondary" />
</p>
```

This example demonstrates a standard unstyled button as compared to the WordPress styled button. As you can tell, the WordPress-styled button looks familiar and uses the proper styling, as shown in Figure 4-13.

You can also use the `button-highlighted` class to put an emphasis on a particular button.

FIGURE 4-13

```html
<input type="submit" name="secondary" value="Secondary Button"
    class="button-secondary" />
<input type="submit" name="highlighted" value="Button Highlighted"
    class="button-highlighted" />
```

The button is now bold and stands out more than a normal Secondary button, as shown in Figure 4-14. This is useful if you want to focus the users' attention on a button.

Links can also take the form of a button by using the appropriate class.

FIGURE 4-14

```html
<a href="#">Search</a>
<a href='#' class='button-secondary'>Search</a>
<a href='#' class='button-highlighted'>Search</a>
<a href='#' class='button-primary'>Search</a>
```

This example shows how a standard `<a href>` link can be styled to look like a button, as shown in Figure 4-15. To normal users they would never know these are regular text links because they look just like a button.

FIGURE 4-15

Links

Links inside the `wrap` class automatically assume the standard WordPress admin link style. However, you can modify the default styling in different ways.

```
<div class="wrap">
    <?php screen_icon( 'plugins' ); ?>        <h2>My Plugin</h2>
    <h2><a href="#">Testing Link</a></h2>
    <h3><a href="#">Testing Link</a></h3>
    <h4><a href="#">Testing Link</a></h4>
    <h5><a href="#">Testing Link</a></h5>
    <a href="#">Testing Link</a>
</div>
```

Wrapping any link in a heading tag enables you to adjust the size of the link, as shown in Figure 4-16.

FIGURE 4-16

Form Fields

WordPress has a special table class just for forms called `form-table`. This class is used on all WordPress admin dashboard forms, including every Settings page. This is a useful class when creating any type of options in your plugin.

```
<div class="wrap">
    <?php screen_icon( 'plugins' ); ?>
    <h2>My Plugin</h2>
    <form method="POST" action="">
    <table class="form-table">
    <tr valign="top">
        <th scope="row"><label for="fname">First Name</label></th>
        <td><input maxlength="45" size="25" name="fname" /></td>
    </tr>
    <tr valign="top">
        <th scope="row"><label for="lname">Last Name</label></th>
        <td><input id="lname" maxlength="45" size="25" name="lname" /></td>
    </tr>
    <tr valign="top">
        <th scope="row"><label for="color">Favorite Color</label></th>
        <td>
            <select name="color">
                <option value="orange">Orange</option>
                <option value="black">Black</option>
            </ select>
        </td>
    </tr>
```

```
            <tr valign="top">
                <th scope="row"><label for="featured">Featured?</label></th>
                <td><input type="checkbox" name="favorite" /></td>
            </tr>
            <tr valign="top">
                <th scope="row"><label for="gender">Gender</label></th>
                <td>
                    <input type="radio" name="gender" value="male" /> Male
                    <input type="radio" name="gender" value="female" /> Female
                </td>
            </tr>
            <tr valign="top">
                <th scope="row"><label for="bio">Bio</label></th>
                <td><textarea name="bio"></textarea></td>
            </tr>
            <tr valign="top">
                <td>
                <input type="submit" name="save" value="Save Options"
                    class="button-primary" />
                <input type="submit" name="reset" value="Reset"
                    class="button-secondary" />
                </td>
            </tr>
            </table>
            </form>
        </div>
```

Using the `form-table` can give your options a
familiar look to your plugin users. This makes for a
better user experience, as shown in Figure 4-17.

Tables

HTML tables are a great way to display rows and
columns of data in an easy-to-read layout. Tables
can easily be styled in WordPress using the
`widefat` class.

FIGURE 4-17

```
<table class="widefat">
<thead>
    <tr>
        <th>Name</th>
        <th>Favorite Holiday</th>
    </tr>
</thead>
<tfoot>
    <tr>
        <th>Name</th>
        <th>Favorite Holiday</th>
    </tr>
</tfoot>
<tbody>
    <tr>
```

```
        <td>Brad Williams</td>
        <td>Halloween</td>
    </tr>
    <tr>
        <td>Ozh Richard</td>
        <td>Talk Like a Pirate</td>
    </tr>
    <tr>
        <td>Justin Tadlock</td>
        <td>Christmas</td>
    </tr>
</tbody>
</table>
```

The `widefat` class has specific styles set
for the `thead` and `tfoot` HTML tags. This styles
the header and footer of your table to match
all other tables on the admin dashboard. The
class can also style all table data, as shown in
Figure 4-18.

FIGURE 4-18

Pagination

If your plugin contains a list of records, you may have a need for pagination, which is the method to
break lists of data into multiple pages and have links to load each individual page. This helps reduce
the load times and makes it a much cleaner user experience to navigate through the data. Would you
rather view 500 records on a page or 10 pages with 50 records on each page?

WordPress has a few different classes to style your pagination. Following is an example.

```
<div class="tablenav">
    <div class="tablenav-pages">
        <span class="displaying-num">Displaying 1-20 of 69</span>
        <span class="page-numbers current">1</span>
        <a href="#" class="page-numbers">2</a>
        <a href="#" class="page-numbers">3</a>
        <a href="#" class="page-numbers">4</a>
        <a href="#" class="next page-numbers">&raquo;</a>
    </div>
</div>
```

First, you need to wrap your pagination links in the `tablenav` and
`tablenav-pages` div classes. The `displaying-num` class styles the
records you view. The `page-numbers` class styles the page links in the
familiar WordPress format. Adding `current` or `next` to the link class
can add some unique styles to those elements, as shown in Figure 4-19.

FIGURE 4-19

Keeping your plugin design consistent with the WordPress user interface can reduce your
plugins' learning curve because users will feel comfortable with the design and styles used. This

can also make your plugins' design future-proof. If the WordPress core styles change down the road, your plugins' design will also change to match the new user interface, and you won't need to edit a single line of code!

SUMMARY

This chapter covered many different methods for integrating your plugin in WordPress. You certainly won't use every method discussed in every plugin you develop, but it's essential to understand what's available for use in your plugin.

5

Internationalization

WHAT'S IN THIS CHAPTER?

➤ Understanding the description of internationalization and localization

➤ Determining the benefits of internationalizing plugins

➤ Preparing plugins for translation

➤ Using the WordPress internationalization functions

➤ Internationalizing JavaScript

➤ Using translation tools

Internationalization is the act of preparing your plugin for use in any number of languages. WordPress uses U.S. English as its default language, but it has a large community of users who don't read and write in English. This community pulls together to create translations of WordPress in languages used all around the world.

One of the goals of WordPress is to make it easy for people across the world to publish content. As a plugin developer, you can help democratize the publishing process for users of many different cultures. WordPress makes this easy for developers, so there are no development hurdles to cross when internationalizing your plugins.

INTERNATIONALIZATION AND LOCALIZATION

Using the built-in translation functions in WordPress, you can easily make your plugin available to a wide variety of people without any knowledge of your users' written languages. The process of translation is handled for you by WordPress if you follow a few simple steps during the development process.

Internationalization deals with making sure strings of text are wrapped in specific function calls. It is the practice of making text ready for localization. The shorthand term for internationalization is "i18n," which you may encounter in some situations.

Localization is the process of translating text for a specific locale. WordPress handles the localization process by checking for specific translation files and performing the translation. It's a plugin's job to handle internationalization so that localization can take place. The shorthand term for localization is "L10n."

 You may notice that we're not taking our own advice throughout this book and making our code snippets ready for translation. The reason for this is that we want to provide short and to-the-point code samples that allow for the best readability. In real-world practice, you should always internationalize your plugin.

Why Internationalize?

Internationalizing your plugin can benefit both you and your plugin users. Compared to the more complex functionality you'll likely use when developing a plugin, internationalization will seem much easier after you follow the guidelines set out in this chapter.

➤ You benefit by having a larger audience of people using your plugin.

➤ Users benefit by using the plugin in their language.

Some plugin authors even develop relationships with translators of their plugins after working closely together to get a translation done. Forming relationships with new people is always a benefit of working on open source projects, and by internationalizing your plugin, you open the door for more possibilities than with plugins that aren't internationalized.

 One fun thing to do is to create your own translation based on your language and region. For example, if you're from the southern part of the United States, you could create a translation of your plugin with a bit of southern slang. This can allow you to get a feel for the process that translators go through when translating plugins.

Understanding Internationalization in Professional Work

Generally, when preparing your plugin for translation, you would do so if it is intended for public release because many of your users may run sites in languages other than your own.

Not all plugins are for use by the public. When performing custom client development, it's not always necessary to follow the steps outlined in this chapter. If your client's site is only in a single language, there might not be a need for translation. However, some clients run multilingual sites and may use a multilingual plugin that enables their content to be read in several languages. In this case, your plugin should be internationalized. You should always check with your client to see if internationalization is a requirement.

Although it's not always necessary to internationalize text for client work, it is considered best practice to internationalize all text. It saves you from potentially having to recode it for translation later if the client changes their mind about needing translatable text, and it's always good to stick to best practices when coding.

Also, a potential benefit to learning the tools in this chapter is having an extra bullet point on your resume for clients in need of this skill.

Getting Your Plugin Ready for Translation

The first step to make your plugin translatable is to use the `load_plugin_textdomain()` function. This function tells WordPress to load a translation file if it exists for the user's language.

```php
<?php
load_plugin_textdomain( $domain, $abs_rel_path, $plugin_rel_path );
?>
```

➤ `$domain` — A unique string that identifies text in your plugin that has been prepared for translation. For organizational purposes, you should give this the same value as the name of your plugin folder.

➤ `$abs_rel_path` — A deprecated parameter that should no longer be used. Setting this to `false` is best.

➤ `$plugin_rel_path` — Relative path to the translations of your plugin from the user's plugin directory (`WP_PLUGIN_DIR`).

If you were creating a plugin with a folder name of `boj-plugin`, your code would like this:

```php
<?php
load_plugin_textdomain( 'boj-plugin', false, 'boj-plugin/languages' );
?>
```

Here, the `$domain` is `boj-plugin` to match the plugin folder name, the `$abs_rel_path` has a value of `false` because it's unneeded, and the `$plugin_rel_path` has a value of `boj-plugin/languages` because this is where you store translation files.

The last parameter is the directory of the plugin (`boj-plugin`) and a subdirectory of the plugin (`languages`). It's good practice to create an extra folder in your plugin called `languages` to house any translations for your plugin. If you ever get more than a handful of translations, you'll want this folder because placing all those files in the top directory of your plugin can get messy.

Echoing and Returning Strings

WordPress has many useful functions for making internationalization easy. Every time you add textual content in your plugin, you should wrap it in one of the WordPress translation functions.

Nearly each of these functions has at least one variable that you'll use: $domain. This is the unique variable used in the "Getting Your Plugin Ready for Translation" section: boj-plugin. The value of this variable enables WordPress to recognize it as a part of your plugin's translation files.

When viewing the core WordPress files, you'll likely notice that $domain is never set. WordPress uses the default, so your plugin should have a unique string to set it apart from the core.

The __() Function

The __() function works by making your text ready for translation and returning it for use in PHP. In this example, you will assign the return value of __() to a PHP variable. Note that this function uses a double underscore, not a single underscore.

```php
<?php

$text = __( 'WordPress is a wonderful publishing platform.', 'boj-plugin' );

?>
```

The _e() Function

_e() makes your text ready for localization. It works similarly to echo in PHP by displaying text on the screen. The $text variable is the content you want translated. Now add a fun message to the site's footer using an action hook (see Chapter 3, "Hooks").

```php
<?php

/* Hook our message function to the footer. */
add_action( 'wp_footer', 'boj_footer_message' );

/* Function that outputs a message in the footer of the site. */
function boj_footer_message() {

    /* Output the translated text. */
    _e( 'This site runs off the coolest platform ever &mdash; WordPress.',
    'boj-plugin' );
}

?>
```

The esc_attr__() Function

esc_attr__() is the internationalization equivalent of the esc_attr() WordPress function (see Chapter 6, "Plugin Security"). It escapes HTML attributes, so anything passed to it won't break HTML validation standards or open a site up to potential security vulnerabilities.

esc_attr__() returns the translation for use in PHP. Now create a function that returns a link to a terms of service page on an example site and display it.

```php
<?php

/* A function that returns a link to the site's terms of service page. */
function boj_terms_of_service_link() {
    return '<a href="http://example.com/tos" title="' .
    esc_attr__( 'Visit the Terms of Service page', 'boj-plugin' ) . '">' .
    __( 'Terms of Service', 'boj-plugin' ) . '</a>';
}

/* Display the output of the boj_terms_of_service_link() function. */
echo boj_terms_of_service_link();

?>
```

The esc_attr_e() Function

esc_attr_e() works the same as the esc_attr__() function except that displays the translation on the screen. For example, you might display a link to the dashboard page in the WordPress admin, so you want to make sure the title attribute of the link works correctly. You can also use the _e() function from earlier.

```php
<a href="<?php echo admin_url( 'dashboard.php' ); ?>"
title="<?php esc_attr_e( 'Visit the WordPress dashboard', 'boj-plugin' ); ?>">
<?php _e( 'Dashboard', 'boj-plugin' ); ?></a>
```

The esc_html__() Function

esc_html__() is the equivalent of the WordPress function esc_html() (see Chapter 6) for translations. You need to use this function in situations in which HTML would be inappropriate for use. This function returns its output for use in PHP.

Suppose a form was submitted with the content of a <textarea> in which a default text message is provided. You'd escape the input the user submitted or escape the default message that the translator provides.

```php
<?php

function boj_get_text_message() {

    /* If the user input any text, escape it. */
    if ( !empty( $_POST['boj-text'] ) )
        $message = esc_html( $_POST['boj-text'] );

    /* If no text was input, use a default, translated message. */
    else
        $message = esc_html__( 'No message input by the user.', 'boj-plugin' );

    return $message;
}

?>
```

The esc_html_e() Function

esc_html_e() behaves the same as the esc_html__() function except that it displays the translated text on the screen instead of returning it. For example, you may be adding a form with some default text in a `<textarea>` but want to make sure no HTML is shown.

```
<textarea name="boj-text" id="boj-text">
    <?php esc_html_e( 'Please input a description.', 'boj-plugin' ); ?>
</textarea>
```

The _x() Function

Sometimes, you need to provide context for translations. The _x() function enables plugin developers to use the same text string multiple times within a plugin. This function's purpose is to provide a context in which a specific text string is used.

Suppose you're creating an SEO plugin in which you use the text "SEO" in several places. In this example, you add a meta box (see Chapter 4, "Integrate in WordPress") for SEO settings on the post editor screen in the admin. You can provide a context for this particular instance of "SEO."

```php
<?php

add_action( 'admin_menu', 'boj_add_seo_meta_box' );

function boj_add_seo_meta_box() {
    add_meta_box(
        'boj_seo_meta_box',
        _x( 'SEO', 'meta box', 'boj-plugin' ),
        'boj_seo_meta_box_callback',
        'post',
        'advanced'
    );
}

function boj_seo_meta_box_callback() {
    _e( 'An example meta box.', 'boj-plugin' );
}

?>
```

The _ex() Function

_ex() is a function to use when you need to note a specific context for a string of text. It works the same as the _x() function except that it echoes its output instead of returning it.

You may use the same text in several places throughout your plugin, but each instance means something different. The term Post is often used in blogging systems as both a noun and a verb. When internationalizing, you need to mark the difference between the two by using a context.

Use the second parameter, $context, to provide a context to translators on how the term is used in this instance.

The following example shows two uses of the term Post and how it can be used as both a noun and a verb.

```php
<?php

/* Displaying "Post" as a noun. */
_ex( 'Post', 'noun', 'boj-plugin' );

/* Displaying "Post" as a verb. */
_ex( 'Post', 'verb', 'boj-plugin' );

?>
```

Well-written text is important. Before using a contextual translation function, ask yourself if the text itself can be written in a more intuitive manner. Instead of using a generic term such as Post, you can make this easier to understand for plugin users and translators.

Post as a noun can be better written as Select a post, and Post as a verb could be better written as Submit post. Therefore, you wouldn't need to use the _ex() function in either case. You could use _e() instead.

```php
<?php

_e( 'Select a post', 'boj-plugin' );

_e( 'Submit post', 'boj-plugin' );

?>
```

The esc_attr_x() Function

esc_attr_x() is a marriage between two of the earlier translation functions: esc_attr__() and _x(). It enables you to translate text, provide a context for translation, and escape it for use in HTML attributes. This function returns translated text for use in PHP, but it does not have a similar function for printing text to the screen.

In the following example, the function displays a link to the WordPress admin. Use the esc_attr_x() function in the title attribute of the link so that any unwanted characters are properly escaped and to provide a context for the text string "Admin."

```php
<?php

function boj_plugin_display_post_link( $post_id ) {

    /* The text for the link. */
    $boj_link_text = _x(
        'Admin',
        'admin link',
        'boj-plugin'
    );
```

```php
    /* The text for the "title" attribute of the link. */
    $boj_link_title = esc_attr_x(
        'Admin',
        'admin link',
        'boj-plugin'
    );

    /* Display the link on the screen. */
    echo '<a href="' . admin_url( 'dashboard.php' ) . '"
    title="' . $boj_link_title . '">' . $boj_link_text . '</a>';
}

?>
```

The esc_html_x() Function

esc_html_x() merges the esc_html__() and _x() functions into a single function that allows for text translation, escapes unwanted HTML, and provides a context to translators.

Suppose you created a plugin that allows users to fill in a form about their favorite things and submit it to the site owner for review. Further suppose you have an optional input field called boj-favorite-food that needs a default value translated in the case of the users not disclosing their favorite food. In this example, you use the term "None," which is a common word and may be used in various circumstances. You should provide a context such as "favorite food" or "favorite item" to differentiate this instance of "None" from others.

```php
<?php

function boj_get_favorite_food() {

    /* If the user input a favorite food. */
    if ( !empty( $_POST['favorite-food'] ) )
        $boj_favorite_food = esc_html( $_POST['favorite-food'] );

    /* If no favorite food was chosen, set a default. */
    else {
        $boj_favorite_food = esc_html_x(
            'None',
            'favorite item',
            'boj-plugin'
        );
    }

    return $boj_favorite_food;
}

?>
```

The _n() Function

As a developer, you may not always know how many items will be returned for use in your PHP code. You can use the _n() function to differentiate between the singular and plural forms of text.

Not only will this function figure out which form should be used, it also will enable you to make each form translatable. Both the singular and plural forms need to be internationalized because the order that words appear for plural and singular forms is different in various languages.

This function's parameters are different from some of the other translation functions. $single represents the singular version of the text, and $plural represents the plural version of the text. $number is a parameter that you cannot know at the moment of writing your code. It's an unknown integer that can have various values.

Not all languages use only two forms (singular and plural). However, you only need to take care of these two forms. If a language requires more than two forms, translators will provide this in the translation files and WordPress's localization process will use the correct form.

Now create a function that counts the number of posts published on the site and prints the value in a sentence using the printf() function (see the "Using Placeholders" section).

```php
<?php

function boj_count_published_posts() {

    /* Count the number of posts. */
    $boj_count_posts = wp_count_posts();

    /* Get the count for the number of posts with a post_status of 'publish'. */
    $count = $boj_count_posts->publish;

    /* Display a sentence, letting the user know how many posts are published. */
    printf( _n(
        'You have published %s post.', 'You have published %s posts.',
        $count,
        'boj-plugin' ),
    $count );
}

?>
```

The two sentences used look similar in English, and many developers may think it's easier to get away with "You have published %s post(s)." Although this works in some languages, it likely won't work in most.

For an example of why this method wouldn't work, look at the word *journal* in French. Using "journal(s)" in this case wouldn't apply because the plural form of *journal* is *journaux*.

The _nx() Function

The _nx() function is a combination of the _n() and _x() translation functions. It allows for the differentiation of singular and plural forms of text and a context for the text.

In this example, you create a function that grabs all of a site's post tags and lists the number of posts that have been given each particular tag. The _nx() function provides a way for you to display the text based on the post count of each tag and provide a context for translation of the text.

```php
<?php

function boj_list_post_tag_counts() {

    /* Get all post tags in an alphabetical list. */
    $tags = get_terms( 'post_tag', array( 'orderby' => 'name', 'order' => 'ASC' ) );

    /* Open unordered list. */
    echo '<ul>';

    /* Loop through each post tag and display its post count and name. */
    foreach ( $tags as $tag ) {
        echo '<li>';
        printf(
            _nx(
                '%s post',
                '%s posts',
                $tag->count,
                'post count',
                'boj-plugin'
            ),
            $tag->count
        );
        echo '</li>';
    }

    /* Close unordered list. */
    echo '</ul>';
}

?>
```

The _n_noop() Function

There are some cases in which you might have singular and plural forms of text that you don't want translated on the spot but need translated later. This is useful when you have large lists of messages but don't know which to display until a variable has been set.

The _n_noop() function adds these values to the translation files. Rather than returning translated string like most other translation functions, it returns an array with both values.

Suppose you created two custom post types (see Chapter 11, "Extending Posts") called video and music to give your plugin users some nifty features for their site. You have some messages you'd like translated, but you want to keep the code easy to reuse and short. In the following example, you create a function that takes a parameter of $post_type. This displays the appropriate message depending on the value of this parameter.

```php
<?php

function boj_count_posts_of_cusboj_types( $post_type = 'video' ) {

    /* Get a count of all posts of the given post type. */
    $all_posts = wp_count_posts( $post_type );
```

```php
    /* Get the count of the published posts. */
    $count = $all_posts->publish;

    /* Prepare an array of messages. */
    $boj_messages = array(
        'video' => _n_noop( 'You have %s video.', 'You have %s videos.' ),
        'music' => _n_noop( 'You have %s music file.', 'You have %s music files.' )
    );

    /* Get the message for the custom post type given. */
    $boj_message = $boj_messages[$post_type];

    /* Print the message for the custom post type given and its count. */

    printf( _n(
        $boj_message['singular'],
        $boj_message['plural'],
        $count
    ), $count );
}

?>
```

The function used the _n_noop() function to build the array of messages, but it used the _n() function to display the translated message. This enabled you to translate only the message needed at the moment instead of each message.

The _nx_noop() Function

_nx_noop() combines the _n_noop() function and the _x() function to enable setting up text for later translation and providing a context for translators on how the text is used in the plugin. It works the same as _n_noop() by adding the text to translation files but not translating it when used in PHP.

Building off the previous example of showing the number of posts published by type, you can use the _nx_noop() function to add a context.

```php
<?php

function boj_count_posts_of_custom_types( $post_type = 'video' ) {

    /* Get a count of all posts of the given post type. */
    $all_posts = wp_count_posts( $post_type );

    /* Get the count of the published posts. */
    $count = $all_posts->publish;

    /* Prepare an array of messages. */
    $boj_messages = array(
        'video' => _n_noop(
            '%s video',
            '%s videos',
            'post count'
        ),
```

```
        'music' => _n_noop(
            '%s music file',
            '%s music files',
            'post count'
        )
    );

    /* Get the message for the custom post type given. */
    $boj_message = $boj_messages[$post_type];

    /* Print the message for the custom post type given and its count. */
    printf( _n(
        $boj_message['singular'],
        $boj_message['plural'],
        $count
    ), $count );
}

?>
```

Using Placeholders

You may have noticed the use of symbols such as `%s` and `%1$s` in previous examples. These are placeholders for variables. Placeholders are useful because they enable you to translate strings without breaking them apart.

The translation functions in WordPress cannot output placeholders on their own. The placeholders are merely there for translators to properly set within the text of their translation files. Placeholders must be converted to a given variable in PHP.

The `printf()` and `sprintf()` PHP functions are useful when using placeholders. Both functions can replace the placeholder with a given variable. Use `printf()` to print text to the screen and `sprintf()` to return text. Each function takes in a first parameter of `$text`, which is the text you're translating. Both can then receive any number of extra parameters that represent the placeholders in the `$text` variable.

Now take a look at an example of a translated sentence that works in English but breaks in many other languages.

```
<?php
function boj_display_blog_name() {
    _e( 'The name of your blog is ', 'boj-plugin' );
    echo get_bloginfo( 'name' );
    _e( '.', 'boj-plugin' );
}
?>
```

Although the text in that function is internationalized, it's not done in a way that's easily translatable. This is where placeholders come in. They enable you to set a variable in the text and keep it as one sentence.

Now rewrite that function in a way that makes it easier for translators to translate. Use `printf()` to print the sentence to the screen and convert the placeholders.

```php
<?php
function boj_display_blog_name() {
    printf(
        __( 'The name of your blog is %s.', 'boj-plugin' ),
        get_bloginfo( 'name' )
    );
}?>
```

Now create a function that returns the tagline of the site in a sentence using the `sprintf()` function.

```php
<?php
function boj_get_blog_tagline() {
    return sprint(
        __( 'The tagline of your site is %s.', 'boj-plugin' ),
        get_bloginfo('description' )
    );
}
?>
```

Sometimes you need multiple placeholders in one text string. Luckily, both `printf()` and `sprintf()` handle this wonderfully. The big difference here is that you shouldn't use `%s`. It's best to use numbered placeholders instead because the order of words in other languages may be different than your own.

In the following example, you use multiple placeholders to display a sentence depending on the number of posts published on the blog, along with the blog title.

```php
<?php

function boj_display_blog_name_and_post_count() {

    /* Get the number of posts. */
    $count_posts = wp_count_posts();

    /* Get the number of published posts. */
    $count = $count_posts->publish;

    /* Get the site name. */
    $site_name = get_bloginfo( 'name' );

    /* Display a sentence based on the number of posts published. */
    printf(
        _n(
            'There is %1$s post published on %2$s.',
            'There are %1$s posts published on %2$s.',
            $count,
            'boj-plugin'
        ),
        $count, $site_name
    );
}

?>
```

In the example function, the `%1$s` placeholder represents the `$count` variable, which returns the number of published posts. The `%2$s` placeholder represents the value of `$site_name`, which was set to the name of the site.

Internationalizing JavaScript

Some plugins require JavaScript to function properly (see Chapter 12, "JavaScript and AJAX"). Because the internationalization functions in WordPress are written in PHP, you can't use them inside of JavaScript files. This makes it a little tougher to translate but not impossible.

WordPress provides a function called `wp_localize_script()` that enables you to pass translated text to an external file. You can then use the translated strings within your JavaScript. Take a look at what this function looks like.

```php
<?php
wp_localize_script( $handle, $object_name, $l10n );
?>
```

➤ `$handle` must match the `$handle` parameter of a script that's already registered with WordPress (see Chapter 12).

➤ `$object_name` is a unique identifier that represents this set of translations.

➤ `$l10n` is an array of translations with named keys that each has a value of a single translated string.

To understand how all this comes together, you need to create a plugin that uses JavaScript. You use a simple script here. To delve more into the process of using JavaScript, read the thorough explanation in Chapter 12. Your plugin will add two input buttons to the site's footer. When either of the buttons is clicked, a translated message appears.

The first step is to create a new plugin folder called `boj-alert-box` and place a new PHP file called `boj-alert-box.php` in this folder. In the `boj-alert-box.php` file, add your plugin information (Chapter 2, "Plugin Foundation").

```php
<?php
/**
 * Plugin Name: BOJ Alert Box
 * Plugin URI: http://example.com
 * Description: A plugin example that places two input buttons in the blog footer
   that when clicked display an alert box.
 * Version: 0.1
 * Author: WROX
 * Author URI: http://wrox.com
 */
```

Code snippet boj-alert-box.php

Next, you need to load your translation as described in the "Getting Your Plugin Ready for Translation" section.

```
/* Add the translation function after the plugins loaded hook. */
add_action( 'plugins_loaded', 'boj_alert_box_load_translation' );

/**
 * Loads a translation file if the paged being viewed isn't in the admin.
 *
 * @since 0.1
 */
function boj_alert_box_load_translation() {

    /* If we're not in the admin, load any translation of our plugin. */
    if ( !is_admin() )
        load_plugin_textdomain( 'boj-alert-box', false, 'boj-alert-box/languages' );
}
```

Code snippet boj-alert-box.php

At this point, you need to load your script using the `wp_enqueue_script()` function. After calling that function, you can localize your script using the `wp_localize_script()` function. It is important that this function is called after the script has been registered because the `$handle` variable has to be set.

```
/* Add our script function to the print scripts action. */
add_action( 'wp_print_scripts', 'boj_alert_box_load_script' );

/**
 * Loads the alert box script and localizes text strings that need translation.
 *
 * @since 0.1
 */
function boj_alert_box_load_script() {

    /* If we're in the WordPress admin, don't go any farther. */
    if ( is_admin() )
        return;

    /* Get script path and file name. */
    $script = trailingslashit( plugins_url( 'boj-alert-box' ) ) .
    'boj-alert-box-script.js';

    /* Enqueue our script for use. */
    wp_enqueue_script( 'boj-alert-box', $script, false, 0.1 );

    /* Localize text strings used in the JavaScript file. */
    wp_localize_script( 'boj-alert-box', 'boj_alert_box_L10n', array(
        'boj_box_1' => __( 'Alert boxes are annoying!', 'boj-alert-box' ),
        'boj_box_2' => __( 'They are really annoying!', 'boj-alert-box' ),
    ) );
}
```

Code snippet boj-alert-box.php

Now you add a couple of fun input buttons to the footer of the site. Notice the use of the esc_attr__() function from earlier in the chapter to translate and escape the value attributes of the buttons.

```php
/* Add our alert box buttons to the site footer. */
add_action( 'wp_footer', 'boj_alert_box_display_buttons' );

/**
 * Displays two input buttons with a paragraph.  Each button has an onClick()
 * event that loads a JavaScript alert box.
 *
 * @since 0.1
 */
function boj_alert_box_display_buttons() {

    /* Get the HTML for the first input button. */
    $boj_alert_box_buttons = '<input type="button" onclick="boj_show_alert_box_1()"
    value="' . esc_attr__( 'Press me!', 'boj-alert-box' ) . '" />';

    /* Get the HTML for the second input button. */
    $boj_alert_box_buttons .= '<input type="button" onclick="boj_show_alert_box_2()"
    value="' . esc_attr__( 'Now press me!', 'boj-alert-box' ) . '" />';

    /* Wrap the buttons in a paragraph tag. */
    echo '<p>' . $boj_alert_box_buttons . '</p>';
}

?>
```

Code snippet boj-alert-box.php

Your plugin's PHP file is complete. You now need to add a JavaScript file called boj-alert-box-script.js to your plugin folder. After it's created, you can add two functions for displaying the alert boxes on screen. Within the boj-alert-box-script.js file, add the JavaScript.

```javascript
/**
 * Displays an alert box with our first translated message when called.
 */
function boj_show_alert_box_1() {
    alert( boj_alert_box_L10n.boj_box_1 );
}

/**
 * Displays an alert box with our second translated message when called.
 */
function boj_show_alert_box_2() {
    alert( boj_alert_box_L10n.boj_box_2 );
}
```

Code snippet boj-alert-box-script.js

Because you're working across multiple files, it may be hard to see how the files interact with one another.

The two most important parameters from the call to `wp_localize_script()` are the `$object_name` and `$l10n` parameters. In the example plugin, you specifically set `$object_name` to `boj_alert_box_L10n` and `$l10n` to an array of key/value pairs.

When needing a translation in the JavaScript file, you used `$object_name.$l10n[$key]`. In the JavaScript function for the first alert box, this looks like this:

```
alert( boj_alert_box_L10n.boj_box_2 );
```

CREATING TRANSLATION FILES

Now that you've done all the hard work of internationalizing the text strings in your plugin, you have one more step to complete. This step requires much less work than the previous steps. You need to create a default translation file to kick start the translation process for potential translators.

To provide a consistent look at how this process works, you can work with the BOJ Alert Box plugin from the "Internationalizing JavaScript" section.

The MO and PO Files

When translators create translations of your plugin, they use your plugin's POT file to create two files: `boj-alert-box-$locale.mo` and `boj-alert-box-$locale.po`.

`boj-alert-box` is the `$domain` parameter used in the translation functions throughout the plugin. `$locale` is a variable that represents the language and regional dialect. For example, WordPress uses `en_US` as its default language. `en` represents English, and `US` represents the region.

The PO file is the file used by translation tools to allow for human-readable text. Translators work with this file to provide a translation. The PO file isn't necessary to run a translation of your plugin, but it's always nice to package it with your plugin download for use by other users that may want to update any text to suit their needs.

The MO file is created from the finished translation. WordPress uses it to translate internationalized text strings from your plugin.

WordPress users set their locale in their `wp-config.php` file. This tells WordPress to look for any translations with that locale and load them. If users set their locale to `fr_FR` (French), WordPress would load a file called `boj-alert-box-fr_FR.mo` if it existed in your plugin.

Translation Tools

Many translation tools around the Web are open source and free to download. Each tool isn't covered in detail here because they all have different ways to create translations. However, there is a list of supported translation tools for WordPress.

Following are available tools for translation:

➤ Poedit: `http://poedit.net`

➤ GlotPress: `http://glotpress.org`

➤ Launchpad: `https://translations.launchpad.net`

➤ Pootle: `http://pootle.locamotion.org`

➤ KBabel: `http://i18n.kde.org`

➤ GNU Gettext: `http://gnu.org/software/gettext`

One of the most common tools for plugin developers is Poedit. It has a simple, point-and-click interface that enables developers to create a POT file from their plugin.

GlotPress is a new Web-based tool from the people behind the WordPress project that promises to enable a single person or a team to work on translating software. It is now being used to facilitate the translation process for the WordPress software at `http://translate.wordpress.org`.

How to Create a POT File

Using Poedit from the "Translating Tools" section, you can create a POT file. You need to input only a few pieces of information, and Poedit does the rest for you.

1. Click File under the main menu.

2. Click New Catalog. A Settings box appears with three tabs, as shown in Figure 5-1.

3. In the Project info tab, fill in the input boxes that are relevant to your plugin, leaving the Charset box as `UTF-8`.

4. In the Paths tab, change the Base Path to `../` and add an extra path of `.` if you're placing your translations in the `languages` folder of your plugin. If not, leave this at the default.

5. In the Keywords tab, enter each function name from the "Echoing and Returning Strings" section of this chapter as a new keyword. For example, enter `esc_attr_e()` as `esc_attr_e`.

6. Click OK to save your POT file settings.

7. Save your file as `plugin-name.pot` in your plugin's `languages` folder. For example, the BOJ Alert Box plugin would be `boj-alert-box.pot`.

FIGURE 5-1

After you complete this process, Poedit synchronizes your POT file with your plugin, and you will have completed the process of preparing your plugin for translation.

Where to Store Translation Files

Many plugins add translation files in the top level of their plugin folder. Although translations will work when using this method, it can get a bit messy and is discouraged. If you have a plugin with many other files, it may become much too unorganized if you take this route.

For the cleanest, most organized system, create an extra directory in your plugin folder called `languages`. When you release your plugin, you can store your default translation files in this folder. When translators send you translation files for your plugin, you simply drop those files in the `languages` folder. Be sure to add both the PO file (for translators) and MO file (for WordPress) of the translation you're given.

SUMMARY

The biggest lesson to take away from this chapter is that people use WordPress in all corners of the world. To have a good plugin for public download, it is essential that you prepare it for translation. This can set your plugin apart from the many thousands of plugins that aren't internationalized. After you start putting the tools of this chapter into practice, you can see how easy it is to make your plugin more powerful and build a larger community around your work.

Plugin Security

WHAT'S IN THIS CHAPTER?

➤ Understanding what security is

➤ Learning to identify weak spots in code

➤ Preventing malicious attacks such as XSS or CSRF

➤ Checking user permissions

➤ Validating and sanitizing data

➤ Formatting robust and secure SQL queries

➤ Keeping good practices in mind

In computer language, "security" often refers to scary buzzwords such as Cross Site Scripting (XSS), Cross Site Request Forgery (CSRF), SQL Injection, Privilege Escalation, Vulnerabilities, and Holes.

Are you frightened yet?

You should be scared because these are real threats and, as you will read, trivial to execute against shabby code. But then, you should not be scared because, fortunately, WordPress comes with all the tools you need to make your code safe and secure.

SECURING YOUR PLUGIN

Weak code may be subject to abuse and eventually compromise your server security, or retrieve otherwise hidden data about you or your users. This is the worst-case scenario.

But before letting Internet pirates wander in your files and directories, feeble code will simply fail at making sure that data entered by an honest user is valid and sanitary. As you can see in this chapter, a poorly coded form can, for instance, truncate user input and as a result process partial content.

What Securing Your Plugin Is

Making your plugin secure is dealing with vulnerabilities and data integrity and reliability. It's both preventing malicious attacks and making sure legitimate use cannot produce unexpected behavior.

What Securing Your Plugin Is Not

In WordPress' environment, securing your plugin is not a difficult task, nor is it cumbersome or time consuming: WordPress implements several functions to address the various potential issues.

USER PERMISSIONS

You probably have already noticed it: When you try to access an admin page of a WordPress blog while being logged in as a user that is not an administrator, you may be shown a message stating that you don't have sufficient privileges, as shown in Figure 6-1.

FIGURE 6-1

To guarantee that specific actions (such as managing plugins or changing the site options) are restricted to a population with specific rights, in other words to block privilege escalation attacks, WordPress makes extensive use of a function named `current_user_can()`. You too, of course, can and should use this function in your plugins.

How to Check current_user_can()

The usage of `current_user_can()` is straightforward: You either check if a user has a capability or a role before proceeding to a sensitive action, or die with a meaningful message. For example:

```php
<?php

// Capability:
if ( !current_user_can('install_plugins') )
    wp_die( 'Insufficient permissions' );

// Role:
if( !current_user_can('editor') )
    wp_die( 'You cannot edit this setting' );
?>
```

You can either use default roles and capabilities or create custom ones. You learn how to do this in Chapter 8, which is devoted to user management.

Do Not Check Too Early

The function `current_user_can()` depends on `get_currentuserinfo()`, which has a particularity: It is a pluggable function. Pluggable functions can be replaced by plugins: They can be found in file `wp-includes/pluggable.php`, which is loaded after active plugins.

Because of this particularity you cannot check user permissions at plugin loading and instead will need to wait until WordPress has fully started and instantiated (for instance, after the action 'init').

For example, picture a plugin that outputs debug information when you append `?debug=1` to any URL of the blog, but only if the user is an administrator.

The debug output function here prints out all SQL queries that WordPress ran, provided that the constant `SAVEQUERIES` is set to true:

```php
<?php
// Print debug information
function boj_debug_output() {
    global $wpdb;
    echo "<pre>";
    print_r($wpdb->queries);
    echo "</pre>";
}
?>
```

Now how can you make this function dependant on the query parameter `debug=1`?

The worst way to do so would be the following:

```php
<?php
if( isset( $_GET['debug'] ) )
    boj_debug_output();
?>
```

This is bad practice because debug information can potentially reveal sensitive information such as physical paths or table names, and with such a conditional test, anyone would see them by simply adding `?debug=1` to any URL of the site.

Because you want to restrict the debug data to the administrator of the blog, you need to code a more evolved condition:

```php
<?php
if( isset( $_GET['debug'] ) && current_user_can( 'manage_options' ) )
    boj_debug_output();
?>
```

But this won't work: Remember, when the plugin is loaded and the server parses and compiles its code, pluggable functions are not in memory yet. What you need to do is to hook this check to an action that occurs only when everything is loaded.

Following is the complete plugin:

```php
<?php
/*
Plugin Name: Simple Debug
Plugin URI: http://example.com/
Description: Append ?debug=1 to display debug info if you are an admin
Author: WROX
Author URI: http://wrox.com
*/

add_action( 'init', 'boj_debug_check' );

function boj_debug_check() {
    if( isset( $_GET['debug'] ) && current_user_can( 'manage_options' ) ) {
        if( !defined( 'SAVEQUERIES' ) )
            define( 'SAVEQUERIES', true );
        add_action( 'wp_footer', 'boj_debug_output' );
    }
}

// Print debug information
function boj_debug_output() {
    global $wpdb;
    echo "<pre>";
    print_r($wpdb->queries);
    echo "</pre>";
}
?>
```

Code snippet plugin-simple-debug.php

 In your plugins, always hook function calls to an appropriate action, such as 'init' or 'plugins_loaded'. This way you can ensure that all WordPress functions have been declared and your function won't be triggered too soon.

NONCES

In the previous section about user permissions, you learned how to check that people have authority before they can perform an operation, and doing so, you protect their blog against nonprivileged users. But you also need to protect users from . . . themselves.

Authority Versus Intention

When you are logged into your WordPress install, you can click links that perform various actions, such as delete a post, update plugin settings, or create a category. Before proceeding, all these operations should verify that you are actually logged in and have sufficient permission, using the function `current_user_can()`. They verify that you have authority.

Now imagine people maliciously crafting a link that would delete a post on your blog. They could not use it themselves, of course, because they have no admin account on your blog and thus, no authority. But what if they trick you into clicking on this link? Because you are logged in, the action would occur, and the post would be deleted. You had authority but no intention. The malicious users just completed a Cross Site Request Forgery, or CSRF.

 To trick people into clicking a link on their own site is trivial. For instance, hide the link with a URL shortener such as `bit.ly` *and share it via instant messaging with a compelling message such as "Look at this pic, very funny!" In the age of Twitter and Facebook, CSRF attacks are flourishing.*

Of course, WordPress has a built-in solution to prevent these attacks.

What Is a Nonce?

In computer language, a nonce, or cryptographic nonce, is the abbreviation of "number used once." In WordPress, it is a short and apparently random string such as a password, which is specific to the following:

➤ One WordPress user

➤ One action (delete, update, save, and such)

➤ One object (a post, a link, a plugin setting, and such)

➤ One time frame of 24 hours

For example, the link to delete the post #43 in your WordPress blog could be something such as `http://example.com/wp-admin/post.php?post=43&action=trash&_wpnonce=83a08fcbc2`. The nonce, here `83a08fcbc2`, is valid for only 24 hours, only if used by you and only to delete post #43.

When you click that link, WordPress verifies that this nonce meets all these specifications before actually deleting the link.

More important, a nonce cannot be guessed by a malicious user, and loading a link without the correct nonce goes nowhere, as shown in Figure 6-2, which shows the result of trying to activate a plugin without knowing the valid nonce.

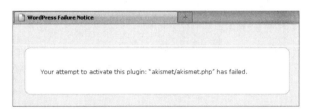

FIGURE 6-2

How to Create and Verify Nonces

WordPress employs two different functions to create nonces in forms, as hidden fields, or in URLs, as a GET parameter.

To become acquainted with nonces, you can code a useful plugin to enhance WordPress native tag management features. This plugin identifies post tags not used in any post and enables you to either rename or delete them. Call this plugin Unused Tags and use the prefix `boj_utags`.

Creating a URL Nonce

To create and add a nonce to a URL, just like in the previous example with links deleting a post, use function `wp_nonce_url()` as follows:

```php
<?php
$url = wp_nonce_url( $url, $action );
?>
```

The first parameter `$url` is a string of the URL address to which you want to append a nonce in the query string. The links in the Unused Tags plugin to delete a link will be of the form `http://example.com/wp-admin/edit.php?page=boj_utags&boj_action=delete&id=6`; in this URL notice the parameter `boj_action` and the tag ID.

The second parameter `$action` is the string with which you make the nonce specific to one action and one object. The link you want to protect with a nonce here is tied to the action "delete" and the tag id 6, so the `$action` parameter could be 'boj_utags-delete_tag6'.

The nonce action can be any string, but to make it unique to your plugin and one action over one object (besides the current user and the 24-hour window), it is good practice to adhere to the `plugin-action_object` *model.*

To sum it up, in your plugin, given a tag ID `$id`, the code to generate a nonce protected URL to delete this tag will be the following:

```php
<?php

$delete_url = add_query_arg( array('boj_action'=>'delete','id'=>$id) );
$nonced_url = wp_nonce_url( $delete_url, 'boj_utags-delete_tag'.$id );
?>
<a href="<?php echo $nonced_url; ?>">delete</a> this tag
```

To craft the delete link, you have used the handy function `add_query_arg()`, which adds to the current URL the query parameters defined in its array parameter. In other words, it adds `?boj_action=delete&id=6`, or `&boj_action=delete&id=6` if the current URL already has a query string.

Creating a Form Nonce

Nonces also protect forms, with function `wp_nonce_field()`. This function needs a single string parameter, the nonce action `plugin-action_object`.

Given the `$name` and `$id` of a post tag, the proper form to allow renaming it follows:

```
<form action="" method="post">
    <?php wp_nonce_field( 'boj_utags-rename_tag'.$id ); ?>
    <input type="hidden" name="boj_action" value="rename" />
    <input type="hidden" name="id" value="<?php echo $id; ?>" />
    <input type="text" name="name" value="<?php echo esc_attr($name); ?>" />
    <input type="submit" value="Rename" />
</form>
```

Notice how you used a new function named `esc_attr()` here: It is to ensure that, should `$name` contain quotes, it will not break the display and the form. You learn all about this in the next section about data sanitization.

Verifying a Nonce

Adding nonces to URLs or forms is only the first part of the job: On the other end, the function that executes the expected operation needs to verify before that the nonce is valid and tied to that operation.

The function you use is named `check_admin_referer()`: It authenticates the nonce, silently does nothing if valid, or dies with an "Are you sure" error screen, as shown in Figure 6-2. This function must be called before any output is sent to the screen.

In your plugin, parameters such as the action or the tag ID are either passed via GET (the URL query string) or POST (the submitted form): Instead of checking both arrays `$_GET` and `$_POST`, you simply examine `$_REQUEST` to get the parameter values.

The complete code block to check nonces and then rename or delete a post tag follows:

```
<?php

if( !current_user_can( 'manage_options' ) )
    wp_die( 'Insufficient privileges!' );

$id     = $_REQUEST['id'];
$action = $_REQUEST['boj_action'];

check_admin_referer( 'boj_utags-'.$action.'_tag'.$id );

switch( $action ) {
    case 'rename':
        $newtag = array( 'name' => $_POST['name'], 'slug' => $_POST['name'] );
        wp_update_term( $id, 'post_tag', $newtag );
        break;
    case 'delete':
        wp_delete_term( $id, 'post_tag' );
        break;
}
?>
```

Notice how you first check user permissions: Nonces check a user's intention, but you still need to validate their authority.

Wrapping It Up: The Entire "Unused Tags" Plugin

To be fully operational, your plugin now needs a proper plugin header, a complete administration page with a new entry in the menu, and of course the function that lists the unused tags.

```php
<?php
/*
Plugin Name: Unused Tags
Plugin URI: http://example.com/
Description: Find unused tags and rename or delete them
Author: WROX
Author URI: http://wrox.com
*/

// Add an entry for our option page to the Posts menu
add_action('admin_menu', 'boj_utags_add_page');
function boj_utags_add_page() {
    add_posts_page( 'Unused Tags', 'Unused Tags', 'manage_options',
        'boj_utags', 'boj_utags_option_page' );
}

// Catch any boj_action parameter in query string
add_action( 'admin_init', 'boj_utags_do_action' );

// Proceed to requested boj_action if applicable
function boj_utags_do_action() {
    if( !isset( $_REQUEST['boj_action'] ) )
        return;

    if( !current_user_can( 'manage_options' ) )
        wp_die( 'Insufficient privileges!' );

    $id     = $_REQUEST['id'];
    $action = $_REQUEST['boj_action'];

    if( $action == 'done' ) {
        add_action( 'admin_notices', 'boj_utags_message' );
        return;
    }

    check_admin_referer( 'boj_utags-'.$action.'_tag'.$id );

    switch( $action ) {
        case 'rename':
            $newtag = array( 'name' => $_POST['name'], 'slug' => $_POST['name'] );
            wp_update_term( $id, 'post_tag', $newtag );
            break;
        case 'delete':
            wp_delete_term( $id, 'post_tag' );
```

```php
                break;
        }

    wp_redirect( add_query_arg( array( 'boj_action' => 'done' ) ) );

}

// Admin notice
function boj_utags_message() {
    echo "<div class='updated'><p>Action completed</p></div>";
}

// Draw the tag management page
function boj_utags_option_page() {
    ?>
    <div class="wrap">
        <?php screen_icon(); ?>
        <h2>Unused Tags</h2>

        <?php

        if( $tags = boj_utags_find_orphans() ):

        echo '<p>You currently have '.count( $tags ). ' unused tags:</p>';
        echo '<ol>';

        foreach( $tags as $tag ) {
            $id   = $tag->term_id;
            $name = esc_attr( $tag->name );

            $delete_url= add_query_arg( array('boj_action'=>'delete','id'=>$id) );
            $nonced_url= wp_nonce_url( $delete_url, 'boj_utags-delete_tag'.$id );
            ?>
            <li>
            <form action="" method="post">
            <?php wp_nonce_field( 'boj_utags-rename_tag'.$id ); ?>
            <input type="hidden" name="boj_action" value="rename" />
            <input type="hidden" name="id" value="<?php echo $id; ?>" />
            <input type="text" name="name" value="<?php echo $name; ?>" />
            <input type="submit" value="Rename" /> or
            <a href="<?php echo $nonced_url; ?>">delete</a> this tag
            </form>
            </li>

        <?php }

        else: ?>
        <p>You have no unused tags.</p>

        <?php endif; ?>

        </ol>
    </div>
```

```php
    <?php
}

// Find unused tags, return them in an array
function boj_utags_find_orphans() {
    global $wpdb;

    $sql = "SELECT terms.term_id, terms.name FROM {$wpdb->terms} terms
            INNER JOIN {$wpdb->term_taxonomy} taxo
            ON terms.term_id=taxo.term_id
            WHERE taxo.taxonomy = 'post_tag'
            AND taxo.count=0";

    return $wpdb->get_results( $sql );
}
?>
```

Code snippet plugin-unused-tags.php

Copy or download this plugin, activate it, and you can access a new page under the Posts menu that resembles Figure 6-3:

FIGURE 6-3

Spot a few more good practices in this plugin:

1. Function `boj_utags_do_action()`, which checks for the presence of a `boj_action` parameter in the query string or the POST data, is hooked to action `admin_init`. This way, the plugin actually does something only when the user is in the admin area. When viewing the public part (the blog itself), no event is triggered. The gain here is negligible because the plugin is simple, but this technique applied to complex plugins does speed up execution.

2. When a tag has been deleted or renamed, the plugin redirects the user to the current page with the additional query parameter `'boj_action=done'`. Doing so, you prevent any unwanted repeated action if the user accidentally reloads the page and resubmits data. The function hooks into `'admin_notices'` to display an informational message.

Nonces in Ajax Scripts

Ajax scripts are particular types of JavaScripts that enable updating a part of the browser's screen without reloading the entire page. Ajax scripts can consist of forms or links and as such need to be protected with nonces as well.

You learn how to add such nonces in Chapter 12, "JavaScript and Ajax," which is entirely about JavaScript and Ajax.

DATA VALIDATION AND SANITIZATION

As you read in the introduction of this chapter, the golden rule in data filtering is to consider all data invalid unless it can be proven valid. Otherwise stated, now is a good time for some healthy suspicion and a little bit of welcome paranoia.

In this practical section, you now learn why data filtering is important, how to validate and sanitize the various types of data your WordPress plugins process (raw text strings, emails, integers, and so on), and what WordPress built-in function can help you do this.

The Need for Data Validation and Sanitization

Consider a few lines of simple and innocent looking HTML and PHP code:

Available for download on Wrox.com

```php
<?php $name = $_POST['fullname']; ?>

<form action="" method="POST">
    Full name:
    <input type="text" name="fullname" value="<?php echo $name; ?>" />
    <input type="submit" value="Save" />
</form>
```

Code snippet bad_form.php

This minimal form has just one field, named fullname, which is prepopulated with any previously entered value. For future reference, name this form Bad Form.

For instance, if you enter Ozh RICHARD as a full name and press Save, everything seems fine with this form (see Figure 6-4).

So, what could possibly go wrong with such a simple form?

Full name: Ozh RICHARD   Save

FIGURE 6-4

The potential problem here is that inputs are not validated, and outputs are not sanitized. In other words, consider the following:

➤ The script does not make sure that the string entered actually looks like a full name.

➤ The script does not make sure that the string entered can be printed out without breaking the form.

To illustrate this trivial lack in security, input the following full names and see the results (see Figure 6-5):

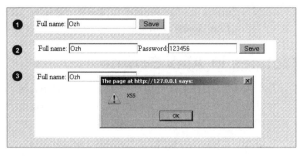

FIGURE 6-5

1. Nonmalicious input: `Ozh "Funny Guy" RICHARD`

2. Malicious input: `Ozh"/>Password:<input name="password" value="123456"`

3. Malicious input: `Ozh"<script>alert('XSS');</script>`

What just happened?

Case 1 is an example of a legit, nonmalicious, yet form-breaking example: Although the data entered is a valid full name, the lack of sanitization at output breaks the input field because of the quotation marks. A correct way to render the form in that case would have been to convert these quotation marks into HTML entities.

In case 2, the user has joined the Dark Side and deliberately tries to exploit the form. Again, the quotation mark breaks the input field, so the output shows another field that would be actually submitted if the user pressed Save again. Not only is the output not sanitized (by encoding quotation marks before printing the value of the field) but the input is also questionable and should have been validated first, for instance by removing all nonalphanumeric characters and stripping HTML tags.

Case 3 is a variation on the same principle: Instead of adding arbitrary content to the form, the user here injects JavaScript that could, for instance, fetch a session cookie value from your site and send it to another one.

The third case is an example of Cross Site Scripting, or XSS: a vulnerability in web applications that enables malicious attackers to inject client-side script into web pages viewed by other users. Via XSS, an attacker can gain elevated access privileges to sensitive page content, session cookies, and a variety of other information maintained by the browser on behalf of the user.

These examples demonstrate how the lack of data validation measures can, at best, corrupt data or, at worst, exploit security holes in your web applications.

 At output, you must sanitize content before sending it to the user's browser screen. At input, you must validate data (make sure it is valid) or sanitize data (fix it to make it valid).

Good Practice: Identifying Potentially Tainted Data

Imagine you are coding a plugin with an interface asking users to enter their age and to pick a color between red, green, or blue.

Consider the following code fragment:

```php
<?php

$clean = array();

// Age: positive integer only
$clean['age'] = absint( $_POST['age'] );

// Color: red, green or blue only
switch( $_POST['color'] ) {
    case 'red':
    case 'green':
    case 'blue':
        $clean['color'] = $_POST['color'];
        break;
}

?>
```

Notice how this validating snippet makes use of an array named $clean. This illustrates a good practice that can help developers identify whether data is potentially unsanitary or can be considered safe. Because you cannot be sure of what the submitted array $_POST contains, don't validate it. Instead, select the expected part of it.

This snippet also introduces a WordPress function that is a convenient wrapper for PHP functions intval() and abs(), used to return a positive integer.

> *You should never validate data and leave it in $_POST, $_GET or $_REQUEST because it is important for developers to always be suspicious of data within these superglobal arrays.*

Initializing variables, such as $clean at the beginning of the snippet here, is another good practice because you make sure the result of your validating procedure contains only what you expect.

Using PHP's error_reporting and setting WordPress constant WP_DEBUG to true can help to enforce the initialization of variables because a reference to an undefined variable generates a notice on the screen. For more details about debugging, see Chapter 16.

The previous snippet validated only data: User input is accepted if it is valid and ignored otherwise. It does not sanitize, or "fix," the input: If incorrect data is submitted (such as the user entering a string instead of their age), the resulting array $clean simply ignores the item.

You can write a similar code block to sanitize data instead of simply validating it:

```php
<?php

$clean = array();

// Age: positive integer only
$clean['age'] = absint( $_POST['age'] );

// Color: red, green or blue only. Default is blue.
switch( $_POST['color'] ) {
    case 'red':
    case 'green':
        $clean['color'] = $_POST['color'];
        break;
    case 'blue':
        default:
        $clean['color'] = 'blue';
        break;
}

?>
```

Now, if users enter an invalid age, such as abc, the result will be 0. If they enter an invalid color (for instance purple), the result will be blue because of the default statement.

The validation philosophy applied here is called white listing: You accept data only from a finite list of known and trusted values. The opposite, reject data from a finite list of untrusted values, is called black listing, which is rarely a good idea. White listing is not always possible, but whenever you can enforce this policy, you should.

Validating or Sanitizing Input?

Whether you want to validate or sanitize user input is a design decision and depends mostly on the kind of data expected. Imagine a form containing a field to receive an integer (age for instance), an email address, and a longer paragraph for raw text with no HTML tags (such as a short bio).

Before you decide that you will just validate or also sanitize data, the first thing to consider is the potential inconvenience of simply validating and rejecting invalid data submitted:

➤ In the age field, the user has to re-enter a simple integer. No big deal and quickly done.

➤ In the bio field, if the entire text is ignored because the user has used an HTML tag, this may be a lot more annoying to start over and rewrite it. Here, sanitizing the input (stripping HTML tags out) would probably make more sense.

A second decisive factor to consider is your ability to interpret and guess what a sanitized value would be:

➤ If the user enters ABC in the age field, does that mean anything? You cannot sanitize here because it's impossible to deduce from invalid information what valid data could be. Your only option is to validate and ignore unacceptable data.

➤ On the contrary, if the user enters unauthorized HTML tags in the bio field, you can strip out HTML tags and propose valid sanitized data that will be close to what the user wanted to input.

A third characteristic to reflect on is what you will do right away with the input data if you sanitize, hence possibly modify it:

➤ If a slightly weird looking or badly formatted bio is published on a profile page, this may not be a severe incident (assuming the user can later edit and amend it, obviously).

➤ If the user enters an invalid email such as joe@joe,co.uk and you send a confirmation email to the sanitized but invalid joe@joeco.uk, the user will never get it. It would be a better choice to validate only the email field, thus rejecting invalid data and asking the user to re-input it.

Validating and Sanitizing Cookbook

You now learn how to validate and sanitize various types of data, and what WordPress functions exist to do so.

Integers

Most of the time, PHP functions such as intval() or is_int() can do the job:

```php
<?php
$data = 43;

// validate integers
return( intval( $data ) == $data );

// sanitize integers
return( intval( $data ) );
?>
```

WordPress's function absint() is also applicable whenever you want a positive integer, such as an age.

The possible problem you may run into is when dealing with large numbers: 32-bit systems have a maximum signed integer range of –2147483648 to 2147483647. So for example on such a system, intval('1000000000000') will return 2147483647. On the same principle, the maximum signed integer value for 64-bit systems is 9223372036854775807.

If you have to deal with large numbers, your best bet is to consider the data a string instead of an integer, and make sure it consists only of digits:

```php
<?php
$num = '100000000000000000';

// Validate large integers
return( ctype_digit( $num ) );
?>
```

Note that the `ctype` library may not be available on all servers. Before using it for a particular client, check that their server supports it.

Arbitrary Pure Text Strings

You often need to validate text strings of arbitrary length, such as a username or a country of birth. PHP functions of the `ctype_` family are fine for validating them. They return Boolean `true` or `false`.

If you are expecting only letters:

```php
<?php
// Validate alphabetic strings
return( ctype_alpha( $num ) );
?>
```

If you are expecting alphanumeric strings, such as for a nickname (for example, "Bob43"):

```php
<?php
// Validate alphanumeric strings
return( ctype_alnum( $num ) );
?>
```

 In version 5.2 and newer, PHP includes filter functions to validate various types of data: integers, Booleans, emails, strings, and so on. You can learn more about them at `http://php.net/filter`. *WordPress does not use them though, as they are still in development.*

Arbitrary Mixed Text Strings

Text strings can also consist of special characters such as punctuation. WordPress offers a function that is handy to sanitize general text strings from user input: `sanitize_text_field()`. This function removes invalid UTF-8 characters, converts single < into HTML entities, and removes all HTML tags, line breaks, and extra white space.

```php
<?php

var_dump( sanitize_text_field( "I am nice.\n Very <em>nice</em>!   " ) );

// result:
// string(21) "I am nice. Very nice!"

?>
```

In a less destructive manner, you may want to simply strip HTML tags but keep other formatting such as line breaks. WordPress provides `wp_strip_all_tags()` because PHP's built-in `strip_tags()`

does not properly filter out complex markup such as `<script></script>` as you can see in the following example:

```php
<?php

$test = '<a href="xx">site</a> <b>bold<b> <script>alert("fail")</script>';

// PHP's strip_tags()
var_dump( htmlentities( strip_tags( $test ) ) );
// result: string(33) "site bold alert("fail")"

// WordPress' wp_strip_all_tags()
var_dump( htmlentities( wp_strip_all_tags( $test ) ) );
// result: string(9) "site bold"
?>
```

Internal Identifier Strings

WordPress comes with a function named `sanitize_key()` used to sanitize internal identifiers, such as option names, which accepts lowercase characters, dashes, and underscores.

```php
<?php
$data = 'option_43;';

// Validate:
return( preg_match('/^[a-z0-9-_]+$/', $data ) );

// Sanitize:
return( sanitize_key( $data ) );
?>
```

The validating line introduces a powerful tool: regular expression pattern matching. Basically, this line says "return `true` if $data matches the pattern". This seemingly cryptic pattern is constructed as shown in Figure 6-6:

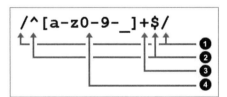

FIGURE 6-6

The four parts of this regular expression follow:

1. The pattern delimiters. It can be any character and is usually a forward slash /.

2. When used as the first character after the opening pattern delimiter, the caret ^ identifies the beginning of the string. Similarly, when used as the last character before the closing delimiter, a dollar sign $ means "end of the string."

3. The plus sign + means "one or more of the preceding pattern."

4. And finally the pattern itself, between square brackets: any character from lowercase a to lowercase z, from 0 to 9, or a dash -, or an underscore _.

You will use more complex regular expressions in the following examples.

String Patterns

Occasionally you need to validate or sanitize text strings that adhere to a predefined and known pattern, such as dates of birth, credit card numbers, ZIP codes, or telephone numbers.

Example 1: Telephone Number

For example, you can now write a function to validate telephone numbers of the following form: 123-456-7890 (3 digits, dash, 3 digits, dash, and four digits).

In regular expressions, \d means a digit (this is equivalent to [0-9] but shorter). If you expect exactly three digits, you can use: \d{3}.

Knowing this, you can now define and test the following function:

```php
<?php
// Validate phone numbers like 123-456-7890
function boj_validate_phone( $num ) {
    return preg_match( '/^\d{3}-\d{3}-\d{4}$/', $num );
}

// Test your function:

var_dump( boj_validate_phone( '132-456-7890' ) );
// echoes: int(1)

var_dump( boj_validate_phone( '555-8882' ) );
// echoes: int(0)
?>
```

Example 2: Product Serial Number

Now if you want to validate a product serial number such as A145-B3D5-KK43, what pattern can you use?

```php
<?php

// Validate product serial number like A145-B3D5-KK43
function boj_validate_serial( $string ) {
    return preg_match( '/^[A-Z0-9]{4}-[A-Z0-9]{4}-[A-Z0-9]{4}$/', $string );
}
?>
```

Example 3: Dates

In this third example, you can write a function to validate a date for an upcoming event. This one is slightly trickier: The data must comply to the pattern mm/dd/yyyy but also be a real and future date. (30/30/2010 cannot be accepted, for instance.)

The pattern used to match the input will be \d{2}/\d{2}/\d{4}. Because this pattern contains forward slashes, the regular expression delimiters will need to be another character, for instance the exclamation mark ! (You can also escape the slashes in the pattern with backslashes, but it makes the pattern even less readable: \d{2}\/\d{2}\/\d{4}.)

To check if the date exists, use the PHP function strtotime(), which converts textual dates into a UNIX timestamp if valid and into −1 or false otherwise.

The complete validating function would be the following:

```php
<?php

// Validate future dates like mm/dd/yyyy.
// Returns true or an error message
function boj_validate_date( $date ) {
    // first test: pattern matching
    if( !preg_match( '!\d{2}/\d{2}/\d{4}!', $date ) )
        return 'wrong pattern';

    // second test: is date valid?
    $timestamp = strtotime( $date );
    if( !$ timestamp )
        return 'date invalid';

    // third test: is the date from the past?
    if( $timestamp <= time() )
        return 'past date';

    // So far, so good
    return true;
}

// Test it:

var_dump( boj_validate_date( '12/12/99' ) );
// string(12) "wrong pattern"

var_dump( boj_validate_date( '35/30/1980' ) );
// string(12) "date invalid"

var_dump( boj_validate_date( '03/30/1980' ) );
// string(9) "past date"

var_dump( boj_validate_date( '03/30/2020' ) );
// bool(true)

?>
```

Code snippet validate_date.php

Because this function returns either the Boolean true for success, or an error message for any further diagnosis, to validate a date you need to strictly compare the validated date with true, using the triple equal sign:

```php
<?php

$date = '30/30/3030';

if( boj_validate_date( $date ) === true ) {
```

```
       // date is valid
} else {
       // date is invalid
}
?>
```

Regular expressions are an extremely powerful tool designed to match any structured pattern. You can find more about this subject at http://php.net/pcre.

Email Strings

Emails are a type of pattern text string that is easy to validate or sanitize within WordPress, thanks to functions is_email() and sanitize_email():

```php
<?php

$email = 'wrox@example.com';

// Validate:
return( is_email( $email ) );

// Sanitize:
return( sanitize_email( $email ) );
?>
```

Function is_email() returns either false or the email address if valid. Consider the following examples:

```php
<?php

var_dump( is_email( 'wrox@example' ) );
// bool(false)

var_dump( is_email( 'wrox@example.com' ) );
// string(11) "wrox@example.com"
?>
```

To use this function, you need to strictly compare an email and the result of is_email():

```php
<?php

if( is_email( $email ) === email ) {
       // email seems valid
} else {
       // email is invalid
}
?>
```

Be aware that in a LAN environment and some corporate networks, possibly functional email addresses such as admin@localhost or webmaster@server will not be considered valid. In such a case, you can simply check for the presence of the @ character, or maybe if possible test against a finite list of valid email addresses.

Function `sanitize_email()` either returns an empty string or a sanitized email address, depending on how malformed the input was. Consider the following sample outputs:

```php
<?php

var_dump( sanitize_email( 'ozh@ozh' ) );
// string(0) ""

var_dump( sanitize_email( 'ozh@ozh..org' ) );
// string(0) ""

var_dump( sanitize_email( '(ozh)@(ozh).org' ) );
// string(11) "ozh@ozh.org"

var_dump( sanitize_email( 'ozh@ozh.org' ) );
// string(11) "ozh@ozh.org"
?>
```

In any case, you should compare the sanitized emails with the original input, and if different ask the users to confirm their address.

Note that these functions do not check whether the email is actually an existing address, but only whether the pattern looks correct: one or more allowed characters, an at sign @, more characters, a dot, and again a few characters for the top-level domain. A blatantly fake email address such as kk@kk.kk will pass the test.

 The only way to test the existence of an email address is to send a mail to that address and ask the recipients to confirm they have received it by completing an action (usually clicking on a link that contains a unique identifier).

HTML (or XML)

HTML in this section can either be a full HTML fragment (a comment on a blog post, for instance), or single nodes, that is, an HTML element with text and attributes.

HTML Fragments

HTML fragments can be sanitized at input with WordPress function `force_balance_tags()`, although this cannot be considered as an HTML validator but more a helper function to achieve validity. This function finds incorrectly nested or missing closing tags and fixes the markup:

```php
<?php

// 1. Fixing missing closing tags:

$html = '<p>Please close my <strong>tags!';
var_dump( force_balance_tags( $html ) );
```

```
// string(45) "<p>Please close my <strong>tags!</strong></p>"

// 2. Fixing incorrectly nested tags:

$html = '<p>Please <strong><em>fix</strong></em> nesting!</p>';
var_dump( force_balance_tags( $html ) );
// string(52) "<p>Please <strong><em>fix</em></strong> nesting!</p>"

?>
```

WordPress ships with a script named KSES (a recursive acronym: KSES Strips Evil Scripts) that should process and sanitize all untrusted HTML, both at input and output. The wrapper function, wp_kses() enables advanced filtering of HTML snippets, for instance with a custom set of authorized tags.

You can now write a function to strip all HTML tags except <strong> and <a href='' title=''>. All other tags (<em>, <b>. . .) or attributes (class='', style='',...) need to be taken out.

First, define an array of allowed tags and attributes:

```
<?php

$allowed = array(
    'strong' => array(),
    'a'      => array(
        'href'  => array(),
        'title' => array()
    )
);
?>
```

You are now ready to filter and sanitize HTML fragments:

```
<?php

$html = '<a href="#" class="external">site</a>
         <b>bold?</b> <strong>bold!</strong>';

var_dump( wp_kses( $html, $allowed ) );
// string(58) "<a href="#">site</a> bold? <strong>bold!</strong>"
?>
```

Notice how selective this function is in removing tags and attributes as you have defined them. This function is used for instance to filter comments and enable only a minimal common set of HTML tags.

Note that the KSES library in WordPress defines default sets of HTML tags and attributes, as you can see at the beginning of the file wp-includes/kses.php. The global variable $allowedtags contains a rather restrictive set of tags that are typically what you will want to accept in comments or user input.

Using the function wp_kses_data() and passing as a single argument the chunk of HTML you want to sanitize, you will make use of this default list:

```php
<?php

$html = '<a href="http://site.com">site</a>
    <script src="script.js"></script>
    <img src="image.png" />
    <junk>random</junk>';

var_dump( wp_kses_data( $html ) );
// string(41) "<a href="http://site.com">site</a> random"
?>
```

HTML Nodes

A node is a part of an HTML (or, again, XML) document. It consists of three parts, as shown in Figure 6-7.

FIGURE 6-7

1. The element node (span, h1, em. . . or any custom XML element)

2. The attribute node (class, style, title, alt. . .)

3. The text node (any text found outside attributes and elements)

What you need to sanitize are the attribute and the text nodes at output to make sure they are valid and cannot break the display.

Consider the following code block, and try to spot its weaknesses before you read more:

```php
<h1><?php echo $page_title; ?></h1>
<a href="#anchor" title="<?php echo $link_title; ?>" >link</a>
```

In a similar manner to how the previous example Bad Form was breakable, the problem here is that the text node $page_title and the attribute node $link_title are not sanitized for display, which can produce unexpected and potentially dreadful results with values such as the following:

```php
<?php

$page_title = 'break</h1><h1>the tag';
$link_title = '" onmouseover="alert(\'XSS\');';

?>
```

WordPress contains two functions specifically designed to sanitize HTML attributes and text nodes, escape illegal characters, and convert to HTML entities when needed: esc_attr() and esc_html(). The same code block, now bullet proof, would be the following:

```php
<h1><?php echo esc_html( $page_title; ) ?></h1>
<a href="#anchor" title="<?php echo esc_attr( $link_title; ) ?>" >link</a>
```

In a localized environment, functions `esc_html()` and `esc_attr()` have variations that can translate and escape at the same time (such as `esc_html_e()` for example). Chapter 5, "Internationalization," has a detailed description of these functions.

URLs

Whether they are used as output in an HTML attribute node (`<a href="">`) or as standalone information (for example a field asking for a site URL in a form), URLs should be sanitized for input and output using WordPress' function `esc_url()`. This function checks and cleans a URL by removing unacceptable characters and optionally filtering protocols.

For output, use the function as following:

```php
<?php
// dangerous URL
$url = 'javascript:alert("XSS");';
?>

<a href="<?php echo esc_url( $url ); ?> ">Link Text</a>
```

In this example, the link would be safely displayed with an empty `href` attribute. For input, pass either one parameter (the URL) or two parameters (the URL and an array of allowed protocols) to sanitize data before storing or returning it.

In the following example, see how various URLs are sanitized:

```php
<?php

$url1 = 'http://example.com/"<script>alert(\'XSS\')</script>';
var_dump( esc_url( $url1 ) );
// string(54) "http://example.com/scriptalert('XSS')/script"

$url2 = 'http://example.com/"&lt;script&gt;alert(\'XSS\')&lt;/script&gt;';
var_dump( esc_url( $url2 ) );
// string(90) "http://example.com/&lt;script&gt;alert('XSS')&lt;/script&gt;"

$url3 = 'onmouseover="alert(\'XSS\')';
var_dump( esc_url( $url3 ) );
// string(41) "http://onmouseover=alert('XSS')"

$url4 = 'c:\dir\dir\dir\dir';
var_dump( esc_url( $url4 ) );
// string(0) ""

$url5 = 'http://ex[]amp[]le.co[]m/';
var_dump( esc_url( $url5 ) );
// string(19) "http://example.com/"
?>
```

As you can see, the purpose of function `esc_url()` is not to make sure a URL is valid (for instance, `http://onmouseover=alert('XSS')` does not look like one) but to sanitize it drastically so that it is harmless when used.

With a second array parameter, this function is also great at limiting the protocols you want to authorize:

```php
<?php

$allowed = array( 'http', 'https', 'ftp' );

$url1 = 'https://example.com';
var_dump( esc_url( $url1, $allowed ) );
// string(19) "https://example.com"

$url2 = 'irc://example.com';
var_dump( esc_url( $url2, $allowed ) );
// string(0) ""

$url3 = 'xyz123://example.com';
var_dump( esc_url( $url3, $allowed ) );
// string(0) ""
?>
```

URLs in a Database

Function `esc_url()` converts ampersands and single quotes into HTML entities to make sure displaying the URL will not break any output. To sanitize a URL for database usage, prefer `esc_url_raw()`, which sanitizes without entity translation:

```php
<?php

$url = "http://ex[a]mple.com/?q=1&s=2'";

var_dump( esc_url( $url ) );
// string(38) "http://example.com/?q=1&#038;s=2&#039;"

var_dump( esc_url_raw( $url ) );
// string(28) "http://example.com/?q=1&s=2'"
?>
```

URLs in Redirects

You may have to redirect users to a page where the location depends on a user generated value, such as `"http://example.com/profile.php?user=$user"`. The wrong way to do it in a WordPress environment would be to simply use header redirection:

```php
<?php
header( "Location: http://example.com/profile.php?user=$user" );
?>
```

Omitting to sanitize variable `$user` could allow unwanted redirection on some server setups (depending on the version of PHP installed), with values such as `"Joe\nLocation: http://evilsite/"`.

The correct way to handle redirections within WordPress is to use its function `wp_redirect()`, which first sanitizes the redirection location:

```php
<?php
wp_redirect( "http://example.com/profile.php?user=$user" );
?>
```

JavaScript

Inline JavaScript (such as `onclick="doSomething();"` for example) is another type of HTML node attribute that gets particular treatment and its own sanitization function: `esc_js()`.

You can use this function to ensure that JavaScript snippets using dynamic variables from PHP will not break, as in the following example:

```php
<?php
$user = 'Joe';
?>

<script type="text/javascript">
var user = '<?php echo esc_js( $user ); ?>';

function confirm_delete() {
    return confirm('Really delete user '+user+'?');
}
</script>

<a href="<?php echo esc_url( "delete.php?user=$user" ); ?>"
   onclick="javascript:return( confirm_delete() )"
   title="Delete">Delete user <?php echo esc_html( $user ) ?></a>
```

Notice how this neat example uses different `esc_` functions to sanitize the various parts of the "delete" link.

Server or Environment Variables

The superglobal array `$_SERVER`, as its name may not imply, contains information received by the server from the client, that is, a user's browser. As such, consider its values unsafe. Depending on what server variable you need, be sure to always sanitize it with the appropriate functions.

For instance, if you want to display on a page the referring URL that presumably sent a visitor to your site, don't use the following:

```php
<?php if( isset( $_SERVER['HTTP_REFERER'] ) ) { ?>
Welcome visitor from <?php echo $_SERVER['HTTP_REFERER']; ?> !
<?php } ?>
```

Because the referrer URL is extremely easy to spoof and may contain anything a malicious user can imagine, let `esc_url()` handle it for you:

```php
<?php if( isset( $_SERVER['HTTP_REFERER'] ) ) { ?>
Welcome visitor from <?php echo esc_url( $_SERVER['HTTP_REFERER'] ); ?> !
<?php } ?>
```

In the same way, don't trust the user-agent signature stored in `$_SERVER['HTTP_USER_AGENT']`. If you want to display this data, you should treat it as unsafe HTML and sanitize it with `wp_kses()` first.

Other often-used server variables are `$_SERVER['REQUEST_URI']` or `$_SERVER['PHP_SELF']`, containing the location of the currently loaded page or executed script. When not sanitized, these server variables are easily exploitable. For example, craft the following form that will point to itself in its action parameter:

```php
<form action="<?php echo $_SERVER['PHP_SELF']; ?>" method="post" >
<input type="text" name="fullname" />
<input type="submit" value="Save" />
</form>
```

Save this form as self_form.php, and then point your browser to `http://localhost/self_form .php/"><script>alert(1337)</script>` and see what happens in Figure 6-8.

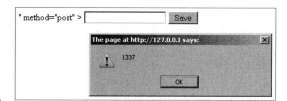

The best option is to always hardcode form action parameters, or to leave the form action empty (`<form action="" method="post">`) to send data back to the same place. If you need to make it dynamic and use a server variable, sanitize it with `esc_url()`.

FIGURE 6-8

Cookies

Just as you must not trust `$_GET` or `$_POST`, be suspicious toward the `$_COOKIE` array. Indeed, cookies are simple text files stored on the client's computer and as such easy to edit with tools such as Firebug for Firefox. Give cookies the same treatment as data from a submitted form: Validate and sanitize values.

In PHP, `$_REQUEST` usually contains `$_GET`, `$_POST`, and `$_COOKIE`. Note that upon start, WordPress removes the `$_COOKIE` array from `$_REQUEST`. Thus, if you need to check the value of a cookie, do not rely on `$_REQUEST` in a WordPress environment, but check `$_COOKIE` directly.

Arrays of Data

You can easily validate or sanitize an array of similar data using PHP's function `array_map()`.

Imagine for instance a form where a user has to enter several positive integers (age, number of children, and household income). To sanitize this information, you need `absint()`. You can process each data one by one, or use this more compact and efficient code:

```php
<?php

// sanitize the whole $_POST array
$_POST = array_map( 'absint', $_POST );

// extract only expected values
$clean = array();
$clean['age'] = $_POST['age'];
$clean['numchild'] = $_POST['numchild'];
$clean['income'] = $_POST['income'];
?>
```

This technique is particularly useful when you don't know how many values you need to sanitize. Picture a form textarea field in which you would ask users to enter a list of URLs, such as their favorite sites, one per line.

To sanitize such a list, you can split it into individual URLs and pass the resulting array to `esc_url()` all at once:

```php
<?php

$clean_urls = array();

// Split the textarea value into an array of URLs
$urls = split( "\n", $_POST['urls'] );

// Sanitize the whole array
$clean_urls = array_map( 'esc_url', $urls );
?>
```

Data from a Defined Set

Even when your form seems to lock down the number of possible values of a given field, such as a radio button being only Yes or No, always validate the submitted value. Indeed, it's trivial to post arbitrary data to any form, as the following example demonstrates.

First, create a script showing a simple form with radio buttons, check boxes, and a drop-down, similar to Figure 6-9. To mimic storing information, the script can also save any submitted information to a local text file.

FIGURE 6-9

Available for download on Wrox.com

```php
<?php

if( $_POST ) {
    $post = print_r( $_POST, true );
    error_log( $post, 3, dirname( __FILE__ ).'/post.log' );
}

?>

<form action="" method="post">

    Gender:
    <input type="radio" name="gender" value="male" />male
    <input type="radio" name="gender" value="female" />female

    Food dislikes:
    <input type="checkbox" name="food[]" value="spinach"/>spinach
    <input type="checkbox" name="food[]" value="anchovy"/>anchovy
    <input type="checkbox" name="food[]" value="liver"/>liver

    Country of residence:
    <select name="country">
        <option value="usa">USA</option>
        <option value="canada">Canada</option>
        <option value="uk">United Kingdom</option>
        <option value="other">Other</option>
    </select>

    <input type="submit" />

</form>
```

Code snippet locked_form.php

At the beginning of the script, if array $_POST is defined, its content is sent to a file named 'log.txt' in the same directory. You can learn more about error and message logging in Chapter 16, which is about debugging and code optimization.

This form looks pretty much locked down: Every field value belongs to a limited set, and at first you would probably confidently think that the submitted data will always be along the lines of the following array as read in log.txt:

```
Array
(
    [gender] => male
    [food] => Array
        (
            [0] => anchovy
            [1] => liver
        )
    [country] => usa
)
```

Just because the input fields seem to enforce values does not mean you cannot post anything to the form. You can now take the role of a malicious user and try to abuse this seemingly locked-down form with a script that posts random data to it:

```html
<form action="locked_form.php" method="post">
    <input name="gender" value="hello" />
    <input name="food[]" value="<script>alert('hello');</script>" />
    <input name="country" value="bleh" />
    <input name="random" value="1337" />
    <input type="submit" />
</form>
```

Code snippet locked_form_abuse.php

Notice how values passed to the script referenced in the action attribute contain totally random values that could not be generated by the legitimate form.

All it takes is a plain HTML file, hosted anywhere including a desktop computer with no web server, to submit any information to a script. Never take for granted that all users will always post only what you expect.

Back to the first form, locked_form.php: You can now make it secure and sanitize submitted values before storing them. Because you know the different values every field can take, you can code efficient and straightforward filters, using a white list principle. The storing code block will now be the following:

```php
<?php

if( $_POST ) {

    $clean = array();

    // Gender: 2 possible values, default to 'male'
    $clean['gender'] = ( $_POST['gender'] == 'female' ? 'female' : 'male' );

    // Food: arbitrary number of possible values, no default
    $foods = array( 'spinach', 'anchovy', 'liver' );
    if( in_array( $_POST['food'], $foods ) )
        $clean['food'] = $_POST['food'];

    // Country: arbitrary number of possible values, default to 'other'
    switch( $_POST['country'] ) {
        case 'canada':
        case 'uk':
        case 'usa':
            $clean['country'] = $_POST['country'];
            break;
```

```
            default:
                $clean['country'] = 'other';
        }

        $post = print_r( $clean, true );
        error_log( $post, 3, dirname( __FILE__ ).'/post.log' );

    }

?>
```

Notice how different test syntaxes are involved. The first comparison and sanitization, for gender, uses PHP's ternary operator. This compact line means, Is $_POST['gender'] female? Then $clean['gender'] equals female, otherwise it will equal male.

Database Queries

Database queries are obviously crucial strings regarding security. Consider for instance a web application in which the following query would authenticate users after they submit their login and password:

```
<?php
$sql = "SELECT * FROM users
        WHERE `user_login` = '$login' AND `user_pass`= '$password'";
?>
```

Because that SQL statement is not escaped and not sanitized, a malicious user could log in with the following credentials:

```
<?php
$login = 'anything';
$password = "123456' OR 1='1";
?>
```

Indeed, setting these variables, the SQL statement becomes a simple 1=1 condition, which is obviously always true:

```
SELECT * FROM users
WHERE `user_login` = 'adminzzz'
AND `user_pass`= '123456'
OR 1='1'
```

This would be a successful SQL injection attack: A user manipulates the statement performed on the database, as humorously depicted in Figure 6-10, a strip by Randall Munroe, titled "Exploits of a Mom" and reproduced here with permission (original URL: http://xkcd.com/327/).

FIGURE 6-10

Opportunely, WordPress comes with functions to help you sanitize your queries properly.

Function `esc_sql()` escapes content for inclusion into the database, which means it adds backslashes before characters that need to be quoted in queries (quotes and backslashes). The particularity of `esc_sql()` is that it can process indifferently a query string or an array of query strings.

```php
<?php

$login = 'back\slash';
$sql = 'SELECT * FROM `users` WHERE `login` = "'. esc_sql( $login ) .'"';
var_dump( $sql );
// string(55) "SELECT * FROM `users` WHERE `login` = "back\\slash""
?>
```

Function `like_escape()` takes care of escaping text used in LIKE clauses, where special characters percent % and ampersand _ are used:

```php
<?php

$pattern = 'joe';

$like = like_escape( 'LIKE "%'.$pattern.'%"' );

$sql = 'SELECT * FROM `users` WHERE `username` '.$like;

var_dump( $sql );
// string(53) "SELECT * FROM `users` WHERE `username` LIKE "\%joe\%""
?>
```

Function `sanitize_sql_orderby()` sanitizes ORDER BY clauses before they are included into an SQL string:

```php
<?php

$order_by   = 'last_name';
$order_sort = 'DESC';
```

```
$order = sanitize_sql_orderby( "$order_by $order_sort" );

$sql = 'SELECT * FROM `users` ORDER BY '. $order;

var_dump( $sql );
// string(45) "SELECT * FROM `users` ORDER BY last_name DESC"
?>
```

WordPress provides much more than simple escaping functions to sanitize queries: It has a complete set of functions designed to help you securely format your SQL statements.

FORMATTING SQL STATEMENTS

WordPress offers numerous functions you learn to use throughout this section to access information from the database.

The $wpdb Object

All database interactions within WordPress can be done through a class called wpdb, which (if you have some PHP background) you will see derives from the popular ezSQL class.

You should not run SQL queries using PHP's functions such as mysql_query() or mysql_fetch_array() for two reasons:

➤   WordPress' wpdb class provides enhanced security functions to protect your queries against SQL injection attacks.

➤   It is possible for a blog owner to replace the database engine from MySQL to something else (PostgreSQL, for instance) and MySQL functions could therefore be not be functional.

Methods from this class, which you learn to use in this section, should not be called directly: Instead, always use the $wpdb object WordPress instantiates on every page load.

 Don't forget to "globalize" $wpdb *(that is, adding line* global $wpdb;*) before using it within your functions.*

The $wpdb object can be used to access data from any table in the database used by WordPress: All the standard tables created upon installation or upgrade of your blog, but also any custom table created by a plugin, for example. In Chapter 7, "Plugin Settings," you learn when and how to create such a custom table.

Why wpdb Methods Are Superior

The $wpdb object contains several methods you can use to read, insert, update, or delete information from tables. The following examples would produce the same results, but notice how readable and foolproof it gets:

```php
<?php

// Example 1
mysql_connect( DB_HOST, DB_USER, DB_PASSWORD ) or
    die("Could not connect: " . mysql_error());
mysql_select_db( DB_NAME );
mysql_query( "UPDATE wp_posts SET post_title= '$newtitle' WHERE ID= $id" );

// Example 2
$newtitle = esc_sql( $newtitle );
$my_id = absint( $my_id );
$wpdb->query( "UPDATE $wpdb->posts SET post_title='$newtitle' WHERE ID=$id");

// Example 3
$new_values = array( 'post_title' => $newtitle );
$where = array( 'ID' => $my_id );
$wpdb->update( $wpdb->posts, $new_values, $where );
?>
```

What do these three examples tell you?

➤   Example 1, the old manual way, is cumbersome: Establish a connection to the database and run the query. The query itself is questionable: The table name is hardcoded even though a blog owner can change the table prefix; variables $newtitle and $id are not sanitized.

➤   Example 2 is good: Variables are sanitized with functions you've just learned to use, the table name complies with the local table prefix, and the query is run through the $wpdb object with the update() method.

➤   Example 3 is just as good but even easier: Define an array of values to update in column => value pairs, define an array of WHERE clause with the same structure, and let the method handle sanitization and query for you. You don't need to remember the exact SQL syntax; you don't need to make mental notes about data sanitization; and you completely rely on the WordPress API.

 Always use the $wpdb *methods: These functions can make your code easier to read, faster to maintain, and safer to execute.*

All-in-One Methods

As in the previous example #3, all-in-one methods are foolproof functions that exempt you from memorizing the boring parts (SQL syntax, sanitization functions) and manage everything for you. Count on `update()` and `insert()`.

$wpdb->update()

This method needs three parameters:

➤ A table name. (Remember to use `$wpdb->prefix`.)

➤ An array of data to update, in column => value pairs, unescaped.

➤ An array of WHERE clauses, in unescaped column => value pairs. If there are several clauses, they will be joined with an AND.

You can optionally pass two other parameters:

➤ An array of formats to be mapped to each of the data to update (or a string instead of an array if the same format is to be used for all the values). A format can be `'%d'` for decimal, `'%s'` for string, or `'%f'` for float. If omitted, all values will be treated as strings, unless otherwise specified in WordPress standard table definitions.

➤ An array of formats (or a string if one format applies) to be mapped to each of the values in the WHERE clause. If omitted, they get a string treatment.

To exemplify the usage of this function, imagine a table named `wp_custom` with a simple structure, as in Table 6-1:

TABLE 6-1: table wp_custom Structure

COL_ID	COL_STRING	COL_INTEGER
int(11) NOT NULL AUTO_INCREMENT	varchar(100) NOT NULL	int(11)

You can now update a row of table `wp_custom`, where the ID is 1, the value in the second column is a string, and the value in the third column is an integer:

```php
<?php

$values = array(
    'column1' => 'some string',
    'column2' => 43
);

$where = array(
```

```php
        'ID' => 1
);

$formats_values = array( '%s', '%d' );

$formats_where = array( '%d' );

$wpdb->update( $wpdb->custom, $values, $where, $formats_values, $formats_where );
?>
```

As you can see, this method grants a structured way to declare the SQL query, in particular the format of the data to sanitize. The method returns either `false` on error, or an integer with the number of rows affected by the update.

 Do not hardcode the WordPress database table prefix (usually `"wp_"`) into your plugins. Be sure to use the `$wpdb->prefix` variable instead. Not only will it use the proper prefix, but it will also include the proper blog ID in a multisite environment.

$wpdb->insert()

You can use this method to insert data in a similar operation, with three parameters:

➤ A table name

➤ An array of data to insert, in unescaped column => value pairs

➤ An optional array of formats to be mapped to these values, otherwise treated and sanitized as strings

Use this method to insert in a row in the same `$wpdb->custom` table, the first field being a string and the second one being an integer:

```php
<?php

$values = array(
    'column1' => 'new string',
    'column2' => 44
);

$formats_values = array( '%s', '%d' );

$wpdb->insert( $wpdb->custom, $values, $formats_values );
?>
```

Similarly to the `update()` method, this function also returns false on error or an integer for the number of rows inserted.

Common Methods

Not all the queries you'll run will be simple UPDATE or INSERT, so the wpdb class provides numerous other methods you'll peruse now, for instance to fetch a single value or an entire row, or perform custom complex statements.

SELECT a Variable

The get_var() method returns a single variable from WordPress' database (or NULL if no value is found).

For instance, to fetch the number of posts you have published on your blog, you can use the following query:

```php
<?php

$sql = "SELECT COUNT(ID) FROM {$wpdb->posts}
        WHERE post_status = 'publish' AND post_type = 'post'";

$num_of_posts = $wpdb->get_var( $sql );
?>
```

SELECT a Row

To fetch an entire row (or parts of a row), use method get_row(), which can return results as an object, an associative array, or a numerically indexed array. The syntax of this method follows:

```php
<?php
$wpdb->get_row( $sql, $output_type, $row_offset );
?>
```

This methods requires the following parameters:

➤ $sql — The SQL query

➤ $output_type — Optionally, one of the three predefined constants OBJECT (return result as an object), ARRAY_A (return as an associative array), or ARRAY_N (numerically indexed array). If omitted, the default is OBJECT.

➤ $row_offset — Optionally, the desired row, default value being 0.

For example, fetch from the users table the email and URL of user 'admin' and compare different output types. The SQL statement for such a query follows:

```php
<?php
$sql = "SELECT `user_email`, `user_url`
        FROM $wpdb->users
        WHERE user_login = 'admin'";

$object  = $wpdb->get_row( $sql, OBJECT );
$array_a = $wpdb->get_row( $sql, ARRAY_A );
$array_n = $wpdb->get_row( $sql, ARRAY_N );
?>
```

Examine now with `var_dump()` the nature of each result, depending on the output type selected:

```php
<?php

var_dump( $object );
/*
object(stdClass)#824 (2) {
  ["user_email"] => string(17) "ozh@ozh.org"
  ["user_url"] => string(21) "http://ozh.org/"
}
*/

var_dump( $array_a );
/*
array(2) {
  ["user_email"] => string(17) "ozh@ozh.org"
  ["user_url"] => string(21) "http://ozh.org/"
}
*/

var_dump( $array_n );
/*
array(2) {
  [0] => string(17) "ozh@ozh.org"
  [1] => string(21) "http://ozh.org/"
}
*/
?>
```

The nature of the result can affect how you now access individual records. For instance, to get the email address of the selected user, you can use one of the three following syntax constructions:

```php
<?php
$email = $object->user_email;

$email = $array_a['user_email'];

$email = $array_n[0];
?>
```

Notice how the first two syntaxes refer to `'user_email'`, which is the name of the column in the database.

 When fetching values from a database, prefer results returned as an object or an associative array. These two output formats can retain the database column names for better clarity.

SELECT a Column

This method can select an entire column, or part of a column, and return a dimensional array. It needs a query as first parameter and an optional column offset as second parameter, used if more than one column is returned. (The default value is zero.)

Imagine you want to send an email to all registered users of your WordPress setup, telling them the site will go temporarily offline for maintenance.

First, query the `$wpdb->users` table and get column `'user_email'`:

```php
<?php

$sql = "SELECT `user_email` FROM $wpdb->users";

$emails = $wpdb->get_col( $sql );
?>
```

Now, send the short email notice to each of these registered users:

```php
<?php

$subject = 'Blog maintenance';
$message = 'Dear user, the blog will be offline for 15 minutes.';

foreach( $emails as $email ) {
    wp_mail( $email, $subject, $message );
}
?>
```

SELECT Generic Results

If you need to fetch generic multiple row results, you can use method `get_results()`. This function needs a SQL statement parameter of course, and like `get_row()` an optional output format between `OBJECT`, `ARRAY_N` or `ARRAY_A` (as discussed earlier in the "Select a Row" section).

As an example of a more complex query, use this method to get the number of posts you have published each year on your blog:

```php
<?php

$sql = "SELECT YEAR(post_date) AS `year`, count(ID) as posts
        FROM $wpdb->posts
        WHERE post_type = 'post' AND post_status = 'publish'
        GROUP BY YEAR(post_date)
        ORDER BY post_date DESC";

$results = $wpdb->get_results( $sql, ARRAY_A );
?>
```

If you use print_r($results), the resulting associative array will be something like the following:

```
Array (
    [0] => Array (
            [year] => 2010
            [posts] => 13
        )
    [1] => Array (
            [year] => 2009
            [posts] => 37
        )
    [2] => Array (
            [year] => 2008
            [posts] => 9
        )
)
```

To display a human readable summary of your yearly activity, you can loop over each subarray of $results, like the following:

```php
<?php

foreach( $results as $sum ) {
    $year  = $sum['year'];
    $count = $sum['posts'];
    echo "<p>Posts published in $year: $count</p>";
}
?>
```

 *A good habit is to SELECT only what you need and avoid the lazy "SELECT * FROM". Trimming your selection only to fields you need helps to reduce the database's load and memory usage.*

This is especially crucial in shared host environments, where hundreds of other processes may be polling data from or writing to the database at the same time. Learning how to minimize hits against the database will ensure that your plugin will not be the one blamed for abuse of resources.

Generic Queries

Of course, common methods of the $wpdb object are not limited to SELECT statements. Any query can be processed by method query(), which returns an integer corresponding to the number of rows affected or selected, or false if an error occurred.

For illustration, you can delete all comments from your blog if they point to an unwanted website:

```php
<?php

$sql = "DELETE from wp_comments
        WHERE comment_author_url
        LIKE '%evil.example.com%'";

$deleted = $wpdb->query( $sql );
?>
```

Now the variable `$deleted` is either false if there were an error (for instance if the table prefix is not `'wp_'` and thus table `'wp_comments'` does not exist) or an integer of the number of records deleted.

You can also use the `query()` method in place of any other method when you need more flexibility in the syntax and parameters. In this practical example, you can disable comments on all posts older than 90 days:

```php
<?php

$sql = "UPDATE $wpdb->posts
        SET comment_status = 'closed'
        WHERE post_date < DATE_SUB( NOW(), INTERVAL 90 DAY )
        AND post_status = 'publish'";

$wpdb->query( $sql );
?>
```

As a last example, imagine a friend of yours who is also a frequent commentator on your site just moved his personal blog to another URL. You can hopefully update all comment author URLs with a single query:

```php
<?php

$sql = "UPDATE $wpdb->comments
        SET comment_author_url =
        REPLACE( comment_author_url, 'http://oldsite/', 'http://newsite/' )";

$wpdb->query( $sql );
?>
```

Protecting Queries Against SQL Injections

You may have noticed that the previous queries are not sanitized. This was indeed not needed because they are completely hardcoded and do not contain any dynamic and potentially unsanitary or malformed data.

If you need to create a dynamic custom query where you cannot hardcode every component, you already know that you need to sanitize and escape it with function `esc_sql()` before your run it. This preparation step can be handily done with the `prepare()` method, which enables the same kind of format strict validation as `insert()` or `update()`.

The process becomes twofold:

1. Prepare the SQL query with `prepare()`, which returns a sanitized and escaped statement.

2. Run the query with this statement, using any of the previously mentioned common methods.

For instance, how can you fetch the titles of all posts written by an author with a given user ID during a particular month? The SQL query for such a request is similar to the following:

```
SELECT `post_title`
    FROM $wpdb->posts
    WHERE `post_author` = 1
    AND post_status = 'publish'
    AND post_type = 'post'
    AND DATE_FORMAT( `post_date`, '%Y-%m' ) = '2010-11'
```

From this example, define a generic SQL query with format placeholders:

```php
<?php
$sql = "SELECT `post_title`
        FROM $wpdb->posts
        WHERE `post_author` = %d
        AND post_status = 'publish'
        AND post_type = 'post'
        AND DATE_FORMAT( `post_date`, '%%Y-%%m') = %s ";

?>
```

Think of it as a template query, where `%d` will be an integer and `%s` a string. Notice how percent signs `%` are double-escaped as `%%` and how you don't need quotes around these placeholders.

Now you can "prepare" the query and then process it. Get all posts titles from author ID 1 from the month of November 2010:

```php
<?php

$id = 1;
$month = '2010-11'

$safe_sql = $wpdb->prepare( $sql, $id, $month );

$posts = $wpdb->get_results( $safe_sql );
?>
```

The `prepare()` method takes an arbitrary number of parameters: first the SQL template with its placeholders and then as many values as there are placeholders, either one by one or grouped in an array. What is important here is to pass these values in the same order as their placeholders in the query, much like you would use PHP's function `printf()`.

If you `var_dump()` the resulting `$posts` variable, you get something like the following:

```
array(3) {
  [0]=>
  object(stdClass)#251 (1) {
```

```
    ["post_title"] => string(30) "Halloween over, Christmas soon"
  }
  [1]=>
  object(stdClass)#250 (1) {
    ["post_title"] => string(25) "Happy Birthday Mike Muir"
  }
  [2]=>
  object(stdClass)#249 (1) {
    ["post_title"] => string(27) "Ditched My Mac, Bought a PC"
  }
```

Miscellaneous wpdb Methods and Properties

The $wpdb object contains a few methods and properties you might use, particularly for debugging purposes.

Toggling Error Display

You can turn error echoing on and off:

```php
<?php

// On:
$wpdb->show_errors();

// Off:
$wpdb->hide_errors();
?>
```

You can also echo the error (if any occurred) generated by the most recent query using either the print_error() method or the last_error property:

```php
<?php
echo $wpdb->last_error;

$wpdb->print_error();
?>
```

Refer to Chapter 16, which is about debugging, for more tips.

Tracking the Number of Queries

The wpdb class variable num_queries keeps record of the number of queries issued. You can also more simply use function get_num_queries(). Again, you learn more about this in Chapter 16, which is about debugging and optimizing.

Other Class Variables

Table 6-2 shows a list of other noteworthy class variables and what they contain:

TABLE 6-2: wpdb Class Variables

VARIABLE	CONTENT
`$wpdb->insert_id`	The ID generated for an `AUTO_INCREMENT` column by the most recent `INSERT` query
`$wpdb->num_rows`	The number of rows returned by the last query
`$wpdb->rows_affected`	Count of affected rows by previous query

SECURITY GOOD HABITS

Security is a subtle cocktail involving design, reflection, and general common sense. Everything you have read in this chapter can aid you and provide the right tools, but you also need to develop a few good habits.

➤ Always try to break your plugins: Think about illegitimate, evil, and malicious ways to exploit your code, but also consider just plain stupid use. Some users don't always read the documentation, just as some plugin authors may be poor at writing clear documentation. Don't assume users will do what you expect them to do.

➤ Make security a part of your reflection from the start of the project: If you do not design your plugin with security in mind, you are doomed to be sooner or later addressing security issues or vulnerabilities.

➤ WordPress developers take security seriously. When vulnerability is reported and confirmed, a new version of WordPress with a fix is made available, generally under a few hours. But these developers do not maintain older versions: As a result, make sure you code with the latest, therefore most secure, existing version. Coding plugins using deprecated functions or API could expose your work to security holes.

➤ WordPress developers take security seriously because they know WordPress is not perfect: If you happen to discover a new security hole while playing with WordPress code, make sure you play your role in WordPress's improvement. Do so in a "white hat" (ethical) approach: Don't make your findings public; instead alert security@wordpress.org.

➤ Some of the functions described in this chapter are relatively recent: If you started coding plugins several years ago and did not stay up to par with WordPress code improvements, now is a good time to get back to your plugins and improve the code.

➤ Document your code. Your future self will thank you when working back on a plugin coded several months ago; this can make maintenance much easier, and you can quickly spot security weaknesses.

➤ Be open to your user community and responsive: You are bound to be addressing security issues one day, and receiving an alarming security report about one product is not something a coder should be ashamed of. But pride yourself in fixing your code quickly, and publicly disclose that you're releasing a security upgrade: This can encourage users to upgrade.

➤ Above all, be distrustful and consider all dynamic data to be unclean.

 The golden rule in security, as per Mark Jaquith's words (lead developer of WordPress and security expert) can be summed up as this: Anything that isn't hardcoded is suspect.

Although there is no official WordPress plugin security audit team that can help you improve or validate your plugin, this does not mean you're on your own. Publicly releasing a plugin and getting involved in the WordPress community will connect you not only with users but also with seasoned developers and WordPress contributors. It's a common practice in the WordPress community to suggest patches to other plugin authors. You will learn more about getting involved in Chapter 17.

SUMMARY

One thing you should retain from this chapter is that security is not difficult to implement in WordPress plugins, thanks to convenient functions designed to address the various aspects of security.

The most important rule to remember is to always check both entrance and exit "gateways": places where users can send data to your server (URLs, form fields, cookies, and so on) and places where you send data back to the user (data outputs on the browser screen). Any interaction between a user and a web site is both dangerous by nature and easy to secure.

Plugin Settings

WHAT'S IN THIS CHAPTER?

➤   Using a WordPress database to save and get data

➤   Leveraging the API functions to write compact and future proof code

➤   Saving global options, or per-user options

➤   Saving special option types: expiring options

➤   Creating a custom database table, when and how to do it

WordPress enables easy access to the database to store and retrieve data, such as options end users can modify and save in settings pages or internal information plugins you need to know. You learn how to save and fetch this data using internal WordPress functions and API.

THE OPTIONS API

The Options API is a set of functions that enable easy access to the database where WordPress, plugins, and themes save and fetch needed information.

Options are stored in a database table named, by default, *wp_options* and can be text, integers, arrays, or objects. For example, WordPress keeps in this table the title of your blog, the list of active plugins, the news articles displayed on the Dashboard, or the time when to check if a new version is available.

You'll now learn how to use the functions to access, update, and save options: `add_option()`, `update_option()`, `get_option()`, and `delete_option()`.

Saving Options

You start by saving your first plugin option, which will be named `boj_myplugin_color` and have a value of red. The function call to do so is the following:

```php
<?php
add_option( 'boj_myplugin_color', 'red' );
?>
```

The first parameter is your option name. It is crucial that you make it unique and self-explanatory.

➤ **Unique:** It shall never conflict with internal existing or future WordPress options, nor with settings that might be created by another plugin.

➤ **Self-explanatory:** Name it so that it's obvious it's a plugin setting and not something created by WP.

 Using the same prefix, for example, `boj_myplugin`, *for function names, options, and variables is highly recommended for code consistency and preventing conflict with other plugins. The golden rule "Prefix Everything," first introduced in Chapter 2, applies here.*

The second parameter is the option value that can be practically anything a variable can hold: string, integer, float number, Boolean, object, or array.

Updating an option value is a similar function call:

```php
<?php
update_option( 'boj_myplugin_color', 'blue' );
?>
```

The difference between `add_option()` and `update_option()` is that the first function does nothing if the option name already exists, whereas `update_option()` checks if the option already exists before updating its value and creates it if needed.

Saving an Array of Options

Every option saved adds a new record in WordPress' option table. You can simply store several options at once, in one array: This avoids cluttering the database and updates the values in one single MySQL query for greater efficiency and speed.

```php
<?php
$options = array(
    'color'    => 'red',
    'fontsize' => '120%',
```

```php
    'border'   => '2px solid red'
);
update_option( 'boj_myplugin_options', $options );
?>
```

Saving your plugin options in one array rather than individual records can have a huge impact on WordPress' loading time, especially if you save or update many options. Most of the time, PHP code executes fast, but SQL queries usually hinder performance, so save them whenever possible.

Retrieving Options

To fetch an option value from the database, use the function `get_option()`:

```php
<?php
$myplugin_color = get_option( 'boj_myplugin_color' );
?>
```

The first thing to know about `get_option()` is that if the option does not exist, it will return `false`. The second thing is that if you store Booleans, you might get integers in return.

As an illustration of this behavior, consider the following code block that creates a couple of new options with various variable types:

```php
<?php
update_option( 'test_bool_true',  true );
update_option( 'test_bool_false', false );
?>
```

You can now retrieve these options, along with another one that does not exist, and see what variable types are returned, shown as an inline comment below each `get_option()` call:

```php
<?php
var_dump( get_option( 'nonexistent_option' ) );
// bool(false)

var_dump( get_option( 'test_bool_true' ) );
// string(1) "1"

var_dump( get_option( 'test_bool_false' ) );
// bool(false)
?>
```

To avoid an error when checking option values, you should store `true` and `false` as `1` and `0`. This means also that you need to strictly compare the return of `get_option()` with Boolean `false` to check if the option exists:

```php
<?php
if( get_option( 'boj_myplugin_someoption' ) === false ) {
    // option has not been defined yet
    // ...
```

```php
    } else {
        // option exists
        // ...
    }
    ?>
```

You can also specify what value you want to be returned if the option is not found in the database, with a second option parameter to get_option(), like in the following example:

```php
    <?php
    $option = get_option( 'boj_myplugin_option', 'option not found' );
    ?>
```

Loading an Array of Options

You have seen that saving multiple options in a single array is best practice. A complete example of saving and then getting values from one array would be as follows:

```php
    <?php
    // To store all of them in a single function call:
    $myplugin_options = array(
        'color'    => 'red',
        'fontsize' => '120%',
        'border'   => '2px solid red'
    );
    update_option( 'boj_myplugin_options', $myplugin_options ) ;

    // Now to fetch individual values from one single call:
    $options  = get_option( 'boj_myplugin_options' );
    $color    = $options[ 'color' ];
    $fontsize = $options[ 'fontsize' ];
    $border   = $options[ 'border' ];
    ?>
```

Saving and retrieving options enclosed in an array has another advantage: Variable Boolean types within the array are preserved. Consider the following example:

```php
    <?php
    add_option( 'test_bool', array(
        'booltrue'  => true,
        'boolfalse' => false
        )
    );
    ?>
```

Now get the option value from the database with var_dump(get_option('test_bool')). See how Boolean types are retained, contrary to the previous example:

```php
    // output result of var_dump(get_option('test_bool'))
    array(2) {
      ["booltrue"] => bool(true)
      ["boolfalse"]=> bool(false)
    }
```

Deleting Options

Deleting an option needs a self-explanatory function call:

```php
<?php
delete_option( 'boj_myplugin_options' );
?>
```

This function call returns `false` if the option to delete cannot be found and returns `true` otherwise. You will mostly delete options when writing uninstall functions or files (see Chapter 2).

The Autoload Parameter

By default, all the options stored in the database are fetched by a single SQL query when WordPress initializes and then caches. This applies to internal WordPress core settings and options created and stored by plugins.

This is efficient behavior: No matter how many `get_option()` calls you issue in your plugins, they won't generate extra SQL queries and slow down the whole site. Still, the potential drawback of this autoload technique is that rarely used options are always loaded in memory, even when not needed. For instance, there is no point in fetching backend options when a reader accesses a blog post.

To address this issue when saving an option for the first time, you can specify its autoload behavior, as in the following example:

```php
<?php
add_option( 'boj_myplugin_option', $value, '', $autoload );
?>
```

Note the empty third parameter: This is a parameter that was deprecated several WordPress versions ago and is not needed any more. Any value passed to it will do; just be sure not to omit it.

The fourth parameter is what matters here. If `$autoload` is anything but `'no'` (or simply not specified), option `boj_myplugin_option` will be read when WordPress starts, and subsequent `get_option()` function calls will not issue any supplemental SQL query. Setting `$autoload` to `'no'` can invert this: This option will not be fetched during startup of WordPress, saving memory and execution time, but it will trigger an extra SQL query the first time your code fetches its value.

 If you want to specify the autoload parameter, you need to use `add_option()` instead of `update_option()` when creating an option the first time. If you don't need this parameter, always using `update_option()` to both create and update will make your code more simple and consistent.

Of course, specifying the autoload parameter upon creation of an option does not change the way you fetch, update, or delete its value.

Segregating Plugin Options

A function to initiate your plugin options, run on plugin activation as covered in Chapter 2, could then look like the following:

```php
<?php
function boj_myplugin_create_options() {
    // front-end options: autoloaded
    add_option( 'boj_myplugin_options', array(
        'color'    => 'red',
        'fontsize' => '120%',
        'border'   => '2px solid red'
    );

    // back-end options: loaded only if explicitly needed
    add_option( 'boj_myplugin_admin_options', array(
        'version'    => '1.0',
        'donate_url' => 'http://x.y/z/',
        'advanced_options' => '1'
    ), '', 'no' );
}
?>
```

Again, don't forget the empty third parameter before the autoload value. This might seem a bit convoluted, and actually it is for so few options set. This professional technique makes sense if your plugin features dozens of options, or options containing long text strings.

> *As a rule of thumb, if your options are needed by the public part of the blog, save them with autoload. If they are only needed in the admin area, save them without autoload.*

Toggling the Autoload Parameter

The autoload parameter is set when an option is created with `add_option()` and is not supposed to change afterward. With this said, if you believe that it would improve your plugin's efficiency to modify the autoload behavior, it is possible and easy: simply delete and then re-create the option with an explicit autoload parameter:

```php
<?php
function boj_myplugin_recreate_options() {
    // get old value
    $old = get_option( 'boj_myplugin_admin_options' );

    // delete then recreate without autoload
    delete_option( 'boj_myplugin_admin_options' );
    add_option( 'boj_myplugin_admin_options', $old, '', 'no' );
}
?>
```

THE SETTINGS API

Options can be internally created and updated by your plugin (for instance, storing the timestamp of the next iteration of a procedure). But they are also frequently used to store settings the end user will modify through your plugin administration page.

When creating or updating user-defined options for a plugin, relying on the Settings API can make your code both simpler and more efficient.

Benefits of the Settings API

Dealing with user inputs introduces new constraints in the option process: You need to design a user interface, monitor form submissions, handle security checks, and validate user inputs. To easily manage these common tasks, WordPress wraps the option functions into a comprehensive Settings API.

The Settings API enables you to handle the simple tasks:

➤ Tell WordPress that you are going to use some new options and how you want them displayed.

➤ Specify a function that will sanitize user inputs.

. . . and let WordPress transparently manage for you the cumbersome and repetitive parts:

➤ Draw most of the option page itself.

➤ Monitor form submission and handle $_POST data.

➤ Create and update options if needed.

➤ Wield all the required security measures and hidden fields for nonces, as covered in Chapter 6.

Now dissect the Settings API: you learn to use it through a step-by-step example.

Settings API Functions

The Settings API functions consist of three steps:

1. First tell WordPress the new settings you want it to manage for you. Doing so adds your settings into a list of authorized options (also known as whitelisting).

2. Next define the settings (text areas, input boxes, and any HTML form element) and how they will be visually grouped together in sections.

3. Tell WordPress to display your settings in an actual form.

But first, you create a setting management page for your plugin.

Creating the Plugin Administration Page

The plugin page will be located at `/wp-admin/options-general.php?page=boj_myplugin`:

```php
<?php
// Add the admin options page
add_action('admin_menu', 'boj_myplugin_add_page');
function boj_myplugin_add_page() {
    add_options_page( 'My Plugin', 'My Plugin', 'manage_options',
        'boj_myplugin', 'boj_myplugin_options_page' );
}

// Draw the options page
function boj_myplugin_options_page() {
    ?>
    <div class="wrap">
    <?php screen_icon(); ?>
    <h2>My plugin</h2>
    <form action="options.php" method="post">
    </form></div>
    <?php
}
?>
```

This page is empty for now (see Figure 7-1). You will add form inputs later.

FIGURE 7-1

Creating pages for plugins is covered in detail in Chapter 4, "Integrating in WordPress," so refer to it for more explanation about this code.

Registering New Settings

The function you need here is `register_setting()` and three parameters, used as follows:

```php
<?php
register_setting(
    'boj_myplugin_options',
    'boj_myplugin_options',
    'boj_myplugin_validate_options'
);
?>
```

The first parameter is the setting group name, and the second parameter is the option name as you would use it in a `get_option()` call. The group name can be anything actually, but it's just simpler to name it the same as the option that will get stored in the database.

The third parameter is an optional function callback: It's a string that references a function, here named `boj_myplugin_validate_options()`, that will be passed all the settings saved in your form. You define this function later.

Defining Sections and Settings

Now define what the settings will be more precisely by using the function `add_settings_field()` and how they will be visually grouped with the function `add_settings_section()`:

```php
<?php
add_settings_section(
    'boj_myplugin_main',
    'My Plugin Settings',
    'boj_myplugin_section_text',
    'boj_myplugin'
);

add_settings_field(
    'boj_myplugin_text_string',
    'Enter text here',
    'boj_myplugin_setting_input',
    'boj_myplugin',
    'boj_myplugin_main'
);
?>
```

The first function call, `add_settings_section()`, defines how the section on the page will show. The four required parameters it uses follow:

➤   An HTML ID tag for the section

➤   The section title text that will show within an `<H3>` tag

➤ The name of the callback function that will echo some explanations about that section

➤ The settings page on which to show the section (that is, the `?page=boj_myplugin` part of the page URL)

The second function call, `add_settings_field()`, describes how to add the form input. Its five required parameters follow:

➤ An HTML ID tag for the section

➤ The text printed next to the field

➤ The name of the callback function that will echo the form field

➤ The settings page on which to show the section

➤ The section of the settings page in which to show the field, as defined previously by the `add_settings_section()` function call

You now need to define two simple callback functions: One to display a few explanations about the section and one to output and fill the form field.

```php
<?php
// Explanations about this section
function boj_myplugin_section_text() {
    echo '<p>Enter your settings here.</p>';
}

// Display and fill the form field
function boj_myplugin_setting_input() {
    // get option 'text_string' value from the database
    $options = get_option( 'boj_myplugin_options' );
    $text_string = $options['text_string'];
    // echo the field
    echo "<input id='text_string' name='boj_myplugin_options[text_string]'
        type='text' value='{$options['text_string']}' />";
}
?>
```

This second function call fetches the option value `'text_string'` that is stored in an array.

When outputting the HTML input field, note its name. This is how you tell the browser to pass this value back into an array with the same name as the option you'll save, as defined earlier in the `register_setting()` function call. Any field that has not been previously registered and whitelisted will be ignored by WordPress.

Validating User Input

There is still one callback function to define: `boj_myplugin_validate_options()`, as mentioned at the beginning when registering the settings.

In this example, users are asked to enter text, so your validation function simply makes sure that the input contains only letters:

```php
<?php
function boj_myplugin_validate_options( $input ) {
    $valid = array();
    $valid['text_string'] = preg_replace(
        '/[^a-zA-Z]/',
        '',
        $input['text_string'] );
    return $valid;
}?>
```

To validate the user input as letters only, a simple pattern matching (also known as regular expression) that strips all other characters is used here.

This function is passed the `$_POST` data as a parameter. For enhanced security, start creating a new empty array named `$valid` and collect in this array only the values you are expecting. This way, if for some reason an unanticipated field is submitted in the form, your function not only validates the information you want but also blocks everything else. Refer to Chapter 6 for more tips and functions about data validation.

Rendering the Form

Now that you have defined these function calls, it's time to use them. At the beginning of this step-by-step example, you created an empty page: Go back to that and add the form fields and a Submit button:

```php
<?php
// Draw the options page
function boj_myplugin_options_page() {
    ?>

    <div class="wrap">
    <?php screen_icon(); ?>
    <h2>My plugin</h2>
    <form action="options.php" method="post">

    <?php
    settings_fields('boj_myplugin_options');
    do_settings_sections('boj_myplugin');
    ?>

    <input name="Submit" type="submit" value="Save Changes" />
    </form></div>

    <?php
}?>
```

The `settings_fields()` function call references the whitelisted option you have declared with `register_setting()`. It takes care of the hidden fields, security checks, and form redirection after it has been submitted.

The second function call, `do_settings_sections()`, outputs all the sections and form fields you have previously defined.

All Done!

Notice how little HTML you have laid down, and yet the plugin page is now complete and functional. This is a major reason this Settings API is rock solid: You focus on features and let WordPress create all the HTML with relevant tags and classes, handle the data submission, and escape strings before inserting them to the database.

> *Designing plugin pages using the Settings API is future-proof: Imagine that you are creating a plugin for a client on a particular version of WordPress. Later, when the administration interface of WordPress changes (different layout, colors, HTML classes), your plugin will still seamlessly integrate because you did not hardcode any HTML in it.*

Wrapping It Up: A Complete Plugin Management Page

Some of the function calls used here need to be hooked into WordPress actions such as `'admin_init'`. Now recapitulate all the steps covered bit by bit into a full-fledged plugin.

```php
<?php
/*
Plugin Name: Settings API example
Plugin URI: http://example.com/
Description: A complete and practical example of use of the Settings API
Author: WROX
Author URI: http://wrox.com
*/

// Add a menu for our option page
add_action('admin_menu', 'boj_myplugin_add_page');
function boj_myplugin_add_page() {
    add_options_page( 'My Plugin', 'My Plugin', 'manage_options',
        'boj_myplugin', 'boj_myplugin_option_page'
    );
}

// Draw the option page
function boj_myplugin_option_page() {
    ?>
    <div class="wrap">
    <?php screen_icon(); ?>
    <h2>My plugin</h2>
```

```php
        <form action="options.php" method="post">
        <?php settings_fields('boj_myplugin_options'); ?>
        <?php do_settings_sections('boj_myplugin'); ?>
        <input name="Submit" type="submit" value="Save Changes" />
        </form></div>
        <?php
}

// Register and define the settings
add_action('admin_init', 'boj_myplugin_admin_init');
function boj_myplugin_admin_init(){
    register_setting( 'boj_myplugin_options', 'boj_myplugin_options',
        'boj_myplugin_validate_options' );
    add_settings_section( 'boj_myplugin_main', 'My Plugin Settings',
        'boj_myplugin_section_text', 'boj_myplugin' );
    add_settings_field( 'boj_myplugin_text_string', 'Enter text here',
        'boj_myplugin_setting_input', 'boj_myplugin', 'boj_myplugin_main' );
}
// Draw the section header
function boj_myplugin_section_text() {
    echo '<p>Enter your settings here.</p>';
}

// Display and fill the form field
function boj_myplugin_setting_input() {
    // get option 'text_string' value from the database
    $options = get_option( 'boj_myplugin_options' );
    $text_string = $options['text_string'];
    // echo the field
    echo "<input id='text_string' name='boj_myplugin_options[text_string]'
        type='text' value='$text_string' />";
}

// Validate user input (we want text only)
function boj_myplugin_validate_options( $input ) {
    $valid = array();
    $valid['text_string'] = preg_replace(
        '/[^a-zA-Z]/',
        '',
        $input['text_string'] );
    return $valid;
}?>
```

Code snippet plugin1-standalone-page.php

Activate this plugin and head to `/wp-admin/options-general.php?page=boj_myplugin` . You see a similar interface to the one shown in Figure 7-2.

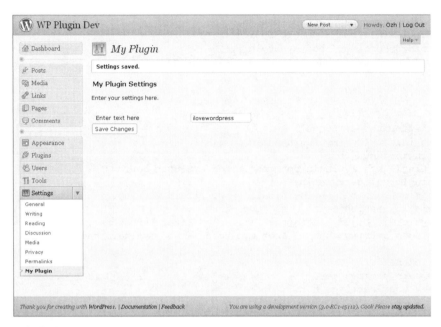

FIGURE 7-2

Improving Feedback on Validation Errors

The validation function you've previously defined could be slightly improved by letting the users know they have entered an unexpected value and that it has been modified so that they can pay attention to it and maybe amend their input.

The relatively unknown function `add_settings_error()` of the Settings API can handle this case. Here's how it is used:

```php
<?php
add_settings_error(
    'boj_myplugin_text_string',
    'boj_myplugin_texterror',
    'Incorrect value entered!',
    'error'
);
?>
```

This function call registers an error message that displays to the user. The first parameter is the title of the setting to which this error applies. The second parameter is an HTML ID tag. Then comes the error message itself, which WordPress encloses in appropriate `<div>` and `<p>` tags. The last parameter is the HTML class and can be either `'error'` or `'update'`.

You can improve the validating function with a user notice if applicable:

```php
<?php
function boj_myplugin_validate_options( $input ) {
    $valid['text_string'] = preg_replace(
```

```
                '/[^a-zA-Z]/',
                '',
                $input['text_string'] );

        if( $valid['text_string'] != $input['text_string'] ) {
            add_settings_error(
                'boj_myplugin_text_string',
                'boj_myplugin_texterror',
                'Incorrect value entered!',
                'error'
            );
        }

        return $valid;
    }
    ?>
```

The function now compares the validated
data with the original input and displays an
error message if they differ (see Figure 7-3).

Adding Fields to an
Existing Page

You have seen how to create a complete
settings page for a plugin and its associated

FIGURE 7-3

entry in the administration menus. Doing so makes sense if your plugin features a lot of settings and
its administration page shows a lot of content.

Sometimes though, it is not worth adding a new menu entry for just one or a few plugin options.
Here again the Settings API will prove to be useful, allowing plugin setting fields to easily be added
to the existing WordPress setting pages.

How It Works

Two internal functions, do_settings_sections() and do_settings_fields(), are triggered to
draw sections and fields that have been previously registered, like you did in the example plugin.

Each core setting page calls these two functions, so you can hook into them if you know their
slug name.

Adding a Section to an Existing Page

Your previous plugin was adding a whole new section and its input field on a standalone page: You
now modify it to insert this content into WordPress' Privacy Settings page.

```
<?php
function boj_myplugin_admin_init(){
    register_setting(
        'privacy',
        'boj_myplugin_options',
```

```
            'boj_myplugin_validate_options'
        );

        add_settings_section(
            'boj_myplugin_options',
            'My Plugin Settings',
            'boj_myplugin_section_text',
            'privacy'
        );

        add_settings_field(
            'boj_myplugin_text_string',
            'Enter text here',
            'boj_myplugin_setting_input',
            'privacy',
            'boj_myplugin_options'
        );
    }?>
```

This function now adds your custom section into the `'privacy'` section, which is located within the Privacy Settings page, as shown in Figure 7-4. Replace all `'privacy'` instances with `'media'`, and your section will be appended at the end of the Media Settings page.

You still need to whitelist this setting, with `register_setting()`. Omitting this step would make WordPress ignore the setting when submitting the form.

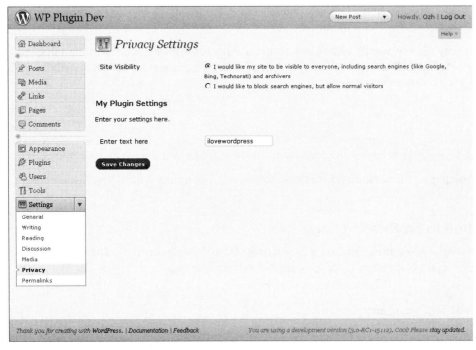

FIGURE 7-4

Adding Only Fields

Of course, it can even make sense to add just one field and no section header to an existing page. Now modify the function in the previous example:

Available for download on Wrox.com

```php
<?php
function boj_myplugin_admin_init(){
    register_setting(
        'privacy',
        'boj_myplugin_options',
        'boj_myplugin_validate_options'
    );

    add_settings_field(
        'boj_myplugin_text_string',
        'Enter text here',
        'boj_myplugin_setting_input',
        'privacy',
        'default'
    );
}?>
```

Code snippet plugin2-add-to-page.php

Your singular field will be added to the `'default'` field set of the `'privacy'` section, as seen in Figure 7-5.

WordPress' Sections and Setting Fields

To add a section to an existing page or a field to an existing section, all you need to know is the slug name of the page. Table 7-1 includes every section and field set names found in WordPress 3.0's Settings pages.

FIGURE 7-5

TABLE 7-1: List of Core Sections and Fields

WORDPRESS' SETTINGS PAGES	SECTION NAMES	FIELD SET NAMES
General Settings (options-general.php)	'general'	'default'
Writing Settings (options-writing.php)	'writing'	'default' 'remote_publishing' 'post_via_email'

continues

TABLE 7-1 *(continued)*

WORDPRESS' SETTINGS PAGES	SECTION NAMES	FIELD SET NAMES
Reading Settings (options-reading.php)	'reading'	'default'
Discussion Settings (options-discussion.php)	'discussion'	'default' 'avatars'
Media Settings (options-media.php)	'media'	'default' 'embeds' 'uploads'
Privacy Settings (options-privacy.php)	'privacy'	'default'
Permalink Settings (options-permalink.php)	'permalink'	'optional'

User Interface Concerns

Electing to add your plugin settings to a separate page or to a core WordPress page is often a matter of choosing the right user interface for the right end user.

When working on a site for a client, you may focus on delivering a key-in-hand CMS solution and not on explaining what is WordPress and what is a plugin extending its features. Adding your plugin settings to a core Settings page can enhance its integration into WordPress' backend because it won't appear different from other core settings. From the client's point of view, your plugin is a core element just as any other built-in feature.

On the contrary, if you intend to make your plugin available for download, you can target people who probably understand the concept of adding new features to a core set. These people will naturally search for a custom menu where they can manage your plugin. If you opt for adding fields to an existing page, be sure to explicitly tell users about it, for instance in the plugin documentation.

THE TRANSIENTS API

You sometimes need to store volatile values in the database. For instance, picture a plugin that would retrieve the name of the song currently on air from an online radio site. In essence, such data has a short life span because it usually changes every three or four minutes.

To be efficient and avoid polling the online radio too often, your plugin could then fetch the song title and keep it for at least three minutes before checking for a fresher value.

The Transients API offers a simple way to temporarily store cached data in the database. It is similar to the Options API, with the added attribute of an expiration time after which the option will be considered expired and deleted.

The Transients API uses three functions: `set_transient()`, `get_transient()`, and `delete_transient()`. In the following sections you learn how to use them.

Saving an Expiring Option

Imagine that your plugin has determined the current song on the online radio to be "I Heart WordPress" by the famous fictional band WROX Hackers. You are going to save this information, stating that it will be valid for 3 minutes:

```php
<?php
set_transient( 'boj_myplugin_song', 'I Heart WordPress', 180 );
?>
```

As you can see, the analogy with `add_option()` is obvious: first a transient name and then its value. The novelty here is a number of seconds as a third parameter, which indicates the duration of the transient validity.

Retrieving an Expiring Option

On every page request, your plugin would now get this transient value:

```php
<?php
$song = get_transient( 'boj_myplugin_song' );
?>
```

The behavior of function `get_transient()` is as follows:

➤ If the transient exists and is still valid, return its value.

➤ If the transient has expired or has never been set before, return Boolean `false`.

Deleting an Expiring Option

To manually delete a transient, use function `delete_transient()`:

```php
<?php
delete_transient( 'boj_myplugin_song' );
?>
```

This function returns `true` if successful, `false` otherwise, for the instance when the transient cannot be found in the database.

Using transients does not clutter the database because expired ones are automatically deleted when you attempt to get their value. Typically, you will not have to use this function, except during an uninstall procedure.

A Practical Example Using Transients

Now see what your plugin would look like.

```php
<?php

// Fetches from an online radio a song title currently on air
function boj_myplugin_fetch_song_title_from_radio() {
    // ... code to fetch data from the remote website
    return $title;
}

// Get song title from database, using a 3 minute transient, and return it
function boj_myplugin_get_song_title() {
    // Get transient value
    $title = get_transient( 'boj_myplugin_song' );

    // If the transient does not exists or has expired, refresh it
    if( false === $title ) {
        $title = boj_myplugin_fetch_song_title_from_radio();
        set_transient( 'boj_myplugin_song', $title, 180 );
    }

    return $title;
}?>
```

Code snippet plugin3-transients.php

The `boj_myplugin_fetch_song_title_from_radio()` function would do the following:

➤ Fetch data from the remote radio website

➤ Parse this data to extract the current song title

➤ Return this song title

Such tasks are beyond the scope of this chapter, but you learn how to do them in Chapter 9, which deals with HTTP requests.

Function `boj_myplugin_get_song_title()` is a complete example of how to use transient functions: Get a transient, and if it's false then refresh its value and restore it.

Technical Details

Due to their volatile nature, transients benefit from caching plugins, where normal options don't. For example, on server setups using memcached (a memory caching system) and a memcached plugin, WordPress stores transient values in fast memory instead of in the database. For this reason, never assume transients live in the database because they may not be stored there at all.

Transient Ideas

Any time you want to store data with a short time to live, you should probably use the transients. Following are a few examples of tasks or plugin features that would be a perfect application of the Transient API:

➤ A corporate blog where the clients want to display the current value of their share price

➤ Current number of Facebook friends

➤ Last tweet from a Twitter account

➤ Latest article fetched from an RSS feed

SAVING PER-USER SETTINGS

The plugins give WordPress users more control over their site with more options. Usually, a plugin adds a page under the Settings menu where you can modify the options and tweak how WordPress works.

There are situations in which such a feature implementation (that is, affecting the way an entire WordPress setup operate) is not ideal. In a single site with multiple users for instance, you might want to allow per-user settings instead of global options.

Crafting a Plugin

Imagine your newest client being a corporation with both English and Spanish employees. Your job, while working on its corporate intranet CMS (based on WordPress, of course), is to allow employees to select the language in which the interface of WordPress' backend will display.

As per your naming conventions, you can name this plugin BOJ's Admin Lang and use `boj_adminlang` as a prefix. While learning how to use functions needed to save and get per-user settings, you can build this plugin.

User Metadata

Data about users are kept in two places in WordPress' database:

➤ Core information primarily used by the login process (name, email address, date of registration, and password) is stored in table `wp_users`.

➤ Meta information, that is, the other data about the user (bio, contact info, Visual Editor preference and so on) resides in table `wp_usermeta`.

The user metadata table has been designed to store anything related to a user and to be easily extensible. To do so, a set of functions enables easy access to these records: `add_user_meta()`, `update_user_meta()`, `get_user_meta()`, and `delete_user_meta()`.

These four functions are similar to the ones from the Options API, with an interesting twist: They enable duplicate data.

Saving User Metadata

The function call to save user metadata has the following syntax:

```php
<?php
add_user_meta( $user_id, $meta_key, $meta_value, $unique );
?>
```

Its parameters follow:

➤ `$user_id` — In user tables, users are identified by an integer, their user ID. You'll see later how to get a user's ID.

➤ `$meta_key` and `$meta_value` — The pair of metadata name and value, like in previous functions covered such as `add_option()`.

➤ `$unique` — Optional, a Boolean. If `true`, you cannot add a given user several metadata with the same name. Its default value is `false`, meaning that if you don't specify it, you implicitly allow duplicate meta keys. For code clarity, it's recommended that you don't omit this parameter.

The various option types previously covered have to be unique, but several metadata for a given user can have the same key. This can make sense to store, for instance, multiple book titles a user would own:

```php
<?php
add_user_meta( 3, 'books', 'Professional WordPress', false);
add_user_meta( 3, 'books', 'I Love WP', false);
?>
```

Depending on the context, it also can make sense to state that a particular metadata key needs to be unique. Back to BOJ's Admin Lang: Storing a user's choice for an interface language is an example of a setting that cannot have multiple values:

```php
<?php
add_user_meta( 3, 'boj_adminlang_lang', 'es_ES', true );
?>
```

This says that user #3 will want the interface to be translated using locale `es_ES` (see Chapter 5, "Internationalization," for more details on locales).

Updating User Metadata

The syntax of function `update_user_meta()` follows:

```php
<?php
update_user_meta( $user_id, $meta_key, $meta_value, $prev_value );
?>
```

The first three parameters are obvious by now. The fourth parameter, if specified, states which metadata key should be updated. If omitted, all the user's metadata with this `$meta_key` will be updated.

In a previous example, you have saved two book titles for user #3. Now update the second title to replace WP with WordPress:

```php
<?php
update_user_meta( 3, 'books', 'I Love WordPress', 'I Love WP' );
?>
```

Omitting the fourth parameter would have updated all the book titles. Back to your polyglot plugin: Because this metadata key is unique, you don't need to pass a fourth parameter. Now set user #3's interface language to empty:

```php
<?php
update_user_meta( 3, 'boj_adminlang_lang', '' );
?>
```

Getting User Metadata

Prior to displaying WordPress' backend interface when a user loads it, your bilingual plugin can check if that particular user has a metadata stating a locale preference. Now see what user #3 prefers:

```php
<?php
$lang = get_user_meta( 3, 'boj_adminlang_lang', true );
?>
```

The first and second parameters are the user ID and the metadata key. The third parameter is a bit less obvious: It's a Boolean stating whether you want the return value to be a single value (`true`) or an array (`false`).

Your dashboard language plugin stores unique metadata with the name `boj_adminlang_lang`, so you want that unique value as a string. To fetch the list of books from the previous example, set this third parameter to false to get the following array. (The results are shown as a comment below the function call.)

```php
<?php
$book = get_user_meta( 3, 'books', false );
// array( 'Professional WordPress', 'I Love WordPress' );
?>
```

Deleting User Metadata

The last function you will learn to use is `delete_user_meta()`, which returns `true` if successful and `false` otherwise (for instance, when the metadata key could not be found in the database). Its syntax follows:

```php
<?php
delete_user_meta( $user_id, $meta_key, $meta_value )
?>
```

You can match records based on key only, or on key and value, to deal with duplicate metadata keys. When you know the metadata key is unique, you can omit the third parameter:

```php
<?php
delete_user_meta( 3, 'boj_adminlang_lang' );
?>
```

If the metadata key is not unique, as in the example with the book title, you can specify which record to delete or simply delete all records with that key:

```php
<?php
// Delete one record:
delete_user_meta( 3, 'books', 'I Love WordPress' );

// Delete all records:
delete_user_meta( 3, 'books' );
?>
```

Getting a User's ID

You have been reading about user IDs and have been using 3 in previous examples, but how do you get the current user ID?

Some actions and filters in WordPress pass the current user ID as an argument, as you see when you build your bilingual plugin from the ground up. If the current user ID is not known, use the following code:

```php
<?php
$user = wp_get_current_user();
$userid = $user->ID;
?>
```

In this code, $user becomes an object containing all known data about the current user: login name, email, privileges in the admin area, Visual Editor preference, metadata, and so on. One of the properties of this object is ID, which is the integer you are looking for.

Adding Input Fields to a Profile Page

Because you are going to store per-user settings, it would not make sense to make a global plugin option page. Instead, you can add an input field to every user's Profile page. Profile pages trigger several actions to which you can hook if you want to add content to the page:

➤   'personal_options' — Add content at the end of the "Personal Options" section.

➤   'profile_personal_options' — Append content after the "Personal Options" section.

➤   'show_user_profile' — Add content before the "Update Profile" button.

Now you can add a simple drop-down list from which to choose between English or Español in the "Personal Options" section:

```php
<?php
// Add and fill an extra input field to user's profile
function boj_adminlang_display_field( $user ) {
    $userid = $user->ID;
    $lang = get_user_meta( $userid, 'boj_adminlang_lang', true );
    ?>

    <tr>
        <th scope="row">Language</th>
        <td>
        <select name="boj_adminlang_lang">
        <option value=""
            <?php selected( '', $lang); ?> >English</option>
        <option value="es_ES"
            <?php selected( 'es_ES', $lang); ?> >Spanish</option>
        </select>
        </td>
    </tr>

    <?php
}
// Trigger this function on 'personal_options' action
add_action( 'personal_options', 'boj_adminlang_display_field' );
?>
```

The action 'personal_options' passes to your custom function boj_adminlang_display_field() the user object. Your function gets the user ID, the language preference from the user's metadata, and then outputs the HTML that adds the select input field, as shown in Figure 7-6.

The input field uses WordPress' function selected() to automatically select the appropriate option, as per user choice if previously saved.

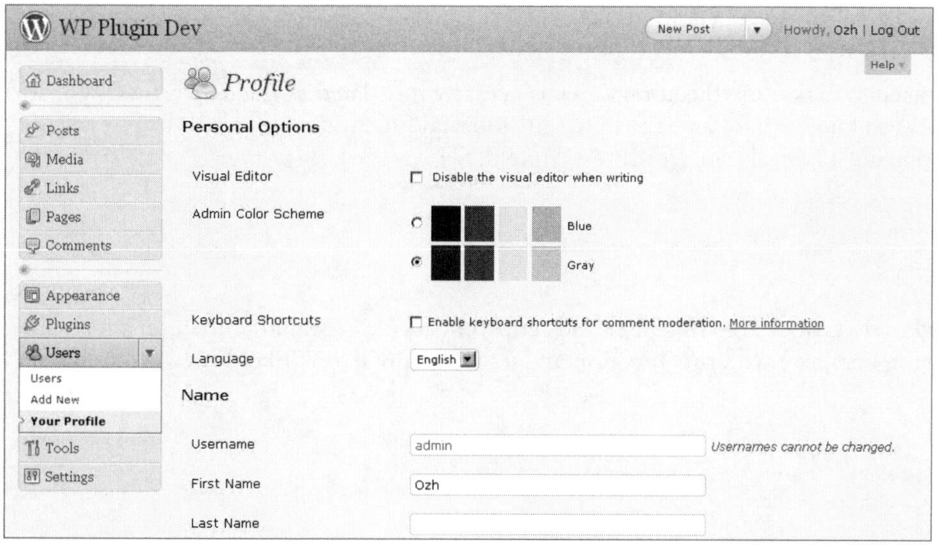

FIGURE 7-6

On profile pages, you need to monitor form submissions and verify if the user entered any custom metadata. To do so, you can rely on action 'personal_options_update' and check the $_POST data:

```php
<?php
// Monitor form submits and update user's setting if applicable
function boj_adminlang_update_field( $userid ) {
    if( isset( $_POST['boj_adminlang_lang'] ) ) {
        $lang = $_POST['boj_adminlang_lang'] == 'es_ES' ? 'es_ES' : '';
        update_user_meta( $userid, 'boj_adminlang_lang', $lang );
    }
}
add_action( 'personal_options_update', 'boj_adminlang_update_field' );
?>
```

The plugin is now finished in its visible part: A custom field on every user's Profile page asks for and saves a preference setting.

Notice how you used a ternary operator for shorter code. The following single line:

```php
<?php
$lang = $_POST['boj_adminlang_lang'] == 'es_ES' ? 'es_ES' : '';
?>
```

is equivalent to the longer structure:

```php
<?php
if( $_POST['boj_adminlang_lang'] == 'es_ES' ) {
    $lang = 'es_ES';
} else {
    $lang = '';
}?>
```

BOJ's Admin Lang Plugin

Now you just need to make sure the admin area is actually translated as the user wants. Whenever WordPress needs to know what language to use, its internal function get_locale() returns the locale, after applying a filter. From WordPress' source, file wp-includes/l10n.php:

```php
<?php
return apply_filters( 'locale', $locale );
?>
```

What you need to do is hook into this filter and return the locale as stored in the user's metadata. The entire plugin, complete with this function and its header, will look like this:

Available for
download on
Wrox.com

```php
<?php
/*
Plugin Name: Per User Setting example
Plugin URI: http://example.com/
```

```
Description: Allow choosing either English or Spanish in the admin area
Author: WROX
Author URI: http://wrox.com
*/

// Return user's locale
function boj_adminlang_set_user_locale() {
    $user = wp_get_current_user();
    $userid = $user->ID;
    $locale = get_user_meta( $userid, 'boj_adminlang_lang', true );
    return $locale;
}
// Trigger this function every time WP checks the locale value
add_filter( 'locale', 'boj_adminlang_set_user_locale' );

// Add and fill an extra input field to user's profile
function boj_adminlang_display_field( $user ) {
    $userid = $user->ID;
    $lang = get_user_meta( $userid, 'boj_adminlang_lang', true );
    ?>

    <tr>
    <th scope="row">Language</th>
        <td>
        <select name="boj_adminlang_lang">
        <option value=""
            <?php selected( '', $lang); ?> >English</option>
        <option value="es_ES"
            <?php selected( 'es_ES', $lang); ?> >Spanish</option>
        </select>
        </td>
    </tr>

    <?php
}
add_action( 'personal_options', 'boj_adminlang_display_field' );
// Monitor form submits and update user's setting if applicable
function boj_adminlang_update_field( $userid ) {
    if( isset( $_POST['boj_adminlang_lang'] ) ) {
        $lang = $_POST['boj_adminlang_lang'] == 'es_ES' ? 'es_ES' : '';
        update_user_meta( $userid, 'boj_adminlang_lang', $lang );
    }
}
add_action( 'personal_options_update', 'boj_adminlang_update_field' );
?>
```

Code snippet plugin4-per-user-option.php

Now activate the plugin, pick the Spanish option and . . . ¡ole!, your blog now speaks Spanish, as shown in Figure 7-7.

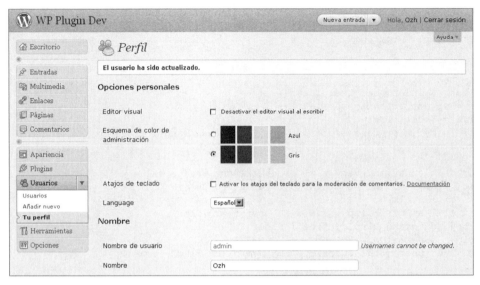

FIGURE 7-7

 For this plugin to work, the WordPress installation needs to include the Spanish translation files you can get from http://es.wordpress.org/. *Put the es_ES files in the directory* wp-content/languages *(which you might need to create first).*

Per-User Settings: Best Practices

If you want a plugin to store per-user settings, make sure it includes the following attributes:

➤ Visually well integrated into WordPress

➤ Wisely implemented

Visual integration — Because you add content to Profile pages, such content must match the look and feel of the original WordPress interface. Use proper HTML and classes, as in the plugin example. More than ever your plugin settings will look like core settings because you won't create an extra administration page, so make it integrate impeccably.

Wise implementation — Sometimes it makes more sense to have a standalone plugin option page, or to add a few options to the WordPress Settings page, with global settings instead of per-user settings. Most WordPress blogs are single-user blogs, where people may not head to their Profile to check for new settings.

STORING DATA IN CUSTOM TABLES

So far in this chapter, you have learned how to store and manage standard options, expiring options, and user metadata. WordPress comes with a number of database tables, and in most cases anything you want to store can fit perfectly in these tables. Still, there might be cases in which you need to create custom tables to save and get data from.

Types of Data

Following are two types of records you can store:

➤ Setup information

➤ Collected data

Setup information is typically plugin options: Users configure and save some settings the first time they install a plugin; they might modify these settings in the future, but the number of records won't grow. This is typically what needs to be stored in the Options table.

Collected data is information added as the users continue to use their blog. This data might be related to posts, comments, or any WordPress component. Data expanding over time might be appropriate candidates for a custom table.

WordPress' Standard Tables

WordPress installs 11 tables, and specifically tables that are more likely to store a lot of custom data; default names are as follows:

➤ wp_posts — The site's content

➤ wp_postmeta — Metadata about posts

➤ wp_commentmeta — Comments metadata

➤ wp_usermeta — Metadata for users

➤ wp_options — Options

Not only can these tables store practically everything you need to store, but they all also have convenient API functions to save and get data. Try to make a connection between information you want to store and a metadata table.

Sometimes you need to think outside of the box to realize that a particular table will be just fine for your data. Consider for instance the wp_post table with stored custom menus, which at first you probably wouldn't have considered a particular post type.

This cannot be emphasized enough: In 99% of the cases, these tables will suffice, and most of the time you will store data in the options table.

Creating a Custom Table

Imagine a statistics plugin that can store the IP address and timestamp of every visitor on your blog. This plugin would need a custom table with three fields, as shown in Table 7-2.

TABLE 7-2: Data Set Structure and Type

HIT_ID	HIT_IP	HIT_DATE
int(11) NOT NULL AUTO_INCREMENT	varchar(100) NOT NULL	datetime

The SQL statement to create such a table structure follows:

```
CREATE TABLE `wp_hits` (
    `hit_id` INT( 11 ) NOT NULL AUTO_INCREMENT,
    `chitin` VARCHAR( 100 ) NOT NULL ,
    `hit_date` DATETIME
);
```

You now can use a powerful built-in WordPress tool: function dbDelta(). This function is not loaded by default, so you need to manually include it in your plugin. Now create your custom table:

```
<?php
$tablename = $wpdb->prefix . "hits";

$sql = "CREATE TABLE `$tablename` (
    `hit_id` INT( 11 ) NOT NULL AUTO_INCREMENT,
    `hit_ip` VARCHAR( 100 ) NOT NULL ,
    `hit_date` DATETIME
);";

require_once(ABSPATH . 'wp-admin/includes/upgrade.php');

dbDelta($sql);
?>
```

What you have just done follows:

1. Got the database table prefix and used it to name your custom table.

2. Defined a SQL statement, one field per line.

3. Included the file that defines function dbDelta().

4. Ran this function.

In wp-config.php a WordPress site owner can define a custom database table prefix, which is by default wp_. When you create a custom table, don't hardcode its full name, and always use the $wpdb->prefix.

Checking if a Table Already Exists

Before creating a table, you might want to check its existence first. To do so, compare the result of SQL command SHOW TABLE with your actual table name:

```php
<?php
$tablename = $wpdb->prefix . "hits";

if( $wpdb->get_var("SHOW TABLES LIKE '$tablename'") != $tablename ) {
    // table does not exist!
}
?>
```

The function dbDelta() includes a check for the table existence before attempting to create or update it. Doing this by yourself can make sense, for instance to determine if your plugin needs to include an otherwise unneeded file containing upgrade functions.

Updating the Structure of a Custom Table

The power of function dbDelta() resides in its capability to update a table with the same syntax used to create it: It examines the current table structure if found, compares it to the desired table structure, and either adds or modifies the table as required.

This can make your code much easier to maintain: The install and the upgrade functions actually share this one function call.

Back to your statistics plugin: You can now add a fourth field to hold the WordPress post ID that has been visited. You can also improve the table structure with a primary key on first field hit_id.

Following is a complete create and upgrade function:

```php
<?php
// Create / Update the custom table
function boj_hits_create_table() {
    global $wpdb;

    $tablename = $wpdb->prefix . "hits";

    $sql = "CREATE TABLE `$tablename` (
        `hit_id` int(11) NOT NULL AUTO_INCREMENT,
        `hit_ip` varchar(100) NOT NULL,
        `hit_date` datetime,
        `post_id` int(11) NOT NULL,
        PRIMARY KEY (`hit_id`)
      );";

    require_once(ABSPATH . 'wp-admin/includes/upgrade.php');

    dbDelta($sql);
}?>
```

Don't forget to bring in your function the $wpdb *object from the global scope.*

dbDelta() Tips for Success

Function dbDelta() can be tricky to use. MySQL's tolerance for syntax errors or approximations is limited, and so is dbDelta(), which is basically a wrapper function. It takes a single space (missing or extra) to fail the function call and sometimes to fail silently.

Watching Your SQL Syntax and Style

dbDelta() is touchy and needs the SQL statement to be formatted with care:

➤ Put each field on its own line in your SQL statement.

➤ Use the key word KEY rather than its synonym INDEX.

➤ Don't use extra spaces between MySQL keywords.

The simplest way to make sure your SQL statement is cleanly formatted is to design your table in a tool such as phpMyAdmin (see Chapter 18, "The Developer Toolbox") and then export your table structure, as shown in Figure 7-8. The SQL generated will generally be formatted and indented in a suitable way for dbDelta().

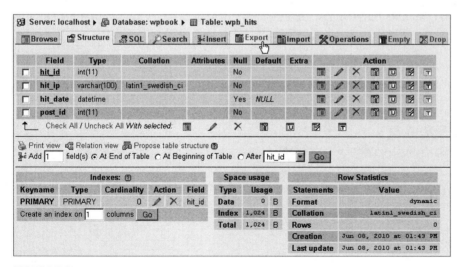

FIGURE 7-8

Checking the Return Value in a Debug Sandbox

dbDelta() does not output any message in case of success or error, but it does return some valuable information about what it did.

You cannot make your plugin install function display debug information because that can trigger a fatal error and prevent your plugin from activating. Instead, it is easy to make a simple sandbox in which you can test your function and inspect dbDelta()'s results with print_r().

In the WordPress root directory of your test install, create an empty file named testsql.php and paste the following code:

```php
<?php
require('./wp-load.php');
?>
<pre>
<?php
$wpdb->show_errors();

$tablename = $wpdb->prefix . "hits";

$sql = "CREATE TABLE `$tablename` (
    `hit_id` int(11) NOT NULL AUTO_INCREMENT,
    `hit_ip` varchar(100) NOT NULL,
    `hit_date` datetime,
    `post_id` int(11) NOT NULL,
    PRIMARY KEY (`hit_id`)
);";
require_once(ABSPATH . 'wp-admin/includes/upgrade.php');

var_dump( dbDelta($sql) );

$wpdb->print_error();
?>
</pre>
```

This file loads the WordPress environment and then runs your install code. Point your browser to this file (its location would be, for instance, http://example.com/testsql.php) and you can see a result like the following:

```
Array
(
    [`wpb_hits`] => Created table `wpb_hits`
)
```

If your SQL statement is incorrect, the resulting array would be empty. Note that you also explicitly turned error echoing on at the top of the file and printed the last SQL error, if any.

Test Running Your SQL Statement

Function `dbDelta()` accepts two parameters: a mandatory SQL statement and an optional Boolean that can prevent the statement from actually executing if set to `false`:

```php
<?php
// Execute statement and print execution result
var_dump( dbDelta( $sql ) );

// Test-run statement without executing it, and print result
var_dump( dbDelta( $sql, false ) );
?>
```

You will probably never use this optional parameter in a production situation (on a client's site or within a released plugin) but this can be an insightful debugging option in a sandbox as just shown.

Accessing Your Custom Table

Now that your custom table is created, you can access it using the global `$wpdb` object. The following code snippet shows standard SQL queries:

```php
<?php

$tablename = $wpdb->prefix . "hits";

// Insert a record
$newdata = array(
    'hit_ip' => '127.0.0.1',
    'hit_date' => current_time( 'mysql' ),
    'post_id' => '123'
);
$wpdb->insert(
    $tablename,
    $newdata
);

// Update a record
$newdata = array( 'post_id' => '456' );
$where   = array( 'post_id' => '123', 'hit_id' => 1 );
$wpdb->update( $tablename, $newdata, $where );


?>
```

Refer to Chapter 6 to learn how to use the `wpdb` class in detail.

SUMMARY

Saving data is a key part of writing plugins: It enables your plugin to be customized and personally set by your users, who will appreciate the ability to fine-tune new features. Using the functions described here, you can integrate your plugins seamlessly into WordPress with efficient, compact, and future-proof code.

Users

WHAT'S IN THIS CHAPTER?

➤ Working with users and user functions

➤ Adding, updating, and retrieving user data

➤ Developing for roles and capabilities

➤ Limiting access with user permissions

➤ Customizing user roles

Just a couple of years ago, a chapter on users would probably not have been too exciting to potential plugin developers. At the time, WordPress was largely used as a pure blogging system with one or a few bloggers writing posts. Developing plugins to integrate with the users system most likely wouldn't have earned you a lot of popularity within the plugin community.

Today, WordPress powers many large sites with thousands and even hundreds of thousands of users. Knowing how WordPress handles users is now an important tool in any plugin developer's toolbox. You'll deal with various user scenarios in many of your plugins.

Perhaps, more important, understanding the roles and capabilities system is paramount to developing a solid and secure plugin. Roles and capabilities define what users can do within individual sites created with WordPress.

People use WordPress for private membership sites, social networks, online newspapers, medical databases, centers for education, and much more. All these might require plugins to handle users and permissions. When creating plugins for these types of sites, it's often important to make sure you use the correct WordPress functions so that private information is not shown to users without permission to see it.

This chapter gives you the tools to work within the WordPress users, roles, and capabilities systems and show you how each interact with each other within the WordPress environment.

WORKING WITH USERS

In WordPress, users are people who have registered a unique username for the site. The user has an account within that installation of WordPress. The term "user" shouldn't be confused with "visitor." A visitor is someone reading the site without an account. This chapter's main focus is on registered users.

All WordPress installations have at minimum one user. This is the person that installed WordPress and initially set it up. This account has been traditionally known as the "admin" user because older versions of WordPress automatically created an account with the "admin" username. Today, WordPress allows a different username upon registration.

 Some older plugins relied on there being a user account called "admin," which was wrong in the past and is wrong now. Never assume that a specific username is in use, and never assume that if the username is in use that the user has particular permissions.

User Functions

WordPress has many functions for working with users. In this section, you learn how to use some of these basic functions.

 Many user functions aren't loaded until after plugins are loaded and the current user isn't authenticated until the init *action hook (see Chapter 3, "Hooks"). Using a user function before* init *in the WordPress flow will most likely cause a fatal error.*

is_user_logged_in()

The `is_user_logged_in()` function is a conditional tag that enables you to check if a user is logged into the site. It returns either `true` or `false` based on whether the current user has an ID. It is also pluggable, so you can create a custom `is_user_logged_in()` function to overwrite its functionality completely. People logged in are users, and people who are not logged in are visitors.

In the following example, you display a message for users based on the return value of this function in the footer of the site. Logged-in users will get one message and users not logged in will get a different message.

```php
<?php

add_action( 'wp_footer', 'boj_footer_user_logged_in' );

function boj_footer_user_logged_in() {

    if ( is_user_logged_in() )
```

```
        echo 'You are currently logged into this site.';

    else
        echo 'You are not logged into the site.';
}

?>
```

This function is important because it enables you to run specific code only when needed. Although it is useful, you'll likely rely more on capabilities for more specific checks within your plugins (see the "Roles and Capabilities" section of this chapter).

get_users()

The `get_users()` function enables you to query users from the database based on the arguments passed into the function through the `$args` parameter. The `$args` parameter is an array of arguments that you can define to limit the users returned by the function.

```php
<?php
get_users( $args );
?>
```

After you query a set of users, you receive an array that you can use to perform some specific functionality based on the results. For example, you could display a list of users based on the date they registered for the site.

The `$args` parameter gives you many options for limiting which users are returned in the query. The parameter is optional and returns all users if you do not define any arguments.

➤ `blog_id` — Get users registered for a specific blog within the network. This is only useful for multisite installs (Chapter 15, "Multisite"). It defaults to the current blog ID.

➤ `role` — The name of a user role. This defaults to an empty string and uses all roles.

➤ `meta_key` — A meta key from the `$wpdb->usermeta` table.

➤ `meta_value` — A meta value from the `$wpdb->usermeta` table.

➤ `meta_compare` — A conditional operator to compare the `meta_value` argument against. Some values are =, !=, >, >=, <, and <=.

➤ `include` — An array of user IDs to specifically include in the query.

➤ `exclude` — An array of user IDs that should be excluded from the query.

➤ `search` — A string used to search for users. The search will be on the `user_login`, `user_nicename`, `user_email`, `user_url`, and `display_name` fields from the `$wpdb->users` table.

➤ `orderby` — The field in which to order the users by. By default, this is `login`. You can also order by `email`, `url`, `registered`, `name`, `user_login`, and `post_count`.

➤ `order` — Whether to order the users in ascending (`ASC`) or descending (`DESC`) order. It defaults to `ASC`.

> ➤ offset — Number of users to skip over in the query before getting the users from the database.

> ➤ number — An integer that limits the user query to a set number of users. By default, all users that match the given arguments will be returned.

It's time to put the get_users() function to some good use. In this section, you build a small plugin that displays the avatar (photo of the user) of all users based on a given role. This plugin will be a simple function that enables the plugin user to input the role they want to show the user avatars for.

```php
<?php
/*
Plugin Name: User Avatars
Plugin URI: http://example.com
Description: Displays user avatars based on role.
Author: WROX
Author URI: http://wrox.com
*/

function boj_user_avatars( $role = 'subscriber' ) {

    /* Get the users based on role. */
    $users = get_users(
        array(
            'role' => $role
        )
    );

    /* Check if any users were returned. */
    if ( is_array( $users ) ) {

        /* Loop through each user. */
        foreach ( $users as $user ) {

            /* Display the user's avatar. */
            echo get_avatar( $user );
        }
    }
}

?>
```

Code snippet boj-user-avatars.php

To use this plugin on a live site, the plugin user needs to use the following code and input a role name. This example uses the editor as the role.

```php
<?php
boj_user_avatars( 'editor' );
?>
```

get_users_of_blog()

If you need to get all the users of the blog, you don't have to use the `get_users()` function from the previous section. The `get_users_of_blog()` function returns an array of all user IDs registered for the current blog being viewed.

```php
<?php
get_users_of_blog( $id );
?>
```

The function takes in a single parameter: `$id`. This parameter is only useful in multisite setups where `$id` would be a specific site ID.

In the next example, you create a function that lists of all the users for the blog. This list displays the user's name and links to the user's archive page.

```php
<?php

function boj_list_users_of_blog() {

    /* Get the users of the current blog. */
    $users = get_users_of_blog();

    /* Check if users are returned. */
    if ( !empty( $users ) ) {

        /* Open the users list. */
        echo '<ul class="users-list">';

        /* Loop through each user returned. */
        foreach ( $users as $user ) {

            /* Create a list item linking to the user archive page. */
            echo '<li><a href="' . get_author_posts_url( $user->ID ) . '">';
            echo get_the_author_meta( 'display_name', $user->ID );
            echo '</a></li>';
        }

        /* Close the users list. */
        echo '</ul>';
    }
}

?>
```

You now have a function for creating a nice list of all the users for a blog. You can build this functionality into a shortcode (see Chapter 10, "The Shortcode API") or a widget (refer to Chapter 4) by calling the `boj_list_users_of_blog()` function. You can also have plugin users input the following code where they want the users list to appear within their theme.

```php
<?php boj_list_users_of_blog(); ?>
```

count_users

The `count_users()` function enables you to count users of the site. It keeps track of the count of all users and the number of users for each role. It takes in a single parameter called `$strategy`, which determines how the users are counted and can be one of two values.

> ➤ `time` — This value is CPU-intensive and is the default.

> ➤ `memory` — This value is memory-intensive.

With the next code example, you get the user count for the site. You then list the total number of users for the site, followed by the user count for each role.

```php
<?php

/* Get the user counts. */
$user_count = count_users();

/* Open an unordered list. */
echo '<ul class="user-counts">';

/* List the total number of users. */
echo '<li>Total users: ' . $user_count['total_users'] . '</li>';

/* Loop through each of the roles. */
foreach ( $user_count['avail_roles'] as $role => $count ) {

    /* List the role and its number of users. */
    echo '<li>' . $role . ': ' . $count . '</li>';
}

/* Close the unordered list. */
echo '</ul>';

?>
```

Creating, Updating, and Deleting Users

WordPress has a built-in user interface for creating, updating, and deleting users that most people will use. However, you may find yourself in a situation where you would need to create a plugin that handles these things outside of the normal WordPress interface.

Following are some examples of reasons why you need to code a plugin to handle this:

> ➤ A client needs to import thousands of users from a different system into WordPress, and creating these users individually would be out of the question.

> ➤ You're building a social networking plugin that needs a front-end interface for registering user accounts.

> ➤ A plugin that enables administrators to bulk edit/update various forms of user data in a quick and efficient manner.

> ➤ You need to create a sidebar widget for use in multiple WordPress themes to handle user registration.

As you should see by now, there can be many reasons for stepping outside of the standard WordPress interface for handling users. Although you won't be using the standard interface, you will be using standard functions that WordPress has conveniently provided for doing these types of things.

wp_insert_user

The wp_insert_user() function inserts new users into the database. It also handles the update of currently registered user accounts if a user ID is passed into the function.

The function has a single parameter: $userdata. This is an array of arguments for inputting data into the $wpdb->users and $wpdb->usermeta tables for the specific user.

```php
<?php
wp_insert_user( $userdata );
?>
```

➤ ID — A current user's ID. You should use this only if you're updating a user. WordPress automatically creates new user IDs.

➤ user_pass — A password for the new user account.

➤ user_login — This is the "username" for the user. This is a required argument and returns an error if not unique.

➤ user_nicename — An alternative name to use in things such as permalinks to user archives. This defaults to the user_login argument.

➤ user_url — A link to the user's personal web site.

➤ user_email — The email address of the user. This is a required argument and returns an error if not given or if the email address is already in use.

➤ display_name — The name to display for the user. This defaults to the user_login argument.

➤ nickname — A nickname for the user. This defaults to the user_login argument.

➤ first_name — The first name of the user.

➤ last_name — The last name (surname) of the user.

➤ description — A biographical information argument that describes the user.

➤ rich_editing — Whether to use the visual editor when writing posts. This is set to true by default.

➤ user_registered — The date and time of the user registration. WordPress automatically sets this to the current date and time if no argument is given.

➤ role — The role the user should have. This defaults to the default role the site administrator has set in the WordPress options.

➤ admin_color — The color scheme for the WordPress administration area.

➤ comment_shortcuts — Whether the user should use keyboard shortcuts when moderating comments. This defaults to false.

Now, you can take these arguments and create a new user with the `wp_insert_user()` function. You can mix and match the preceding arguments but make sure you use the required arguments (`user_login`, `user_pass`, and `user_email`). The user you create next has the "editor" role and is named Wrox. You also make sure the user was created by displaying a WordPress-generated error message in the instance that something went wrong.

Create a new plugin file named `boj-insert-user.php` and use the following code to create a plugin that will insert a new user into your database using the `wp_insert_user()` function.

```php
<?php
/*
Plugin Name: Insert User
Plugin URI: http://example.com
Description: Plugin that inserts a user.
Version: 0.1
Author: WROX
Author URI: http://wrox.com
*/

/* Insert the new user on the 'init' hook. */
add_action( 'init', 'boj_insert_user' );

/* Inserts a new user. */
function boj_insert_user() {

    /* Do nothing if the 'wrox' username exists. */
    if ( username_exists( 'wrox' ) )
        return;

    /* Set up the user data. */
    $userdata = array(
        'user_login' => 'wrox',
        'user_email' => 'wrox@example.com',
        'user_pass' => '123456789',
        'user_url' => 'http://example.com',
        'display_name' => 'Wrox',
        'description' => 'Loves to publish awesome books on WordPress!',
        'role' => 'editor'
    );

    /* Create the user. */
    $user = wp_insert_user( $userdata );

    /* If the user wasn't created, display the error message. */
    if ( is_wp_error( $user ) )
        echo $result->get_error_message();
}

?>
```

Code snippet boj-insert-user.php

wp_create_user

You may be wondering why there's a function named `wp_create_user()` when the `wp_insert_user()` can get the job done. This function can actually be a useful alternative that enables you to quickly create new users and not worry about dealing with all the arguments from `wp_insert_user()`.

```php
<?php
wp_create_user( $username, $password, $email );
?>
```

This function enables you to insert the minimum arguments for creating a user, which simplifies creating users greatly. It's especially useful if you don't have any other data you want to input.

➤   `$username` — A unique login name for the user.

➤   `$password` — A password the user will use to log into the site.

➤   `$email` — A unique email address for the user account.

With the next code, you create a new user called wrox2. This user is given the default user role set by the site administrator. Create a new plugin file named `boj-create-user.php` and use the following code to create a new user with the `wp_create_user()` function.

Available for download on Wrox.com

```php
<?php
/*
Plugin Name: Create User
Plugin URI: http://example.com
Description: Plugin that creates a user.
Version: 0.1
Author: WROX
Author URI: http://wrox.com
*/

/* Create the new user on the 'init' hook. */
add_action( 'init', 'boj_create_user' );

/* Creates a new user. */
function boj_create_user() {

    /* Do nothing if the 'wrox2' username exists. */
    if ( username_exists( 'wrox2' ) )
        return;

    /* Create the 'wrox2' user. */
    wp_create_user(
        'wrox2',
        '123456789',
        'wrox2@example.com'
    );
}

?>
```

Code snippet boj-create-user.php

wp_update_user

This is another function that can be done with `wp_insert_user()`. This function is a wrapper function for it with one important difference: If the user password (`user_pass` argument) is updated, the function automatically resets the cookies for the user's browser.

```php
<?php
wp_update_user( $userdata );
?>
```

This function takes in a single parameter called `$userdata`, which accepts all the same arguments covered in the section on `wp_insert_user()`. However, the ID argument is required for updating the user. If the ID argument isn't present, a new user will be created.

In the next example, you use the `wp_update_user()` function to force the currently logged-in user to use the "fresh" color scheme in the admin. This can be useful for making sure all users have a consistent experience in the admin. Create a new file called `boj-force-admin-color.php` and use the following code to update the user.

```php
<?php
/*
Plugin Name: Force Admin Color
Plugin URI: http://example.com
Description: Forces the 'fresh' admin color scheme.
Version: 0.1
Author: WROX
Author URI: http://wrox.com
*/

/* Only load change the color scheme in the admin. */
add_action( 'admin_init', 'boj_force_admin_color' );

/* Forces the current user to use the 'fresh' admin color. */
function boj_force_admin_color() {

    /* Get the current user object. */
    $user = wp_get_current_user();

    /* If the $user variable is not empty, continue. */
    if ( !empty( $user ) ) {

        /* Get the user's admin color scheme. */
        $admin_color = get_user_meta( $user->ID, 'admin_color', true );

        /* If the admin color is not 'fresh', change it. */
        if ( $admin_color !== 'fresh' ) {

            /* Set up the user data. */
            $userdata = array(
                'ID' => $user->ID,
                'admin_color' => 'fresh'
            );

            /* Update the user. */
```

```
                    wp_update_user( $userdata );
                }
            }
        }

    ?>
```

Code snippet boj-force-admin-color.php

wp_delete_user

The wp_delete_user() function is a little different than the previous user functions because it exists only in the WordPress admin. Therefore, you should call the function only while in the admin. Otherwise, you get a PHP error.

```php
<?php
wp_delete_user( $user_id, $reassign );
?>
```

The function is used for deleting individual users and reassigning their posts and links to an alternative user. It takes in two parameters.

➤ $id — The ID of the user to delete.

➤ $reassign — The ID of the user to set as the author of posts and links in which the user you're deleting has published. If this parameter is not set, the posts and links will be deleted from the database.

In this next example, you delete a user with the ID of 100 and reassign the user's posts and links to a user with the ID of 1.

```php
<?php

/* Delete user 100 and assign posts to user 1. */
wp_delete_user( 100, 1 );

?>
```

User Data

User data in WordPress is saved in two different tables in the database: $wpdb->users and $wpdb->usermeta. The users table saves information about the user that WordPress needs to function. The usermeta table is for storing additional metadata about users. You sometimes need to load, create, update, and delete this data within your plugins.

When working with user data from the users table, you work with a few different values set for every user on the site.

➤ ID — The ID of the registered user.

➤ user_login — The login name (username).

➤ user_pass — The user's password. Note that you should never display this publicly.

➤ user_nicename — A "pretty" version of the user login that works in URLs.

➤ user_url — The web site address of the user.

➤ user_email — The email address of the user. You should never display this publicly without the user's permission.

➤ user_registered — The date the user registered for the site.

➤ display_name — The name the user would like displayed.

get_userdata

The get_userdata() function is for getting a user's data from the users table. It also returns data from the usermeta table, but WordPress has other functions that will be covered for getting this information. It takes in a single parameter of $user_id, which is the ID of a registered user for the site. It returns an object of user data if a user were found or false if no user were found.

Remember, this function can also return metadata, but you shouldn't worry about using this function for displaying metadata with it. This is covered later in the chapter.

Suppose you needed a function to quickly display a specific user's name and web site address. Use the following code to create a function to display this data.

```php
<?php
function boj_display_user_website( $user_id ) {

    /* Get the user data. */
    $data = get_userdata( $user_id );

    /* Check if data was returned. */
    if ( !empty( $data ) ) {

        /* Check if a URL has been given. */
        if ( !empty( $data->user_url ) ) {

            /* Display the user display name and URL. */
            echo $data->display_name . ': ' . $data->user_url;
        }
    }
}

?>
```

Now you can use the boj_display_user_website() function to display any user's name and site address by inputting the user ID as the $user_id parameter. For example, you could use the following code to display this information for a user with the ID of 100.

```php
<?php
boj_display_user_website( 100 );
?>
```

wp_get_current_user

The wp_get_current_user() function gets the user data from the users table for the currently logged-in user. It can be useful for displaying information when a specific user is logged into the site. The function takes in no parameters and returns an object of the user data.

In the next example, you display a welcome message based on the user's display name in the WordPress admin footer.

```php
<?php

/* Display user welcome message in the admin footer. */
add_action( 'in_admin_footer', 'boj_user_welcome_message' );

function boj_user_welcome_message() {

    /* Get the current user's data. */
    $data = wp_get_current_user();

    /* Display a message for the user. */
    echo "Hello, {$data->display_name}.<br />";
}

?>
```

get_currentuserinfo

The get_currentuserinfo() function is similar to the function from the previous section. wp_get_current_user() actually calls it to get the user's information. The big difference between the two functions is that get_currentuserinfo() doesn't return a variable. It sets a global variable of $current_user instead.

In most scenarios, the wp_get_current_user() function is preferable. However, both functions are pluggable (you can create your own versions of the functions), so this needs to be taken into consideration when building plugins that do overwrite the functions.

Following is the code you can use to display the current user's registration date. Create a new plugin file named boj-user-registration-date.php and use the code to display the user's registration date for the site in the admin footer.

```php
<?php
/*
Plugin Name: User Registration Date
Plugin URI: http://example.com
Description: Displays user's registration date in admin footer.
Version: 0.1
Author: WROX
Author URI: http://wrox.com
*/

/* Display user registration date in the admin footer. */
```

```
add_action( 'in_admin_footer', 'boj_display_user_registration_date' );

function boj_display_user_registration_date() {

    /* Globalize the $current_user variable. */
    global $current_user;

    /* Call the current user function. */
    get_currentuserinfo();

    /* Format user registration date. */
    $date = mysql2date( 'F j, Y', $current_user->user_registered );

    /* Display the user's registration date. */
    echo "You registered on {$date}.<br />";
}

?>
```

Code snippet boj-user-registration-date.php

count_user_posts

If you need to count the number of posts a user has written, use the `count_user_posts()` function. This function counts only the number of posts of the "post" post type. For example, it doesn't count the number of pages or entries of custom post types. It takes in a single parameter of `$user_id`, which is the ID of the user you'd like to count the posts of.

Suppose you have a rating system for users depending on the number of posts each user has written. You want to give a user a "silver" rating for writing 25 posts or a "gold" rating for writing 50 posts. To do this, you only need to execute the code when a post is saved. Create a new plugin file called `boj-user-ratings.php` and use the following code to update the logged-in user's rating. Remember, the user's rating is saved as user meta only when a post is saved. (See the section on user metadata for details on how to handle metadata.)

```
<?php
/*
Plugin Name: User Ratings
Plugin URI: http://example.com
Description: Updates user rating based on number of posts.
Version: 0.1
Author: WROX
Author URI: http://wrox.com
*/

/* Only update the user rating when a post is saved. */
add_action( 'save_post', 'boj_add_user_rating' );

function boj_add_user_rating() {

    /* Get the current user. */
```

```php
$user = wp_get_current_user();

/* Get the current user rating. */
$rating = get_user_meta( $user->ID, 'user_rating', true );

/* If user already has 'gold' rating, do nothing. */
if ( 'gold' == $rating )
    return;

/* Get the user's post count. */
$posts = count_user_posts( $user->ID );

/* Check if the number of posts is equal to or greater than 50. */
if ( 50 <= $posts ) {

    /* Give the user a 'gold' rating. */
    update_user_meta( $user->ID, 'user_rating', 'gold' );
}

/* Check if the number of posts is equal to or greater than 25. */
elseif ( 25 <= $posts ) {

    /* Give the user a 'silver' rating. */
    update_user_meta( $user->ID, 'user_rating', 'silver' );
}
}

?>
```

Code snippet boj-user-ratings.php

count_many_users_posts

Sometimes you may want to count the number of posts for multiple users rather than a single user. Any time you need post counts from multiple users, you should use this function instead of using the count_user_posts() function multiple times so that you're not querying the database multiple times.

The count_many_users_posts() function accepts a single parameter of $users, which should be an array of user IDs. It returns an array with the user IDs as the array keys and the post counts as the array values.

In this next example, you create a function that accepts an array of user IDs and lists the number of posts each user has written.

```php
<?php

function boj_list_users_posts_counts( $user_ids = array() ) {

    /* Make sure user IDs were given. */
    if ( empty( $user_ids ) )
```

```php
        return '';

    /* Get the post counts for the users. */
    $users_counts = count_many_users_posts( $user_ids );

    /* Open an unordered list. */
    echo '<ul class="users-posts-counts">';

    /* Loop through each of the user counts. */
    foreach ( $users_counts as $user => $count ) {

        /* Display a message with user ID and post count. */
        echo "<li>The user with an ID of {$user} has {$count} posts.</li>";
    }

    /* Close the unordered list. */
    echo '</ul>';
}

?>
```

A plugin user can use this code to display a formatted list of post counts for the users of their choosing. Suppose the plugin user wanted to list the post counts for users with the IDs of 100, 200, and 300. They'd need to only input those user IDs into the function call as shown in the following code.

```php
<?php boj_list_users_posts_counts( array( 100, 200, 300 ) ); ?>
```

User Metadata

User metadata is data about the user that is saved in the `$wpdb->usermeta` table in the database. This is additional data that plugins can add about the user outside of the predefined WordPress fields in the `$wpdb->users` table.

This type of data can be anything you need to develop user-based settings for your plugin. This data is saved in key/value pairs; however, a single key may have multiple values. Meta keys are a way to represent the information provided by the meta values. Think of them as a human-readable ID that represents the information you're working with. Meta values are the pieces of data you retrieved based on the given meta key.

Metadata can literally be any type of data you want to save for the user. Some examples include the following:

➤ Twitter or Facebook account

➤ Location (country, city, state)

➤ Phone number

➤ Favorite book

➤ Personal settings for the site

➤ Private membership information

Keep in mind that when saving sensitive information about users, you should make sure this data is not publicly displayed by your plugin.

This section focuses on adding, displaying, updating, and deleting specific data for a user. This can enable you to see how the user meta functions work when manipulating data.

You work with a user ID of 100 and a meta key of favorite_books. This meta key saves the values of the user's three favorite books.

add_user_meta

To add new user metadata, use the add_user_meta() function. This function returns true when the data is successfully entered into the database and false when it fails.

```php
<?php
add_user_meta( $user_id, $meta_key, $meta_value, $unique );
?>
```

➤ $user_id — The ID of the user to add metadata to.

➤ $meta_key — The metadata key in the database.

➤ $meta_value — A single value to add to pair with $meta_key.

➤ $unique — Whether the function should force a single row (true) in the usermeta table or create multiple rows for multiple meta values (false). This defaults to false.

Now, you give three favorite books to a user with the ID of 100. These book titles are *WordPress Dev Champ*, *WordPress Lazy Coder*, and *WordPress The Hard Way*.

```php
<?php

add_user_meta( 100, 'favorite_books', 'WordPress Dev Champ', false );
add_user_meta( 100, 'favorite_books', 'WordPress Lazy Coder', false );
add_user_meta( 100, 'favorite_books', 'WordPress The Hard Way', false );

?>
```

The $unique parameter is set to false. This must be false to set multiple values for the same meta key, favorite_books. You would set this to true if the meta value should be a single value.

get_user_meta

Now that you've learned how to add custom user metadata, you might want to display it. The get_user_meta() function pulls the meta from the database based on the user ID and meta key.

```php
<?php
get_user_meta( $user_id, $meta_key, $single );
?>
```

➤   `$user_id` — The ID of the user to get the metadata for.

➤   `$meta_key` — The metadata key to get the metadata value(s) for.

➤   `$single` — Whether to return an array of meta values (`false`) or a single value (`true`). This defaults to `false`.

To display a list of the user's favorite books that you added with the `add_user_meta()` function, use the following code.

```php
<?php

/* Get the user's favorite books. */
$favorite_books = get_user_meta( 100, 'favorite_books', false );

/* Check if there are any favorite books. */
if ( !empty( $favorite_books ) ) {

    /* Open an unordered list. */
    echo '<ul class="favorite-books">';

    /* Loop through each of the books. */
    foreach ( $favorite_books as $book ) {

        /* Display the book name. */
        echo '<li>' . $book . '</li>';
    }
}

?>
```

If the `favorite_books` meta key had only a single meta value instead of multiple values, you wouldn't need to loop through an array. You could simply print the return value to the screen.

```php
<?php

/* Get the user's favorite book (single book). */
$favorite_book = get_user_meta( 100, 'favorite_books', true );

/* Display the favorite book. */
echo $favorite_book;

?>
```

update_user_meta

The `update_user_meta()` enables you to update a single meta value whether there is a single or multiple values. You can also completely overwrite all of the meta values if the meta key has multiple values. This function can also be used to insert new metadata if it doesn't already exist for the user.

```php
<?php
update_user_meta( $user_id, $meta_key, $meta_value, $prev_value );
?>
```

➤ `$user_id` — The ID of the user you want to get metadata for.

➤ `$meta_key` — The metadata key to update meta values for.

➤ `$meta_value` — The new value for the meta key.

➤ `$prev_value` — The previous meta value to overwrite. If this is not set, all meta values will be overwritten with the single, new `$meta_value` parameter.

Suppose you want to change one of the user's favorite books, *WordPress Dev Champ*, to a new book, *WordPress Design Champ*. You need to set the `$meta_value` parameter to the new book name and the `$prev_value` parameter to the old book name.

```php
<?php

update_user_meta(
    100,
    'favorite_books',
    'WordPress Design Champ',
    'WordPress Dev Champ'
);

?>
```

If you want to overwrite all the favorite books with a single book, you can pass the `$meta_value` parameter and leave the `$prev_value` parameter empty.

```php
<?php

update_user_meta( 100, 'favorite_books', 'WordPress Design Champ' );

?>
```

delete_user_meta

The `delete_user_meta()` function enables you to delete all the meta values and meta key or a single meta value for a given meta key.

```php
<?php
delete_user_meta( $user_id, $meta_key, $meta_value = '' );
?>
```

➤ `$user_id` — The ID of the user to delete metadata for.

➤ `$meta_key` — The meta key to delete or the meta key to delete meta value(s) for.

➤ `$meta_value` — The specific meta value to delete. If this is left empty, all meta values and the meta key will be deleted for the user.

If you want to delete a single book from the user's list of favorite books, you need to set the `$meta_value` parameter to the name of the book. With the following code, you delete the *WordPress Lazy Coder* book from the user's favorite books.

```php
<?php

delete_user_meta( 100, 'favorite_books', 'WordPress Lazy Coder' );

?>
```

If you want to delete all the user's favorite books, leave the `$meta_value` parameter empty.

```php
<?php

delete_user_meta( 100, 'favorite_books' );

?>
```

user_contactmethods

user_contactmethods is a hook (Chapter 3, "Hooks"), not a function like what this chapter has focused on. It is important because it's a quick method for adding user metadata for alternative contact methods such as a Twitter username, Facebook profile, or phone numbers.

It enables you to create additional fields on the user edit screen with a few lines of code. By default, WordPress adds five methods. The last three are metadata as covered in this section of the chapter:

➤ Email

➤ Website

➤ AIM

➤ Yahoo IM

➤ Jabber/Google Talk

The user_contactmethods filter hook returns an array of meta keys and labels for these label keys. To add new meta keys, you need to add new values to the array, as shown in the next code.

Available for download on Wrox.com

```php
<?php
/*
Plugin Name: User Contact Methods
Plugin URI: http://example.com
Description: Additional user contact methods.
Author: WROX
Author URI: http://wrox.com
*/

/* Add a filter to the hook. */
add_filter( 'user_contactmethods', 'boj_user_contactmethods' );

/* Function for adding new contact methods. */
function boj_user_contactmethods( $user_contactmethods ) {

    /* Add the Twitter contact method. */
    $user_contactmethods['twitter'] = 'Twitter Username';

    /* Add the phone number contact method. */
```

```
        $user_contactmethods['phone'] = 'Phone Number';

        /* Return the array with the new values added. */
        return $user_contactmethods;
    }

    ?>
```

Code snippet boj-user-contact-methods.php

This adds the extra fields to the contact info section of the user profile screen, as shown in Figure 8-1.

Contact Info

E-mail *(required)*	example@example.com
Website	http://example.com
AIM	example
Yahoo IM	example
Jabber / Google Talk	example
Twitter Username	example
Phone Number	555-555-5555

FIGURE 8-1

WordPress handles all the heavy lifting of adding, updating, and deleting the metadata in the admin. To retrieve these values, use the `get_user_meta()` function covered earlier in this section.

Creating a Plugin with User Metadata

Now that you've learned how to manipulate user metadata, it's time to use that knowledge for a practical test. In many cases, custom user metadata your plugin might use needs to be set by the user from the user's profile page.

What you will do is build a plugin that adds an extra section to the user edit screen in the WordPress admin. This form will have a select box of the site's blog posts. The users can select one of these posts as their favorite.

The first step would be to create a new file in your plugin directory with a filename `boj-user-favorite-post.php`. You would then need to create the plugin header and add the form to the user edit page.

```
<?php
/*
Plugin Name: User Favorite Post
Plugin URI: http://example.com
Description: Allows users to select their favorite post from the site.
Version: 0.1
```

```
Author: WROX
Author URI: http://wrox.com
*/

/* Add the post form to the user/profile edit page in the admin. */
add_action( 'show_user_profile', 'boj_user_favorite_post_form' );
add_action( 'edit_user_profile', 'boj_user_favorite_post_form' );

/* Function for displaying an extra form on the user edit page. */
function boj_user_favorite_post_form( $user ) {

    /* Get the current user's favorite post. */
    $favorite_post = get_user_meta( $user->ID, 'favorite_post', true );

    /* Get a list of all the posts. */
    $posts = get_posts( array( 'numberposts' => -1 ) );
?>

<h3>Favorites</h3>

<table class="form-table">

    <tr>
        <th><label for="favorite_post">Favorite Post</label></th>

        <td>
            <select name="favorite_post" id="favorite_post">
                <option value=""></option>

            <?php foreach ( $posts as $post ) { ?>
                <option value="<?php echo esc_attr( $post->ID ); ?>"
                <?php selected( $favorite_post, $post->ID ); ?>>
                    <?php echo esc_html( $post->post_title ); ?>
                </option>
            <?php } ?>

            </select>
            <br />
            <span class="description">Select your favorite post.</span>
        </td>
    </tr>

</table>
<?php }
```

Code snippet boj-user-favorite-post.php

This gives you an extra section on the user edit page, as shown in Figure 8-2.

The form is only displayed at this point. The next step would be to save the user's favorite post as metadata.

FIGURE 8-2

```php
/* Add the update function to the user update hooks. */
add_action( 'personal_options_update', 'boj_user_favorite_post_update' );
add_action( 'edit_user_profile_update', 'boj_user_favorite_post_update' );

/* Function for updating the user's favorite post. */
function boj_user_favorite_post_update( $user_id ) {

    /* Check if the current user has permission to edit the user. */
    if ( !current_user_can( 'edit_user', $user_id ) )
        return false;

    /* Only accept numbers 0-9 since it's a post ID. */
    $favorite_post = preg_replace( "/[^0-9]/", '', $_POST['favorite_post'] );

    /* Update the user's favorite post. */
    update_user_meta( $user_id, 'favorite_post', $favorite_post );
}

?>
```

Code snippet boj-user-favorite-post.php

The plugin is complete at this point. However, this information is saved only in the database and shown on the user's profile screen in the admin. If you want to show the user's favorite post, you need to use the `get_user_meta()` function to pull the information from the database.

With the following code, you get the favorite post selected by a user with the ID of 100 and display its title. Because the post ID is the saved meta value, you need to use the `get_post()` function to retrieve additional information about the post, such as the post title.

```php
<?php

/* Get the user's favorite post (ID). */
$favorite_post = get_user_meta( 100, 'favorite_post', true );

/* Check if the favorite post is set. */
if ( !empty( $favorite_post ) ) {

    /* Get the post object based on the post ID. */
    $post = get_post( $favorite_post );

    /* Display the post title. */
    echo $post->post_title;
}

?>
```

ROLES AND CAPABILITIES

WordPress provides a flexible user system as you've seen in the previous half of this chapter. However, this system represents data about individual users. Alone, it doesn't define what a user can do within the site. For that, WordPress has a roles and capabilities system, which enables complete control over what permissions users have.

Roles are what define users in the WordPress system. More precisely, they grant users a set of permissions called capabilities.

What Are Roles and Capabilities?

Roles are what users are grouped by in WordPress. They're a way of giving a label to various sets of users. One of the most important things to note is that roles are not hierarchical. For example, an administrator is not necessarily "higher" than an editor. Roles are merely defined by what the role can and can't do. It's a permissions system.

Capabilities are that permissions system. Roles are assigned capabilities that define what that role can or can't do. These can be set up with the WordPress defaults or be completely custom, depending on the site. As a plugin developer, you can't make too many assumptions about what certain roles have permission to do.

Imagine having to define what individual users could do on a site with thousands of users, each user having a custom set of permissions. It'd be nearly impossible to maintain. Roles enable you to group users into distinguishable sets, each group with its own permissions.

Understanding how users, roles, and capabilities work and their relationship to one another is an important aspect of plugin development.

> ➤ **Users** are registered accounts on a site. Each user's role determines what the user can do on a site.

> ➤ **Roles** are sets of capabilities assigned to users. Multiple roles may be given to users, although this is not evident in the WordPress interface.

> ➤ **Capabilities** are the permissions for roles, which are extended to the users of that role.

In general, most plugins won't need to know what roles users have. Most plugins work directly with capabilities because they are what define whether a user has permission to perform a task within the site.

 A common mistake many plugin authors make is to check a user's role before executing code. There is rarely a good reason to do this. Your plugin should check for a capability because capabilities determine a user's permission to do something on the site.

Default Roles

WordPress ships with five default roles, which work well for most installs. Although roles are not hierarchical, the default roles do set up what appears to be a hierarchical system.

> ➤ **Administrator** — Has control over everything on the site

> ➤ **Editor** — Has publishing permission and editing access over everyone's posts

> ➤ **Author** — Has publishing access and can edit its own posts but doesn't have control over others' content

> ➤ **Contributor** — Can submit posts but not publish them

> ➤ **Subscriber** — Enables access to edit its user profile and the WordPress dashboard

This list is a general overview of the default roles. Even though these are the defaults, plugin users can install role management plugins that enable them to change what each role can do.

You should note the context in which the term "author" is used because it might refer to either the default author role or a post author. It's usually not an issue, but it is one those WordPress quirks you have to learn to live with.

Custom Roles

WordPress allows custom roles, which can be created by plugins and themes. There is no user interface in WordPress for creating custom roles; however, several role management plugins exist that enable users to create new roles for their site.

Therefore, as a plugin developer, you can never know exactly what roles exist or might exist for a site unless you have direct access to the install, such as when doing client work. Keep this in mind when developing your plugins.

You may be faced with the task of creating custom roles in your plugins as well. Imagine that you were creating a plugin that implemented a forum within a WordPress install. Because WordPress wouldn't know how to manage a forum, you would have to define these custom roles within your plugin. Some example roles for a forum might include the following:

➤ Forum Administrator

➤ Forum Moderator

➤ Forum Member

➤ Forum Suspended

See the "Customizing Roles" section later in this chapter for more details on creating custom roles.

LIMITING ACCESS

"Limiting access" is a way to describe the process of working with WordPress capabilities to see if a user has permission to access something or perform a specific task within a WordPress install.

By default, most access in WordPress is restricted within the admin. The admin can expose potentially vital information about a site, so making sure only users with the correct permissions have access to particular parts of it is important. WordPress can handle this when it needs to. Security issues arise when your plugin doesn't take into account a user's capabilities.

WordPress has two types of capabilities:

➤ **Role capabilities** — Added to individual roles, which are extended to the role's users

➤ **Meta capabilities** — Based on a specific object (user, post, link, and so on)

A good way to differentiate between the two is to consider this example. User A has the `edit_posts` capability (given to his role). This capability enables the user to edit posts. However, this user shouldn't be able to edit User B's posts based on that capability. That's where meta capabilities come into play. If User A is trying to edit User B's post, the `edit_post` meta capability is called, but it's not the actual capability checked for. The `map_meta_cap()` function in WordPress decides whether the user can edit the post by returning an array of role capabilities to check against based on the user and post.

When adding settings pages for your plugin, you input a capability. However, WordPress handles the capability checks for you, so you don't need to worry about limiting access to those pages with custom code. See Chapter 7, "Plugin Settings," for more information on adding settings pages.

This chapter reviews only a few of the possible capabilities. For an in-depth list of the available capabilities, reference the Roles and Capabilities page on the WordPress Codex: http://codex.wordpress.org/Roles_and_Capabilities.

Checking User Permissions

When you check a user's permissions, you're checking if a user's role has been granted a specific capability or if the user is given a meta capability for a specific object. Plugins won't need to deal with meta capabilities in most cases, but there are instances in which meta capabilities are needed.

current_user_can

The `current_user_can()` function enables you to check if the currently logged-in user has permission to perform a given capability. If the user has permission, the function returns `true`. If the user is not logged in or doesn't have permission, it returns `false`.

```php
<?php
current_user_can( $capability, $args );
?>
```

➤ `$capability` — A single capability to check against a user's role.

➤ `$args` — Extra argument that's usually an object ID (like a post ID) when checking if the user has a meta capability.

You will most likely use this function when checking for permissions within your plugin. You can use it to check for default WordPress capabilities or custom capabilities implemented by your plugin.

Suppose you wanted to check if a user has permission to edit posts before creating a link to the posts page in the admin on the front end of the site. You would use the `current_user_can()` function and the `edit_posts` capability.

```php
<?php

/* Check if the current user can edit posts. */
if ( current_user_can( 'edit_posts' ) ) {

    /* Link to the edit posts page in the admin. */
    echo '<a href="' . admin_url( 'edit.php' ) . '">Edit Posts</a>';
}

?>
```

If you want to check for a meta capability, you would use the same technique. However, you need to insert the second parameter of the object ID into the current_user_can() function. For example, suppose you want to save some post metadata for a post with the ID of 100 but need to check if the user can edit the post before updating the metadata (see Chapter 11, "Extending Posts").

```php
<?php

/* Check if the current user can edit the specific post. */
if ( current_user_can( 'edit_post', 100 ) {

    /* Update the post meta. */
    update_post_meta( 100, 'boj_example_meta', 'Example' );
}

?>
```

 Your plugin shouldn't check for permissions based on role. Remember, roles are not hierarchical, so you cannot assume a role has permission to perform a specific task. Always check for permission by capability.

current_user_can_for_blog

This function is specifically for use with multisite installations. It works almost exactly the same as current_user_can() with the added expectation of the blog ID parameter.

```php
<?php
current_user_can_for_blog( $blog_id, $capability );
?>
```

➤ $blog_id — The ID of the blog in the multisite install to check the capability against

➤ $capability — The capability to check if the user has, for the given blog ID

You can learn more about working within a multisite environment in Chapter 15, "Multisite."

author_can

The `author_can()` function works similarly to `current_user_can()` function. It enables you to check if a post author (not the author role) can perform a specific task based on the capability for a given post. This function checks for the author of the post. It does not extend to other users.

```php
<?php
author_can( $post, $capability );
?>
```

➤ `$post` — A post object or the ID of a post

➤ `$capability` — The capability to check against the author of the post

In most scenarios, you would use the `current_user_can()` function. However, this function has its place and should be used when you want to specifically check if the post author has permission to perform a specific task.

With this next code, you can check if the author of a post with the ID of `100` has permission to publish posts and display a message depending on the result.

```php
<?php

/* Check if the post author can publish posts. */
if ( author_can( 100, 'publish_posts' ) ) {

    /* Display a message. */
    echo 'The author of this post has publishing access.';
}

/* If the author can't publish posts. */
else {

    /* Display a message. */
    echo 'The author of this post cannot publish this post.';
}

?>
```

This can be a useful function if you want to build a notification system for editors or administrators of the site to let them know when a post has been written but not published. That way, users with the `publish_posts` capability could come in and press the Publish button.

user_can

The `user_can()` function works similarly to the previous functions. The difference is that you can check if any user on the WordPress install has a specific capability.

```php
<?php
user_can( $user, $capability );
?>
```

➤ $user_id — A user ID or object to check the capability for

➤ $capability — A capability to check against the given user

You use this function when you only need to check for a capability against a specific user rather than the currently logged-in user or the author of a post. It returns true if the user has the capability and false if not.

map_meta_cap

The map_meta_cap filter hook is applied to the return value of the map_meta_cap() function, which is a function that maps role capabilities to the meta capability of a given object. For example, it's called when current_user_can() is used to check a meta capability. The function returns an array of role capabilities the user's role must have based on the meta capability and object.

To simplify that description, imagine that you're checking if a specific user can edit a specific post. The map_meta_cap() function determines this for you. However, plugins have the option of overwriting this using the map_meta_cap filter hook.

```
<?php
apply_filters( 'map_meta_cap', $caps, $cap, $user_id, $args );
?>
```

➤ $caps — Array of capabilities the user must have. The user must have each of the capabilities in the array for the current_user_can() function to return true.

➤ $cap — The meta capability to check if the user can perform the given check.

➤ $user_id — The user's ID to check the capabilities against.

➤ $args — Array of additional arguments passed to the map_meta_cap() function. Generally, the object ID will be the first argument in the array.

Imagine you want to create a plugin that restricted other users from editing or deleting an admin's blog posts. Remember, because roles are not hierarchical, any user with the edit_others_posts capability can edit the admin's posts, or any user with the delete_others_posts capability can delete them.

You're going to create a plugin that limits the editing of admin posts to only users that are admins by checking for an admin-related capability: delete_users. Therefore, a user with the edit_others_posts capability cannot edit admin posts, and a user with the delete_others_posts cannot delete admin posts.

You're overwriting the default WordPress functionality to present more of a hierarchical-type role system by doing this.

```
<?php
/*
Plugin Name: Restrict Admin Post Editing
Plugin URI: http://example.com
Description: Only admins can edit posts made by admins.
Version: 0.1
```

```
Author: WROX
Author URI: http://wrox.com
*/

/* Filter the 'map_meta_cap' hook. */
add_filter( 'map_meta_cap', 'boj_restrict_admin_post_editing', 10, 4 );

/* Function for restricting users from editing admin posts. */
function boj_restrict_admin_post_editing( $caps, $cap, $user_id, $args ) {

    /* If user is trying to edit or delete a post. */
    if ( 'edit_post' == $cap || 'delete_post' == $cap ) {

        /* Get the post object. */
        $post = get_post( $args[0] );

        /* If an admin is the post author. */
        if ( author_can( $post, 'delete_users' ) ) {

            /* Add a capability that only admins might have to the caps array. */
            $caps[] = 'delete_users';
        }
    }

    /* Return the array of capabilities. */
    return $caps;
}

?>
```

Code snippet boj-restrict-admin-post-editing.php

Ideally, if you were creating a plugin that made a hierarchical system like this, you'd create custom capabilities and check for those. Custom capabilities are outlined later in this chapter.

Is the User an Admin?

Sometimes, your plugin might need to check if a user is an admin on the site. This can be confusing as a plugin developer because roles are not hierarchical. Remember, users with the "administrator" role are not always in full control of the site. However, they will be in most cases.

Generally, you wouldn't check whether a user is an admin. It's nearly always better to check for a capability based on the specific task the user might be performing.

Determining admin status can be dangerous territory without understanding how roles and capabilities work because there is no single capability that defines a user as an admin. WordPress does provide a function for checking if a user is an admin, but it should be used only if a specific capability isn't evident.

is_super_admin

The is_super_admin() function was added as part of the multisite package of features, but it works great for single-site installs of WordPress as well. It gives an accurate view of who is an admin on the site.

The function accepts a single parameter of $user_id, which is the ID of the user you want to check admin status for. It returns `true` if the user is an admin or `false` if the user is not an admin.

`is_super_admin()` works a bit differently for multisite installs and single-site installs. A super admin in a multisite setup has full control over the site. You can read more about how super admins work within a multisite environment in Chapter 15.

On single-site installations, the `is_super_admin()` function checks if the current user has the `delete_users` capability because it's a capability that would essentially give the user the most power on the site. This could just as easily be done with the `current_user_can()` function. It almost seems silly to check if someone is an admin by checking if they have the `delete_users` capability, especially if the task to be performed has nothing to do with deleting users.

Suppose your plugin needed to check if a user with the ID of `100` was an admin before performing a specific task. You would use the following code to handle that check.

```php
<?php

/* Check if the user is an admin. */
if ( is_super_admin( 100 ) ) {

    /* Display a message. */
    echo 'User 100 is an admin. */
}

?>
```

 Keep in mind that being an admin and having the administrator role is not the same thing in some custom setups.

Allowing Custom Permissions

WordPress ships with many default capabilities that extend all the control average users will ever need. Most plugins will never need custom capabilities. However, some plugins may want to use custom capabilities to control permissions related to their functionality.

Suppose you want to create a plugin that allows users to create private sections of content within their posts with a simple shortcode (see Chapter 10, "The Shortcode API"). You would need to create a custom capability to control who could see that particular content and use the `current_user_can()` function to check for that capability.

```php
<?php
/*
Plugin Name: Private Content
Plugin URI: http://example.com
Description: Shortcode for hiding private content.
Version: 0.1
```

```
Author: WROX
Author URI: http://wrox.com
*/

/* Register shortcodes in 'init'. */
add_action( 'init', 'boj_private_content_register_shortcodes' );

/* Function for registering the shortcode. */
function boj_private_content_register_shortcodes() {

    /* Adds the [boj-private] shortcode. */
    add_shortcode( 'boj-private', 'boj_private_content_shortcode' );
}

/* Function for handling shortcode output. */
function boj_private_content_shortcode( $attr, $content = null ) {

    /* If there is no content, return. */
    if ( is_null( $content ) )
        return $content;

    /* Check if the current user has the 'read_private_content' capability. */
    if ( current_user_can( 'read_private_content' ) ) {

        /* Return the private content. */
        return $content;
    }


    /* Return an empty string as a fallback. */
    return '';
}

?>
```

Code snippet boj-private-content.php

Post authors can then hide content using the `[boj-private]` shortcode within the post editor. For example, a post author might hide content as shown here.

```
[boj-private]
You can only see this content if you have permission to see it.
[/boj-private]
```

When creating this plugin, you may have noticed that no user has permission to read the content. This is because no roles have been assigned the capability of `read_private_content`. To assign this capability to a role, a user would need to install a role management plugin, or your plugin would need to assign the capability upon activation.

See the later section, "Adding Capabilities to a Role," for information on how to assign capabilities to roles.

CUSTOMIZING ROLES

WordPress roles are flexible, and plugins can bend them in any way that suits their purposes. This section covers customizing roles, creating new roles, and adding capabilities to new or existing roles.

You need to know that any changes you make to roles are saved in the database. If your plugin makes a change, this change won't undo itself when it's deactivated. Your plugin should remove custom capabilities that it has added and remove any roles it adds if no users are assigned to that role.

Creating a Role

WordPress enables the creation of custom roles by plugins. The best time to create a new role for your plugin is on the activation hook for your plugin (see Chapter 2, "Plugin Foundation"). Role creation needs to be done only once, so this is a good hook to use because it's fired only when your plugin is activated.

add_role

The `add_role()` function enables plugin developers to easily add new roles. The function returns a role object if a new role was successfully added and `null` if the role already exists.

```php
<?php
add_role( $role, $display_name, $capabilities );
?>
```

➤ `$role` — The name of the role to add. This should act as a key and contain only alphanumeric characters or underscores.

➤ `$display_name` — The label for the role. This is the name used for the role in public-facing areas.

➤ `$capabilities` — An array of capabilities to assign to the role. Capabilities can also be added or removed later.

Now go back to the previous forum example from the "Custom Roles" section. The section outlined four roles that a forum plugin might define.

➤ Forum Administrator

➤ Forum Moderator

➤ Forum Member

➤ Forum Suspended

In the next code, you create these roles and give each a basic capability of `read`, which enables the user to see only their profile and the dashboard in the admin.

```php
<?php

/* Create the forum administrator role. */
```

```
add_role( 'forum_administrator', 'Forum Administrator', array( 'read' ) );

/* Create the forum moderator role. */
add_role( 'forum_moderator', 'Forum Moderator', array( 'read' ) );

/* Create the forum member role. */
add_role( 'forum_member', 'Forum Member', array( 'read' ) );

/* Create the forum suspended role. */
add_role( 'forum_suspended', 'Forum Suspended', array( 'read' ) );

?>
```

Adding a new role can make it appear in the role selection box on the user profile page, as shown in Figure 8-3, and on the Users screen in the admin.

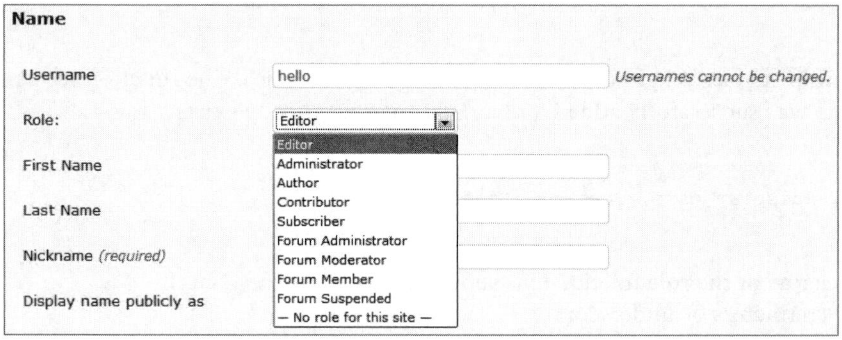

FIGURE 8-3

Deleting a Role

Deleting a role is as simple as adding a new role by using the correct WordPress function. However, if your plugin needs to delete a role, it should check that no users on the site have the given role before deleting it. Otherwise, you might potentially break the plugin user's custom setup.

The best time to delete a role is on the activation or deactivation hook for your plugin (see Chapter 2, "Plugin Foundation"). You need to delete a role only once, so these are good hooks to use because they're fired only when your plugin is activated or deactivated.

remove_role

The remove_role() function can remove a role from the list of saved roles in the database. It accepts a single parameter of $role, which is the name of the role (not the label or display name).

Suppose you wanted to delete the Forum Moderator role you created in the previous section. You need to set the $role parameter to forum_moderator.

```php
<?php

/* Remove the forum moderator role. */
remove_role( 'forum_moderator' );

?>
```

If you want to check if a user has the role before deleting it, you need to use the `get_users()` function outlined earlier. If the function doesn't return any users, delete the role. If it does, simply skip the role deletion.

```php
<?php

add_action( 'admin_init', 'boj_remove_forum_moderator' );

function boj_remove_forum_moderator() {

    /* Get at least one user with the forum moderator role. */
    $users = get_users( array( 'role' => 'forum_moderator', 'number' => 1 ) );

    /* Check if there are no forum moderators. */
    if ( empty( $users ) ) {

        /* Remove the forum moderator role. */
        remove_role( 'forum_moderator' );
    }
}

?>
```

For the purposes of this example, your code is executing on the `admin_init` hook, which WordPress executes on every admin page. In real-world use, it should be executing only once, most likely on a plugin deactivation hook. This is the hook you will use when creating your plugin in the "A Custom Role and Capability Plugin" section later.

Adding Capabilities to a Role

Like creating custom roles, you can create custom capabilities. You can also add WordPress capabilities to new or existing roles. A capability doesn't technically exist if it's not given to a role. Your plugin should add capabilities to a role only once. Most likely, it will run this code on the plugin activation hook (see Chapter 2, "Plugin Foundation").

get_role

To add a capability to a role, you must first get the role object, which requires the `get_role()` function. This function accepts a single parameter of `$role`, which is the name of the role. After you get the role object, you would use the `add_cap()` method to grant a capability to the role.

Suppose you want to grant the default WordPress Contributor role the ability to publish posts. Using this code, you can make the change.

```php
<?php

/* Get the contributor role. */
$role =& get_role( 'contributor' );

/* Check if the role exists. */
if ( !empty( $role ) ) {

    /* Add the 'publish_posts' capability to the role. */
    $role->add_cap( 'publish_posts' );
}

?>
```

Going back to the idea of a forum plugin and the custom roles you added in the previous section, you can easily use this method for adding extra capabilities to those roles. Suppose you want to give two custom capabilities to the forum administrator role called `publish_forum_topics` and `delete_forum_topics`.

```php
<?php

/* Get the forum administrator role. */
$role =& get_role( 'forum_administrator' );

/* Check if the role exists. */
if ( !empty( $role ) ) {

    /* Add the 'publish_forum_topics' capability to the role. */
    $role->add_cap( 'publish_forum_topics' );

    /* Add the 'delete_forum_topics' capability to the role. */
    $role->add_cap( 'delete_forum_topics' );
}

?>
```

Removing Capabilities from a Role

WordPress has you covered when it comes to deleting capabilities from a role. Any time you create a plugin that assigns custom capabilities for use with just your plugin, your plugin needs to clean up after itself and remove the capabilities it added. Your plugin should remove capabilities from a role only once instead of on every page load. Most likely, it will run this code on the plugin activation or deactivation hook (see Chapter 2, "Plugin Foundation").

Like with adding capabilities, you must first get the role you want to remove capabilities from using the `get_role()` function. The difference is that you would use the `remove_cap()` method for removing the capability from the role.

In the previous section, you added the `publish_posts` capability to the contributor role. In your plugin's uninstall method or on its deactivation hook (See Chapter 2, "Plugin Foundation"), you would remove this capability.

```php
<?php

/* Get the contributor role. */
$role =& get_role( 'contributor' );

/* Check if the role exists. */
if ( !empty( $role ) ) {

    /* Remove the 'publish_posts' capability to the role. */
    $role->remove_cap( 'publish_posts' );
}

?>
```

A Custom Role and Capability Plugin

Now that you've learned how to create custom roles and capabilities, it's time to put this knowledge to the test. In this section, you create a plugin that puts it all together.

The forum plugin you've been keeping in mind throughout the roles section of this chapter will be your starting point. Before starting with code, you need to outline what capabilities each role should have. Because capabilities handle permissions, you need to define what each capability should do. Let's outline four fictional capabilities a forum plugin might have. (A real forum plugin would likely have many more.)

➤ `publish_forum_topics` — Permission to publish new forum topics

➤ `edit_others_forum_topics` — Permission to edit other users' forum topics

➤ `delete_forum_topics` — Permission to delete forum topics

➤ `read_forum_topics` — Permission to read forum topics

After you outline your capabilities, focus on which roles should have each capability. Use the four custom roles outlined earlier and the default WordPress administrator role.

➤ **Administrator** — Default WordPress administrator role should have all the capabilities for the forum.

➤ **Forum Administrator** — Should have all the capabilities and full control over the forum.

➤ **Forum Moderator** — Should have the `publish_forum_topics`, `edit_others_forum_topics`, and `read_forum_topics` capabilities.

➤ **Forum Member** — Should have the `publish_forum_topics` and `read_forum_topics` capabilities.

➤ **Forum Suspended** — Because these users are suspended, they should have only the `read_forum_topics` capability.

You create a forum administrator role because the plugin users might want to assign forum administrators outside of their normal administrator role and not grant full access to the site to those users.

Now that you've outlined the roles and capabilities needed for your plugin, you can start building it.

```php
<?php
/*
Plugin Name: Forum Roles
Plugin URI: http://example.com
Description: Creates custom roles and capabilities for a fictional forum plugin.
Version: 0.1
Author: WROX
Author URI: http://wrox.com
*/

/* Custom forum roles and capabilities class. */
class BOJ_Forum_Roles {

    /* PHP4 Constructor method. */
    function BOJ_Forum_Roles() {

        /* Register plugin activation hook. */
        register_activation_hook( __FILE__, array( &$this, 'activation' ) );

        /* Register plugin deactivation hook. */
        register_deactivation_hook( __FILE__, array( &$this, 'deactivation' ) );
    }

    /* Plugin activation method. */
    function activation() {

        /* Get the default administrator role. */
        $role =& get_role( 'administrator' );

        /* Add forum capabilities to the administrator role. */
        if ( !empty( $role ) ) {
            $role->add_cap( 'publish_forum_topics' );
            $role->add_cap( 'edit_others_forum_topics' );
            $role->add_cap( 'delete_forum_topics' );
            $role->add_cap( 'read_forum_topics' );
        }

        /* Create the forum administrator role. */
        add_role(
            'forum_administrator',
            'Forum Administrator',
            array(
                'publish_forum_topics',
                'edit_others_forum_topics',
                'delete_forum_topics',
                'read_forum_topics'
            )
        );

        /* Create the forum moderator role. */
```

```php
    add_role(
        'forum_moderator',
        'Forum Moderator',
        array(
            'publish_forum_topics',
            'edit_others_forum_topics',
            'read_forum_topics'
        )
    );

    /* Create the forum member role. */
    add_role(
        'forum_member',
        'Forum Member',
        array(
            'publish_forum_topics',
            'read_forum_topics'
        )
    );

    /* Create the forum suspended role. */
    add_role(
        'forum_suspended',
        'Forum Suspended',
        array( 'read_forum_topics' )
    );
}

/* Plugin deactivation method. */
function deactivation() {

    /* Get the default administrator role. */
    $role =& get_role( 'administrator' );

    /* Remove forum capabilities to the administrator role. */
    if ( !empty( $role ) ) {
        $role->remove_cap( 'publish_forum_topics' );
        $role->remove_cap( 'edit_others_forum_topics' );
        $role->remove_cap( 'delete_forum_topics' );
        $role->remove_cap( 'read_forum_topics' );
    }

    /* Set up an array of roles to delete. */
    $roles_to_delete = array(
        'forum_administrator',
        'forum_moderator',
        'forum_member',
        'forum_suspended'
    );

    /* Loop through each role, deleting the role if necessary. */
    foreach ( $roles_to_delete as $role ) {

        /* Get the users of the role. */
```

```
            $users = get_users( array( 'role' => $role ) );

            /* Check if there are no users for the role. */
            if ( count( $users ) <= 0 ) {

                /* Remove the role from the site. */
                remove_role( $role );
            }
        }
    }
}

$forum_roles = new BOJ_Forum_Roles();

?>
```

Code snippet boj-forum-roles.php

This plugin can make the four extra roles you created available on the Users screen in the admin, as shown in Figure 8-4. Your plugin users could add the users they want to these forum-type roles.

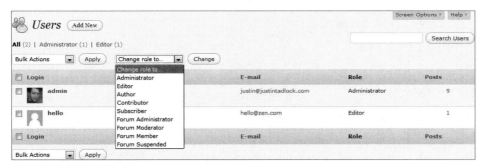

FIGURE 8-4

SUMMARY

The user, role, and capability systems in WordPress are powerful and flexible, enabling you to build any type of plugin to manipulate how these systems work. Each section in this chapter has briefly touched on possibilities. The best thing you can do as a plugin developer is set up a test install and create several fictional test users. Then, take what you've learned throughout this chapter and start coding.

If you take away anything from this chapter, you need to remember how the relationship of users, roles, and capabilities works. Capabilities control permissions. Roles are given capabilities. Users are assigned roles, and each role's capabilities are extended to its users. Keeping this in mind when developing your plugins can make the development process much smoother.

HTTP API

In the modern web, dubbed "2.0," Internet-based services communicate with each other: web-based readers gather data from blog feeds and Twitter accounts; personal web sites display Facebook badges or YouTube videos.

Your site should be no exception to this interoperability: In this chapter you learn how to make WordPress exchange information with remote services API and open it to a whole new level of perspective.

HTTP REQUESTS CRASH COURSE

This opening section explains what exactly an HTTP request is, what it can be used for, and why you will once again thank WordPress for lending a convenient hand and doing the cumbersome parts for you.

What Is an HTTP Request?

Hyper Text Transfer Protocol (HTTP) is the networking protocol that is no less than the foundation of data communication for the World Wide Web.

HTTP Request Concepts

Even if you cannot name or explain the following concepts yet, you have already experienced them in your everyday life online, using a web browser: HTTP is a request/response protocol in the client/server computing model.

➤ **Client/server** — An application (the client) talks to another application (the server) that itself can respond to many clients at the same time. In the HTTP model, a client is, for example, a web browser, such as Firefox running on your computer, and the server is a web server powered, for instance, by Apache, PHP, and MySQL and running WordPress. A client can also be a web indexing spider robot or a PHP script that fetches and parses a web page to retrieve information. You do this later in this chapter.

➤ **Request/response protocol** — The client submits an HTTP request (basically "Hello, I'm Firefox, please send me file example.html") and the server sends back a response ("Hello, I'm the Apache running PHP; here is the file, it is 4kb in size," followed by the file itself). Both requests contain potentially interesting information you learn to decipher and use.

Dissecting an HTTP Transaction

An HTTP transaction is a simple and clear text communication between the client and the server.

The Client Sends a Request

The client request typically consists of a few lines sent in clear text to the server. Using Firefox as a web browser and trying to load `http://example.com/file.html` from a Google result page would translate into the following query:

```
GET /file.html HTTP/1.1
Host: www.example.com
User-Agent: Mozilla/5.0 (Windows; U; Windows NT 5.0) Firefox/3.6
Referer: http://www.google.com/search?q=example.com
Cookie: lastvisit=235456684
```

The first line starts with GET: A GET session is how you tell the server you want to retrieve a document, here `file.html` from host `example.com`. Other main requests methods you can use are HEAD (to just receive the server response headers) and POST (to submit data to a form).

Notice also how information such as the referrer URL or the user agent string is also sent by the client. In Chapter 6, "Plugin Security," you read that these data should not be trusted: Indeed, in an example later, you learn how to forge these values to anything.

The Server Sends a Response

The server response consists of three parts: the headers, with information about the response, a blank line, and then the response body.

The headers are a few lines of information and can be something like this:

```
HTTP/1.1 200 OK
Date: Mon, 23 May 2012 22:38:34 GMT
Server: Apache/1.3.3.7 (Unix)  (Red-Hat/Linux)
```

```
Last-Modified: Wed, 08 Jan 2003 23:11:55 GMT
Set-Cookie: lastvisit=235456951
Content-Length: 438
Content-Type: text/html; charset=UTF-8
```

The first interesting information is the status code, here 200. Each server response should have a status code giving details on how the transaction was handled by the server: 200 means OK, 404 means not found. Table 9-1 lists the main HTTP status codes you can use.

TABLE 9-1: Main HTTP Status Codes

STATUS CODE	SIGNIFICATION
200	OK
301	Moved Permanently
302	Moved Temporarily
403	Forbidden
404	Not Found
500	Internal Server Error
503	Service Unavailable

Source: http://en.wikipedia.org/wiki/List_of_HTTP_status_codes

Of course, you don't have to memorize all these status codes, but with some experience you can quickly remember the main classes, as detailed in Table 9-2.

TABLE 9-2: HTTP Status Code Classes

STATUS CODE	SIGNIFICATION
2xx	Request was successful.
3xx	Request was redirected to another resource (like in the case of a URL shortener).
4xx	Request failed because of a client error (for instance, a wrong username/ password combination).
5xx	Request failed because of a server error (like a bad configuration or a broken script).

The server response also generally discloses information about the software running on the server, the content-type of the document it serves, and its length.

Possibilities for Crafting HTTP Requests

The first obvious use of HTTP requests is to retrieve a remote document or particular information within a remote document: a Twitter user's last message, the current value of share stock, or JSON encoded data from a remote API service.

You can also send information to a remote document, such as a form or an HTTP API, and modify data from a client script.

These requests would be done using either GET or POST methods, sometimes with credentials (a login and password or another authentication mechanism) or other parameters. You can make such requests later in this chapter.

Another interesting application, using HEAD requests, is to check the state of a remote document without bothering downloading its content. For instance, a broken link checker plugin could make sure your bookmarks in WordPress don't return a 404 header.

How to Make HTTP Requests in PHP

In basic PHP, without WordPress that is, there are several common ways to send HTTP requests. It is interesting to know the basics because you sometimes need to code a portion of code in a non-WordPress environment.

The following examples all do the same thing: send a GET request to http://wordpress.org/ and display the content received (that is, their index page).

Using the HTTP Extension

You can use the HTTP extension to send a GET request to http://wordpress.org/ and display the content received.

```php
<?php

$r= new HttpRequest( 'http://wordpress.org/', HttpRequest::METH_GET );
$r->send () ;
echo $r->getResponseBody();
?>
```

Using fopen() Streams

You can use fopen() streams to send a GET request to http://wordpress.org/ and display the content received.

```php
<?php

if( $stream = fopen( 'http://wordpress.org/', 'r' ) ) {
    echo stream_get_contents( $stream );
    fclose($stream);
}
?>
```

Using a Standard fopen()

You can use a standard `fopen()` to send a GET request to `http://wordpress.org/` and display the content received.

```php
<?php

$handle = fopen( "http://wordpress.org/", "rb" );
$contents = '';
while( !feof( $handle ) ) {
    $contents .= fread( $handle, 8192 );
}
fclose( $handle );
echo $contents;
?>
```

Using fsockopen()

You can use `fsockopen()` to send a GET request to `http://wordpress.org/` and display the content received.

```php
<?php

$fp = fsockopen( "wordpress.org", 80, $errno, $errstr, 30 );
if (!$fp) {
    echo "$errstr ($errno)<br />\n";
} else {
    $out = "GET / HTTP/1.1\r\n";
    $out .= "Host: wordpress.org\r\n";
    $out .= "Connection: Close\r\n\r\n";
    fwrite($fp, $out);
    while (!feof($fp)) {
        echo fgets($fp, 128);
    }
    fclose($fp);
}
?>
```

Using the CURL Extension

You can use the CURL extension to send a GET request to `http://wordpress.org/` and display the content received.

Available for download on Wrox.com

```php
<?php

$ch = curl_init();

curl_setopt( $ch, CURLOPT_URL, "http://wordpress.org/" );
curl_setopt( $ch, CURLOPT_HEADER, 0 );
curl_exec($ch);
curl_close($ch);
?>
```

Code snippet http_request_tests.php

Too Many Ways?

Each way has drawbacks and advantages over others: Some are simple and quicker to write, and some allow more parameters for finer control, support different request methods, or are faster to execute. Notice for instance how burdensome it is to use fsockopen(), which needs the complete request headers, compared to using streams or the HTTP extension.

The problem is this: Depending on the server setup and configuration, PHP version, or security settings, some methods won't be allowed or even available. When working for a specific client, you could adapt to its specific server architecture and use a method you know will work, but this is simply impossible when authoring a plugin you intend to release for broad use.

What you have to do, simply put, boils down to this alternative: Either test each method prior to using one, or rely on WordPress' HTTP API.

WORDPRESS' HTTP FUNCTIONS

WordPress implements a smart and powerful class, named WP_Http and found in wp-includes/class-http.php, which can test each previously described method and automatically select the best one available on the current machine.

The HTTP API supports all the methods you need to use (GET, POST and HEAD) and enables fine-tuning several parameters such as proxy tunneling.

 Don't use PHP native methods to perform HTTP requests: Remember, they may be not installed or have restrictive configurations on many web hosts. Always use the WordPress HTTP API and its functions described next.

The wp_remote_ Functions

You can execute an HTTP request within WordPress mostly using three functions: wp_remote_get(), wp_remote_post(), and wp_remote_head(), obviously for GET, POST, and HEAD requests.

These functions all operate the same way:

➤   The HTTP request is performed using the eponymous method.

➤   They accept two parameters, one required and one optional.

➤   They return an array or an object.

The syntax of these three functions follows:

```php
<?php

$get_result  = wp_remote_get( $url, $args );
$post_result = wp_remote_post( $url, $args );
$head_result = wp_remote_head( $url, $args );

?>
```

These three functions can actually be considered as simple shortcuts to the more generic wp_remote_request(). Indeed, the three preceding lines are equivalent to the three following ones:

```php
<?php

$get_result  = wp_remote_request( $url, array( 'method' => 'GET' ) );
$post_result = wp_remote_request( $url, array( 'method' => 'POST' ) );
$head_result = wp_remote_request( $url, array( 'method' => 'HEAD' ) );

?>
```

The function wp_remote_request() works the same way as the other wp_remote_* functions, so everything that follows applies to any wp_remote_ function.

You now learn what parameters they need, what data they return, and then play with them.

wp_remote_* Input Parameters

The first parameter $url these functions need is a string representing a valid site URL to which the HTTP request will be sent. Supported protocols are HTTP and HTTPS; some transports might work with other protocols such as FTP but don't assume this.

The second parameter $args is an optional array of parameters to override the defaults. The default parameters are the following array:

```php
<?php

$defaults = array (
    'method' => 'GET',
    'timeout' => 5,
    'redirection' => 5,
    'httpversion' => '1.0',
    'user-agent' => 'WordPress/3.1; http://example.com/',
    'blocking' => true,
    'headers' => array (),
    'cookies' => array (),
    'body' => NULL,
    'compress' => false,
    'decompress' => true,
    'sslverify' => true,
)

?>
```

This array contains the default values when omitted. For instance, instead of identifying your blog in the user-agent string and if you want to disguise your HTTP request as one made by a generic browser, you would write the following:

```php
<?php

$args = array(
    'user-agent' => 'Mozilla/5.0 (Windows NT 5.1; en-US) Firefox/3.6.8',
);

$result = wp_remote_get( $url, $args );

?>
```

In Chapter 6, you learned that despite its trustful name, the PHP generated array `$_SERVER` should not be trusted. As you can see, it takes a single PHP line to forge and fake the content of, for example, `$_SERVER['HTTP_USER_AGENT']`.

Table 9-3 contains a comprehensive description of the most important default values. You can consider the others either partially implemented, not always functional depending on the transport used, or simply of minor interest.

TABLE 9-3: Default Settings of wp_remote_ Functions Optional Parameters

PARAMETER	SIGNIFICATION
`'method'`	Either `'GET'`, `'POST'`, or `'HEAD'`. Some transports (the HTTP or the CURL extension for instance) may accept other rarely used methods such as `'PUT'` or `'TRACE'`, but should not be assumed.
`'timeout'`	A number of seconds: how long the connection should stay open before failing when no response.
`'user-agent'`	The user-agent used to identify "who" is performing the request. Defaults to `"WordPress/"` followed by the version of WordPress running and the URL of the blog issuing the request.
`'headers'`	An array of additional headers.
`'cookies'`	An array of cookie values passed to the server.
`'body'`	The body of the request, either a string or an array, which is data submitted to the URL.

wp_remote_* Return Values

All `wp_remote_*` functions return an array if the request has completed, or an error object if it was unsuccessful.

Unsuccessful Requests

In case of a malformed HTTP request, or if the request cannot be performed for any other reason (site not responding, temporary connection problem, etc.), the result will be an object instance of WordPress' class WP_Error, containing an error code and an error message, as illustrated in the following code snippet:

```php
<?php

var_dump( wp_remote_get( 'malformed-url' ) );

?>
```

The result of this ill-fated GET request follows:

```
object(WP_Error)#259 (2) {
  ["errors"]=>
  array(1) {
    ["http_request_failed"]=>
    array(1) {
      [0]=>
      string(29) "A valid URL was not provided."
    }
  }
  ["error_data"]=>
  array(0) {
  }
}
```

Error objects returned by HTTP requests will contain the error code "http_request_failed" and a meaningful detailed diagnosis. Consider the following attempts:

Available for download on Wrox.com

```php
<?php

$bad_urls = array(
    'malformed',
    'http://0.0.0.0/',
    'irc://example.com/',
    'http://inexistant',
);

foreach( $bad_urls as $bad_url ) {
    $response = wp_remote_head( $bad_url, array('timeout'=>1) );
    if( is_wp_error( $response ) ) {
        $error = $response->get_error_message();
        echo "<p>$bad_url returned: <br/> $error </p>";
    }
}

?>
```

Code snippet wp_remote_errors.php

Notice a couple of things in this snippet:

➤ To speed up things because it's obvious these requests will fail, and you don't want to wait for 5 seconds each, an additional timeout parameter is set, to 1 second.

➤ Because HTTP requests return a `WP_Error` object on failure, you can test the response using function `is_wp_error()`. You learn more about dealing with errors and the `WP_Error` class in Chapter 16, "Debugging and Optimizing."

Finally, look at the actual result of this code snippet:

```
Trying malformed returned:
A valid URL was not provided.

Trying http://0.0.0.0/ returned:
couldn't connect to host

Trying irc://example.com/ returned:
Unsupported protocol: irc

Trying http://inexistant returned:
Could not resolve host: inexistant; No data record of requested type
```

As you can see, the HTTP request functions can diagnose most scenarios, so you know you can rely on them if you need to troubleshoot unexpected behavior within your code.

Successful Requests

When the HTTP request has completed, `wp_remote_` functions return a multidimensional array of four elements, containing the raw server response in four parts: `'headers'`, `'body'`, `'response'`, and `'cookies'`.

Consider the following request:

```php
<?php

var_dump( wp_remote_get( 'http://example.com/asdfgh' ) );

?>
```

The output of this request will be akin to the following:

```
array(4) {

  ["headers"] => array(5) {
    ["date"] => string(29) "Wed, 01 Sep 2010 14:39:21 GMT"
    ["server"] => string(85) "Apache/2.2.8 mod_ssl/2.2.8 PHP/5.2.5"
    ["content-length"] => string(3) "461"
    ["connection"] => string(5) "close"
    ["content-type"] => string(25) "text/html; charset=utf-8"
  }

  ["body"]=> string(461) "<html><head>
<title>404 Not Found</title>
```

```
</head><body>
(... snip ...)
</body></html>
"

  ["response"] => array(2) {
    ["code"] => int(404)
    ["message"] => string(9) "Not Found"
  }

  ["cookies"] => array(0) {}
}
```

The first thing you should note here is that despite sending an HTTP request to a nonexistent page, the request is still considered successful: Whenever the web server replies to the client request, no matter its reply, the HTTP transaction is complete.

The four elements of the response array consist of the following:

> `'headers'` — The raw list of the server response as detailed in the first section of this chapter, minus the HTTP response code.

> `'body'` — The body of the server response, which is typically the page HTML content itself but can be JSON or XML encoded data when polling a remote API for instance.

> `'response'` — The server response code and its signification, as detailed in Table 9-1 and Table 9-2. This particular information is especially valuable: Despite the HTTP transaction being successful, its result may be totally different from what you expect. You should always check that you obtain 200 as a response code.

> `'cookies'` — If the server wants the client to store cookie information, they will be included here. In case you need this info for any subsequent HTTP request, include them as additional optional parameter in the next `wp_remote_` function call.

wp_remote_ Companion Functions

The array returned by `wp_remote_` functions enclose exhaustive information, and as such may contain too much data if you need just a part of it.

Along with functions performing HTTP requests, you can use "companion" functions that enable quick access to a part of the returned array. These functions follow:

> `wp_remote_retrieve_response_code()` — Returns just the response code (for example, 200) of an HTTP response

> `wp_remote_retrieve_response_message()` — Returns just the response message (for example, "OK")

> `wp_remote_retrieve_body()` — Returns the body of the response

> `wp_remote_retrieve_headers()` — Returns all the headers of a server response

> `wp_remote_retrieve_header()` — Returns just one particular header from a server response

For example, to check if a link exists and does not return a 404 Not Found error, you can use the following code:

```php
<?php

$url = 'http://www.example.com/bleh';

// Send GET request
$response = wp_remote_get( $url );

// Check for server response
if( is_wp_error( $response ) ) {

    $code = $response->get_error_message();
    wp_die( 'Requests could not execute. Error was: ' . $code );

}

// Check that the server sent a "404 Not Found" HTTP status code
if( wp_remote_retrieve_response_code( $response ) == 404 ) {

    wp_die( 'Link not found' );

}

// So far, so good
echo 'Link found';

?>
```

Code snippet wp_remote_check_404.php

You can use these simple companion functions more in the next examples and plugins.

Advanced Configuration and Tips

Thanks to these `wp_remote_` functions, you are now able to perform most tasks involving HTTP requests in a standard WordPress environment. But not all environments are customary, and not all tasks are basic. Fortunately, the HTTP API is extensible and versatile.

For instance, it is frequent that networks in corporate environments are isolated behind a firewall or a proxy. You will now read how to bypass this, and maybe treat HTTP responses differently.

In the following sections, you will also learn how to fine-tune the behavior of the HTTP API, utilizing its hooks and filters, for example to log requests for troubleshooting.

Proxy Support

In computer networks, a proxy server is a server that acts as an intermediary between the client and the requested server.

A great aspect of the HTTP API, and another reason why it is superior to PHP native functions as detailed in the first section, is that it supports connections through proxy without additional complex configuration.

To enable proxy support, you simply need to have the user define the following constants:

```php
<?php

define( 'WP_PROXY_HOST', 'firewall.corp.example.com' );
define( 'WP_PROXY_PORT', '3128' );
define( 'WP_PROXY_USERNAME', 'mylogin' );
define( 'WP_PROXY_PASSWORD', 'mypassword' );

?>
```

This is especially important for users in a corporate environment where proxies are common and can block all WordPress' outgoing requests if not, or incorrectly, configured.

On a corporate network, where a firewall architecture can characteristically handle different connections toward the Internet and those staying on the intranet, another constant can be used to specify domains that should not go through the proxy, in a comma-separated list:

```php
<?php

// these hosts will not go through the proxy
define( 'WP_PROXY_BYPASS_HOSTS', 'sales.example.com, hr.example.com' );
?>
```

The blog domain and `localhost` are automatically added to this list, so you don't have to include them.

Also, when working with clients on a firewalled corporate intranet, a concern of your client's IT department may be to limit outgoing connections to a restricted white list of web sites. If so, use constants `WP_HTTP_BLOCK_EXTERNAL` and `WP_ACCESSIBLE_HOSTS` like so:

```php
<?php

// block all requests through the HTTP API
define( 'WP_HTTP_BLOCK_EXTERNAL', true );

// except for these hosts
define( 'WP_ACCESSIBLE_HOSTS',
    'api.wordpress.org, sales.example.com, partner.web' );
?>
```

Including `api.wordpress.org` in the list of accessible hosts can ensure that the built-in upgrading for core, plugins, and themes still work.

Filtering Requests and Responses

As any other piece of WordPress code poetry, the HTTP API makes considerable use of hooks, and reading the source file of the `WP_Http` class you can find several filters and actions triggered.

Example: Modify a Default Parameter

For instance, if you want all your plugins to show off your WordPress skills in server logs whenever they perform queries, add the following filter and function:

```php
<?php

// Hook into the filter that sets user agent for HTTP requests
add_filter( 'http_headers_useragent', 'boj_myplugin_user_agent' );

// Set your own user agent
function boj_myplugin_user_agent() {
    global $wp_version;

    return "WordPress version $wp_version ; ".
            "Need a WordPress specialist? Contact us! ".
            "BOJ Studio www.example.com";
}

?>
```

This filter can set the new default value for the user agent string, which means that on a per-request basis you can still override it, as in the previous example where you disguised as a generic Internet browser.

Example: Log HTTP Requests and Responses

Hooks that can come handy when debugging requests and server responses are the `'http_request_args'` and `'http_response'` filters, used to allow modification of the request's parameters right before it is executed or just before the server responses are returned.

In the `WP_Http` class source (located in `wp-includes/class-http.php`), you can see that each request applied these two filters:

```php
<?php

// before the request is sent, you will find:
$r = apply_filters( 'http_request_args', $r, $url );

// once the response is processed, you will read:
return apply_filters( 'http_response', $response, $r, $url );

?>
```

You are now going to code a plugin that logs each HTTP request and its parameters, and each server response into a flat text file. You can use `boj_loghttp` as a prefix throughout this plugin.

Available for download on Wrox.com

```php
<?php
/*
Plugin Name: Log HTTP requests
Plugin URI: http://example.com/
Description: Log each HTTP requests into a flat text file for further analysis
```

```php
Author: WROX
Author URI: http://wrox.com
*/

// Hook into filters
add_filter( 'http_request_args', 'boj_loghttp_log_request', 10, 2 );
add_filter( 'http_response', 'boj_loghttp_log_response', 10, 3 );

// Log requests.
// Parameters passed: request parameters and URL
function boj_loghttp_log_request( $r, $url ) {

    // Get request parameters formatted for display
    $params = print_r( $r, true );

    // Get date with format 2010-11-25 @ 13:37:00
    $date = date( 'Y-m-d @ H:i:s' );

    // Message to log:
    $log = <<<LOG
$date: request sent to $url
Parameters: $params
--------------

LOG;

    // Log message into flat file
    error_log( $log, 3, dirname( __FILE__ ).'/http.log' );

    // Don't forget to return the requests arguments!
    return $r;
}

// Log responses
// Parameters passed: server response, requests parameters and URL
function boj_loghttp_log_response( $response, $r, $url ) {

    // Get server response formatted for display
    $resp = print_r( $response, true );

    // Get date with format 2010-11-25 @ 13:37:00
    $date = date( 'Y-m-d @ H:i:s' );

    // Message to log:
    $log = <<<LOG
$date: response received from $url
Response: $resp
--------------

LOG;

    // Log message into flat file
    error_log( $log, 3, dirname( __FILE__ ).'/http.log' );
```

```
            // Don't forget to return the response!
            return $response;

    }

    ?>
```

Code snippet plugin_boj_loghttp.php

The two logging functions are similar: They receive from the filters a number of parameters that are then printed into a flat text file using PHP function `error_log()`; then they eventually return the unmodified filtered value.

Notice the particular syntax used here to delimit strings, called the heredoc syntax. The opening string delimiter is an identifier after <<<, and the closing delimiter is the identifier, not indented.

After you activate this plugin, it starts appending entries to the file http.log in the plugin's directory. This is an interesting plugin that demonstrates the inner working of WordPress' core, because it will, for instance, log all transactions with `api.wordpress.org` when checking the latest version of plugins, themes, and core, or when fetching the feeds displayed in your dashboard.

Remember that logging events is for debugging only and is not suitable for production environments, as it could leak sensitive information or even fill up disk space with log data.

Example: Advanced Filtering

Filters and actions in the `WP_Http` class enable specific customization of how WordPress handles HTTP requests.

Imagine working for a client who wants a plugin that can monitor the content of an FTP directory. As a seasoned plugin author, you know that the HTTP API supports only the HTTP and HTTPS protocols, but as an experienced PHP hacker you also remember that the CURL extension can perform FTP requests.

You could obviously code something using CURL directly instead of the HTTP API functions, but that would not be best practice because you would lose access to the hooks of this API.

When you are confident the client server will have CURL support, you can code a specific plugin to leverage CURL's capability to work with the FTP protocol.

You can now write the part of such a plugin to do the following:

➤   Disable all transports except CURL.

➤   Add custom parameters to the CURL session.

➤   Fetch and display the content of an FTP directory (for example, `ftp://ftp.gnu.org`, a public repository).

```php
<?php

// Disable all transports but curl
function boj_onlycurl_force_curl() {
    add_filter( 'use_fsockopen_transport', '__return_false' );
    add_filter( 'use_fopen_transport', '__return_false' );
    add_filter( 'use_streams_transport', '__return_false' );
    add_filter( 'use_http_extension_transport', '__return_false' );
}

// Add a custom parameter to the CURL requests:
// display only file names of FTP directories (no attributes, size etc...)
function boj_onlycurl_hack_curl_handle( $handle ) {
    curl_setopt( $handle, CURLOPT_FTPLISTONLY, true );
    return $handle;
}

// Hook CURL requests to the above function
add_action( 'http_api_curl', 'boj_onlycurl_hack_curl_handle' );

// Now do the job
boj_onlycurl_force_curl();

var_dump( wp_remote_get( 'ftp://ftp.gnu.org' ) );

?>
```

Code snippet plugin_boj_onlycurl.php

By using the HTTP API, even if reducing it to use the CURL extension, your code still interacts easily with WordPress, for instance with your previously defined filter that modifies the user agent string.

Notice a convenient function you used here: __return_false(). A few shortcut functions in WordPress can be used to return always the same value: __return_true(), __return_false(), __return_zero() and __return_empty_array().

These shortcut functions are designed to be used in a filter context for simpler code. The three following examples are equivalent:

```php
<?php

// 1. The old way
// You need to create an extra function that may be used only once
add_filter( 'somefilter', 'boj_always_return_false' );
function boj_always_return_false() {
    return false;
}

// 2. The convoluted short way
add_filter( 'somefilter', create_function('$a', 'return false;') );
```

```
// 3. The elegant and simple way
add_filter( 'somefilter', '__return_false' );

?>
```

Using anonymous (or lambda) functions in PHP with `create_function()` has several drawbacks for which it is wise to avoid:

➤ The argument list and body are strings, so you have to pay extra attention to escaping and quotes.

➤ Your favorite editor or IDE cannot highlight properly the code within the string body, making it more difficult to code more complex operations.

➤ Opcode caches such as APC or PHP Accelerator cannot cache these dynamic functions.

Some Caveats on Checking HTTP Responses

When you want to programmatically check the existence and validity of a link with an HTTP request, you can break your analysis down into two steps: If the request is successful and the response code is 404, you know the link does not exist. Otherwise, you may have to check things more carefully, depending on the context:

➤ If the request is an `is_wp_error()`, it can be because the URL to check is malformed but also because there is a temporary glitch preventing your web server from accessing the URL (connection problem, DNS timeout, and so on).

➤ If the response code is in the 5xx family (a server error, remember Table 9-2) this is probably a temporary server error, so you need to check again later.

➤ Some web servers are configured to handle "Not Found" errors differently than expected. For instance, `http://example.com/icons` will return a 404 when you would have expected the server to redirect to `http://example.com/icons/`, which actually exists.

➤ Some proxies or DNS servers, especially in corporate environments, are configured to handle all requests successfully, even though they should have returned an error: The following result is the actual return of `wp_remote_head( 'http://example.xom' )` (notice the typo in the top-level domain) behind such a proxy, treating a nonexistent domain as a regular 404 error. (See Figure 9-1 for the human readable result in a browser when trying to access this URL.)

```
array(4) {
  ["headers"]=>
  array(6) {
    ["cache-control"]=>
    string(8) "no-cache"
    ["pragma"]=>
    string(8) "no-cache"
    ["content-type"]=>
    string(24) "text/html; charset=utf-8"
    ["proxy-connection"]=>
    string(10) "Keep-Alive"
```

```
          ["connection"]=>
          string(10) "Keep-Alive"
          ["content-length"]=>
          string(3) "762"
        }
        ["body"]=>
        string(0) ""
        ["response"]=>
        array(2) {
          ["code"]=>
          int(404)
          ["message"]=>
          string(9) "Not Found"
        }
        ["cookies"]=>
        array(0) {
        }
      }
```

Corporate Proxy

Network Error (dns_unresolved_hostname)

Your requested host "www.example.xom" could
not be resolved by DNS.

FIGURE 9-1

PRACTICE: READING JSON FROM A REMOTE API

Now that you know mostly everything about the HTTP API, it's time to put your knowledge into practice.

Twitter is an interesting practical playground because its API is developer-friendly, has extensive documentation (see http://dev.twitter.com/doc/), and can output results in various formats such as JSON, XML, or RSS.

 When working with remote APIs, always check the current documentation for recent changes. More often than not, third-party services introduce new methods and deprecate some, possibly breaking previously functional code.

In this section you create a plugin that can fetch the number of followers of a given Twitter username and the latest status update. You also learn how to get and parse JSON data, a format you often deal with when playing with remote APIs.

Getting and Reading JSON

The API URL you will poll is `http://api.twitter.com/1/users/show.json?screen_name=$username`, with a simple GET request. This returns data presented in JSON format, which looks like this, when formatted and indented for human eyes:

```
{
  "followers_count" : 1731,
  "friends_count" : 108,
  "name" : "Ozh RICHARD",
  "description" : "WordPress & PHP hacker.",
  "screen_name" : "ozh",
  "status" : {
      "created_at" : "Sun Sep 05 09:01:56 +0000 2010",
      "id" : 23045381793,
      "retweet_count" : 1337,
      "text" : "I'm writing a book about WordPress plugins!",
    },
  "statuses_count" : 1730,
  "time_zone" : "Paris",
  "url" : "http://ozh.org/",
}
```

JSON (JavaScript Object Notation) is a popular data text format with a `"name":"value"` pair structure, which resembles a PHP multidimensional array. A reason for its popularity is that it is easy to programmatically parse and generate it, using functions `json_encode()` and `json_decode()`.

> For your information, functions `json_encode()` and `json_decode()` are built in PHP as of version 5.2 and newer. Fortunately, WordPress versions with looser requirements include emulations of these functions for older platforms, to be found in `wp-includes/compat.php`.

After you have your JSON data collected into string `$json`, the function `json_decode()` converts it to an object or an array, as follows:

```php
<?php

// Convert JSON string to an object
$json_object = json_decode( $json );
$followers   = $json_object->followers_count;
$last_tweet  = $json_object->status->text;

// Convert JSON string to an array: pass bool true as second parameter
$json_array = json_decode( $json, true );
```

```
$followers   = $json_array['followers_count'];
$last_tweet  = $json_array['status']['text'];

?>
```

Your Functional Plugin

Your complete plugin, named "Twitter Info" and using `boj_ti_` as a prefix, follows:

Available for download on Wrox.com

```php
<?php
/*
Plugin Name: Twitter Info
Plugin URI: http://example.com/
Description: Get number of followers and last tweet of a Twitter user
Author: WROX
Author URI: http://wrox.com
*/

// Define the Twitter username. Edit this.
define( 'BOJ_TI_USERNAME', 'ozh' );

// Name of the transient key to cache values
define( 'BOJ_TI_KEY', 'boj_ti_key' );

// Poll Twitter API
// Return array of (follower count, last tweet), or false on error
function boj_ti_ask_twitter() {

    // Send GET request to Twitter API
    $api_url = 'http://api.twitter.com/1/users/show.json?screen_name=';
    $api_response = wp_remote_get( $api_url . urlencode( BOJ_TI_USERNAME ) );

    // Get the JSON object
    $json = wp_remote_retrieve_body( $api_response );

    // Make sure the request was successful or return false
    if( empty( $json ) )
        return false;

    // Decode the JSON object
    // Return an array with follower count and last tweet
    $json = json_decode( $json );

    return array(
        'followers'  => $json->followers_count,
        'last_tweet' => $json->status->text
    );
}

// Return array of followers and last tweet, either from cache or fresh
function boj_ti_get_infos( $info = 'followers' ) {
```

```php
        // first, look for a cached result
        if ( false !== $cache = get_transient( BOJ_TI_KEY ) )
            return $cache[$info];

        // no cache? Then get fresh value
        $fresh = boj_ti_ask_twitter();

        // Default cache life span is 1 hour (3600 seconds)
        $cache = 3600;

        // If Twitter query unsuccessful, store dummy values for 5 minutes
        if( $fresh === false ) {
            $fresh = array(
                'followers' => 0,
                'last_tweet' => '',
            );
            $cache = 60*5;
        }

        // Store transient
        set_transient( BOJ_TI_KEY, $fresh, 60*5 );

        // Return fresh asked info
        return $fresh[$info];
    }


// Echo number of followers
function boj_ti_followers() {
    $num = boj_ti_get_infos( 'followers' );
    echo "<p>I have $num followers on Twitter!</p>";
}


// Echo last tweet
function boj_ti_last_tweet() {
    $tweet = boj_ti_get_infos( 'last_tweet' );
    echo "<p>My last tweet: $tweet</p>";
}


// Register custom actions
add_action( 'boj_ti_followers' , 'boj_ti_followers' );
add_action( 'boj_ti_last_tweet', 'boj_ti_last_tweet' );

?>
```

Code snippet plugin_boj_twitter_info.php

In this plugin, the function `boj_ti_ask_twitter()` sends a GET request against Twitter's API, makes sure the result is JSON, decodes it, and returns an array of follower count and last tweet.

The function `boj_ti_get_infos()` makes good use of the Transient API as covered in Chapter 7, "Plugin Settings," to avoid hammering Twitter for constantly fresh results. Notice how it also caches dummy results for a shorter time when the API returns an error: It is good practice to cover all possible results when dealing with third-party providers you have no control over.

Because the main function `boj_ti_get_infos()` returns an array with the follower count and last tweet, for more convenience you've added two simple shortcut functions to easily access one data set, `boj_ti_followers()` and `boj_ti_last_tweet()`.

To use your plugin, you would traditionally use the following snippet:

```php
<?php

if( function_exists( 'boj_ti_followers' ) )
    boj_ti_followers()

?>
```

This way, if for some reason your plugin is deactivated, you won't break your blog by calling an undefined function.

But have a closer look at the end of the plugin: You have defined two custom actions. This good practice now enables you to simply use this one-liner:

```php
<?php
do_action( 'boj_ti_followers' );
?>
```

Using this method is simpler for end users (less code to add) and safer. (If the plugin is deactivated, the action simply does not exist and nothing is triggered.)

PRACTICE: SENDING DATA TO A REMOTE API

You can now practice with POST requests.

Code a simple plugin that can automatically back up your blog posts to Tumblr, a popular free blogging platform located at `http://www.tumblr.com/` and with a simple API, documented at `http://www.tumblr.com/docs/api`.

Formatting Parameters for POST Requests

First, you need to create an account there and write down the email used for login and your password.

Sending POST requests is like submitting a form in a web browser; the information you would write into form fields are instead collected in an array that is sent as the body of the request.

When you publish a new post, your plugin can get its title and content into `$post_title` and `$post_content`. You can now send a POST request to the Tumblr write API:

```php
<?php

// URL of the Tumblr API
$api = 'http://www.tumblr.com/api/write';

// Data for the POST request
$data = array(
```

```
            'email' => 'email@example.com',
            'password' => '123456',
            'type' => 'regular',
            'title' => $post_title,
            'body' => $post_body
    );

    // Do the POST
    $response = wp_remote_post( $api,
        array(
            'body' => $data,
            'timeout' => 20
        )
    );
    ?>
```

The data of the POST request is passed as the body item of the request parameter array, along with any other parameter as, for instance here, a longer timeout.

Your Functional Plugin

Your complete plugin, named Simple Tumblr Backup and using boj_stb as a prefix, follows:

```php
<?php
/*
Plugin Name: Simple Tumblr Backup
Plugin URI: http://example.com/
Description: Backup posts to a Tumblr account as you publish them
Author: WROX
Version: 1.00
Author URI: http://wrox.com/
*/

// Edit this:
define( 'BOJ_STB_TUMBLR_EMAIL', 'email@example.com' );
define( 'BOJ_STB_TUMBLR_PASSW', '132456' );

// Actions when new post is published
add_action( 'draft_to_publish',   'boj_stb_newpost' );
add_action( 'pending_to_publish', 'boj_stb_newpost' );
add_action( 'future_to_publish',  'boj_stb_newpost' );

// Function called when new post. Expecting post object.
function boj_stb_newpost( $post ) {

    // Get post information
    $post_title   = $post->post_title;
    $post_content = $post->post_content;

    // URL of the Tumblr API
    $api = 'http://www.tumblr.com/api/write';

    // Data for the POST request
    $data = array(
            'email' => BOJ_STB_TUMBLR_EMAIL,
```

```
                'password' => BOJ_STB_TUMBLR_PASSW,
                    'type' => 'regular',
                   'title' => $post_title,
                    'body' => $post_content
        );

        // Do the POST request
        $response = wp_remote_post( $api,
            array(
                'body' => $data,
                'timeout' => 20
            )
        );

        // All done!
    }



    ?>
```

The simple trick here is to hook your function that sends to Tumblr into each action triggered when a new post is published, which is one of these scenarios:

➤   Draft post that you eventually publish (action: `'draft_to_publish'`)

➤   A post pending review and now published (action: `'pending_to_publish'`)

➤   A post previously written but set with a future date (action: `'future_to_publish'`)

After you activate your plugin, each post you publish on your WordPress blog is automatically backed up on your Tumblr account, as shown in Figure 9-2.

FIGURE 9-2

PRACTICE: READING ARBITRARY CONTENT

You cannot always poll a remote API with neat results presented in formatted JSON or XML. Sometimes, you need to fetch arbitrary content, such as a plain HTML page, and extract the information out of it.

In Chapter 7, the practical example for using the Transients API included a hypothetical function to fetch the current song title from an online radio. The code used follows:

```php
<?php

// Fetches from an online radio a song title currently on air
function boj_myplugin_fetch_song_title_from_radio() {
    // ... code to fetch data from the remote website
    return $title;
}
?>
```

Now it's time you make this function less imaginary and code it to retrieve the song currently on air on, say, radio KNAC located at http://www.knac.com/.

This web site does not offer a convenient API, but after some poking you'll find that its system generates a text file located at http://knac.com/text1.txt and formatted as follow:

```
text1=<b>NOW PLAYING</b>: EL DORADO<br><b>BY:</b> IRON MAIDEN

<current_song> EL DORADO
<current_artist> IRON MAIDEN
<current_album> THE FINAL FRONTIER

<last_5_songs_played> 10:32:37 - SLAYER, WAR ENSEMBLE<br> (... snip ...)
```

There is a slight resemblance to XML but it's not, and you'll be on your own to parse this file. You use regular expressions to extract the requested information from this text.

The working function will now be the following:

Available for
download on
Wrox.com

```php
<?php

function boj_myplugin_fetch_song_title_from_radio() {
    $url = 'http://knac.com/text1.txt';

    $text = wp_remote_retrieve_body( wp_remote_get( $url ) );

    preg_match( '/\<current_song\>(.*)/', $text, $matches );
    $song = trim( $matches[1] );

    preg_match( '/\<current_artist\>(.*)/', $text, $matches );
    $artist = trim( $matches[1] );
```

```
        return "$song by $artist";
    }

?>
```

The regular expression used here to capture the song title, for instance, is `'/\<current_song\>(.*)/'`, which translates to: string `<current_song>` followed by any character (the dot) repeated zero or more times (the *) until the end of the line.

Regular expressions are a key skill when it comes to parsing arbitrary content. If you are not familiar with them, they are introduced in Chapter 6, and then you can learn more at `http://php.net/pcre`.

MAKE YOUR OWN PLUGIN REPOSITORY

A great trait of WordPress is that when plugins are hosted on `http://wordpress.org/extend/plugins`, users see right from their blog administration interface if there is a new version of a particular plugin, and they can update it without leaving their blog. WordPress' central repository is a key feature of plugin marketing, as you see in detail in Chapter 17, "Marketing Your Plugins."

This said, not all plugins you create end up available for public use on WordPress' repository: Clients often require that plugins created for their use remain private, or you may want to code plugins and sell them through your own repository.

Even if you host your plugin yourself, you can still have your users benefit from WordPress' built-in upgrade feature.

How Plugin Upgrades Work in WordPress

Twice daily, WordPress sends a request to `api.wordpress.org` with the list of plugins currently installed. The API server replies with a list of new versions when available and information about these new versions.

For instance, if you have on your blog only one plugin installed and active, the request sent as POST to `http://api.wordpress.org/plugins/update-check/1.0/` would be something like this:

```php
<?php

// Sample request sent to api.wordpress.org to check for new plugins

$request = array(
    'plugins' => array (
        'boj_myplugin/plugin.php' => array (
            'Name' => 'My BOJ Plugin',
            'PluginURI' => 'http://example.com/',
            'Version' => '',
            'Description' => 'This plugin does incredible stuff',
```

```php
            'Author' => 'Ozh',
            'AuthorURI' => 'http://wrox.com/',
            'TextDomain' => '',
            'DomainPath' => '',
            'Network' => false,
            'Title' => 'My BOJ Plugin',
        ),
    ),
    'active' => array (
        0 => 'boj_myplugin/plugin.php',
    ),
)
?>
```

If your plugin is hosted on wordpress.org, and there is a new version available, the API server will reply with the following information array:

```php
<?php

// Sample response from api.wordpress.org with new plugin versions, if any

$response = array(
    'boj_myplugin/plugin.php' => array(
        'id' => 10256,
        'slug' => 'boj_myplugin',
        'new_version' => '2.0',
        'url' => 'http://wordpress.org/extend/plugins/boj_myplugin/',
        'package' => 'http://downloads.wordpress.org/plugin/boj_myplugin.zip'
    )
);

?>
```

So every 12 hours, your blog checks for new plugin versions and stores the request sent and the response received in a site transient named `'update_plugins'`, containing the following information:

1. `'last_checked'`: the last time it checked
2. `'checked'`: the list of plugins and their version currently installed
3. `'response'`: the response from the API server with new version information

The function responsible for this behavior is `wp_update_plugins()`, found in file `wp-includes/update.php`.

Polling an Alternative API from a Plugin

You can now code a plugin that also checks an alternative API for a new version about a particular plugin not hosted on WordPress.

Just before your blog stores the site transient, the filter `'pre_set_site_transient_update_plugins'` is applied to the transient value. At this point, your plugin sends a request to your alternative API and appends its response to the transient value. This response contains information about a new value if applicable, along with a package URL that won't be hosted on wordpress.org.

```php
<?php
/*
Plugin Name: BOJ Alternate Plugin API
Plugin URI: http://example.com/
Description: Checks for a new version of itself against a self hosted API
Version: 1.0
Author: Ozh
Author URI: http://wrox.com/
*/

define( 'BOJ_ALT_API', 'http://example.com/plugin-api/' );
```

This constant defines your alternative API that sends information about a new version of this plugin. You can code the server script for this API later.

Now, the function that checks the API at the moment the transient is about to be stored follows:

```php
// Hook into the plugin update check
add_filter('pre_set_site_transient_update_plugins', 'boj_altapi_check');

// Check alternative API before transient is saved
function boj_altapi_check( $transient ) {

    // Check if the transient contains the 'checked' information
    // If no, just return its value without hacking it
    if( empty( $transient->checked ) )
        return $transient;

    // The transient contains the 'checked' information
    // Now append to it information form your own API

    $plugin_slug = plugin_basename( __FILE__ );

    // POST data to send to your API
    $args = array(
        'action' => 'update-check',
        'plugin_name' => $plugin_slug,
        'version' => $transient->checked[$plugin_slug],
    );

    // Send request checking for an update
    $response = boj_altapi_request( $args );

    // If response is false, don't alter the transient
    if( false !== $response ) {
```

```php
            $transient->response[$plugin_slug] = $response;
        }

    return $transient;
}

// Send a request to the alternative API, return an object or false
function boj_altapi_request( $args ) {

    // Send request
    $request = wp_remote_post( BOJ_ALT_API, array( 'body' => $args ) );

    // Make sure the request was successful
    if( is_wp_error( $request )
    or
    wp_remote_retrieve_response_code( $request ) != 200
    ) {
        // Request failed
        return false;
    }

    // Read server response, which should be an object
    $response = unserialize( wp_remote_retrieve_body( $request ) );
    if( is_object( $response ) ) {
        return $response;
    } else {
        // Unexpected response
        return false;
    }
}
```

The purpose of the function `boj_altapi_check()` is to insert into the transient information about your plugin coming from another place than WordPress' repository, and in particular the URL of the new download package.

At this point, if the alternative API replies that a new version for this plugin is available, you see an upgrade link (see Figure 9-3) and can run the built-in upgrader with your own package URL (see Figure 9-4).

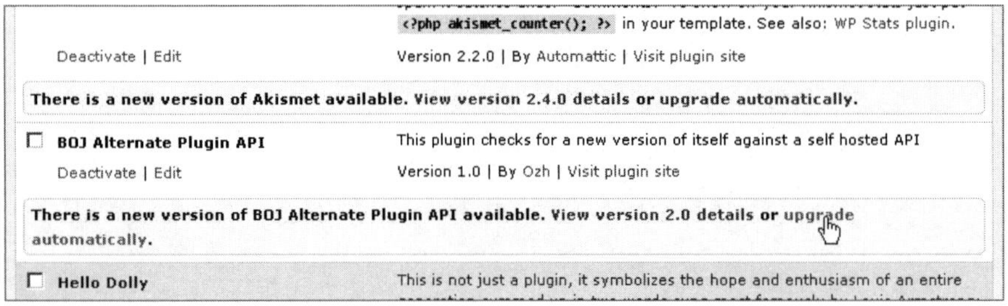

FIGURE 9-3

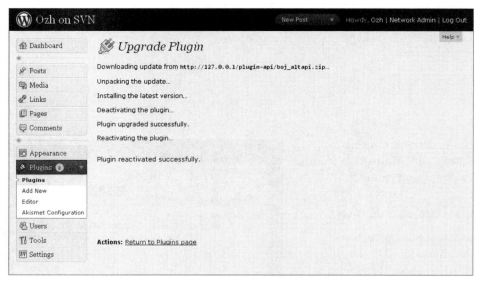

FIGURE 9-4

But things are not perfect yet: You need to also take care of the View Version Details link which, at this point, would still fetch detailed information from api.wordpress.org and thus display a blank screen.

The internal function you need to take over is plugins_api() (found in wp-admin/includes/ plugin-install.php) and that uses the filter 'plugins_api':

Available for download on Wrox.com

```
// Hook into the plugin details screen
add_filter('plugins_api', 'boj_altapi_information', 10, 3);

function boj_altapi_information( $false, $action, $args ) {

    $plugin_slug = plugin_basename( __FILE__ );

    // Check if this plugins API is about this plugin
    if( $args->slug != $plugin_slug ) {
        return false;
    }

    // POST data to send to your API
    $args = array(
        'action' => 'plugin_information',
        'plugin_name' => $plugin_slug,
        'version' => $transient->checked[$plugin_slug],
    );

    // Send request for detailed information
    $response = boj_altapi_request( $args );
```

```
        // Send request checking for information
        $request = wp_remote_post( BOJ_ALT_API, array( 'body' => $args ) );

        return $response;
    }
    ?>
```

Now if you click the detailed information link, your plugin can pull information from your own API, as shown on Figure 9-5.

Building the Alternative API

Of course, your plugin is completely dependent on the alternative API that must reply with information about the plugin. Fortunately, such an API is fairly easy to implement.

On a remote server, defined as `'http://example.com/plugin-api/'` in the plugin, a single script can handle the two types of requests your plugin can issue:

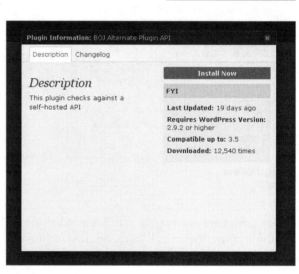

FIGURE 9-5

➤ Check for a new version (action parameter: `'update-check'`) that needs a reply with a newer version number and a package URL where to download the newer plugin.

➤ Check for detailed information about an updated plugin (action parameter: `'plugin_information'`)

```php
<?php

$action = $_REQUEST['action'];
$slug = $_REQUEST['plugin_name'];

// Create new object
$response = new stdClass;

switch( $action ) {

    // API is asked for the existence of a new version of the plugin
    case 'update-check':
        $response->slug = $slug;
        $response->new_version = '2.0';
        $response->url = 'http://example.com/boj-altapi/';
        $response->package = 'http://example.com/plugin-api/boj_altapi.zip';
```

```php
        break;

    // Request for detailed information
    case 'plugin_information':
        $response->slug = 'boj_altapi.php';
        $response->plugin_name = 'boj_altapi.php';
        $response->new_version = '2.0';
        $response->requires = '2.9.2';
        $response->tested = '3.5';
        $response->downloaded = 12540;
        $response->last_updated = "2010-08-23";
        $response->sections = array(
            'description' => 'This plugin checks against a self-hosted API',
            'changelog' => 'New features added!'
        );
        $response->download_link = 'http://example.com/plugin-api/boj_altapi.
zip';
        break;

}

echo serialize( $response );
?>
```

Code snippet plugin-api/index.php

This single script generates a response object, which needs to be serialized (that is, transformed into a string), for printing purpose. The key variable in its response is the URL of a zip package that is not hosted on wordpress.org.

A Few Words of Caution About Self-Hosted API

The flexibility of WordPress' plugin API enables all sorts of customization, including not being tied to wordpress.org if needed.

This being said, you should consider hosting your plugins on wordpress.org if you intend to release them publicly. You learn in Chapter 17 how doing so can play a great role in your promotion strategy.

SPECIAL CASE: FETCHING REMOTE FEEDS

The HTTP API functions can fetch any type of remote content, such as HTML, images, zip archives, or JSON data. To fetch remote RSS feeds though, there is a better alternative: WordPress ships with SimplePie, a third-party popular and efficient RSS and Atom feed parser.

The function you use is fetch_feed(), which needs a single argument (the feed URL such as http://example.com/feed/) and returns either a WP_Error object on failure or a SimplePie object on success.

To illustrate how to use fetch_feed() and its return, you can now get the five latest articles from a web site and display their title, publication date, and link.

```php
<?php

// Get a SimplePie object from a feed source.
$rss = fetch_feed('http://example.com/feed/');

// Make sure the SimplePie object is created correctly
if( is_wp_error( $rss ) )
    wp_die( 'Could not fetch feed' );

echo 'Feed found, contains '. $rss->get_item_quantity() . ' articles.';

// Build an array of 5 elements, starting from item #0
$rss_items = $rss->get_items( 0, 5 );

// Start ordered list
echo '<ol>';

// Loop through each item and display its link, title and date
foreach( $rss_items as $item ) {
    $title = $item->get_title();
    $date  = $item->get_date('Y/m/d @ g:i a');
    $link  = $item->get_permalink();

    echo "<li><a href='$link'>$title</a> ($date)</li>\n";
}

// Close ordered list
echo '</ol>';
?>
```

When polled using `fetch_feed()`, web site feeds are cached for 12 hours by default and stored in a transient.

The `SimplePie` class has numerous methods that you can become acquainted with at this address: http://simplepie.org/wiki/reference/start.

SUMMARY

The HTTP API functions are a bridge between your blog and a whole world of interaction with remote services. Practically all modern web services offer an API for developers to use, and this widens even more the scope of possibilities for WordPress plugins.

The one thing you should retain from this chapter is that you should forget what you have done in a pre-WordPress life, when you probably got used to coding HTTP requests using CURL. As you have learned here, relying on the WordPress API enables much more flexibility (leveraging the internal hooks of the API) and security because you can be confident WordPress will pick the best functions available to perform requests.

10

The Shortcode API

WHAT'S IN THIS CHAPTER?

➤ Creating custom shortcode

➤ Registering complex and parameterized shortcodes

➤ Mastering advanced shortcode tips

➤ Connecting your site with Google Maps

Shortcodes are WordPress-specific code that enables you to do nifty things with little effort, such as embed content or create objects that would normally require lots of complicated, ugly code.

In this chapter, you learn how to allow users of your plugins to enhance their posts with advanced customizable content using just a few characters.

CREATING SHORTCODES

This section teaches you what a shortcode is and how to create new shortcodes, from simple string replacements to advanced functions with parameters.

What Shortcodes Are

The Shortcode API enables creating simple macro codes, sometimes also referred to as bbcodes for their similarity with a popular syntax in various forums and bulletin boards.

In a nutshell, a shortcode is a simple tag syntax between square brackets, such as `[something]`, used in posts. At render time when the post is displayed, the shortcode is dynamically replaced with a more complex and user-defined content. See Figure 10-1 for a simple example of a shortcode plugin that would substitute `[date]` with the current date and time.

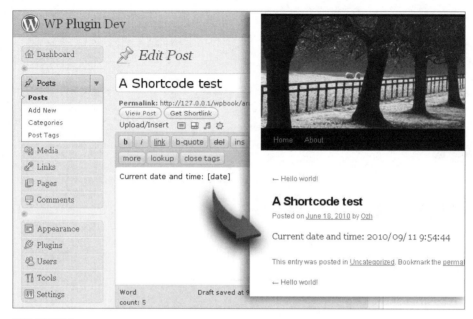

FIGURE 10-1

WordPress out-of-the-box registers shortcodes you can use: When you upload multiple images attached to a given post, you can simply insert [gallery] in your post, and this shortcode will be replaced with a nicely formatted gallery of your images.

Technically, a shortcode can be any string that would fit as an array key. For instance, you could register the following different shortcodes:

➤   [foo]

➤   [Foo]

➤   [123]

➤   [133t]

➤   [Hello My Name Is Inigo Montoya]

In practice, for simplicity, and to avoid potential conflicts between different shortcodes, you register only short, lowercase, simple strings.

 You must not register for your own use the following shortcodes: [wp_caption], [caption], [gallery] *and* [embed]. *These are registered by WordPress.*

Register Custom Shortcodes

You now learn how to register your own shortcodes, with practical usages, from a simple tag replacement to more complex and parameterized output.

The following shortcode plugins use `boj_scX` as a prefix, where X will be a number.

[book]

The simplest usage of shortcodes is to quicken your typing and replace often-used sentences with something shorter to type or easier to remember.

For instance, if you frequently mention a book you want to promote on Amazon, instead of typing "`<a href="http://www.amazon.com/dp/0470560541">book</a>`" each time, wouldn't it be faster to just write `[book]`?

The function you use is `add_shortcode()`, which needs two parameters:

➤   The tag pattern (without the surrounding square brackets)

➤   A callback function used to replace the tag

```php
<?php
/*
Plugin Name: Shortcode Example 1
Plugin URI: http://example.com/
Description: Replace [book] with a long Amazon link
Version: 1.0
Author: Ozh
Author URI: http://wrox.com/
*/

// Register a new shortcode: [book]
add_shortcode( 'book', 'boj_sc1_book' );

// The callback function that will replace [book]
function boj_sc1_book() {
    return '<a href="http://www.amazon.com/dp/0470560541">book</a>';
}


?>
```

Code snippet plugin_boj_sc1.php

What just happened?

1.   With `add_shortcode()`, you have registered `[book]` as a new shortcode, stating that it will be replaced with the output of the function `boj_sc1_book()`

2.   The shortcode callback function, here `boj_sc1_book()`, needs to `return` a value in the end. A frequent beginner error is to have it `echo` a value instead of returning it, which will make the shortcode fail.

Activate the plugin, and from now on, write "Buy my `[book]`" in a post or a page, and it will be replaced with the Amazon link.

Note that WordPress is rather flexible on the shortcode syntax: You can more or less mimic XHTML tags and either type `[book]`, `[book ]`, `[book/]` or `[book /]`. The only requirement is that there is no space between the opening square bracket and the tag.

[books title="xkcd"]

What if you have more than one book to promote?

The first option would be to create several simple shortcodes as previously done, one per book (for instance `[book1]`, `[book2]`, `[book3]`, and so on). A more elegant option you can use is to introduce an attribute to the shortcode, so it enables a smarter syntax such as `[book title="prowp"]` and `[book title="xkcd"]`.

You can use the same function `add_shortcode()` again but now with a new parameter `$attr` that receives an array of attribute => value pairs.

```php
<?php
/*
Plugin Name: Shortcode Example 2
Plugin URI: http://example.com/
Description: Replace [books title="xxx"] with different Amazon links
Version: 1.0
Author: Ozh
Author URI: http://wrox.com/
*/

// Register a new shortcode: [books title="xxx"]
add_shortcode( 'books', 'boj_sc2_multiple_books' );

// The callback function that will replace [books]
function boj_sc2_multiple_books( $attr ) {

    switch( $attr['title'] ) {
        case 'xkcd':
            $asin = '0615314465';
            $title = 'XKCD Volume 0';
            break;

        default:
        case 'prowp':
            $asin = '0470560541';
            $title = 'Professional WordPress';
            break;
    }

    return "<a href='http://www.amazon.com/dp/$asin'>$title</a>";
}
?>
```

Code snippet plugin_boj_sc2.php

What just happened?

1. You have registered a new shortcode, [books].

2. Your callback function boj_sc2_multiple_books() expects a parameter: $attr will be an array of attribute => value pair used in the shortcode. For instance, write [books title="prowp"] and the callback function will receive array('title' => 'prowp') as its parameter.

3. Your callback function can now return different values depending on the attribute used.

4. If you write [books] with no attribute, the callback function receives an empty string. You have coded it to return a default value in such a case.

[amazon asin="12345"]book title[/amazon]

You can continue to push the plugin forward with a new improvement: The anchor text in the Amazon link will now be parameterized.

The function used will still be the same add_shortcode(), this time with a second parameter $content, which will receive any enclosed text as a string:

```php
<?php
/*
Plugin Name: Shortcode Example 3
Plugin URI: http://example.com/
Description: Replace [amazon isbn="xxx"]book title[/amazon]
Version: 1.0
Author: Ozh
Author URI: http://wrox.com/
*/

// Register a new shortcode: [amazon isbn="123"]link title[/amazon]
add_shortcode( 'amazon', 'boj_sc3_amazon' );

// Callback function for the [amazon] shortcode
function boj_sc3_amazon( $attr, $content ) {

    // Get ASIN (Amazon Standard Identification Number)
    if( isset( $attr['asin'] ) ) {
        $asin = preg_replace( '/[^\d]/', '', $attr['asin'] );
    } else {
        $asin = '0470560541';
    }

    // Sanitize content, or set default
    if( !empty( $content ) ) {
        $content = esc_html( $content );
    } else {
        if( $asin == '0470560541' ) {
            $content = 'Professional WordPress';
```

```
            } else {
                $content = 'this book';
            }
        }

        return "<a href='http://www.amazon.com/dp/$asin'>$content</a>";
    }
?>
```

Code snippet plugin_boj_sc3.php

What just happened?

1. You have registered another shortcode, using the tag [amazon].

2. Your callback function, boj_sc3_amazon(), now expects two optional parameters: an array of attribute => value pairs, and a text string enclosed between the opening and the closing shortcodes.

3. The callback function can deal with all the combinations of missing ASIN attribute (Amazon Standard Identification Number) and/or book title: [amazon], [amazon asin="123"], and [amazon]awesome book[/amazon] would flawlessly work.

4. Your shortcode can return arbitrary content, so remember to apply techniques you have learned in Chapter 6, "Plugin Security": Sanitize the ASIN to be only digits and make sure the book title can be safely displayed and your blog and won't break the <a> tag in which it is enclosed.

Wrap Up: add_shortcode() and the callback Function

When you register a new shortcode, the two parameters define the square bracket tag pattern and the callback function:

```
<?php

add_shortcode( 'boj', 'boj_my_shortcode' );

?>
```

The callback function receives two parameters, empty if omitted: an array of attribute => value pairs, and a string of content enclosed within the opening and closing shortcode. Just as in HTML, the attributes are case-insensitive.

You can define default values just as in any other PHP function, and in the end the function must return something.

```
<?php

function boj_my_shortcode( $attr = array( 'var' => 'val' ), $content = 'book' ) {
    // $attr is an associate array
```

```
        // $content is a string

        return $something;
    }

    ?>
```

The shortcode attributes are case-insensitive, can have arbitrary or no value, and support quotes or lack thereof. The following examples show the values of the array $attr in the callback function, depending on how the shortcode is used:

➤ [boj] : $attr will be an empty string.

➤ [boj hello] : $attr will be array('hello').

➤ [boj name=ozh skillz='1337' MAP="q3dm6"] : $attr will be array ('name' => 'ozh', 'skillz' => '1337', 'map' => 'q3dm6').

SHORTCODE TIPS

Shortcodes are a great way to spice up post contents with complex and dynamic content. To guarantee the best end user experience, as a plugin author you should keep in mind two principles:

➤ Make things simple and fool proof.

➤ Remember it's dynamic.

Think Simplicity for the User

As a plugin user, it's great to add new features to one's blog and being allowed to write a simple shortcode that can display much more complex content. But it's cumbersome to remember the shortcode parameter syntax: you end up with the impression that you have to learn a new markup language.

Back to your plugin with the [amazon] shortcode: You can now code a companion plugin that will add the shortcode [amazonimage] to display product images from Amazon. You can specify the ASIN number, the image type (books or CD covers), and its size.

When functional, the plugin permit shortcodes such as [amazonimage asin='123456' type='CD' imagesize='small'].

When users have this plugin installed for a long time, they might have forgotten about the attribute names and syntax. Is it [amazonimage] or [amazonimg]? As for the attributes, is it isbn or asin? And imagesize='large' or 'big'? type='CD' or type='disk'?

Allowing lots of options is neat, but you don't want your users having to check the plugin documentation and give them a bad experience. Instead, make things simple and foolproof so that users can use your plugin instinctively.

Now to the plugin:

```php
<?php
/*
Plugin Name: Shortcode Example 4
Plugin URI: http://example.com/
Description: Replace [amazonimage] with images from Amazon
Version: 1.0
Author: Ozh
Author URI: http://wrox.com/
*/

// Register two shortcodes [amazonimage] and [amazonimg]
add_shortcode( 'amazonimage', 'boj_sc4_amazonimage' );
add_shortcode( 'amazonimg',   'boj_sc4_amazonimage' );

// Callback function for the shortcode
function boj_sc4_amazonimage( $attr, $content ) {

    // Get ASIN or set default
    $possible = array( 'asin', 'isbn' );
    $asin = boj_sc4_find( $possible, $attr, '0470560541' );

    // Get affiliate ID or set default
    $possible = array( 'aff', 'affiliate' );
    $aff = boj_sc4_find( $possible, $attr, 'aff_id' );

    // Get image size if specified
    $possible = array( 'size', 'image', 'imagesize' );
    $size = boj_sc4_find( $possible, $attr, '' );

    // Get type if specified
    if( isset( $attr['type'] ) ) {
        $type = strtolower( $attr['type'] );
        $type = ( $type == 'cd' || $type == 'disc' ) ? 'cd' : '';
    }

    // Now build the Amazon image URL
    $img = 'http://images.amazon.com/images/P/';
    $img .= $asin;
    // Image option: size
    if( $size ) {
        switch( $size ) {
            case 'small':
                $size = '_AA100';
                break;
            default:
            case 'medium':
                $size = '_AA175';
                break;
            case 'big':
            case 'large':
                $size = '_SCLZZZZZZZ';
```

```
                    break;  // Good practice: don't forget the last break
            }
        }
        // Image option: type
        if( $type == 'cd' ) {
            $type = '_PF';
        }
        // Append options to image URL, if any
        if( $type or $size ) {
            $img .= '.01.' . $type . $size;
        }
        // Finish building the image URL
        $img .= '.jpg';

        // Now return the image
        return "<a href='http://www.amazon.com/dp/$asin'><img src='$img' /></a>";
    }

    // Helper function:
    // Search $find_keys in array $in_array, return $default if not found
    function boj_sc4_find( $find_keys, $in_array, $default ) {
        foreach( $find_keys as $key ) {
            if( isset( $in_array[$key] ) )
                return $in_array[$key];
        }
        return $default;
    }
    ?>
```

Code snippet plugin_boj_sc4.php

The first thing you'll notice is that you have registered two shortcodes with the same callback function: This way, the user can either use [amazonimage] or [amazonimg].

Then look at how the plugin considers multiple attributes as synonyms: Using the helper function named boj_sc4_find(), the main callback function checks the value of $attr['asin'] or $attr['isbn'], and if omitted, sets a default value.

As non-WordPress information, it's also worth mentioning that the fun part in this plugin is to leverage the way Amazon crafts image URLs. The base URL is http://images.amazon.com/images/P/, to which you append the following:

➤ The ASIN number, such as 'B002OEBMN4'.

➤ If you want to add options, append '.01.'

➤ A first possible option used here is the size: Append for instance '_AA100' for 100 pixels wide, or '_SCLZZZZZZZ' for a large image.

➤ Another possible option used is to add a CD image beneath the cover: Append '_PF' to the image URL.

➤ Finally, make the image URL end with '.jpg'.

Activate the plugin, write a post with "`Currently listening to [amazonimage asin=
"B00008WT5E" type="cd" size="small"]`" and see the result that should look like Figure 10-2.

FIGURE 10-2

Remember the Dynamicity

Shortcode outputs are dynamically generated: Every time WordPress displays a page (a single post,
an archive), the post content is parsed, and shortcodes are replaced with the returned result of their
callback function.

Replacements such as the one you coded in this chapter so far are lightning fast, and you don't have
to worry about WordPress' performance when you register new shortcodes.

However, performance will be a matter of importance if your shortcodes either pull information
from the database or from remote web sites:

➤ In the first case, your code will issue extra SQL queries, which can hinder performance on
slow web hosts.

➤ In the second case, your shortcode will perform external HTTP requests that could slow down
the whole page rendering, while WordPress is awaiting the remote server response to parse.

In such cases, you should consider caching the result of your shortcode, for instance in the post
metadata. In the next plugin, you implement such a caching technique.

Look Under the Hoods

Besides using `add_shortcode()` to register new ones, here are other interesting functions or facts to know about the Shortcode API and then a fun plugin to make use of them.

$shortcode_tags

All registered shortcodes are stored in the global array `$shortcode_tags`, in `'shortcode'` => `'callback'` pairs:

```php
<?php

global $shortcode_tags;
var_dump( $shortcode_tags );

/* Result:
array (
    'wp_caption'  => 'img_caption_shortcode',
    'caption'     => 'img_caption_shortcode',
    'gallery'     => 'gallery_shortcode',
    'embed'       => '__return_false',
    'amazonimage' => 'boj_sc4_amazonimage',
    'amazonimg'   => 'boj_sc4_amazonimage',
)
*/

?>
```

remove_shortcode()

You can dynamically unregister a shortcode using the function `remove_shortcode()`.

Example: `remove_shortcode( 'amazonimg' );`

remove_all_shortcodes()

Similarly, you can dynamically unregister all the shortcodes, using the function `remove_all_shortcodes()` with no argument. Technically, this function simply resets the global `$shortcode_tags` to an empty array.

strip_shortcodes()

The function `strip_shortcodes()` strips registered shortcodes from string content, as in the following example:

```php
<?php

$content = <<<S
Some existing shortcodes: [amazonimage] [gallery]
These don't exist: [bleh] [123]
S;
```

```
echo strip_shortcodes( $content );

/* Result:
Some existing shortcodes:
These don't exist: [bleh] [123]
*/
?>
```

shortcode_atts()

This function can be used to compare user attributes against a list of supported attributes and fill in defaults when needed.

For instance, look at how the built-in shortcode [gallery] works. Its callback function is gallery_shortcode(), which processes the shortcode attributes like so:

```php
<?php

function gallery_shortcode( $attr ){

    // Define supported attributes and their default values
    $defaults = array(
        'order'      => 'ASC',
        'orderby'    => 'menu_order ID',
        'id'         => $post->ID,
        'itemtag'    => 'dl',
        'icontag'    => 'dt',
        'captiontag' => 'dd',
        'columns'    => 3,
        'size'       => 'thumbnail',
        'include'    => '',
        'exclude'    => ''
    );

    // Filter user entered attributes and set default if omitted
    $options = shortcode_atts( $defaults, $attr );

    //   [.. code continues ..]
    //   File: wp-includes/media.php

}
?>
```

After the exhaustive list of supported attributes and their default values is set in array $defaults, it is combined with the user input attributes in array $attr, and any unknown attribute is ignored.

do_shortcode()

The function do_shortcode() searches the string content passed as its parameter for shortcodes, and processes them. When WordPress initializes, it hooks the filter 'the_content' to this function, so that post contents are taken care of:

```php
<?php

// In wp-includes/shortcodes.php
add_filter( 'the_content', 'do_shortcode', 11 );
?>
```

Recursive Shortcodes

It can happen that the content enclosed in a shortcode may contain other shortcodes. For instance, you can register [b] and [i] to display bold and italic text, and it should work with a nested structure such as "[b]some [i]text[/i] here[/b]".

This is no problem because the callback function of a shortcode can recursively call do_shortcode():

Available for
download on
Wrox.com

```php
<?php
// add shortcodes [b] and [i]
add_shortcode( 'i', 'boj_sc5_italic' );
add_shortcode( 'b', 'boj_sc5_bold' );

// callback function: return bold text
function boj_sc5_bold( $attr, $content ) {
    return '<strong>' . do_shortcode( $content ) . '</strong>';
}

// callback function: return italic text
function boj_sc5_italic( $attr, $content ) {
    return '<em>' . do_shortcode( $content ) . '</em>';
}

?>
```

Code snippet plugin_boj_sc5.php

Each callback function applies shortcodes to its enclosed text to make sure each shortcode is processed.

A "bb code" for Comments Plugin

You can now code a new plugin to enable BB-like tags in comments: Instead of using regular HTML tags such as <a> or <b>, commenters need to use [url] and [b] like in most forums.

The plugin will also have the following traits:

➤ It should not change how authors write their posts (with HTML tags as usual).

➤ It should not apply to comments shortcodes otherwise registered for posts, such as [amazonimage] in your previous plugin or [gallery].

The plugin follows:

```php
<?php
/*
Plugin Name: Shortcode Example 6
Plugin URI: http://example.com/
Description: Enables [url] and [b] shortcodes in comments
Version: 1.0
Author: Ozh
Author URI: http://wrox.com/
*/

// Hook into 'comment_text' to process comment content
add_filter( 'comment_text', 'boj_sc6_comments' );

// This function processes comment content
function boj_sc6_comments( $comment ) {

    // Save registered shortcodes:
    global $shortcode_tags;
    $original = $shortcode_tags;

    // Unregister all shortcodes:
    remove_all_shortcodes();

    // Register new shortcodes:
    add_shortcode( 'url', 'boj_sc6_comments_url' );
    add_shortcode( 'b', 'boj_sc6_comments_bold' );
    add_shortcode( 'strong', 'boj_sc6_comments_bold' );

    // Strip all HTML tags from comments:
    $comment = wp_strip_all_tags( $comment );

    // Process comment content with these shortcodes:
    $comment = do_shortcode( $comment );

    // Unregister comment shortcodes, restore normal shortcodes
    $shortcode_tags = $original;

    // Return comment:
    return $comment;
}

// the [b] or [strong] to <strong> callback
function boj_sc6_comments_bold( $attr, $text ) {
    return '<strong>' . do_shortcode( $text ) . '</strong>';
}

// the [url] to <a> callback
function boj_sc6_comments_url( $attr, $text ) {
    $text = esc_url( $text );
```

```
        return "<a href=\"$text\">$text</a>";
}

?>
```

Code snippet plugin_boj_sc6.php

What just happened?

1. As you can see, your plugin does not register new shortcodes `[url]` and `[b]` directly from the start; otherwise, they would interfere with the post contents. Instead, the plugin starts with capturing each comment's contents.

2. The comment processing function, `boj_sc5_comments()`, first unregisters all shortcodes after making a copy of them.

3. New shortcodes are then registered: `[url]` and `[b]`. (`[strong]` will be equivalent to `[b]`, for user's simplicity.)

4. The comment content, kept in the variable `$comment`, is expurgated from regular HTML tags and then applied to the newly registered shortcodes.

5. Notice how the shortcode callback function for bold text recursively calls `do_shortcode()`, enabling for nested structures.

6. Original shortcodes are restored; the comment shortcodes `[url]` and `[b]` are unregistered by the way.

7. The formatted comment content is returned for display.

Activate the plugin and type in a new comment: See in Figure 10-3 how HTML tags are ignored; `[b]` and `[url]` shortcodes are processed but regular shortcodes such as `[gallery]`, which would otherwise apply to posts, are not.

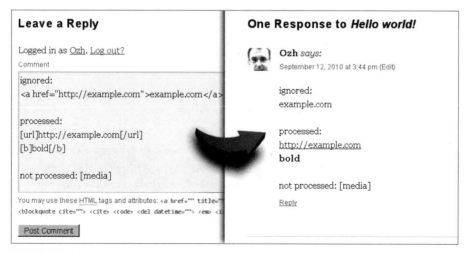

FIGURE 10-3

Shortcode Nesting Limitations

As you have read previously, WordPress can handle nested shortcode structures, provided their callback functions recursively call do_shortcode(). However, this handling has limitations and can sometimes fail, as you will see now.

The following structure is fine because nested shortcodes are different, and each one is correctly enclosed:

```
Works:
[foo]
    [bar]
        [baz]
    [/bar]
[/foo]
```

The parser will fail if you enclose a shortcode within the same shortcode:

```
Fails:
[foo]
    [foo]
    [/foo]
[/foo]
```

Also, remember that shortcodes can be self-closing (a standalone [foo] or [foo/]) or enclose content ([foo]content[/foo]), which can also make some structures impossible to parse correctly:

```
Fails:
[foo]
[foo]
    content
[/foo]
```

INTEGRATING GOOGLE MAPS

As a complete and more complex example using shortcodes, you now make a plugin that can integrate Google Maps into your WordPress-powered web site.

Google offers many different APIs for accessing its services and in particular the mapping service, which uses two related services: a geocoding API and the map API.

 Google provides extensive documentation on the Google Maps API. You can find more information at http://code.google.com/apis/maps/documentation/ javascript/.

In this section, you code a plugin to convert a plain text address (such as "111 River Street Hoboken, NJ 07030") into a dynamically generated interactive Google map.

Accessing the Google Geocoding API

The first step to convert an address into a map is to "geocode" this address. Geocoding is defined as the process of converting a standard address (like "108 Ocean Ave. Amityville, NY 11701") to geographic longitude and latitude coordinates ("40.6665060, -73.4147750"). These coordinates are used by the Google Maps API to locate specific positions on a map and to plot markers on a map based on the coordinates specified.

Currently the Google Geocoding API can return results in two formats: JSON or XML. In this example you use the JSON format and work with the techniques discussed in Chapter 9, "HTTP API," about HTTP requests.

Google has made the process of interacting with its API simple. To retrieve coordinates you can request the following URL: `http://maps.google.com/maps/api/geocode/$output?$parameters` where `$output` will be the format output (for instance `'json'`) and `$parameter` will be a query string of additional parameters to geocode.

You need to pass only two required parameters to this API: `address` or `latlng` and `sensor`:

➤ Because you don't know the latitude and longitude coordinates, you use the `address` parameter. This parameter is the full, plain text address you want to geocode, in its URL encoded form.

➤ The sensor parameter indicates whether the request comes from a device with a location sensor (such as a smartphone). You set this variable to `false`.

You can easily test this by loading the geocoding API URL in any browser and populating the required parameters: `http://maps.google.com/maps/api/geocode/json?address=1600+Pennsylvania+Ave,+Washington,+DC&sensor=false`.

As you can see, the JSON results returned contain the longitude and latitude coordinates of the address and additional data such as the ZIP code (which we didn't send in the request).

Now write the function `boj_gmap_geocode()` that will geocode an address:

```php
<?php

// Geocode an address: return array of latitude & longitude
function boj_gmap_geocode( $address ) {
    // Make Google Geocoding API URL
    $map_url = 'http://maps.google.com/maps/api/geocode/json?address=';
    $map_url .= urlencode( $address ).'&sensor=false';

    // Send GET request
    $request = wp_remote_get( $map_url );

    // Get the JSON object
    $json = wp_remote_retrieve_body( $request );
```

```php
    // Make sure the request was successful or return false
    if( empty( $json ) )
        return false;

    // Decode the JSON object
    $json = json_decode( $json );

    // Get coordinates
    $lat = $json->results[0]->geometry->location->lat;    //latitude
    $long = $json->results[0]->geometry->location->lng;   //longitude

    // Return array of latitude & longitude
    return compact( 'lat', 'long' );
}
?>
```

This function sends a request to the Google Maps Geocoding API, and receives a JSON response which, when decoded, contains latitude and longitude. Test it to check the return value format:

```php
<?php

$coords = boj_gmap_geocode( '108 Ocean Ave. Amityville, NY' );

var_dump( $coords );

/* Result:
array(2) {
  ["lat"]=> float(40.666506)
  ["long"]=> float(-73.414775)
}
*/
?>
```

For more details and explanation on the functions used in this function, refer to Chapter 9.

Storing API Results

One important aspect of shortcodes is that they generate content dynamically each time. But that would not be efficient to issue an HTTP request to the Google Maps Geolocation API each time a post is displayed because it would slow down each page load.

As an alternative, when an address has been geolocated, you can store its coordinates in metadata attached to the post. This way, next time the same post displays, the latitude and longitude will be automatically fetched from the database with all other post metadata, thus saving one HTTP request.

 Post metadata, accessible in the WordPress write interface as "Custom Post Fields," is fetched at the same time as the post data itself, so reading information stored there does not issue an extra SQL query. You learn more about post metadata in Chapter 11, "Extending Posts."

Instead of getting coordinates from Google's API using the function `boj_gmap_geocode()`, you can use the proxy function `boj_gmap_get_coords()` that first checks for the information in the post metadata. If the information is missing, it will be fetched fresh from Google and then stored in the metadata for faster later reuse.

Following is your proxy function:

```php
<?php

// Convert a plain text address into latitude & longitude coordinates
// Retrieved from meta data if possible, or get fresh then cached otherwise
function boj_gmap_get_coords( $address = '111 River Street Hoboken, NJ' ) {

    // Current post id
    global $id;

    // Check if we already have this coordinates in the database
    $saved = get_post_meta( $id, 'boj_gmap_addresses' );
    foreach( (array)$saved as $_saved ) {
        if( isset( $_saved['address'] ) && $_saved['address'] == $address ) {
            extract( $_saved );
            return compact( 'lat', 'long' );
        }
    }

    // Coordinates not cached: let's fetch them from Google
    $coords = boj_gmap_geocode( $address );
    if( !$coords )
        return false;

    // Cache result in a post meta data
    add_post_meta( $id, 'boj_gmap_addresses', array(
        'address' => $address,
        'lat' => $coords['lat'],
        'long' => $coords['long']
        )
    );

    extract( $coords );
    return compact( 'lat', 'long' );
}

?>
```

Each time an address is geolocated for the first time, the `add_post_meta()` call inserts into the post metadata named `'boj_gmap_addresses'` an array like the following:

```php
array(
    "address" => "108 Ocean Ave. Amityville, NY ",
    "lat"     => "40.666506",
    "long"    => "-73.414775"
)
```

On the next page load, the coordinates should be found and retrieved from the post metadata.

Accessing the Google Maps API

Now that you know how to convert an address into longitude and latitude coordinates using the Google Geocoding API, you can plot those coordinates on a Google Map using the Google Maps API.

API Concepts

Interactive Google Maps are created using JavaScript that must be inserted in the page where you want the map to display. Before integrating it straight into your plugin, you learn how to embed such a map in an HTML page:

First, you need to insert the main script:

```
<script type="text/javascript"
    src="http://maps.google.com/maps/api/js?sensor=false">
```

Then, insert the map-specific JavaScript part, enclosed in its own function:

```
function initialize_map() {
```

An object holds a new instance of a Google Map, with specific latitude and longitude parameters:

```
var myLatlng = new google.maps.LatLng(45.124099,-123.113634);
```

Another object can define the map options: its zoom level, where it should be centered, and the map type (terrain, road, satellite, or hybrid):

```
var myOptions = {
    zoom: 4,
    center: myLatlng,
    mapTypeId: google.maps.MapTypeId.SATELLITE
}
```

Now, you attach the map to an HTML object such as a `<div>`; here with attribute id `"map_canvas"`:

```
var map = new google.maps.Map( document.getElementById("map_canvas"), myOptions );
```

The following string holds a custom text that displays in the information window showing when clicking the marker on the map:

```
var contentString = '<div id="content">'+
    '<p><b>Firefox Crop Circle</b>: Somewhere in a field in Oregon'+
    ', this 67 metre wide icon was created by the Oregon State University'+
    'Linux Users Group to celebrate the launch of Firefox version 2</p>'+
    '</div>'+
    '</div>';
```

This string is now attached to a new instance of the `InfoWindow` object:

```
var infowindow = new google.maps.InfoWindow({
    content: contentString
});
```

Now, place a marker on your map:

```
var marker = new google.maps.Marker({
    position: myLatlng,
    map: map,
    title: 'Firefox Crop Circle'
});
```

And finally add behavior so that the information window pops up when the marker is clicked:

```
google.maps.event.addListener(marker, 'click', function() {
    infowindow.open(map,marker);
});
}
```

Almost done! Now create the empty HTML object that will receive the map, and call the JavaScript function that will display it:

```
<p>The map will display here:</p>
<div id="map_canvas" style="width:600px;height:600px"></div>
<script type="text/javascript">initialize_map()</script>
```

Code snippet google_map_api_example.html

This file outlines the concept of the Google Maps API and displays a map, as shown in Figure 10-4.

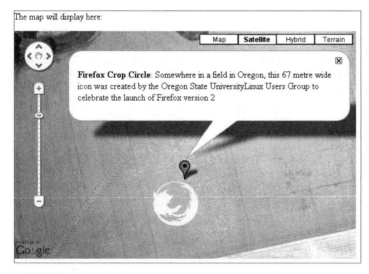

FIGURE 10-4

You are now ready to implement dynamic Google Maps in your plugin.

Plugin Implementation

Now you code the central piece of the plugin: the function to register the shortcode [googlemap] and display the Google Map. The shortcode will be used like so:

```
[googlemap width=500 height=300 zoom=12]Elm Street, Springwood, Ohio[/googlemap]
```

First, register the shortcode itself. You could elect to also register various similar shortcodes pointing to the same callback, such as [googlemaps], [google_map], and [google_maps].

```php
<?php

//add the [googlemap] shortcode support
add_shortcode( 'googlemap', 'boj_gmap_generate_map' );
```

Now start to define the callback function that can parse and process the shortcode attributes and its content:

```php
// The shortcode callback
function boj_gmap_generate_map( $attr, $address ) {

    // Set map default
    $defaults = array(
        'width'  => '500',
        'height' => '500',
        'zoom'   => 12,
    );

    // Get map attributes (set to defaults if omitted)
    extract( shortcode_atts( $defaults, $attr ) );
```

This first part sets an array of default values, merged with the actual attributes using the function shortcode_atts() that returns an array. The extract() call then imports variables from the array so that for instance array('size' => 300) becomes $size = 300.

```php
    // get coordinates
    $coord = boj_gmap_get_coords( $address );

    // Make sure we have coordinates, otherwise return empty string
    if( !$coord )
        return '';
```

What you've done here is geocode the address (either from fresh API data or the post metadata) and, in case the geocoding fails (temporary connection problem between your server and Google's, for instance), return an empty string.

```php
    // Output for the shortcode
    $output = '';

    // populate $lat and $long variables
    extract( $coord );
```

Now that you have all the needed variables, you sanitize them for output. Some are to be included in JavaScript strings and others used as HTML attributes, so you can use the appropriate escaping function as described in Chapter 6:

```
// Sanitize variables depending on the context they will be printed in
$lat     = esc_js( $lat );
$long    = esc_js( $long );
$address = esc_js( $address );
$zoom    = esc_js( $zoom );
$width   = esc_attr( $width );
$height  = esc_attr( $height );
```

Now you insert the JavaScript parts.

Usually, you would insert the main script in the <head> of the document, but in this case this would be counter-performant because the script would be inserted even if no post on the page requires it.

Instead, you insert it inline, as part as the shortcode return, while making sure it's echoed only once per page:

```
// generate a unique map ID so we can have different maps on the same page
$map_id = 'boj_map_'.md5( $address );

// Add the Google Maps main javascript only once per page
static $script_added = false;
if( $script_added == false ) {
    $output .= '<script type="text/javascript"
    src="http://maps.google.com/maps/api/js?sensor=false"></script>';
    $script_added = true;
}
```

Now you can insert the map-specific JavaScript. Each function and each map placeholder will be uniquely named, using the $map_id variable previously generated, so you can have several maps on the same page:

```
// Add the map specific code
$output .= <<<CODE
<div id="$map_id"></div>

<script type="text/javascript">
function generate_$map_id() {
    var latlng = new google.maps.LatLng( $lat, $long );
    var options = {
        zoom: $zoom,
        center: latlng,
        mapTypeId: google.maps.MapTypeId.ROADMAP
    }

    var map = new google.maps.Map(
        document.getElementById("$map_id"),
```

```
                options
            );

            var legend = '<div class="map_legend"><p> $address </p></div>';

            var infowindow = new google.maps.InfoWindow({
                content: legend,
            });

            var marker = new google.maps.Marker({
                position: latlng,
                map: map,
            });

            google.maps.event.addListener(marker, 'click', function() {
                infowindow.open(map,marker);
            });

        }

        generate_$map_id();

        </script>
```

Append to the output some simple styling as per user-defined attributes:

```
    <style type"text/css">
    .map_legend{
        width:200px;
        max-height:200px;
        min-height:100px;
    }
    #$map_id {
        width: {$width}px;
        height: {$height}px;
    }
    </style>

CODE;
```

And, of course, don't forget to return the content of the shortcode replacement:

```
        return $output;
    }
?>
```

Code snippet plugin_boj_sc7.php

Now your plugin is ready to go! Create a new post and, for instance, write the following shortcode:
`[googlemap width=450 height=300 zoom=14]108 Ocean Ave. Amityville, NY[/googlemap]`.
Your post will look like Figure 10-5.

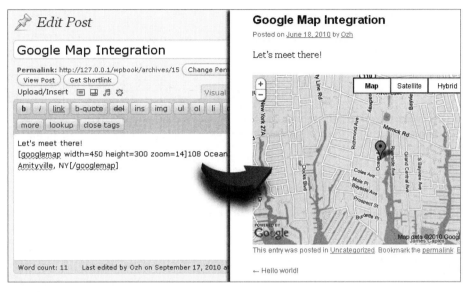

FIGURE 10-5

MORE SHORTCODE QUICK IDEAS

Shortcodes can easily add interesting and practical functions, and again, your imagination will be the limit. You can for instance register shortcodes to display member-only content, display time-limited content, obfuscate email addresses, and more. In the following sections, you'll look at a few of the options.

Display Member-Only Content

The first quick shortcode you will implement now is a neat way to display content to logged in users only. For instance, its usage in posts would be as following:

```
Today's Jedi pro-tip is:
[members]Use the force[/members]
```

The code and function for such a shortcode is the following simple snippet:

Available for
download on
Wrox.com

```php
<?php

add_shortcode( 'members', 'boj_sc8_loggedin' );

function boj_sc8_loggedin( $attr, $content ) {
    if( is_user_logged_in() ) {
        return $content;
    } else {
```

```
            return "<p>Members Eyes Only</p>";
        }
    }
    ?>
```

Code snippet plugin_boj_sc8.php

The result is that you enclose content between a [members] shortcode, and only readers who are logged in can see it. For a more elaborated example on the same concept, refer back to Chapter 8, "Users."

Display Time-Limited Content

Another simple yet valuable shortcode you will code will allow displaying time-limited content, such as a promotional link that is valid only for 24 hours:

```
This promo link valid for 24 hours only:
[24hours] http://example.com/promo/ [/24hours]
```

To implement this shortcode, you need the following snippet that will simply check the current time against the time the post was published:

Available for download on Wrox.com

```
<?php

add_shortcode( '24hours', 'boj_sc8_24hours' );

function boj_sc8_24hours( $attr, $content ) {
    $now = time();
    $post_time = get_the_date( 'U' );
    if( ( $now - $post_time ) > 86400 ) {
        return 'Offer has expired!';
    } else {
        return $content;
    }
}
?>
```

Code snippet plugin_boj_sc8.php

If the current post has been published more than 86400 seconds (that is, 24 hours) ago, the text enclosed in [24hours] tags won't show.

Obfuscate Email Addresses

The next quick shortcode idea you will code is a practical way to convert a plain text email address into a mailto: link that will be obfuscated (that is, less readable) to spam robots. In a post, you would simply type:

```
Email me at [email]ozh@ozh.org[/email]
```

The shortcode function will make use of WordPress' function `antispambot()`, which converts characters into HTML entities that spambots and email harvesters cannot easily read:

```php
<?php

add_shortcode( 'email', 'boj_sc8_email' );

function boj_sc8_email( $attr, $content ) {
    if( is_email( $content ) ) {
        $content = antispambot( $content );
        return sprintf( '<a href="mailto:%s">%s</a>', $content, $content );    }
else {
        return '';
    }
}
?>
```

Code snippet plugin_boj_sc8.php

The result is that you enclose email addresses between `[email][/email]` tags, and the shortcode will obfuscate them. For instance, actual return for `'ozh@ozh.org'` is `'o&#122;&#104;&#64;&#111;z&#104;&#46;org'`.

SUMMARY

Shortcodes open the door to advanced, customizable, and dynamic content for end users who may have no knowledge or will to write complicated HTML, JavaScript, CSS, or PHP.

Using shortcodes, you can propose advanced macros to your clients, adding much value to your work at little cost for development.

11

Extending Posts: Metadata, Custom Post Types, and Taxonomies

WHAT'S IN THIS CHAPTER?

➤ Creating custom post types

➤ Using custom post types

➤ Adding and using post metadata

➤ Creating custom taxonomies

➤ Using custom taxonomies

In WordPress, posts represent the content of the site. Content is typically the most important aspect of having a web site. Taxonomies are a way to classify or categorize posts. Metadata is additional information about individual posts. Each of these things can be brought together to make any type of web site imaginable.

Throughout this chapter, you work on building a single plugin that houses a user's music collection. Both the post types and taxonomies sections of this chapter contribute to the overall plugin. Nearly every snippet of code provided within this chapter contributes to the plugin and gives you a view of how the topics presented work together to manage content.

One important thing to note about post types, post metadata, and taxonomies is that their display is typically controlled by themes when on the frontend of the site, so plugin developers don't always have complete control over how this is handled. Of course, this depends on what functionality the plugin is providing to the user. WordPress theme development is outside the scope of this book, but learning how themes work within the WordPress environment can make your plugin development skills stronger.

CREATING CUSTOM POST TYPES

By default, WordPress has several predefined post types that enable users to create and manage the content of their site. For the average blog user, these post types are all they ever need.

- ➤ **Post** — Blog posts typically presented in order from newest to oldest on the site
- ➤ **Page** — Top-level, hierarchical types of content such as About, Contact, and a myriad of other pages
- ➤ **Attachment** — Media attached to other post types, such as images and videos for a post
- ➤ **Revision** — Revisions of other post types used as a backup system in case a user needs to revert to an older copy
- ➤ **Nav Menu Item** — Items added to nav menus using WordPress' built-in menu management system

As WordPress becomes a more widely used system, other types of content are necessary for running sites that don't fit within this predefined mold, which has traditionally catered to running blogs. WordPress enables plugin developers to create other content types to handle many different scenarios.

Post Type Possibilities

When WordPress 3.0 was released, it opened the door to an endless number of possibilities. Users could use the platform to run any type of web site. WordPress became a serious contender with other, more robust content management systems (CMS). It would no longer need to be considered simply a blogging platform.

Today, you can use custom post types in WordPress to define any type of content. Following is a sample list of ideas that custom post types can handle:

- ➤ Music collection
- ➤ Product testimonials
- ➤ Online store
- ➤ Famous quotes
- ➤ Event calendar
- ➤ Photo portfolio
- ➤ Book database
- ➤ Image slideshows
- ➤ Videos

Registering a Post Type

WordPress makes it easy for developers to step in and create new post types with little code. Before diving into the post type creation process, you need to understand the main function used for creating post types and its arguments.

register_post_type

You use the `register_post_type()` function to create new post types for a site. It's simple to use and gives plugin developers a lot of flexibility when creating post types.

```php
<?php
register_post_type( $post_type, $args );
?>
```

The `register_post_type()` function returns the post type object and accepts two parameters.

➤ `$post_type` — The name of the post type. This should contain only alphanumeric characters and underscores.

➤ `$args` — An array of arguments that define the post type and how it should be handled within WordPress.

WordPress enables many different arguments for the `$args` parameter, each with its own unique functionality that helps define how your post type will work within the WordPress environment. The following descriptions give you a basic understanding of each.

public

The argument that handles whether the post type should be shown on the frontend of the site and backend. By default, this is set to `false`. This is a catchall argument that defines the `show_ui`, `publicly_queryable`, and `exclude_from_search` arguments if they are not set individually.

show_ui

`show_ui` controls whether administration screens should be shown for the post type in the admin. This defaults to the value set by the `public` argument.

publicly_queryable

`publicly_queryable` controls whether the post type should be publicly queryable from the frontend of the site. This defaults to the value set by the `public` argument.

exclude_from_search

This argument enables you to exclude your post type's posts from search results on the site. By default, this is set to the value of the `public` argument.

supports

The `supports` argument enables plugins to define what features their post types support. It accepts an array of values that WordPress checks for internally. However, WordPress-supported features aren't the only features the post type can support. Other plugins/themes may optionally check for support of certain features.

WordPress checks for support of the following features. If your plugin does not set this argument, it defaults to the `title` and `editor` arguments.

➤ `title` — Enables users to enter a post title.

➤ `editor` — Displays a content editor on the post editing screen with a media uploader.

➤ `author` — Offers a select box to choose the author of the post.

➤ `thumbnail` — Presents a featured image box for the post.

➤ `excerpt` — Creates an excerpt editor on the post editing screen.

➤ `comments` — Shows whether comments will be enabled for posts of this type.

➤ `trackbacks` — Shows whether trackbacks and pingbacks will be enabled for posts of this type.

➤ `custom-fields` — Shows the custom field editing area on the post edit screen.

➤ `page-attributes` — Displays the attributes box for choosing the post order. The `hierarchical` argument must be set to `true` for this to work.

➤ `revisions` — Saves revisions of posts of this type.

labels

The `labels` argument is an array of text strings shown in various places in the admin for the post type. See the "Setting Post Type Labels" section for details on each label.

capability_type

This argument enables you to add a custom set of capabilities. It acts as a catchall term from which new capabilities are created. The `capabilities` argument can overwrite individual capabilities set by this argument. By default, its value is `post`.

capabilities

The `capabilities` argument is an array of custom capabilities required for editing, deleting, reading, and publishing posts of this type. See the "Using Custom Capabilities" section for details on each capability.

hierarchical

The `hierarchical` argument enables you to set the posts of this type to be ordered hierarchically (such as the WordPress "page" post type) or nonhierarchically (such as the WordPress "post" post type). If set to `true`, posts can be arranged in a hierarchical, tree-like structure. By default, the argument is set to `false`.

has_archive

The `has_archive` argument creates an archive page for the post type, much like the WordPress posts page that displays the site's latest blog posts. How these posts are displayed is dependent on the theme the user has installed. By default, this argument is set to `false`. If it is set to `true`, WordPress will create the archive.

query_var

This argument is the name of the query variable for posts of this type. For example, you would use this when querying posts of this type from the database.

rewrite

The `rewrite` argument creates unique permalinks for this post type. Valid values for it are `true`, `false`, or an array. If set to `true`, it will create permalinks from the `query_var` argument and the individual post title. If set to `false`, no permalink structure will be created.

If using an array, you may set several values:

➤ `with_front` — Whether to prefix permalinks with the permalink front base. By default, this is set to `true`.

➤ `slug` — A unique string to use before the post title in the permalink. This defaults to the `query_var` argument.

➤ `feeds` — Whether the post type should have feeds for its posts. The `has_archive` argument needs to be set to true for this to take effect. Its value will default to the `has_archive` value if neither is set.

➤ `pages` — Whether post type archive pages should be paginated. By default, it is set to `true`. This feature is only useful if the `has_archive` argument is also set to `true`.

taxonomies

This argument enables you to add support for preexisting taxonomies to the post type. It accepts an array of taxonomy names as its value. See the "Attaching Existing Taxonomies" section for more details on how to do this.

menu_position

`menu_position` enables you to set the position in which the administration menu item shows in the admin menu. By default, new post types are added after the Comments menu item.

menu_icon

This argument accepts an image filename to use as the menu icon in the admin menu.

show_in_nav_menus

If you want to allow posts of this type to appear in WordPress nav menus, set this to `true`; otherwise, set it to `false`. By default, it is set to the value of the `public` argument.

can_export

WordPress has an import/export feature that enables users to import or export posts. This argument enables you to set whether users can export posts of this type. It is set to `true` by default.

register_meta_box_cb

Plugins can add meta boxes to the edit post screen. This argument enables plugins to set a custom callback function for adding custom meta boxes within the `add_meta_box()` function for this post type (see Chapter 4, "Integrating in WordPress," for details on using meta boxes).

permalink_epmask

This is the rewrite endpoint bitmask used for posts of this type. By default, this is set to
`EP_PERMALINK`.

Registering the Music Album Post Type

Now that you've reviewed the arguments of the `register_post_type()` function, it's time to create
your first post type, which is the theme of this chapter.

The first step is to create a new plugin file called `boj-music-collection-post-types.php` to hold
your new plugin called "Music Collection Post Types." Using the following code, you register a post
type called `music_album`.

```php
<?php
/*
Plugin Name: Music Collection Post Types
Plugin URI: http://example.com
Description: Creates the music_album post type.
Version: 0.1
Author: WROX
Author URI: http://wrox.com
*/

/* Set up the post types. */
add_action( 'init', 'boj_music_collection_register_post_types' );

/* Registers post types. */
function boj_music_collection_register_post_types() {

    /* Set up the arguments for the 'music_album' post type. */
    $album_args = array(
        'public' => true,
        'query_var' => 'music_album',
        'rewrite' => array(
            'slug' => 'music/albums',
            'with_front' => false,
        ),
        'supports' => array(
            'title',
            'thumbnail'
        ),
        'labels' => array(
            'name' => 'Albums',
            'singular_name' => 'Album',
            'add_new' => 'Add New Album',
            'add_new_item' => 'Add New Album',
            'edit_item' => 'Edit Album',
            'new_item' => 'New Album',
            'view_item' => 'View Album',
            'search_items' => 'Search Albums',
            'not_found' => 'No Albums Found',
```

```
                    'not_found_in_trash' => 'No Albums Found In Trash'
            ),
        );

        /* Register the music album post type. */
        register_post_type( 'music_album', $album_args );
    }

?>
```

Code snippet boj-music-collection-post-types.php

This creates a new top-level menu item in the WordPress admin called Albums, as shown in Figure 11-1. The new menu item also has two submenu items: Albums and Add New Album. The former links to a page that lists the albums (after they're created) in the order that they've been published. The latter adds a new page for publishing new albums.

FIGURE 11-1

 The function your plugin uses to create post types must be added to the init *action hook. Otherwise, your post type won't be properly registered.*

Setting Post Type Labels

In the WordPress admin, several text strings are shown for the post type. Each piece of text typically represents a link, button, or extra information about the post. By default, hierarchical post types have the term "page" in these strings, and nonhierarchical post types have the term "post" in them.

These strings are placeholders for your plugin to change depending on the post type it creates. For example, you wouldn't want to show View Post when you intend to display View Album. By setting these strings, you can create a much nicer experience for your plugin users.

When you set up your initial music album post type, you set the `labels` array for the `$args` parameter with multiple values as shown in this excerpt from the code in the previous section:

```php
<?php

'labels' => array(
    'name' => 'Albums',
    'singular_name' => 'Album',
    'add_new' => 'Add New Album',
    'add_new_item' => 'Add New Album',
    'edit_item' => 'Edit Album',
    'new_item' => 'New Album',
    'view_item' => 'View Album',
    'search_items' => 'Search Albums',
    'not_found' => 'No Albums Found',
    'not_found_in_trash' => 'No Albums Found In Trash'
),

?>
```

Each of these labels is shown in some way within the admin to make for a better user experience:

➤ `name` — The plural name of the post type, which is sometimes used in the WordPress admin and by other plugins and themes.

➤ `singular_name` — The singular version of the name of the post type. It is also sometimes used in the WordPress admin and by other plugins and themes.

➤ `add_new` — The label used for the add new submenu item. The text defaults to Add New.

➤ `add_new_item` — Used as the button text on the main post listing page to add a new post. By default, the text is Add New Post/Page.

➤ `edit_item` — Used as the text for editing an individual post. Defaults to Edit Post/Page.

➤ `new_item` — Text for creating a new post. By default, it is set to New Post/Page.

➤ `view_item` — The text for viewing an individual post. It defaults to View Post/Page.

➤ `search_items` — Text displayed for searching the posts of this type. It defaults to Search Posts/Pages.

➤ `not_found` — The text shown when no posts were found in a search. By default, it displays No Posts/Pages Found.

➤ `not_found_in_trash` — The text shown when no posts are in the trash. Defaults to No Posts/Pages Found in Trash.

➤ `parent_item_colon` — Text shown when displaying a post's parent. This text is used only with hierarchical post types and displays Parent Page: by default.

Using Custom Capabilities

On some WordPress installations, there are several users, each with their own tasks to perform on the site. You need to keep this in mind when developing custom post types because site administrators often assign different user roles to editing and publishing content to specific sections of the site. Chapter 8, "Users," covers how to manipulate roles and capabilities. However, when registering custom post types, you'll likely want to set up custom capabilities for handling content.

The `capability_type` and `capabilities` arguments for the `$args` array in the `register_post_type()` function enable you to control this. `capability_type` gives you global control over the capabilities. The `capabilities` argument is an array that gives you specific control over individual capabilities.

Suppose you want to create custom capabilities for permission to these types of posts. The first option is to simply define the `capability_type` argument, which can automatically set each option in the `capabilities` array.

```php
<?php

'capability_type' => 'album',

?>
```

This can create several default capabilities for editing, reading, deleting, and publishing posts of this type:

➤ `edit_album`

➤ `edit_albums`

➤ `edit_others_albums`

➤ `publish_albums`

➤ `read_album`

➤ `read_private_albums`

➤ `delete_album`

If you want full control over how each of these capabilities is named, you would use the `capabilities` argument instead of the `capability_type` argument as shown in the following code.

```php
<?php

'capabilities' => array(
    'edit_post' => 'edit_album',
    'edit_posts' => 'edit_albums',
    'edit_others_posts' => 'edit_others_albums',
    'publish_posts' => 'publish_albums',
    'read_post' => 'read_album',
    'read_private_posts' => 'read_private_albums',
    'delete_post' => 'delete_album',
),

?>
```

Each capability grants permission for a specific task in the content publishing process for posts of this type:

➤ `edit_post` — The meta capability used to determine if a user can edit a specific post.

➤ `edit_posts` — A capability that grants access to creating and editing posts but does not enable publishing.

➤ `edit_others_posts` — Gives permission to edit posts created by other users.

➤ `publish_posts` — Grants publishing rights to the user to publish any posts of this type.

➤ `read_post` — The meta capability that determines if a user can read a specific post.

➤ `read_private_posts` — Enables the user to read privately published posts.

➤ `delete_post` — The meta capability used to determine if a user can delete a specific post.

You don't have to stick to a specific formula with custom post types though. Your plugin can mix these up. It can set the same capability for multiple capability options. Or it can set the same capability for each option. For example, you can set each of these capabilities to `manage_music_collection` if you know only certain users will have permission to manage all music album posts.

Another capability you can set is `do_not_allow` if you don't want to allow access to a specific task. Generally, you wouldn't use this, but some situations may call for it, such as setting `edit_others_posts` to `do_not_allow` so that no user can edit posts created by other users.

Attaching Existing Taxonomies

If your post type can make use of existing taxonomies, you can easily set this in the `taxonomies` argument within the `$args` array of `register_post_type()`. For example, WordPress has two general taxonomies that work great for other post types: `category` and `post_tag`. However, you're not limited to taxonomies created by WordPress. Your post type can use taxonomies created by other plugins and themes as well.

Imagine you wanted to add post tags to your music album post type. You would set this as shown in the following code:

```php
<?php

'taxonomies' => array( 'post_tag' ),

?>
```

By adding this to your `$args` array for `register_post_type()`, a new Post Tags submenu item will be added below your Albums menu item in the admin, as shown in Figure 11-2.

FIGURE 11-2

USING CUSTOM POST TYPES

Now that you've learned how to create custom post types, you need to use them. How they'll be used will be highly dependent on what functionality your custom post type should serve, but getting the content created by posts of this type will nearly always rely on WordPress' post-related functions.

To find functions for getting post information, you can look in one of two files within the WordPress install.

➤ `wp-includes/post.php` — Post functions and post utility functions

➤ `wp-includes/post-template.php` — Template functions for displaying post content

Each function serves a specific task within WordPress. By studying and using the functions within these files, you can start grasping how the post functions work.

Generally, it's the job of a WordPress theme to display posts on the frontend of the site. However, not all custom post types need to be displayed in the same manner. It depends on what functionality the custom post type is used for. To use custom post types, you need to learn a few functions typically considered theme territory.

Creating a Custom Post Type Loop

When you want to grab the content of a post or multiple posts, you can query these posts from the database by initializing a new `WP_Query` object and looping through each of the posts retrieved. Within this loop, you would use post template functions for outputting specific parts of the individual post objects.

Suppose you want to create a list of all album titles in alphabetical order with links to the individual albums for your music collection plugin. You're creating something called The Loop, where you use a PHP `while` loop to iterate through each post.

The following code is an example of how to display The Loop using a shortcode that users can place within a shortcode-aware area, such as the page editor (see Chapter 10, "The Shortcode API"). The user only needs to place [music_albums] within this area. You can add the following code to your "Music Collection Post Types" plugin from earlier in this chapter to provide this functionality.

```php
<?php

add_action( 'init', 'boj_music_album_register_shortcodes' );

function boj_music_album_register_shortcodes() {

    /* Register the [music_albums] shortcode. */
    add_shortcode( 'music_albums', 'boj_music_albums_shortcode' );
}

function boj_music_albums_shortcode() {

    /* Query albums from the database. */
    $loop = new WP_Query(
        array(
            'post_type' => 'music_album',
            'orderby' => 'title',
            'order' => 'ASC',
            'posts_per_page' => -1,
        )
    );

    /* Check if any albums were returned. */
    if ( $loop->have_posts() ) {

        /* Open an unordered list. */
        $output = '<ul class="music-collection">';

        /* Loop through the albums (The Loop). */
        while ( $loop->have_posts() ) {

            $loop->the_post();

            /* Display the album title. */
            $output .= the_title(
                '<li><a href="' . get_permalink() . '">',
                '</a></li>',
                false
            );

        }

        /* Close the unordered list. */
        $output .= '</ul>';
    }

    /* If no albums were found. */
```

```
    else {
        $output = '<p>No albums have been published.';
    }

    /* Return the music albums list. */
    return $output;
}

?>
```

Code snippet boj-post-type-loop.php

This custom loop can output a list of items similar to the list shown in Figure 11-3 if any new albums have been published.

The most important part of the previous code is the `post_type` argument in the array passed to `WP_Query`. It must be set to the name of your post type. In this case, you used `music_album` for this value because it is your post type's name.

The only limit to how you can display posts of custom post types is your PHP development skills. You can use The Loop to display posts in any manner you want. You can display them in widgets (refer to Chapter 4) or create a shortcode as you did in the previous code (see Chapter 10, "The Shortcode API"). It's entirely dependent on what you want your plugin to do.

- Gettin' Funky With WordPress
- In Love With Plugins
- Lovin' WordPress
- Rockin' WordPress
- The WordPress Blues
- WordPress Redneck

FIGURE 11-3

Retrieving Custom Post Type Content

WordPress has several functions for retrieving content of posts. This section focuses on the most common functions for retrieving post data; however, other functions exist for getting other data about the post. You should always use these functions within The Loop, which is what you created in the previous section. Typically, WordPress themes use these functions to display content on the frontend of the site; however, your plugin may need them to display posts.

the_title

This function displays the title of the post. It displays something only if a title is given for the post. For example, if your plugin doesn't set `title` in the `supports` argument for `register_post_type()`, you wouldn't use this function to display a title. It accepts three parameters.

```php
<?php
the_title( $before, $after, $echo );
?>
```

➤ `$before` — Content to display before the post title. This defaults to an empty string.

➤ `$after` — Content to display after the post title. This defaults to an empty string.

➤ `$echo` — Whether to print the title to the screen or return it for use in PHP code. By default, it is set to `true`.

the_content

This function enables you to display the content written in the post editor by the user. For it to display any content, post content must be written. Also, the `editor` value needs to be added to the `supports` array for `$args` in `register_post_type()` for users to add content. If this is not set, you probably won't need this function.

```php
<?php
the_content( $more_link_text, $stripteaser );
?>
```

➤ `$more_link_text` — Text to show a continue reading link if a user sets the `<!--more-->` quick tag in the post editor.

➤ `$stripteaser` — Whether to display the content written before the `<!--more-->` quick tag is used. By default, this is set to `false`.

the_excerpt

This function shows an excerpt of the post content. If your post type sets `excerpt` in the `supports` argument for the `$args` parameter in `register_post_type()`, it can create an excerpt box that users can use to write custom excerpts. If this is not set or the user doesn't write a custom excerpt, one will be auto-created from the post content.

```php
<?php
the_excerpt();
?>
```

the_permalink

This function displays the permanent link (the URL) to the given post. It links to the singular view of the post. You would use it as the `href` attribute within HTML hyperlinks.

```php
<?php
the_permalink();
?>
```

Checking if a Post Type Exists

There may be some scenarios in which you need to check if a post type exists before running any particular code. For example, you may want to check if the `music_album` post type exists before registering your own `music_album` post type. Or you may want to offer integration with other plugins' post types with your plugin.

post_type_exists

The `post_type_exists()` function checks whether the post type has been registered with WordPress. It accepts a single parameter of `$post_type`, which should be a string representing the post type name. It returns `true` if the post type exists or `false` if it doesn't exist.

```php
<?php
post_type_exists( $post_type );
?>
```

Suppose you wanted to display a message depending on whether the music_album post type has been registered. Using the following code, you can perform this task.

```php
<?php

/* If music_album post type is registered. */
if ( post_type_exists( 'music_album' ) ) {

    echo 'The music_album post type has been registered.';
}

/* If the music_album post type is not registered. */
else {

    echo 'The music_album post type has not been registered.';
}

?>
```

POST METADATA

In WordPress, posts can have additional information attached to them. This information is called post metadata and is saved in the $wpdb->postmeta table in the database.

Post metadata is often referred to as Custom Fields in WordPress terminology. This is more of a term used for an easier user experience so that users are not scared off by developer terms such as metadata. By default, WordPress adds a meta box on the post/page editor screens for adding custom fields, as shown in Figure 11-4.

For custom post types to use this feature on the post-editing screen, the custom-fields value must be set for the supports argument when using register_post_type() as described in the "Registering a Post Type" section.

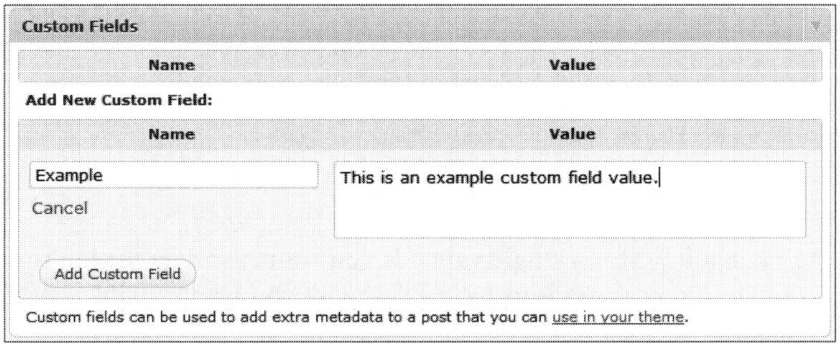

FIGURE 11-4

The true power of post metadata isn't in enabling users to manually create and input keys and values in the Custom Fields section on the post editor screen. Plugins can create, update, and delete these values without the user ever knowing that they're manipulating metadata.

To hide this knowledge from the end user, you would create custom meta boxes for the post screen. (For more information on creating custom meta boxes, refer to Chapter 4.) This chapter focuses on the functions you would use to manipulate metadata.

Throughout this section on post metadata, you create, retrieve, update, and delete a user's favorite song(s) from a music album (your custom post type created in the post type section).

Adding Post Metadata

WordPress provides a simple function for adding new post metadata. Use this to update a user's favorite song. When adding new metadata, it appears in the Custom Fields select box, as shown in Figure 11-4.

add_post_meta

You use the `add_post_meta()` function to add new post metadata to a specific post, which accepts four parameters.

```php
<?php
add_post_meta( $post_id, $meta_key, $meta_value, $unique );
?>
```

➤ `$post_id` — The ID of the post to add metadata to.

➤ `$meta_key` — The metadata key (name) to add meta value(s) to.

➤ `$meta_value` — The value attributed to the meta key. Multiple meta values may be added to a single key.

➤ `$unique` — Whether the meta value provided should be the only meta value. If `true`, there will be only a single meta value. If `false`, multiple meta values can be added. By default, this parameter is set to `false`.

Now that you know how the parameters work for `add_post_meta()`, you can insert some metadata to a specific post. Suppose you have a post (album) with the ID of `100` and the user's favorite song from the album is "If Code Could Talk." You would use the following code to update this value.

```php
<?php

add_post_meta( 100, 'favorite_song', 'If Code Could Talk', true );

?>
```

Setting the `$unique` parameter to `true` allows for a single value. If you want to allow for multiple values for the `favorite_song` meta key, you can set it to `false`. Suppose you want to add another song called "WordPress Makes Me Happy." You can set both values using two instances of `add_post_meta()`.

```php
<?php

add_post_meta( 100, 'favorite_song', 'If Code Could Talk', false );
add_post_meta( 100, 'favorite_song', 'WordPress Makes Me Happy', false );

?>
```

 To hide meta keys from appearing in the Custom Fields select box on the post-editing screen, prefix the meta key with an underscore like _favorite_song. *This makes sure users never see it and is common practice when creating custom meta boxes.*

Retrieving Post Metadata

WordPress makes it easy to get post metadata for display or to use in other PHP functions. A good place to use this functionality is within The Loop, which you learned how to use in the "Using Custom Post Types" section.

get_post_meta

The get_post_meta() function retrieves metadata for a specific post and accepts three parameters.

```php
<?php
get_post_meta( $post_id, $meta_key, $single );
?>
```

➤ $post_id — The ID of the post to get the metadata for.

➤ $meta_key — The meta key name to retrieve meta value(s) for.

➤ $single — Whether to return a single meta value (true) or return an array of values (false). By default, this parameter is set to false.

Suppose you want to get a single meta value for the favorite_song meta key. You can use the following code to display the message "Favorite song from this album: If Code Could Talk."

```php
<?php

/* Get a single favorite song by the favorite_song meta key. */
$favorite_song = get_post_meta( 100, 'favorite_song', true );

/* Display the meta value. */
echo 'Favorite song from this album: ' . $favorite_song;

?>
```

You could also display each of the meta values for the favorite_song meta key. Imagine that you want to create a list of all the favorite songs.

```php
<?php

/* Get all meta values for the favorite_song meta key. */
$favorite_songs = get_post_meta( 100, 'favorite_song', false );

/* Open an unordered list. */
echo '<ul class="favorite-songs">';

/* Loop through each meta value. */
foreach ( $favorite_songs as $song ) {

    /* Display the individual meta value. */
    echo '<li>' . $song . '</li>';
}

/* Close the unordered list. */
echo '</ul>';

?>
```

Updating Post Metadata

WordPress provides the ability to update post metadata as well. You can use this functionality when you need to update a preexisting meta value or completely overwrite all meta values for a given meta key. You can also use it to add a meta key and values if none are present.

update_post_meta

The `update_post_meta()` function exists to update previous metadata for a specific post or to add new metadata if it is not already set. This function accepts four parameters.

```php
<?php
update_post_meta( $post_id, $meta_key, $meta_value, $prev_value );
?>
```

➤ `$post_id` — The post ID to update meta value(s) for.

➤ `$meta_key` — The meta key to update meta value(s) for.

➤ `$meta_value` — The new meta value to add to the meta key.

➤ `$prev_value` — The previous meta value to overwrite. If this parameter is not set, all meta values will be overwritten in favor of the `$meta_value` parameter.

If you want to update an existing meta value, use the `update_post_meta()` function. For example, if you want to change the `favorite_song` value of "If Code Could Talk" to a new value, "WP Blues," you can use the following code to do this.

```php
<?php

update_post_meta( 100, 'favorite_song', 'WP Blues', 'If Code Could Talk' );

?>
```

Alternatively, you can overwrite all meta values for the `favorite_song` meta key by not adding the `$prev_value` parameter. In the next example, you overwrite all previous values with the value of WP Blues.

```php
<?php

update_post_meta( 100, 'favorite_song', 'WP Blues' );

?>
```

Deleting Post Metadata

There will be scenarios in which you need to delete post metadata completely or to delete a single meta value from a given meta key. WordPress makes this process simple for developers.

delete_post_meta

The `delete_post_meta()` function enables you to delete metadata for a specific post, and it accepts three parameters.

```php
<?php
delete_post_meta( $post_id, $meta_key, $meta_value );
?>
```

➤ `$post_id` — The post ID to delete metadata for.

➤ `$meta_key` — The meta key to delete or the meta key to delete a meta value for.

➤ `$meta_value` — The meta value to delete for the given meta key. If this parameter is not set, all meta values for the meta key will be deleted.

If you wanted to delete a single value for the `favorite_song` meta key, you need to make sure the `$meta_value` parameter is set. In this case, you delete the "If Code Could Talk" meta value by setting it as the `$meta_value` parameter.

```php
<?php

delete_post_meta( 100, 'favorite_song', 'If Code Could Talk' );

?>
```

The preceding usage of `delete_post_meta()` deletes a single meta value. If you want to delete all the meta values for the `favorite_song` meta key for this post, leave the `$meta_value` parameter empty.

```php
<?php

delete_post_meta( 100, 'favorite_song' );

?>
```

CREATING CUSTOM TAXONOMIES

Taxonomies are a way to group or categorize objects in WordPress, such as posts, links, and users. For the purposes of this chapter, focus on creating taxonomies for posts.

WordPress ships with several taxonomies by default:

➤   **Category** — A hierarchical taxonomy used to categorize blog posts

➤   **Post Tag** — A nonhierarchical taxonomy used to tag blog posts

➤   **Link Category** — A nonhierarchical taxonomy used to categorize links

➤   **Nav Menu** — A nonhierarchical taxonomy that represents navigation menus and groups nav menu items

The greatest power of custom taxonomies is creating them for custom post types. Creating a custom post type almost makes it necessary to include additional organizational methods for the individual posts of that type.

Understanding Taxonomies

To understand how taxonomies work, you must understand that an individual taxonomy is a group of terms. Each term of the taxonomy would define how posts fit into that taxonomy.

The post types section covered how to create a new post type: music album. Users would use this post type to organize their collection of music albums. Each post would be an album. Users might want a way to further organize their music collection by grouping similar albums within given taxonomies. Some possible taxonomies for music albums follow:

➤   Artist (WP Hot Boys, Code Rockstars)

➤   Genre (Rock, Blues, R&B)

➤   Format (CD, vinyl, cassette)

➤   Studio (WP Productions, Code Is Music)

Each of these taxonomies would enable users to label their music albums with information that further defines the content. Essentially, taxonomies provide clearer organization and definition for content.

This section focuses on creating the Artist and Genre taxonomies for the music album post type you created within the post types section.

 This chapter focuses solely on creating taxonomies for post types because this will be the scenario they'll be used for in most cases. However, you can add taxonomies to any object type in WordPress, such as links and users.

Registering a Custom Taxonomy

Registering a taxonomy requires the use of only a single function provided by WordPress: `register_taxonomy()`. This function enables you to register a new taxonomy and set it up by using custom arguments to define how the taxonomy should be handled within WordPress.

register_taxonomy

In your plugin file, you use the `register_taxonomy()` function to create a new taxonomy. It accepts three parameters.

```php
<?php
register_taxonomy( $taxonomy, $object_type, $args );
?>
```

➤ `$taxonomy` — The name of your plugin's taxonomy. This should contain only alphanumeric characters and underscores.

➤ `$object_type` — A single object or an array of objects to add the taxonomy to.

➤ `$args` — An array of arguments that defines how WordPress should handle your taxonomy.

The `$args` parameter is what enables you to customize your taxonomies. The following descriptions of each argument can give you an understanding of how you can set up taxonomies to your needs.

public

The `public` argument determines whether the taxonomy should be publicly queryable from the frontend of the site. By default, this argument is set to `true`.

show_ui

This argument decides if a WordPress-generated user interface should be added in the admin for managing the taxonomy. This argument is set to the value of the `public` argument by default.

hierarchical

The `hierarchical` argument determines if the taxonomy's terms should be in a hierarchical or nonhierarchical (flat) format. If this argument is set to `true`, terms may have parent terms within the taxonomy. By default, the argument is set to `false`.

query_var

This argument is the name of the query variable for terms of this taxonomy. For example, you would use this when querying posts for a specific term of this taxonomy from the database. You can set it to a custom string, `true`, or `false`. Set it to `true` to use the taxonomy name as the argument, or set it to `false` to prevent queries. By default, this argument is set to the taxonomy name.

rewrite

The rewrite argument creates permalinks (URLs) for the term archive pages for the taxonomy. It accepts one of three values: `true`, `false`, or an array. If set to `true`, it creates permalinks from the taxonomy name and the individual term slug. If set to `false`, no permalink structure will be created.

If your plugin uses an array, you can set a few arguments:

➤ `with_front` — Whether to prefix permalinks with the permalink front base. By default, this is set to `true`.

➤ `slug` — Unique string to use before the term slug in the permalink. This is set to the taxonomy name by default.

➤ `hierarchical` — Whether terms with parents should show the parent terms in their permalink structure. The taxonomy must be hierarchical for this to work. By default, this is set to `false`.

update_count_callback

You may set a custom function for this argument to be called when the term count is updated, which generally happens when a post is saved.

show_tagcloud

This argument determines whether the taxonomy can be used in the WordPress tag cloud widget. If set to `true`, the taxonomy's terms can be shown with the widget. If set to `false`, the terms cannot be shown. The argument defaults to the value of the `show_ui` argument.

show_in_nav_menus

The `show_in_nav_menus` argument decides whether the terms of the taxonomy can be added to user-created nav menus in the admin. By default, this argument is set to the value of the `public` argument.

labels

When creating your taxonomy, you need to provide the best user experience possible. The `labels` argument enables you to set text strings that are generally used in the admin to provide information about the taxonomy or its terms. If you do not set these labels, WordPress automatically creates labels with the term `Tags` for nonhierarchical taxonomies and the term `Categories` for hierarchical taxonomies.

The `labels` argument is an array of text strings. Following is a description of each key in the array.

➤ `name` — The plural name of the taxonomy.

➤ `singular_name` — The singular name of the taxonomy.

➤ `search_items` — The text shown for searching for terms within the taxonomy.

➤ `popular_items` — Text displayed when showing a tag cloud of popular terms of the taxonomy. This text isn't used for hierarchical taxonomies.

➤ `all_items` — Text shown for a link to view all terms of the taxonomy.

➤ `parent_item` — Text used to show a parent term. This isn't used for nonhierarchical taxonomies.

➤ `parent_item_colon` — Text displayed when showing a parent term, followed by a colon at the end of the text. This label isn't used for nonhierarchical taxonomies.

➤ `edit_item` — Text shown when editing a term.

➤ `update_item` — Text shown to update a term.

➤ `add_new_item` — Text displayed to create a new term.

➤ `new_item_name` — Text shown to create a new term name.

➤ `separate_items_with_commas` — A sentence letting users to know to separate individual terms with commas. This label isn't used with hierarchical taxonomies.

➤ `add_or_remove_items` — A sentence telling users to add or remove terms when JavaScript in their browser is disabled. This text isn't used with hierarchical taxonomies.

➤ `choose_from_the_most_used` — A sentence enabling users to choose from the most-used terms of a taxonomy. This label isn't used with hierarchical taxonomies.

capabilities

When developing your custom taxonomy, you need to keep in mind what users should have permission to manage, edit, delete, and assign terms of the taxonomy. The capabilities argument is an array of capabilities that you set to control this. Chapter 8 covers capabilities in detail.

➤ `manage_terms` — Grants users the ability to manage terms of the taxonomy. This enables them to use the category-to-tag converter and to view the taxonomy's terms in the taxonomy page in the admin. Defaults to `manage_categories`.

➤ `edit_terms` — Gives users the ability to edit terms of the taxonomy. Defaults to `manage_categories`.

➤ `delete_terms` — Permission to delete terms from the taxonomy. Defaults to `manage_categories`.

➤ `assign_terms` — Grants the ability to assign terms from the taxonomy to a post. Defaults to `edit_posts`.

Registering the Genre and Artist Taxonomies

Now that you've reviewed the `register_taxonomy()` parameters and arguments in detail, it's time to use that knowledge to create new taxonomies.

In the next example, you create two new taxonomies, `album_artist` and `album_genre`, for the "music album" post type that you created in the first part of this chapter. The artist taxonomy is nonhierarchical and the genre taxonomy is hierarchical.

```php
<?php

/* Set up the taxonomies. */
add_action( 'init', 'boj_music_collection_register_taxonomies' );

/* Registers taxonomies. */
function boj_music_collection_register_taxonomies() {

    /* Set up the artist taxonomy arguments. */
    $artist_args = array(
```

```php
            'hierarchical' => false,
            'query_var' => 'album_artist',
            'show_tagcloud' => true,
            'rewrite' => array(
                'slug' => 'music/artists',
                'with_front' => false
            ),
            'labels' => array(
                'name' => 'Artists',
                'singular_name' => 'Artist',
                'edit_item' => 'Edit Artist',
                'update_item' => 'Update Artist',
                'add_new_item' => 'Add New Artist',
                'new_item_name' => 'New Artist Name',
                'all_items' => 'All Artists',
                'search_items' => 'Search Artists',
                'popular_items' => 'Popular Artists',
                'separate_items_with_commas' => 'Separate artists with commas',
                'add_or_remove_items' => 'Add or remove artists',
                'choose_from_most_used' => 'Choose from the most popular artists',
            ),
        );

        /* Set up the genre taxonomy arguments. */
        $genre_args = array(
            'hierarchical' => true,
            'query_var' => 'album_genre',
            'show_tagcloud' => true,
            'rewrite' => array(
                'slug' => 'music/genres',
                'with_front' => false
            ),
            'labels' => array(
                'name' => 'Genres',
                'singular_name' => 'Genre',
                'edit_item' => 'Edit Genre',
                'update_item' => 'Update Genre',
                'add_new_item' => 'Add New Genre',
                'new_item_name' => 'New Genre Name',
                'all_items' => 'All Genres',
                'search_items' => 'Search Genres',
                'parent_item' => 'Parent Genre',
                'parent_item_colon' => 'Parent Genre:',
            ),
        );

        /* Register the album artist taxonomy. */
        register_taxonomy( 'album_artist', array( 'music_album' ), $artist_args );

        /* Register the album genre taxonomy. */
        register_taxonomy( 'album_genre', array( 'music_album' ), $genre_args );
}

?>
```

Code snippet boj-music-collection-taxonomies.php

After you add the preceding code, you'll be presented with two new submenu items under the Albums menu item in the admin, labeled Artists and Genres. You also have two new meta boxes for assigning artists and genres to individual albums, as shown in Figure 11-5.

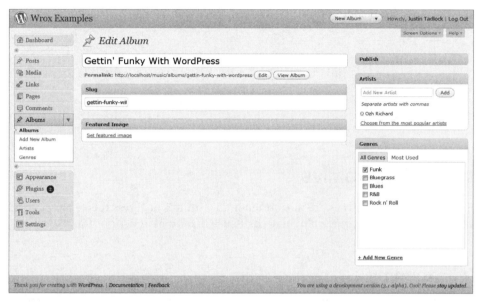

FIGURE 11-5

 Your function for registering new taxonomies must be added to the `init` *action hook for the taxonomies to be properly registered.*

Assigning a Taxonomy to a Post Type

Sometimes, you may need to assign taxonomy to a post type when your plugin does not create the taxonomy or the post type. If your plugin creates the taxonomy, you would do this with the `register_taxonomy()` function, or if your plugin needs to add a preexisting taxonomy, it would set this in the `register_post_type()` function as you've seen earlier. However, you may not always have the benefit of using those functions when you need to assign taxonomy to a post type.

register_taxonomy_for_object_type

This function enables you to set taxonomy to any object type, which will typically be a specific post type. It accepts two parameters and returns `true` if successful and `false` if not.

```php
<?php
register_taxonomy_for_object_type( $taxonomy, $object_type );
?>
```

➤ `$taxonomy` — The name of the taxonomy your plugin will add to the post type.

➤ `$object_type` — The name of the object type to add the taxonomy to. Most of the time, this will be a post type. This value can be a single object type or an array of object types.

One example of setting a specific taxonomy to a post type is giving the "page" post type the "post tag" taxonomy, which is usually used for the "post" post type. Using the following code, you can add this taxonomy to it.

```php
<?php

/* Adds the post_tag taxonomy to the page post type. */
register_taxonomy_for_object_type( 'post_tag', 'page' );

?>
```

USING CUSTOM TAXONOMIES

As with custom post types, taxonomies are most often used within WordPress theme template files. However, there are scenarios where your plugin needs to use taxonomy functions for displaying information.

Retrieving a Taxonomy

In some cases, you may need to get a taxonomy object to retrieve information about a registered taxonomy. The taxonomy object is a PHP object created for registered taxonomies using the arguments supplied for the `$args` array in `register_taxonomy()`.

get_taxonomy

The `get_taxonomy()` function accepts a single parameter of `$taxonomy`, which should be the name of the taxonomy. It returns the taxonomy object.

```php
<?php
get_taxonomy( $taxonomy );
?>
```

Suppose you need to display the `singular_name` label of the `album_genre` taxonomy that you registered. You'd use the following code to get the taxonomy object and display this label.

```php
<?php

/* Get the genre taxonomy object. */
$genre = get_taxonomy( 'album_genre' );

/* Display the singular name of the genre taxonomy. */
echo $genre->labels->singular_name;

?>
```

Using a Taxonomy with Posts

When using taxonomy with posts, you'll generally be listing the taxonomy terms for the given post alongside some or all the content of the post. This would allow viewers to note there is a taxonomy for the post and allow them to find related posts by a given taxonomy term.

the_terms

The the_terms() function returns a formatted list of terms for a given taxonomy of a specific post. It accepts five parameters.

```php
<?php
the_terms( $id, $taxonomy, $before, $sep, $after );
?>
```

➤ $id — The ID of the post to list the taxonomy's terms for.

➤ $taxonomy — The name of the taxonomy to list terms for.

➤ $before — Content to display before the list of terms.

➤ $sep — Any string of text or HTML to separate individual terms in the list. This defaults to a comma.

➤ $after — Content to display after the list of terms.

The the_terms() function is a wrapper function for get_the_term_list(). The former function displays the list of terms for the taxonomy, and the latter returns them for use in PHP.

Now revisit the custom shortcode you created in the section on custom post types in which you listed posts of the music album post type. This time, use the get_the_term_list() function to add each album's artist(s) and genre(s) to the list.

You can add the following two lines of code to your shortcode function for displaying the album artist(s) and genre(s):

```php
$output .= get_the_term_list( get_the_ID(), 'album_artist', 'Artist: ', ', ', ' ' );

$output .= get_the_term_list( get_the_ID(), 'album_genre', 'Genre: ', ', ', ' ' );
```

The following is what the code should now look like to display the album_artist and album_genre taxonomy terms:

Available for download on Wrox.com

```php
<?php

add_action( 'init', 'boj_music_album_register_shortcodes' );

function boj_music_album_register_shortcodes() {

    /* Register the [music_albums] shortcode. */
```

```php
    add_shortcode( 'music_albums', 'boj_music_albums_shortcode' );
}

function boj_music_albums_shortcode() {

    /* Query albums from the database. */
    $loop = new WP_Query(
        array(
            'post_type' => 'music_album',
            'orderby' => 'title',
            'order' => 'ASC',
            'posts_per_page' => -1,
        )
    );

    /* Check if any albums were returned. */
    if ( $loop->have_posts() ) {

        /* Open an unordered list. */
        $output = '<ul class="music-collection">';

        /* Loop through the albums (The Loop). */
        while ( $loop->have_posts() ) {

            $loop->the_post();

            /* Display the album title. */
            $output .= the_title(
                '<li><a href="' . get_permalink() . '">',
                '</a></li>',
                false
            );

            /* Insert a line break. */
            $output .= '<br />';

            /* Show the album artist. */
            $output .= get_the_term_list( get_the_ID(), 'album_artist',
                'Artist: ', ', ', ' ' );

            /* Show the album genre. */
            $output .= get_the_term_list( get_the_ID(), 'album_genre',
                'Genre: ', ', ', ' ' );

        }

        /* Close the unordered list. */
        $output .= '</ul>';
    }

    /* If no albums were found. */
    else {
        $output = '<p>No albums have been published.';
    }

    /* Return the music albums list. */
```

```
        return $output;
    }

    ?>
```

Code snippet boj-post-type-taxonomy-loop.php

This code can give you a list of items similar to the list shown in Figure 11-6.

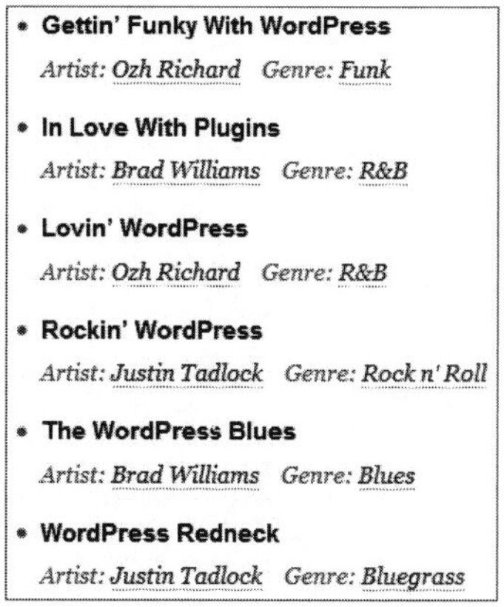
• Gettin' Funky With WordPress
Artist: Ozh Richard Genre: Funk
• In Love With Plugins
Artist: Brad Williams Genre: R&B
• Lovin' WordPress
Artist: Ozh Richard Genre: R&B
• Rockin' WordPress
Artist: Justin Tadlock Genre: Rock n' Roll
• The WordPress Blues
Artist: Brad Williams Genre: Blues
• WordPress Redneck
Artist: Justin Tadlock Genre: Bluegrass

FIGURE 11-6

Taxonomy Conditional Tags

WordPress has a few conditional tags for taxonomies. Conditional tags check a specific condition and return `true` if the condition is met or `false` if the condition is not met.

taxonomy_exists

The `taxonomy_exists()` function checks if a taxonomy has been registered with WordPress. It accepts a single parameter of `$taxonomy`, which should be the name of the taxonomy you're checking.

```
<?php
taxonomy_exists( $taxonomy );
?>
```

Suppose you wanted to check if the artist taxonomy you created earlier exists. Using the following code, you can display a custom message based on the return value of the `taxonomy_exists()` function.

```
<?php

/* If the album artist taxonomy exists. */
if ( taxonomy_exists( 'album_artist' ) ) {

    echo 'The "artist" taxonomy is registered.';
}

/* If the album artist taxonomy doesn't exist. */
else {

    echo 'The "artist" taxonomy is not registered.';
}

?>
```

is_taxonomy_hierarchical

The `is_taxonomy_hierarchical()` function determines if a given taxonomy is hierarchical. It accepts a single parameter of `$taxonomy`, which should be the name of the taxonomy.

```php
<?php
is_taxonomy_hierarchical( $taxonomy );
?>
```

The album genre taxonomy you created is hierarchical, but the album artist taxonomy is not hierarchical. Now create an array of taxonomy names and loop through each, creating a list of messages to determine whether each is hierarchical.

```php
<?php

/* Create an array of custom taxonomies. */
$taxonomies = array(
    'album_artist',
    'album_genre'
);

/* Open an unordered list. */
echo '<ul>';

/* Loop through the array of taxonomies. */
foreach ( $taxonomies as $tax ) {

    /* If the taxonomy is hierarchical. */
    if ( is_taxonomy_hierarchical( $tax ) ) {
        echo '<li>The ' . $tax . ' taxonomy is hierarchical.</li>';
    }

    /* If the taxonomy is non-hierarchical. */
    else {
        echo '<li>The ' . $tax . ' taxonomy is non-hierarchical.</li>';
    }
}

/* Close the unordered list. */
echo '</ul>';

?>
```

is_tax

The is_tax() function determines if a site visitor is on a term archive page on the frontend of the site. When using no parameters, it simply checks if the visitor is on any taxonomy archive. However, you may optionally set either parameter for a more specific check.

```php
<?php
is_tax( $taxonomy, $term );
?>
```

➤ $taxonomy — The name of the taxonomy to check for. Defaults to an empty string.

➤ $term — The name of the term from the taxonomy to check for. Defaults to an empty string.

With the next snippet of code, you display up to three different messages depending on which conditions are true. You first check to see if a visitor is on a taxonomy term archive. You then check for a specific taxonomy: genre. Then, you check if the archive page is in the blues genre.

```php
<?php

/* If on a taxonomy term archive page. */
if ( is_tax() ) {
    echo 'You are viewing a term archive.';
}

/* If viewing a term archive for the album genre taxonomy. */
if ( is_tax( 'album_genre' ) ) {
    echo 'You are viewing a term archive for the genre taxonomy.';
}

/* If viewing the blues archive for the album genre taxonomy. */
if ( is_tax( 'album_genre', 'blues' ) ) {
    echo 'You are viewing the blues archive for the genre taxonomy.';
}

?>
```

A POST TYPE AND TAXONOMY PLUGIN

Now that you covered how to use post types and taxonomies, you can put both techniques together to make a plugin based on this knowledge. The name of your plugin is Music Collection. It enables users to create new music albums and organize the albums by genre and artist. What you're doing here is putting together code you've already covered throughout this chapter.

The first step you'll take is creating a new file in your plugins directory named `boj-music-collection.php` and adding your plugin header at the top of this file.

Available for download on Wrox.com

```php
<?php
/*
Plugin Name: Music Collection
Plugin URI: http://example.com
Description: Keeps track of a music collection by album, artist, and genre.
Version: 0.1
Author: WROX
Author URI: http://wrox.com
*/
```

Code snippet boj-music-collection.php

The next step is to create the `music_album` post type, which was outlined in the "Registering a Post Type" section.

```
/* Set up the post types. */
add_action( 'init', 'boj_music_collection_register_post_types' );

/* Registers post types. */
function boj_music_collection_register_post_types() {

    /* Set up the arguments for the 'music_album' post type. */
    $album_args = array(
        'public' => true,
        'query_var' => 'music_album',
        'rewrite' => array(
            'slug' => 'music/albums',
            'with_front' => false,
        ),
        'supports' => array(
            'title',
            'thumbnail'
        ),
        'labels' => array(
            'name' => 'Albums',
            'singular_name' => 'Album',
            'add_new' => 'Add New Album',
            'add_new_item' => 'Add New Album',
            'edit_item' => 'Edit Album',
            'new_item' => 'New Album',
            'view_item' => 'View Album',
            'search_items' => 'Search Albums',
            'not_found' => 'No Albums Found',
            'not_found_in_trash' => 'No Albums Found In Trash'
        ),
    );

    /* Register the music album post type. */
    register_post_type( 'music_album', $album_args );
}
```

Code snippet boj-music-collection.php

The final step of the process is creating the taxonomies for the music_album post type: album_artist and album_genre. How to register a taxonomy was covered in the "Registering a Custom Taxonomy" section.

```
/* Set up the taxonomies. */
add_action( 'init', 'boj_music_collection_register_taxonomies' );

/* Registers taxonomies. */
function boj_music_collection_register_taxonomies() {

    /* Set up the artist taxonomy arguments. */
    $artist_args = array(
        'hierarchical' => false,
        'query_var' => 'album_artist',
        'show_tagcloud' => true,
```

```php
        'rewrite' => array(
            'slug' => 'music/artists',
            'with_front' => false
        ),
        'labels' => array(
            'name' => 'Artists',
            'singular_name' => 'Artist',
            'edit_item' => 'Edit Artist',
            'update_item' => 'Update Artist',
            'add_new_item' => 'Add New Artist',
            'new_item_name' => 'New Artist Name',
            'all_items' => 'All Artists',
            'search_items' => 'Search Artists',
            'popular_items' => 'Popular Artists',
            'separate_items_with_commas' => 'Separate artists with commas',
            'add_or_remove_items' => 'Add or remove artists',
            'choose_from_most_used' => 'Choose from the most popular artists',
        ),
    );

    /* Set up the genre taxonomy arguments. */
    $genre_args = array(
        'hierarchical' => true,
        'query_var' => 'album_genre',
        'show_tagcloud' => true,
        'rewrite' => array(
            'slug' => 'music/genres',
            'with_front' => false
        ),
        'labels' => array(
            'name' => 'Genres',
            'singular_name' => 'Genre',
            'edit_item' => 'Edit Genre',
            'update_item' => 'Update Genre',
            'add_new_item' => 'Add New Genre',
            'new_item_name' => 'New Genre Name',
            'all_items' => 'All Genres',
            'search_items' => 'Search Genres',
            'parent_item' => 'Parent Genre',
            'parent_item_colon' => 'Parent Genre:',
        ),
    );

    /* Register the album artist taxonomy. */
    register_taxonomy( 'album_artist', array( 'music_album' ), $artist_args );

    /* Register the album genre taxonomy. */
    register_taxonomy( 'album_genre', array( 'music_album' ), $genre_args );
}

?>
```

Code snippet boj-music-collection.php

At this point, you have created an entire plugin with minimal code that creates and organizes a new type of content within WordPress. All that's left is learning other techniques presented throughout this book to make your plugin even stronger, such as adding widgets (refer to Chapter 4) and creating shortcodes (refer to Chapter 10) for your post types and taxonomies.

SUMMARY

This chapter represents a small sampling of what's possible with custom post types, post metadata, and taxonomies. The biggest lesson you should take away is that you can literally use WordPress to create and manage any type of content you can imagine. The platform isn't simply limited to blog posts and pages.

The information presented in this chapter reveals many possibilities for plugin developers. You can make plugins for public use to give thousands of people new ways to manage content. Or you can use these tools for custom client web sites that have unique content needs.

12

JavaScript and Ajax in WordPress

WHAT'S IN THIS CHAPTER?

➤ Understanding jQuery and Ajax

➤ Correctly loading JavaScript in WordPress

➤ Adding scripts only when needed

➤ Making interactive interfaces with Ajax in WordPress

➤ Implementing security checks in your Ajax requests

JavaScript is principally a language used to code plain text script executed on the client side, that is, the browser. In this chapter, occurrences of the term "script" refer to JavaScript script.

This chapter offers a concise introduction to jQuery, a JavaScript library used by WordPress, and to Ajax. Then it focuses on the WordPress specifics, introducing the functions and concepts you need to know, and eventually you author plugins using JavaScript and Ajax.

JQUERY—A BRIEF INTRODUCTION

jQuery is a popular JavaScript framework: It is used by more than 40% of the top million sites followed by Quantcast (source: http://trends.builtwith.com/javascript) and, more specific to this book's subject, is used by WordPress. jQuery on its own deserves more than an entire book, so this will be only a short preamble.

Benefits of Using jQuery

What makes jQuery such a great library and the reasons why it comes with WordPress are among the following:

➤ It is light: The minified and gzipped library is only 24kb.

➤ It uses a quick and terse syntax for faster developing (the write-less-do-more library).

➤ It is completely a cross browser: What you develop works the same in IE 6+, Firefox 2+, Safari 3+, Chrome, and Opera 9+.

➤ It is CSS3-compliant: It supports CSS 1-3 selectors (select document elements such as `div p.asides` or `tr:nth-child(odd) td`).

➤ It makes things easier to work on: Events, DOM object manipulation and traversing, effects, common utilities, and so on.

➤ It makes Ajax much simpler and easily reads JSON and XML.

➤ It has a great documentation, available at `http://docs.jquery.com/`.

It's of course possible to use any other library such as PrototypeJS, Mootools, or YUI with WordPress, but because WordPress uses jQuery for its internal need, you also have lots of great code to dissect and study when you want to understand the innards of a particular behavior.

jQuery Crash Course

The scope of this section is not to teach you how to master this powerful JavaScript library in a few minutes but to give you some basis to read on without being completely lost, and WordPress specific information.

The jQuery Object

In old school JavaScript, you may have written code like

```
document.getElementById('container').getElementsByTagName('a')
```

to select elements that your CSS would simply call `#container a`. With jQuery, you can now simply write the following:

```
$('#container a')
```

The dollar `$` sign is a shortcut to the `jQuery` object.

Syntax and Chaining

JQuery methods can be chained together, which will return the `jQuery` object, as you will see in the following short practical example.

Create a minimalist HTML content that includes the latest jQuery script from the official website:

```
<html>
<head>
<script src='http://code.jquery.com/jquery.js'></script>
<title>Quick jQuery example</title>
</head>
<body>
<p class="target">click on me!</p>
<p class="target">click on me!</p>
<p class="target">click on me!</p>
</body>
</html>
```

Now, right before the closing `</body>` tag, insert a jQuery snippet to add a background and a border to each paragraph, and which, when clicked, changes the background color while shrinking it for 2 seconds before making it disappear:

```
<script type="text/javascript">
$('p.target')
    .css( { background:'#eef', border: '1px solid red' } )
    .click(function(){
    $(this)
        .css('background','#aaf')
        .animate(
            { width:'300px', borderWidth:'30px', marginLeft:'100px'},
            2000,
            function(){
                $(this).fadeOut();
            }
        );
    });
</script>
```

Code snippet jquery-example.html

If you dissect this compact snippet, you can see the main structure:

```
$('p.target').css(    ).click( function(){    } );
```

This applies some styling to the selected paragraph and then defines the behavior when the event `'click'` occurs on this element. Chaining enables a method to return an object itself as a result, reducing usage of temporary variables and enabling a compact syntax.

Similarly, within the function defining the click behavior, you can see several methods applied to the `$(this)` object, referencing the current jQuery object instantiated by the initial `$('p.target')`.

What you have now is three independently animated paragraph blocks, as shown in Figure 12-1.

FIGURE 12-1

No-Conflict Mode in WordPress

jQuery is not the only JavaScript library to use the $ sign. For example, PrototypeJS uses $ as a simple shortcut to the longer function `document.getElementById()`.

To enable coexistence with other libraries, jQuery has a no-conflict mode, activated by default within WordPress, which gives back $ to other libraries. The result of this is that if you port existing jQuery code to a WordPress environment, you need to use one of these solutions:

1. Write `jQuery( )` instead of each `$( )`.
2. Use a jQuery wrapper.

To illustrate this, consider the initial jQuery code you would need to port into a WordPress no-conflict environment:

```
$('.something').each( function(){
    $(this).addClass( 'stuff' );
});
$.data( document.body, 'foo', 1337 );
```

Option one would give the following result:

```
jQuery('.something').each( function(){
    jQuery(this).addClass( 'stuff' );
});
jQuery.data( document.body, 'foo', 1337 );
```

Option two would give the following result:

```
// jQuery noConflict wrapper:
(function($) {
    // $() will work here
    $('.something').each( function(){
        $(this).addClass( 'stuff' );
    });
    $.data( document.body, 'foo', 1337 );
})(jQuery);
```

Both solutions are programmatically equal, but using a no-conflict wrapper will enable you to more conveniently and easily use existing code without having to replace each $ with a longer `jQuery`.

Launching Code on Document Ready

A frequent requirement in JavaScript is to make sure that elements in a page load before you can do something with them. Here is a snippet you may have used before:

```
window.onload = function(){
    /* do something */
}
```

This ancient technique has two weaknesses:

1. Another script can easily overwrite the `window.onload` definition with its own function.

2. The `onload` event in JavaScript waits for everything to be fully loaded before executing, including images, banner ads, external widgets, and so on.

With jQuery you get a much better solution:

```
$(document).ready( function(){
    /* do something */
});
```

Now, as soon as the DOM hierarchy has been fully constructed, the document `"ready"` event triggers: This happens before images load, before ads are shown, so the user experience is much smoother and faster.

You can combine the document-ready function with a jQuery `noConflict()` wrapper, like the following:

```
jQuery(document).ready(function($) {

    // $() will work as an alias for jQuery() inside of this function

});
```

Using this technique, you can use the `$( )` syntax and be sure that you do not reference a DOM element that has not been rendered by the browser yet.

AJAX

In the WordPress interface when you write a new post, you can add or remove tags and categories without refreshing the whole page: This is Ajax.

Ajax is a web development technique that enables a page to retrieve data asynchronously, in the background, and to update parts of the page without reloading it. The word originally stands as an acronym for Asynchronous JavaScript And XML, but despite its name the use of XML is not actually mandatory. You can sometimes read it as AJAX, but the form Ajax is more widely adopted.

Ajax is not a technology or a programming language but a group of technologies: It involves client-side scripts such as JavaScript and server-side script such as PHP that outputs content in HTML, CSS, XML, and JSON — or actually mostly anything.

What Is Ajax?

You can now code a simple yet illustrative example of what Ajax is. The page you write can asynchronously fetch from Twitter the latest tweets of a given user.

First, start with a basic HTML page structure.

```
<html>
<head>
    <title>Ajax Example</title>
    <script src='http://code.jquery.com/jquery.js'></script>
</head>
<body>
    <h1>Ajax example, reading JSON response</h1>
    <p>View <a id="load" href="http://twitter.com/ozh">Ozh' latest tweets</a></p>
    <div id="tweets"></div></body>
</html>
```

The two things you notice in this HTML document follow:

1. The page includes the jQuery script.

2. There is an empty placeholder: `<div id="tweets"></div>`.

Now onto the Ajax bits: When clicking the link to Twitter, it should display the latest tweets in the page rather than redirecting to Twitter. The link click behavior can be overtaken:

```
<script type="text/javascript">

// When the DOM is ready, add behavior to the link
$(document).ready(function(){

    $('#load').click(function(){
        load_tweets();
        // Skip default behavior (ie redirecting to the link href)
        return false;
    });

});

</script>
```

You now need to define the function that fetches and displays the latest tweets:

```
<script type="text/javascript">
// Main function: load tweets in JSON
function load_tweets() {

    // Activity indicator:
    $('#tweets').html('loading tweets...');

    // Ajax JSON request
    $.getJSON(
        // Use a JSONP (with callback) URL
```

```
                'http://twitter.com/status/user_timeline/ozh.json?count=5&callback=?',

                // Function that will handle the JSON response
                function(data) {
                    // Put empty <ul> in the placeholder
                    $('#tweets').html('<ul></ul>');
                    // Read each object in the JSON response
                    $(data).each(function(i, tweet) {
                        $('#tweets ul').append('<li>'+tweet.text+'</li>');
                    });
                }
            );
    }
    </script>
```

What just happened?

When called by a click on the link, the function `load_tweets()` adds some feedback so that the user knows that something is happening in the background ("loading. . .") and then send a JSON request to Twitter, which if successful will be handled by the callback function that goes through each JSON item and adds its text element to the placeholder. These events happen on the same page without reloading the page, as shown in Figure 12-2.

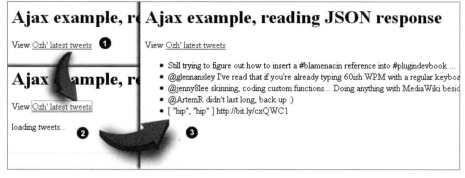

FIGURE 12-2

 An important limitation of Ajax to understand is the Same Origin Policy: Due to browser security restrictions, most Ajax requests cannot successfully retrieve data from a different domain, subdomain, or even protocol. JSONP requests (as used here) are not subject to the same origin policy restrictions.

You have coded a page with a client script that can update a part of the HTML document (the empty `<div>` placeholder) with data asynchronously fetched: This is a typical Ajax example.

Review the entire page with both the HTML and the JavaScript:

```html
<html>
<head>
    <title>Ajax Example</title>
    <script src='http://code.jquery.com/jquery-1.4.2.js'></script>
</head>

<body>
    <h1>Ajax example, reading JSON response</h1>
    <p>View <a id="load" href="http://twitter.com/ozh">Ozh' latest tweets</a></p>
    <div id="tweets"></div>

<script type="text/javascript">

// When the DOM is ready, add behavior to the link
$(document).ready(function(){

    $('#load').click(function(){
        load_tweets();
        // Skip default behavior (ie sending to the link href)
        return false;
    });

});

// Main function: load tweets in JSON
function load_tweets() {

    // Activity indicator:
    $('#tweets').html('loading tweets...');

    // Ajax JSON request
    $.getJSON(
        'http://twitter.com/status/user_timeline/ozh.json?count=5&callback=?',

        // Callback function with JSON response
        function(data) {
            // Put empty <ul> in the placeholder
            $('#tweets').html('<ul></ul>');
            // Read each object in the JSON response and add text to the <ul>
            $(data).each(function(i, tweet) {
                $('#tweets ul').append('<li>'+tweet.text+'</li>');
            });
        }
    );
}
</script>
</body>
</html>
```

Code snippet ajax-example-twitter.html

Ajax Best Practices

This simple page is also a neat example of a few JavaScript and Ajax good practices:

➤ **Unobtrusive JavaScript** — No inelegant `onclick="doSomething()"` bits added to HTML elements; the behavior is added via JavaScript, and the content is separated from the function. First write content; then add functions.

➤ **Accessible content** — A direct consequence of unobtrusive JavaScript is that, on a browser with no JavaScript such as screen readers that sight-impaired people use, the page makes sense with a proper link to Twitter.

➤ **Activity indicator** — When the user clicks the View Tweets links, there is immediate feedback ("loading. . ."). This is important to let the user know that something is happening in the background.

➤ **User feedback** — When a part of the page updates successfully, it should be obvious to the user. (A counter example would be, for instance, a login box at the top of a page that would add content to the bottom of the page.) In more complex applications, it's also important to deal with errors and let the user know when something unexpectedly failed.

 Ajax popularized the usage of tiny animated images, called throbbers, to indicate background activity. Sites such as http://ajaxload.info/ *enable you to create your own images that match your design.*

ADDING JAVASCRIPT IN WORDPRESS

Back to your favorite topic: WordPress! You now learn how to use JavaScript in WordPress: first the important techniques, and then full-fledged plugins illustrating them.

The main skill to master is how to add JavaScript into pages that WordPress generates. As trivial as it may sound at first, it can quickly become a source of conflicts between plugins or with the core if incorrectly done.

A Proper Way to Include Scripts

The main function you use to insert JavaScript into a WordPress page is `wp_enqueue_script()`, which as it name suggests adds a script to a queue of required scripts.

Introducing wp_enqueue_script()

The goal of `wp_enqueue_script()` is to register a script and tell WordPress to properly inject it in the page. The function syntax and its five arguments follow:

```php
<?php
// Add a script to the insert queue
wp_enqueue_script( $handle, $src, $dependencies, $ver, $in_footer );
?>
```

➤ `$handle` — The only mandatory argument of the function, this represents the name of the script in the form of a lowercase string. The name of the script is either provided by WordPress or is a custom name registered by your plugin. In such a case, you should of course make it unique.

➤ `$src` — If provided, this is the URL of the script. WordPress needs this parameter only if it does not know this script yet. If the script is already known, this parameter will be simply ignored.

➤ `$dependencies` — An optional array of handles the script you want to add depends on and as such that must be loaded before. This parameter is needed only if WordPress does not know about this script.

➤ `$ver` — An optional version number, in the liberal form of a string such as 1.0 or 3.0.1-RC1. This makes sure the browser fetches the correct version of a script, regardless of its caching settings.

➤ `$in_footer` — An optional Boolean you set to `true` if instead of having your script injected into the `<head>` of the document, you want it placed at the bottom of the page near the closing `</body>` tag.

Using WordPress' queue system to add scripts has four virtues:

1. No matter how many plugins require the same script, it will be added only once into the page.

2. You can precisely select on what page you want to add your script. You learn how to do this a little bit later.

3. Specifying dependencies as described next, you can expressly set the order in which several scripts will be included in the page, no matter the sequence of `wp_enqueue_script()` function calls.

4. Scripts are added in compliance to the `FORCE_SSL_ADMIN` constant value. (That is, if the user uses WordPress over https in the admin area, scripts will be added over https, too.)

Typically, you will use `wp_enqueue_script()` hooked to an early action that occurs before any content is sent to the browser, such as `'init'` or `'template_redirect'`, and the function call will output a proper `<script>` tag in the resulting HTML document, as in the following snippet:

```
<?php
add_action( 'init', 'boj_js_add_script' );

function boj_js_add_script() {
    wp_enqueue_script( $handle, $src, $dependencies, $ver, $in_footer );
}
?>
```

You will use the various parameters of `wp_enqueue_script()` depending on the scenario, as you will now read in concrete examples of different usages.

Adding a Core Script

You can easily use `wp_enqueue_script()` to add a core script to your PHP code, for instance the Prototype JavaScript library.

```php
<?php

// Example 1: Add prototype.js which is bundled with WordPress
function boj_js_add_script1() {
    wp_enqueue_script( 'prototype' );
}
?>
```

In this first example, no script source is provided: WordPress ships with a version of the JavaScript framework PrototypeJS and thus knows where to find it.

This is equivalent to adding the following line to the document <head>:

```
<script type="text/javascript"
    src="http://example.com/wp-includes/js/prototype.js?ver=1.6.1"></script>
```

Notice the query string appended to the script URL: WordPress affixes the known version number to known scripts.

Adding a Custom Script

To add a custom script to your code with `wp_enqueue_script()` you need to specify its source as well as its handle.

```php
<?php

// Example 2: Add a custom script
function boj_js_add_script2() {
    wp_enqueue_script( 'boj1', 'http://example.com/script1.js' );
}
?>
```

In this example, you need to specify the full location of the script because it's not a core script.

This is equivalent to the following:

```
<script type="text/javascript"
    src="http://example.com/script1.js?ver=3.1"></script>
```

Notice again the version number in the script URL. Because the version number is omitted in the `wp_enqueue_script()` call, WordPress appends its own version number to it.

Adding a Custom Script with Dependencies

Now you will look at how you can clarify that your script has dependencies on other scripts.

```php
<?php

// Example 3: Add a custom script that relies on jQuery components
function boj_js_add_script3() {
    wp_enqueue_script(
        'boj2',
```

```
        'http://example.com/script2.js',
        array( 'jquery-ui-tabs', 'jquery-ui-draggable' )
    );
}
?>
```

Here you have specified that the script depends on other scripts, which therefore need to be loaded before. These scripts are included in WordPress, so their handle is enough information. This single line outputs in the HTML document the following set of script `includes`:

```
<script type='text/javascript'
 src='http://example.com/wp-includes/js/jquery/jquery.js?ver=1.4.2'></script>
<script type='text/javascript'
 src='http://example.com/wp-includes/js/jquery/ui.core.js?ver=1.7.3'></script>
<script type='text/javascript'
 src='http://example.com/wp-includes/js/jquery/ui.tabs.js?ver=1.7.3'></script>
<script type='text/javascript'
 src='http://example.com/wp-includes/js/jquery/ui.draggable.js?ver=1.7.3'></script>
<script type='text/javascript'
 src='http://example.com/script2.js?ver=3.1'></script>
```

Adding a Custom Script with a Version Number

Including version numbers with your scripts is often practical, and it is easy to accomplish.

```
<?php

// Example 4: Add a custom script with version number
function boj_js_add_script4() {
    wp_enqueue_script( 'boj3', 'http://example.com/script3.js', '', '1.3.3.7' );
}
?>
```

This inserts the following bits to the document <head>:

```
<script type='text/javascript'
    src='http://example.com/script3.js?ver=1.3.3.7'></script>
```

If you maintain a plugin and update its JavaScript, keeping track of the version included is a good idea to avoid browser caching issues. Typically, you would, for instance, define a constant that holds the current plugin version and use this constant anywhere needed in your plugin.

Adding Scripts in the Footer

By default, `wp_enqueue_script()` will output the corresponding `<script>` tag within the `<head>` of the resulting HTML document. Instead, you can elect to add it near the end of document with passing `true` as a last parameter:

```
<?php

// Example 5: Add a custom script in the footer
function boj_js_add_script5() {
```

```
        wp_enqueue_script( 'boj4', 'http://example.com/script4.js', '', '', true );
    }
    ?>
```

Example 5 adds the script near the closing `</body>` tag. The potential interest of adding a script to the page footer is discussed later in this chapter, in the section titled "Where To Include Scripts."

 Injecting a script in the footer is possible if WordPress knows that it is currently rendering the footer. In the admin area, this always works, but for the blog part it requires the theme to use the `wp_footer()` *function in its footer. Any good theme should do this, but be warned that bad themes exist!*

All Parameters at Once

As a wrap-up, you will now review a call to the function `wp_enqueue_script()` with all parameters used at once.

```php
<?php

// Example 6: All parameters specified
function boj_js_add_script6() {
    wp_enqueue_script(
        'boj5',
        'http://example.com/script5.js',
        array( 'boj1' ),
        '6.6.6',
        true
    );
}
?>
```

This function call includes the script with version 6.6.6 in the footer. Notice how you have declared a dependency to script `boj1`, which is feasible because the script is now known by WordPress since example 2. Stating dependency to an unknown script would result in nothing being eventually included in the page.

Default Core Scripts

As you've read in this chapter and may already know, WordPress comes with numerous core scripts. You will find these scripts in the following:

➤ `/wp-includes/js` and subdirectories for scripts either used on the public part (the site itself) or the admin backend

➤ `/wp-admin/js` and subdirectories for scripts WordPress uses in the admin area

All these core scripts exist in two versions: a minified `.js` file and a readable (commented and indented) `.dev.js` version. By default, the minified files are included to save bandwidth, but

you can toggle this behavior for debugging purpose by adding the following line to your
`wp-config.php`:

```php
<?php
define( 'SCRIPT_DEBUG', true );
?>
```

Handles for all the core scripts are defined in the function `wp_default_scripts()` to be found in
`wp-includes/script-loader.php`. Refer to this function source if you need to include a core script
and need to know its handle. The most frequently used in plugins follow:

➤   `'jquery'` for the jQuery framework

➤   jQuery components such as `'jquery-ui-core'`, `'jquery-ui-tabs'`, `'jquery-ui-sortable'` or `'jquery-ui-draggable'`

➤   `'thickbox'` for the floating iframe (such as the one popping over when you want to upload
    an image in a post for instance), also known as a "thickbox"

Removing a Queued Script

If you want to prevent a script from loading, you can use function `wp_dequeue_script()` to remove
it from the queue as follows:

```php
<?php
add_action( 'init', 'boj_js_remove_queued' );

function boj_js_remove_queued() {
    // Don't include PrototypeJS
    wp_dequeue_script( 'prototype' );

    // Don't include a script added by another plugin
    wp_dequeue_script( 'some_script' );
}
?>
```

You can also use function `wp_script_is( $handle )` to check if a script is registered and
enqueued. This trick can be useful in the following, and unfortunately not hypothetical, scenario:

Imagine you've authored a new plugin with a neat settings page that makes good use of JavaScript
and Ajax. Quickly, you start to receive support requests about JavaScript functionalities broken
when another particular plugin is activated.

Indeed, it is not uncommon that plugin authors incorrectly add their scripts to all admin pages when
it's actually needed only on their plugin settings page. (You'll see later in this chapter in the section
"Adding Script Only When Needed" how to add scripts to selected particular pages.) Doing so, they
can involuntarily break other plugins' settings pages.

At this point, you have two options to make your plugin compatible with the culprit:

➤   Either contact the other plugin authors and tell them to correctly insert their script only
    where needed; if you're lucky, they will update it.

➤   Or on your own plugin settings page, dequeue the conflicting script.

Replacing a Core Script with Your Own

WordPress comes with its own scripts, but that does not mean you cannot replace them. For instance, instead of using the built-in jQuery framework, you can tell your sites to load it from Google's Content Delivery Network (CDN). By doing so the end user will download the framework from a highly reliable server that is possibly geographically closer than your own server thanks to Google's data centers. You will also increase the chances that the user already has the file in their cache and thus save bandwidth on your own server.

To do this, simply cut and paste the following snippet into all your plugins:

Available for download on Wrox.com

```php
<?php

// Replace in-house jQuery with Google's one
add_action( 'init', 'boj_jquery_from_cdn' );
if( !function_exists( 'boj_jquery_from_cdn' ) ) {
    function boj_jquery_from_cdn() {
        wp_deregister_script( 'jquery' );
        wp_register_script(
            'jquery',
            'http://ajax.googleapis.com/ajax/libs/jquery/1.4.3/jquery.min.js'
        );
    }
}
?>
```

Code snippet boj_jquery_cdn.php

This snippet does the following:

➤ Early in the WordPress instantiation process (on action `'init'`), the function `boj_jquery_from_cdn()` is called.

➤ This function (defined only if it does not already exist because you may have pasted this snippet in several plugins) deregisters jQuery as known by WordPress and then registers it again, this time with another script location.

The function `wp_register_script()` does not enqueue the script for inclusion in the page; it just "introduces" it to WordPress for later use if required.

Registering and Enqueuing Scripts

If you need to enqueue the same script several times in a plugin, you can use the shorthand function `wp_register_script()` introduced in the previous paragraph.

First, define your script, using the same parameters as with function `wp_enqueue_script()`:

```php
<?php
wp_register_script( $handle, $src, $deps, $ver, $in_footer );
?>
```

Now you can enqueue it anytime needed:

```php
<?php
wp_enqueue_script( $handle );
?>
```

Managing Styles in WordPress

This is outside the scope of this chapter but simply too similar not to be mentioned: You can add, register, and enqueue style sheets (that is, CSS files) the same way you add scripts, with similar functions accepting the same parameters:

➤ Core styles are defined in `wp_default_styles()` in file `wp-includes/script-loader.php`.

➤ Add styles with `wp_enqueue_style()`.

Where to Include Scripts

You now know that using `wp_enqueue_script()` you can elect to insert your script in the document header or at the end of the document body. How does this matter?

You've also read that it is important to insert your scripts only when needed, for instance on your plugin's settings page. How can you do this?

Head? Footer? Inline?

The function `wp_enqueue_script()` can insert scripts in the `<head>` or near the closing `</body>` tag. But you can also insert them manually, echoing `<script src="http://example.com/script.js"></script>` in your code. Finally, you can also insert your script inline in your document.

Each situation has its preferred method:

In the Head

The typical script inclusion adds a JavaScript library in the document `<head>`, as `wp_enqueue_script()` does by default:

```html
<head>
    <script type="text/javascript" src="/js/library.js"></script>
</head>
```

Doing so, the page elements may not be available to the script because they are not loaded yet. You can typically include here libraries and function definitions that can then be used later in the page.

Near the Footer

The opposite alternative is to add the `<script>` tag near the end of the HTML document, hence usually in the footer of the page:

```html
<script type="text/javascript" src="/js/script.js"></script>
</body>
</html>
```

This technique has been widely advocated by Yahoo! in its "Best Practices for Speeding Up Your Web Site" (see `http://developer.yahoo.com/performance/rules.html`). This rule can be effective if you need to include a third-party script that can potentially slow down or halt the rendering of your page while it loads and executes, for instance a widget hosted on another site. By adding it late in the page, the reader has a chance to actually view some page content before the widget halts the page rendering, making the overall experience less clunky.

In the Page Content

Another way to add JavaScript in the page is to insert its `<script>` tag in an arbitrary location within the page:

```
    </p>
  </div>
  <div>
      <script type="text/javascript" src="/js/script.js"></script>
```

There are situations when you won't want to always load a script in the head or the footer. Back to Chapter 10, "The Shortcode API," for a moment: In this chapter you've created a plugin that adds a Google map script only if the post contains the appropriate shortcode. Doing this, you load the script only if a post in the page needs it, instead of systematically loading it with `wp_enqueue_script()`.

Inline

The last option to add JavaScript is to add it inline in the document, instead of specifying the `src` attribute of the `<script>` tag:

```
    </p>
  </div>
  <div>
      <script type="text/javascript">
      var something = 123;
      do_something();
      </script>
```

You can also add small chunks of JavaScript inline, typically when it won't clutter the page with too much inline content and does not justify making an external JavaScript file.

If you want to pay attention to HTML or XHTML code validation, remember to use the following syntax:

VALID XHTML SYNTAX

```
<script type="text/javascript">
/* <![CDATA[ */
// content of your Javascript goes here
/* ]]> */
</script>
```

VALID HTML 5 SYNTAX

```
<script>
// content of your Javascript goes here
</script>
```

Pondering the Best Option

The preferred JavaScript library to develop with WordPress is jQuery, which has a convenient method to state that a script should start executing only when the DOM (that is, the page elements) is ready. If you use jQuery's document ready method, it becomes rather unimportant if the script is loaded in the header, the footer, or anywhere in the page.

For scripts that you did not author and do not rely on such a DOM ready technique, it is still relevant to consider the best spot to load them.

Adding Scripts Only When Needed

More important than where in the page to load a script is to load it only when needed. Doing so, you not only reduce site load, page rendering time, and bandwidth usage, but you also decrease the chances of having your scripts conflict with another script they don't relate with.

You can now code a plugin that performs this important task of adding a given script where needed and only where needed. Because the objective of this section is to learn how to target in WordPress specific pages for JavaScript inclusion, the scripts are simple `alert()` boxes to instantly identify which script has loaded.

Getting the Location of Your Plugin's Scripts

Your plugin has to guess its own URL on the user install before it can add to pages the JavaScript it ships with. In Chapter 2, "Plugin Foundation," you learned about an appropriate plugin folder structure, with a subdirectory for each type of file, as shown in Figure 12-3.

FIGURE 12-3

Assuming you follow this sane advice, the following snippet includes a file named `script.js` located within the `/js` subdirectory of your plugin directory:

```php
<?php

// guess current plugin directory URL
$plugin_url = plugin_dir_url( __FILE__ );

// Enqueue script
wp_enqueue_script( 'boj_script', $plugin_url.'js/script.js' );
?>
```

This is a great snippet to reuse: It does not hardcode anything related to the user install specifics (location of the `wp-content` directory, for instance). The function `plugin_dir_url()` returns the URL directory path (with a trailing slash) for the plugin file passed as a parameter. (It will, for instance, return `http://example.com/wp-content/plugins/bj_insertjs/`).

> *Never hardcode the path or URL of your plugin: You cannot assume where the* `wp-content` *folder will be on a user's install because it does not necessarily exist within the main WordPress directory. Instead, opt for this always safe snippet to guess your plugin's location, which works even if the user renames your plugin folder.*

For this plugin you can use `boj_insertjs` as a prefix, and the plugin starts with defining its own script location:

Available for download on Wrox.com

```php
<?php
/*
Plugin Name: Add JavaScript
Plugin URI: http://example.com/
Description: Demonstrates how to properly insert JS into different pages
Author: Ozh
Author URI: http://wrox.com
*/

// URL to the /js directory of the plugin
define( 'BOJ_INSERTJS', plugin_dir_url( __FILE__ ).'js' );
```

Code snippet boj_insertjs/plugin.php

Adding in Admin Pages

The general rule is that `wp_enqueue_script()` needs to be called early and before any content has been printed to the page. The hook and technique to use depends on where exactly you need the script.

The plugin can add a different script on various pages:

➤ One script on all admin pages

➤ One script only on the plugin settings page

➤ One script only on another plugin generated page under the Users menu

➤ One script only on the Edit Comments page

Because the script you want to add here concerns only the admin area, you can rely on a hook that occurs only in this context. Since you add a few pages in the admin menu, the hook `admin_menu` is a perfect candidate:

```
// Add new admin pages
add_action('admin_menu', 'boj_insertjs_add_page');

// Add new admin pages
function boj_insertjs_add_page() {
```

Within this function you will now sequentially add the four scripts, as detailed in the following snippets:

```
// 1. Add JS to all the admin pages
wp_enqueue_script( 'boj_insertjs_1', BOJ_INSERTJS.'/admin.js' );
```

You enqueued a script that can load in all pages of the admin area, either built-in such as the dashboard or created by plugins:

```
// 2. Add a page under Settings
$settings = add_options_page( 'Insert JS', 'Insert JS', 'manage_options',
    'boj_insertjs_settings', 'boj_insertjs_options_page'
);
```

Now you added a menu entry using `add_options_page()`. Using the return value of this function call, you can hook into an interesting hook that is "`load-$pagename`" where the page name is a variable part:

```
// Add JS to the plugin setting page only
add_action( 'load-'.$settings, 'boj_insertjs_add_settings_script' );
```

This action fires only when loading the plugin settings page. Now create another plugin page, and use a different hook to also fire an action only on that page:

```
// 3. Add a page under Users
$users = add_users_page( 'Insert JS', 'Insert JS', 'manage_options',
    'boj_insertjs_users', 'boj_insertjs_users_page'
);

// 4. Add JS to the users page, with a different hook
add_action( 'admin_print_scripts-'.$users, 'boj_insertjs_add_users_script' );

} // end of function boj_insertjs_add_page()
```

These two admin page specific actions now need to be defined: They will be regular `wp_enqueue_script()` calls:

```
// Add JS to the plugin's settings page
function boj_insertjs_add_settings_script() {
    wp_enqueue_script( 'boj_insertjs_2', BOJ_INSERTJS.'/settings.js' );
}

// Add JS to the plugin's users page, in the page footer for a change
function boj_insertjs_add_users_script() {
    wp_enqueue_script( 'boj_insertjs_3', BOJ_INSERTJS.'/users.js',
        '', '', true
    );
}
```

You can now load another script into a specific and core admin page, for instance the Comments page. Again, the load-$pagename hook can prove useful:

Available for download on Wrox.com

```
// Add JS to the Comments page
add_action( 'load-edit-comments.php', 'boj_insertjs_on_comments' );
function boj_insertjs_on_comments() {
    wp_enqueue_script( 'boj_insertjs_4', BOJ_INSERTJS.'/comments.js' );
}
```

Code snippet boj_insertjs/plugin.php

Using wp_enqueue_script() attached to specific admin hooks, you have made sure that given scripts load only where needed in the admin area.

This cannot be emphasized enough: Always be selective regarding where to add JavaScript, and target precisely pages where your scripts will be needed. Most of the time you need to add a custom script to your plugin settings page only: Use the above trick.

Adding in Public Pages

To add scripts to the public area, the principle is similar: Rely on a hook that will be triggered only when the blog part is viewed, for instance 'template_redirect', which is triggered when WordPress is about to load the required theme.

Available for download on Wrox.com

```
// Add JS to pages of the blog
add_action( 'template_redirect', 'boj_insertjs_add_scripts_blog' );
function boj_insertjs_add_scripts_blog() {

    // To all pages of the blog
    wp_enqueue_script( 'boj_insertjs_5', BOJ_INSERTJS.'/blog.js' );

    // To single post pages
    if( is_single() ) {
```

```
            wp_enqueue_script( 'boj_insertjs_6', BOJ_INSERTJS.'/single.js' );
        }

        // To the "About" page
        if( is_page('About') ) {
            wp_enqueue_script( 'boj_insertjs_7', BOJ_INSERTJS.'/about.js' );
        }
    }
```

Code snippet boj_insertjs/plugin.php

What you have done here is hook into an action that occurs only on the public part, and then using conditional tags such as is_single(), you have targeted specific pages. You can learn more about these conditional tags at http://codex.wordpress.org/Conditional_Tags.

Of course, you can select on which page to add JavaScript using other conditions than just the page type. Following are examples on how to add a script if a user is not logged in or add another script only if the single post being viewed has comments:

```
// Add script if user is not logged
add_action( 'template_redirect', 'boj_insertjs_notlogged' );
function boj_insertjs_notlogged() {
    if( !is_user_logged_in() )
        wp_enqueue_script( 'boj_insertjs_8', BOJ_INSERTJS.'/notlogged.js' );
}

// Add script on single post & pages with comments only
add_action( 'template_redirect', 'boj_insertjs_add_ifcomments' );
function boj_insertjs_add_ifcomments() {
    if( is_single() ) {
        global $post;
        if( $post->comment_count )
            wp_enqueue_script( 'boj_insertjs_9', BOJ_INSERTJS.'/hascomments.js' );
    }
}
```

Dynamic Scripts in WordPress

JavaScript files are usually static .js files, but you sometimes need your script to be aware of data coming from WordPress, such as an option value or a plugin path.

How Not to Do It and Why

An obvious way to make your script dynamic would be to serve a dynamic script.js.php file instead of a static one so that PHP generates the JavaScript on-the-fly.

To make such a script aware of WordPress data, a common way adopted by a lot of coders is something along the lines of this:

1. In WordPress, enqueue the dynamic script as usual:

```php
<?php

wp_enqueue_script( 'dyn', $path.'/script.js.php' );
?>
```

2. In the `script.js.php` file, start the file with the following:

```php
<?php

header('Content-type: application/javascript');
include( '../../../wp-load.php' );
?>
/* javascript (and PHP) code here */
```

This (albeit frequent) solution has several critical flaws:

➤ Finding `wp-load.php` or `wp-config.php` can be difficult: The whole `wp-content` directory could be placed somewhere nonstandard and not necessarily as a subdirectory of the folder where `wp-load.php` is. Failing to properly include this file can result in a fatal error when the script tries to access a WordPress function.

➤ Requiring `wp-load.php` in an embedded file wholly instantiates WordPress again, which means that for every page request the load on the web server will be doubled: two WordPress init, both reading all options from memory, each loading plugins, and so on.

➤ Depending on the configuration, browsers may not cache `.js.php` files, which may cause server and bandwidth issues on active web sites.

A Better Solution

The preceding solution is tempting because the `.js.php` file enables flexible code, for instance having the file to output totally different JavaScript code depending on variable values.

If you must use such a file, a better solution is to pass the needed variable as query arguments to the `.js.php` file and make this one completely independent from WordPress (in other words, not loading `wp-load.php`).

1. In WordPress, get the needed information and then enqueue the dynamic script with query arguments:

```php
<?php

// Get info the script needs
$var1 = get_option( 'myplugin_var1' );
$var2 = get_home_url();

// Craft dynamic script query
$script = 'script.js.php?var1=' . $var1 . '&var2=' . $var2 ;
wp_enqueue_script( 'dyn', $path.'/'.$script );
?>
```

2.   Now your `script.js.php` file would look like this:

```php
<?php
header('Content-type: application/javascript');

// Get variable
$var  = isset( $_GET['var1'] ? $_GET['var1'] : '' );
$home = isset( $_GET['var2'] ? $_GET['var2'] : '' );

?>
/* javascript (and PHP) code here using $var and $home */
```

This solution is arguably better because you don't instantiate WordPress another time in the script file, which is now completely independent from WordPress and the folders' location.

There is still a potential problem to address regarding caching because browsers may or may not cache the `script.js.php?args` file. Although this won't be a big deal if the script is to be used in the admin area only, it can be problematic on the public side of the site where page hits are much more frequent and from many more different users.

An Ideal Solution

A more robust solution is to output dynamic variables inline in the WordPress page that needs JavaScript and enqueue a totally static cacheable file. For instance, in the next section of this chapter titled "Ajax in WordPress," you code an Ajax plugin in which you need to know the URL of the file that handles Ajax requests in WordPress, for example, `http://example.com/wp-admin/admin-ajax.php`, and you use the technique explained here.

First, you enqueue a truly static script, the usual way:

```php
<?php

// Enqueue the script
wp_enqueue_script( 'boj_myplugin', plugin_dir_url( __FILE__ ).'js/script.js', );
?>
```

Then, collect in an array all the WordPress data your script needs:

```php
<?php

$params = array(
    'option1' => get_option( 'boj_myplugin_option' ),
    'home'    => get_home_url();
);

?>
```

Now, finally tell WordPress that wherever it includes your static script, it should output inline variables right before it:

```php
<?php

wp_localize_script( 'boj_myplugin', 'boj_myplugin_params', $params );

?>
```

The function `wp_localize_script()` needs three arguments: the script handle, registered by the preceding `wp_enqueue_script()` call; a unique name for the options; and an array of strings that will be converted into a properly escaped and quoted javascript string.

Now review the full snippet and its actual result in the page:

```php
<?php

// Enqueue the script
wp_enqueue_script( 'boj_myplugin', plugin_dir_url( __FILE__ ).'js/script.js', );

$params = array(
    'option1' => get_option( 'boj_myplugin_option' ),
    'home'    => get_home_url();
);

wp_localize_script( 'boj_myplugin', 'boj_myplugin_params', $params );

?>
```

This snippet outputs HTML similar to the following:

```html
<script type='text/javascript'>
/* <![CDATA[ */
var boj_myplugin_params = {
    option1: "it\'s an option value",
    home: "http://example.com/"
};
/* ]]> */
</script>
<script
   type='text/javascript'
   src='http://example.com/wp-content/plugins/boj_myplugin/js/script.js?ver=3.1'>
</script>
```

The JavaScript functions located in `script.js` can now easily access the dynamic variables, which will be respectively here `boj_myplugin_params.option1` and `boj_myplugin_params.home`.

Using the function `wp_localize_script()` (introduced in Chapter 5, "Internationalization") may seem a bit unexpected at first because you're not localizing here, but it does have several benefits:

➤   You can use a completely static script, hence fully cacheable by browsers and not needing any processing by the server.

➤   The inline JavaScript is bound to the main script defined in `wp_enqueue_script()`: You precisely target pages, and if you need to dequeue the main script, there will be no unnecessary inline JavaScript left.

➤ The inline JavaScript is always properly escaped and quoted.

➤ The function takes care of the required CDATA tags not to break XHTML validation.

AJAX IN WORDPRESS

So far, you now know how to flawlessly include JavaScript in pages that WordPress generates. Now it's time to learn how to handle and process Ajax requests and then get your hands greasy with coding.

Ajax in WordPress: Principles

As explained in the introductory section about Ajax, you can break down the Ajax flow of events, as shown in Figure 12-4.

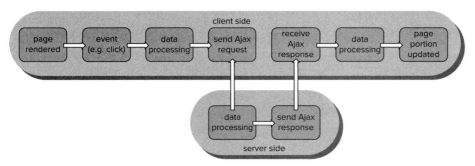

FIGURE 12-4

Implementing Ajax in WordPress is a streamlined process: Using jQuery makes it simple to both send and receive Ajax data, while a dedicated action in WordPress handles all the server-side parts.

Client Side: Send Ajax Request, Receive Response

When the client-side event occurs (element clicked, timer completed, form submitted and such), you process and collect the data that will be sent in the Ajax request:

```
var data = {
    action:    'boj_myplugin_do_ajax_request',
    some_var:  'some value',
    other_var: 'other value'
};
```

Note the `'action'` parameter; it will be used later.

Using jQuery, sending the Ajax request (here via POST) and waiting for the server response is done in one function call to which you pass the `admin-ajax.php` URL the data to post and a callback:

```
jQuery.post( 'http://example.com/wp-admin/admin-ajax.php', data, function( resp ) {
    /*
    1. process response object 'resp'
    2. update part of page
    */
});
```

All Ajax requests are sent to `admin-ajax.php`, located in the `wp-admin` directory. Despite its name and location, this file can indeed handle and process Ajax requests sent both from the admin area and the public side of the site, from both logged in known users and anonymous users.

 Head to http://api.jquery.com/category/ajax/ *to learn more about the syntax of Ajax requests in* `jQuery``type="note"`.

Server-Side: Receive Ajax Request; Send Response

In the client-side part, the JavaScript posts data to `admin-ajax.php`, including a parameter named 'action' with a value of '`boj_myplugin_do_ajax_request`'. You guessed it already: This value must be unique, and prefixing it as usual is a good practice.

The `'action'` parameter is how you connect a function defined in WordPress and an Ajax request, using the two `wp_ajax_` actions:

➤ `wp_ajax_$action` hooks functions if the user is logged in.

➤ `wp_ajax_nopriv_$action` hooks functions if the user is not logged in and has no privilege.

For instance, in your plugin you would define the following action hook:

```
<?php
add_action( 'wp_ajax_boj_myplugin_do_ajax_request', 'boj_myplugin_process_ajax' );
?>
```

Now define the function that will process the request and return data:

```
<?php
// process Ajax data and send response
function boj_myplugin_process_ajax() {

    // check authority and permissions: current_user_can()

    // check intention: wp_verify_nonce()

    // process data sent by the Ajax request

    // echo data response that the Ajax function callback will process

    die();
}

?>
```

Depending on the situation, you need to pay attention to user permissions and intention, as explained in Chapter 6, "Plugin Security."

After security checks conclude, your function can process data in the $_POST array, echoing a result that is understandable by the client-side Ajax callback function and die().

 All Ajax requests, both from the front side and the admin side, are handled by admin-ajax.php. *If this directory is protected at a lower level than WordPress (like with a .htaccess password), this file will not be accessible to anonymous readers, and Ajax requests will fail.*

As a practical application of this implementation process and the techniques to insert JavaScript, you can now code a neat plugin.

A Complete Example: Instant "Read More" Links

As you may know, you can break posts in WordPress using the `<!--more-->` tag. You can now make a sexy plugin that will enable a reader to read the rest of a story without being redirected to a new page: A click on the Read More link can display inline the second part of a post, as shown in Figure 12-5.

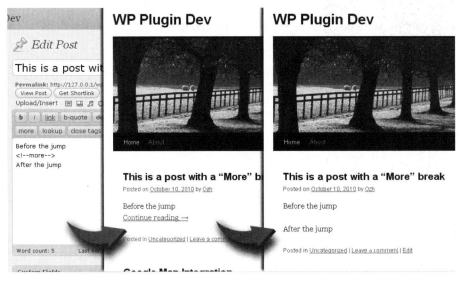

FIGURE 12-5

Your Ajax Read More plugin can use `boj_arm_` as a prefix. The plugin needs to do the following tasks:

➤ Insert a script that monitors clicks on Read More links.

➤ Insert the script only if there is a Read More link on the page.

➤ Get the second part of a post after the Read More break.

Inserting the JavaScript with a Twist

By the time WordPress prints the `<head>` of a page, you cannot know if the page contains a Read More link. You can then use a smarter technique:

1. Enqueue the JavaScript for inclusion in the footer.

2. As every post is displayed, check for the presence of a Read More link.

3. Right before it's actually added to the footer, check if it's actually needed and remove it otherwise.

The first step is to enqueue the JavaScript in the footer.

```php
<?php

// Plugin version, bump it up if you update the plugin
define( 'BOJ_ARM_VERSION', '1.0' );

// Enqueue the script, in the footer
add_action( 'template_redirect', 'boj_arm_add_js' );
function boj_arm_add_js() {

    // Enqueue the script
    wp_enqueue_script( 'boj_arm',
        plugin_dir_url( __FILE__ ).'js/script.js',
        array('jquery'), BOJ_ARM_VERSION, true
    );

    // Get current page protocol
    $protocol = isset( $_SERVER["HTTPS"] ) ? 'https://' : 'http://';

    // Output admin-ajax.php URL with same protocol as current page
    $params = array(
      'ajaxurl' => admin_url( 'admin-ajax.php', $protocol )
    );
    wp_localize_script( 'boj_arm', 'boj_arm', $params );
}

?>
```

As explained before, Ajax actions are handled by `admin-ajax.php`, located in the `wp-admin` folder, and which location is guessed using the function `admin_url()`. But remember an important limitation of Ajax described in the preparatory section: because of the same origin policy, Ajax requests and responses must be processed on the same domain, including same protocol (http or https).

In WordPress you can enforce the https protocol in the admin area even if the public part is on http (defining constant 'FORCE_SSL_ADMIN' to true), but you cannot view a page on http://example.com/ that sends Ajax requests to https://example.com/wp-admin/admin-ajax.php.

That's why you're calling here admin_url() with a second parameter that will enforce the current protocol used in the public part in the location of admin-ajax.php. In other words, even if the admin area has an obligatory https:// preference, viewing the public pages under http:// will return http://example.com/wp-admin/admin-ajax.php.

 Remember: to succeed, Ajax requests must be performed on the same domain, subdomain (http://example.com/ and http://www.example.com/ are different) and protocol (http versus https).

For the second step, as explained, you now check, as each post is displayed, if there is a Read More link that can justify the inclusion of the JavaScript in the footer.

```php
<?php

// Flag to state if the script is needed
global $boj_arm_needjs;
$boj_arm_needjs = false;

// Inspect each post to check if there's a "read more" tag
add_action( 'the_post', 'boj_arm_check_readmore' );
function boj_arm_check_readmore( $post ) {
    if ( preg_match('/<!--more(.*?)?-->/', $post->post_content )
    && !is_single() ) {
        global $boj_arm_needjs;
        $boj_arm_needjs = true;
    }
}

?>
```

Here, during the loop on each unprocessed and unformatted post, you're checking if $post->post_content contains the <!--more--> tag, and if that's not a single page where the post will be displayed entirely, flag a Boolean to true, stating that the page will need the JavaScript.

For the third and final step in JavaScript inclusion, in the footer right before WordPress adds the script, check if it's needed and remove it if not.

```php
<?php

// Don't add the script if actually not needed
add_action( 'wp_print_footer_scripts', 'boj_arm_footer_maybe_remove', 1 );
function boj_arm_footer_maybe_remove() {
```

```
        global $boj_arm_needjs;
        if( !$boj_arm_needjs ) {
            wp_deregister_script( 'boj_arm' );
        }
    }

    ?>
```

WordPress adds scripts in the footer when the action `'wp_print_footer_scripts'` is fired: Hooked into it and if the Boolean flag is `false`, simply deregister the JavaScript file. Because you've also used `wp_localize_script()` to add the inline bits, it will also be removed if the script is dequeued, leaving no superfluous bits on the page.

Client-Side JavaScript

Now that you know that the script will be included only if needed, you can start writing that script. The script will loop over each link that has `class="more-link"` and add to them the following behavior when clicked:

➤ Guess the post ID, from the Read More link anchor that will have a fragment such as `#more-45`.

➤ Change the link text to "Loading. . ." so that the reader knows that something is happening in the background.

➤ Send an Ajax request to `admin-ajax.php` with the post ID, requesting the second part of the post.

➤ Receive the second part of the post from `admin-ajax.php`, and display it inline in place of the Read More link.

Following is the complete script:

```
(function($) {
        $('a.more-link').click(function(){

            // copy the this object for future reference
            var link = this;

            // change link text
            $(link).html('loading...');

            // get post id from its href
            var post_id = $(link).attr('href').replace(/^.*#more-/, '');

            // Prepare Ajax data: action and post id
            var data = {
                action: 'boj_arm_ajax',
                post_id: post_id
            };

            // Send Ajax request with data
            $.get(boj_arm.ajaxurl, data, function(data){
```

```
                // add content after link and remove link
                $(link).after(data).remove();
            });

            // prevent default behavior of the link that was clicked
            return false;
        });
    })(jQuery);
```

Notice how your script uses the URL of admin-ajax.php, contained in boj_arm.ajaxurl and as printed by the call to wp_localize_script().

Server-Side Ajax Processing

The last part of this plugin is now the server-side processing: Admin-ajax.php will receive a post ID, which you use to fetch the second part of the post corresponding to this ID.

First, define the Ajax action and its associated function:

```php
<?php

// Ajax handler
add_action('wp_ajax_nopriv_boj_arm_ajax', 'boj_arm_ajax');
add_action('wp_ajax_boj_arm_ajax', 'boj_arm_ajax');

function boj_arm_ajax() {
    // Modify the way WP gets post content
    add_filter( 'the_content', 'boj_arm_get_2nd_half' );

    // setup the main Query again
    query_posts( 'p='.absint( $_REQUEST['post_id'] ) );

    // "The Loop"
    if ( have_posts() ) : while ( have_posts() ) : the_post();
        the_content();
    endwhile; else:
        echo "post not found :/";
    endif;

    // reset Query
    wp_reset_query();

    // Always die() in functions echoing content for Ajax requests
    die();
}

?>
```

Because the reader can either be anonymous random users or users with privileges, you have used both the wp_ajax_ and the wp_ajax_nopriv_ hooks, pointing to the same function boj_arm_ajax().

The Ajax handler function `boj_arm_ajax()` is mainly a custom loop that just has the one occurring on the blog page to display posts, except that it is limited to one post of a given ID. It has no security measure implemented apart from validating the post ID as an absolute integer: It's used to display post content, just as anyone on the front page can do, so there is no permission to check.

You're almost there: As-is, the function would return the entire post, but you want only the second half of it. The filter introduced in this function will do the trick:

```php
<?php

// Get second part of a post after the "more" jump
function boj_arm_get_2nd_half( $content ) {
    $id = absint( $_REQUEST['post_id'] );
    $content = preg_replace( "!^.*<span id=\"more-$id\"></span>!s", '', $content );
    return $content;
}

?>
```

Hooked into filter `'the_content'`, this function receives the formatted post content and returns it after removing everything until the `<span>` element that WordPress inserts in place of the Read More link.

All done! Review the whole plugin Ajax Read More and its JavaScript component:

```php
<?php
/*
Plugin Name: Ajax Read More
Plugin URI: http://example.com/
Description: Ajaxify the "Read more" links
Version: 1.0
Author: Ozh
Author URI: http://wrox.com
*/

// Flag to state if the script is needed
global $boj_arm_needjs;
$boj_arm_needjs = false;

// Plugin version, bump it up if you update the plugin
define( 'BOJ_ARM_VERSION', '1.0' );

// Enqueue the script, in the footer
add_action( 'template_redirect', 'boj_arm_add_js' );
function boj_arm_add_js() {

    // Enqueue the script
    wp_enqueue_script( 'boj_arm',
        plugin_dir_url( __FILE__ ).'js/script.js',
        array('jquery'), BOJ_ARM_VERSION, true
    );
```

```php
    // Get current page protocol
    $protocol = isset( $_SERVER["HTTPS"]) ? 'https://' : 'http://';

    // Output admin-ajax.php URL with same protocol as current page
    $params = array(
      'ajaxurl' => admin_url( 'admin-ajax.php', $protocol )
    );
    wp_localize_script( 'boj_arm', 'boj_arm', $params );
}

// Don't add the script if actually not needed
add_action( 'wp_print_footer_scripts', 'boj_arm_footer_maybe_remove', 1 );
function boj_arm_footer_maybe_remove() {
    global $boj_arm_needjs;
    if( !$boj_arm_needjs ) {
        wp_deregister_script( 'boj_arm' );
    }
}

// Inspect each post to check if there's a "read more" tag
add_action( 'the_post', 'boj_arm_check_readmore' );
function boj_arm_check_readmore( $post ) {
    if ( preg_match('/<!--more(.*?)?-->/', $post->post_content )
    && !is_single() ) {
        global $boj_arm_needjs;
        $boj_arm_needjs = true;
    }
}

// Ajax handler
add_action('wp_ajax_nopriv_boj_arm_ajax', 'boj_arm_ajax');
add_action('wp_ajax_boj_arm_ajax', 'boj_arm_ajax');
function boj_arm_ajax() {
    // Modify the way WP gets post content
    add_filter( 'the_content', 'boj_arm_get_2nd_half' );

    // setup Query
    query_posts( 'p='.absint( $_REQUEST['post_id'] ) );

    // "The Loop"
    if ( have_posts() ) : while ( have_posts() ) : the_post();
        the_content();
    endwhile; else:
        echo "post not found :/";
    endif;

    // reset Query
    wp_reset_query();
    die();
}

// Get second part of a post after the "more" jump
function boj_arm_get_2nd_half( $content ) {
```

```php
    $id = absint( $_REQUEST['post_id'] );
    $content = preg_replace( "!^.*<span id=\"more-$id\"></span>!s", '', $content );
    return $content;
}
```

Code snippet boj_readmore/plugin.php

```javascript
(function($) {
    $('.more-link').click(function(){
        var link = this;
        $(link).html('loading...');
        var post_id = $(link).attr('href').replace(/^.*#more-/, '');
        var data = {
            action: 'boj_arm_ajax',
            post_id: post_id
        };
        $.get(boj_arm.ajaxurl, data, function(data){
            $(link).after(data).remove();
        });
        return false;
    });
})(jQuery);
```

Code snippet boj_readmore/js/script.js

Another Example: Frontend Comment Deletion

You are now going to make another plugin that can enable a user with sufficient privileges to instantly delete comments from the frontend, on the post page without waiting for the page to refresh, as shown in Figure 12-6.

FIGURE 12-6

You can code the plugin Instant Delete Comment to point out three aspects of Ajax programming in WordPress:

➤ How to implement security in Ajax

➤ The `Wp_Ajax_Response` class and its XML response

➤ How to read an XML response in JavaScript

Plugin Basis

Start the plugin with inserting the JavaScript if needed and adding the Delete Comment link after each comment. Use `boj_idc_` as a prefix.

```php
<?php

/*
Plugin Name: Instant Delete Comment
Plugin URI: http://example.com/
Description: Add a quick link to instantly delete comments
Author: Ozh
Version: 1.0
Author URI: http://wrox.com/
*/

// Add script on single post & pages with comments only, if user has edit rights
add_action( 'template_redirect', 'boj_idc_addjs_ifcomments' );
function boj_idc_addjs_ifcomments() {
    if( is_single() && current_user_can( 'moderate_comments' ) ) {
        global $post;
        if( $post->comment_count ) {
            $path = plugin_dir_url( __FILE__ );

            wp_enqueue_script( 'boj_idc', $path.'js/script.js' );
            $protocol = isset( $_SERVER["HTTPS"]) ? 'https://' : 'http://';
            $params = array(
               'ajaxurl' => admin_url( 'admin-ajax.php', $protocol )
            );
            wp_localize_script( 'boj_idc', 'boj_idc', $params );
        }
    }
}

// Add an admin link to each comment
add_filter( 'comment_text', 'boj_idc_add_link' );
function boj_idc_add_link( $text ) {
    // Get current comment ID
    global $comment;
    $comment_id = $comment->comment_ID;

    // Get link to admin page to trash comment, and add nonces to it
    $link = admin_url( 'comment.php?action=trash&c='.$comment_id );
    $link = wp_nonce_url( $link, 'boj_idc-delete-'.$comment_id );
    $link = "<a href='$link' class='boj_idc_link'>delete comment</a>";
```

```
    // Append link to comment text
    return $text."<p>[admin: $link]</p>";
}

?>
```

Code snippet boj_deletecomment/plugin.php

The function `boj_idc_addjs_ifcomments()` is self-explanatory. In the function `boj_idc_add_link()` that modifies the comment text, however, you can notice the use of `wp_nonce_url()` (refer to Chapter 6 for details on this function).

The link added to each comment has the class attribute `boj_idc_link` and the following location pattern: `http://example.com/wp-admin/comment.php?action=trash&c=11&_wpnonce=551e407bc1`. When clicked, this link posts via Ajax the parameter `c` (the comment ID) and the nonce value.

Server-Side Ajax Handler: Security Checks and XML Response Parsing

The server-side Ajax handler will be the following function:

Available for
download on
Wrox.com

```php
<?php

// Ajax handler
add_action( 'wp_ajax_boj_idc_ajax_delete', 'boj_idc_ajax_delete' );
function boj_idc_ajax_delete() {
    $cid = absint( $_POST['cid'] );

    $response = new WP_Ajax_Response;

    if(
        current_user_can( 'moderate_comments' ) &&
        check_ajax_referer( 'boj_idc-delete-'.$cid, 'nonce', false ) &&
        wp_delete_comment( $cid  )
    ) {
        // Request successful
        $response->add( array(
            'data' => 'success',
            'supplemental' => array(
                'cid'     => $cid,
                'message' => 'this comment has been deleted'
            ),
        ) );
    } else {
        // Request failed
        $response->add( array(
            'data' => 'error',
            'supplemental' => array(
                'cid'     => $cid,
                'message' => 'an error occurred'
            ),
        ) );
    }
```

```
        $response->send();

        exit();
    }

?>
```

First, notice the security measures and then the use of a new class: `WP_Ajax_Response`.

Ajax Security: Nonces and Permissions

Similarly to what you have practiced in the Chapter 6, before executing any request here, you first verify the user's permission and intention.

The function `check_ajax_referer()` is similar to `check_admin_referer()` and takes up to three parameters:

1. `$action` — A string corresponding to the unique action used to compute the nonce string, here `'boj_idc-delete-'.$comment_id`.

2. `$query_arg` — The name of the parameter passed to the Ajax request and containing the nonce string. If this parameter is omitted, the function will look in `$_REQUEST` for `_ajax_nonce` or `_wpnonce`. In this case, you are looking for the nonce string in the parameter `nonce`.

3. `$die` — A Boolean with a default value of true telling WordPress to die with message –1, which can then be interpreted as a failure by the client-side JavaScript. In this plugin you handle the error checking yourself; therefore, the value of `false` passed.

The WP_Ajax_Response Class

Notice how the function `boj_idc_ajax_delete()` uses an instance of this new class:

```php
<?php

// New class instance
$response = new WP_Ajax_Response;

// Add data to the response
$response->add( array(
    'data' => 'success',
    'supplemental' => array(
        'cid'     => $cid,
        'message' => 'this comment has been deleted'
    ),
) );

// Output the response
$response->send();

?>
```

The purpose of this class is to output a well-formed XML response that will be then easy to parse with jQuery. Its method add() appends the argument to the XML response. It expects a string into its element data and an arbitrary array passed to supplemental. You can for instance here easily return translated strings to the static JavaScript in the frontend.

Its method send() prints the data as an XML document and then dies to prevent any further output. For instance, the result of the previous snippet will be the following XML:

```xml
<?xml version='1.0' standalone='yes'?>
<wp_ajax>
    <response action="boj_idc_ajax_delete_0">
        <object id="0" position="1">
            <response_data>success</response_data>
            <supplemental>
                <cid>12</cid>
                <message>this comment has been deleted</message>
            </supplemental>
        </object>
    </response>
</wp_ajax>
```

Now write the client-side JavaScript to see how you will parse this XML response.

Client-Side XML Response Parsing

The script will be this:

```javascript
jQuery(document).ready(function($) {

    $('.boj_idc_link').click(function(){
        var link = this;
        // get comment id and nonce
        var href = $(link).attr( 'href' );
        var id =    href.replace(/^.*c=(\d+).*$/, '$1');
        var nonce = href.replace(/^.*_wpnonce=([a-z0-9]+).*$/, '$1');

        var data = {
            action: 'boj_idc_ajax_delete',
            cid: id,
            nonce: nonce
        }

        $.post( boj_idc.ajaxurl, data, function(data){
            var status  = $(data).find('response_data').text();
            var message = $(data).find('supplemental message').text();
            if( status == 'success' ) {
                $(link).parent().after( '<p><b>'+message+'</b></p>' ).remove();
            } else {
                alert( message );
            }
        });
```

```
        return false;

    });

});
```

Code snippet boj_deletecomment/js/script.js

As in the previous plugin, this function modifies the click behavior and parses the link `href` attribute to get the comment ID and the nonce value that are then posted in the Ajax request.

The callback of the Ajax function shows how easy it is with jQuery to parse an XML response, using `$.find()` to literally find an element into the document tree, just as you would select an element into an HTML page.

Debugging Ajax

When you write PHP code, you instantly notice if your code has an error: The server prints an error in bold, and you can use functions such as `var_dump()` to check what variables or objects contain. The difficulty with Ajax is that everything happens in the background, so if your script fails on the client side or server side, it can be more difficult to diagnose.

The browser Firefox has an invaluable and free addon called Firebug that can prove indispensable to inspect an Ajax request. You can, for instance, check the parameters passed and the XML response, as shown in Figure 12-7.

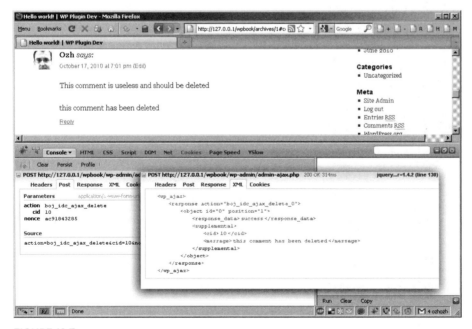

FIGURE 12-7

You can download Firebug for Firefox at `http://getfirebug.com/`. The browser Chrome has a built-in inspector tool that provides the same kind of functionalities.

Firefox with Firebug and Chrome can also let you easily check the JavaScript variables, array, or object as you would do it in PHP with `var_dump()`, using the function `console.log()`:

```
if( typeof(console) == 'object' ) {
    console.log( 'script loaded' );
    console.log( an_array, an_object, some_string );
}
```

SUMMARY

If you were to memorize just one thing from this chapter, it should be that when adding JavaScript to your WordPress pages, you should always target where you will need the script, using a proper `wp_enqueue_script()` call.

The other thing that this chapter should have shown is that adding Ajax to WordPress is fairly easy because of the dedicated actions `wp_ajax_` and `wp_ajax_nopriv_`. The only difficulty here will be mastering JavaScript and the awesome jQuery library.

13

Cron

The execution of certain functions on a schedule is a key feature of the WordPress API. In this chapter you learn how to schedule events in cron, unschedule events, and set custom cron schedule intervals. You also create more advanced, practical-use example plugins using cron.

WHAT IS CRON?

Cron is how WordPress handles scheduled events. The term cron comes from the time-based job scheduler in UNIX. WordPress uses cron for various core functionality. These scheduled jobs include checking for new versions of WordPress, checking for plugin and theme updates, and publishing scheduled posts.

How Is Cron Executed?

One of the common misconceptions about cron in WordPress is that cron is always running, looking for tasks to execute. This actually isn't true. Cron is run when a frontend or admin page is loaded on your web site. Every time a page is requested, WordPress checks if there are any cron jobs to run. Any visit to your Web site can trigger cron, whether from a visitor or a search engine bot.

This is also one of the caveats of cron. Because cron runs on page load, it is not 100% precise. If you have a scheduled cron job to run at midnight, but your Web site lacks adequate traffic, the scheduled job may not run until 12:30 a.m. or later because no one is on your Web site that late.

SCHEDULING CRON EVENTS

Two types of cron events can be scheduled in WordPress: single and recurring. A recurring event is a cron job that runs on a schedule and has a set recurring time in which it will run again. A single event runs once and never runs again until it is rescheduled.

Scheduling a Recurring Event

When scheduling an event to execute using cron, you actually start by creating a custom action hook. That hook will be registered with the cron scheduler to execute at the scheduled time. When the action hook runs, it will trigger the custom function you set in your hook and process any code in that function.

To schedule an event in WordPress, use the `wp_schedule_event()` function.

```php
<?php wp_schedule_event( timestamp, recurrence, hook, args ); ?>
```

The function accepts the following parameters:

➤ `timestamp` — The time you want the event to occur

➤ `recurrence` — How often the event should reoccur

➤ `hook` — The action hook name to execute

➤ `args` — Arguments to pass to the hook's callback function

Now build a simple example plugin to demonstrate the power of a cron scheduled task. As with most plugins, you create a settings menu option and page.

```php
<?php
add_action( 'admin_menu', 'boj_cron_menu' );

function boj_cron_menu() {

    //create cron example settings page
    add_options_page( 'Cron Example Settings', 'Cron Settings',
'manage_options', 'boj-cron', 'boj_cron_settings' );

}
?>
```

In this example, you schedule the cron event when the user visits your settings page for the first time. You can schedule your cron event in many different ways, for example, on plugin activation or when the user enables a specific option value, but for this example the settings page will work just fine.

Next you create a custom action hook and function to execute when the cron runs the scheduled task.

```php
<?php
add_action('boj_cron_hook', 'boj_cron_email_reminder');

function boj_cron_email_reminder() {

    //send scheduled email
    wp_mail( 'you@example.com', 'Elm St. Reminder',
        'Don\'t fall asleep!' );

}
?>
```

As you can see, you first create a custom action hook named `boj_cron_hook`. When that hook is called, it executes your custom `boj_email_reminder()` function. This is the function that runs when the cron scheduled job runs. This example uses the `wp_mail()` function to send an email to make sure you stay awake!

Now create the custom `boj_cron_settings()` function to display your settings page and schedule the cron job.

```php
<?php
function boj_cron_settings() {

    //verify event has not been scheduled
    if ( !wp_next_scheduled( 'boj_cron_hook' ) ) {

        //schedule the event to run hourly
        wp_schedule_event( time(), 'hourly', 'boj_cron_hook' );

    }

}
?>
```

First, use the `wp_next_scheduled()` function to verify your cron job hasn't been scheduled already. This function returns the timestamp for the cron event, and if that event doesn't exist it will return `false`.

After you have verified the cron job hasn't been scheduled, it's time to schedule it! You do this using the `wp_schedule_event()` function. The first parameter set is the current time. The second parameter is the recurrence in which this task should run. By default WordPress has three recurrence settings: `hourly`, `daily`, and `twicedaily`. In this example you set the task to run hourly. The final parameter you send is the name of the action hook to execute when the cron job runs. This is set to the custom action hook you created earlier: `boj_cron_hook`.

You have successfully created a scheduled cron job in WordPress! Every hour WordPress will automatically send an email reminding you to stay awake.

Now review the full plugin source code:

```php
<?php
/*
Plugin Name: Cron Example Plugin
Plugin URI: http://example.com/wordpress-plugins/my-plugin
Description: A plugin demonstrating Cron in WordPress
Version: 1.0
Author: Brad Williams
Author URI: http://wrox.com
License: GPLv2
*/

add_action( 'admin_menu', 'boj_cron_menu' );

function boj_cron_menu() {

    //create cron example settings page
    add_options_page( 'Cron Example Settings', 'Cron Settings',
        'manage_options', 'boj-cron', 'boj_cron_settings' );

}

add_action('boj_cron_hook', 'boj_cron_email_reminder');

function boj_cron_email_reminder() {

    //send scheduled email
    wp_mail( 'you@example.com', 'Elm St. Reminder',
        'Don\'t fall asleep!' );

}

function boj_cron_settings() {

    //verify event has not been scheduled
    if ( !wp_next_scheduled( 'boj_cron_hook' ) ) {

        //schedule the event to run hourly
        wp_schedule_event( time(), 'hourly', 'boj_cron_hook' );

    }

}
?>
```

Code snippet boj-cron.php

Scheduling a Single Event

Typically events scheduled in cron are recurring, but there may be an occasion when you want to schedule a single event in cron. This means the event would run once and not be scheduled to run again. To schedule a single event use the `wp_schedule_single_event()` function:

```php
<?php wp_schedule_single_event( timestamp, hook, args ); ?>
```

The function accepts the following parameters:

➤   `timestamp` — The time you want the event to run

➤   `hook` — The action hook name to execute

➤   `args` — Arguments to pass to the hook's callback function

Now look at a working example. Just as before start by adding a menu item that links to your settings page.

```php
<?php
//create the plugin menu
add_action( 'admin_menu', 'boj_cron_single_menu' );

function boj_cron_single_menu() {

    //create cron example settings page
    add_options_page( 'Cron Example Settings', 'Cron Settings',
        'manage_options', 'boj-single-cron', 'boj_cron_single_settings' );

}
?>
```

Next create the settings page that will schedule the single event to run.

```php
<?php
function boj_cron_single_settings() {

    //verify event has not been scheduled
    if ( !wp_next_scheduled( 'boj_single_cron_hook' ) ) {

        //schedule the event to in one hour
        wp_schedule_single_event( time()+3600,
            'boj_single_cron_hook' );

    }

}
?>
```

Using the `wp_schedule_single_event()` function, you set the execution time to `time()+3600`, which is exactly one hour from the time the cron event is scheduled. The second parameter, `boj_single_cron_hook`, is the custom hook the cron job will execute. Now create the hook.

```php
<?php
//create the custom hook for cron scheduling
add_action( 'boj_single_cron_hook',
    'boj_cron_single_email_reminder' );

function boj_cron_single_email_reminder () {

    //send scheduled email
    wp_mail( 'you@example.com', 'Reminder', 'You have a meeting' );

}
?>
```

Now look at the full plugin source code.

```php
<?php
/*
Plugin Name: Schedule Single Event Cron
Plugin URI: http://example.com/wordpress-plugins/my-plugin
Description: schedules a single event to run in cron
Version: 1.0
Author: Brad Williams
Author URI: http://wrox.com
License: GPLv2
*/

//create the plugin menu
add_action( 'admin_menu', 'boj_cron_single_menu' );

function boj_cron_single_menu() {

    //create cron example settings page
    add_options_page( 'Cron Example Settings', 'Cron Settings',
        'manage_options', 'boj-single-cron', 'boj_cron_single_settings' );

}

//create the custom hook for cron scheduling
add_action( 'boj_single_cron_hook',
    'boj_cron_single_email_reminder' );

function boj_cron_single_email_reminder () {

    //send scheduled email
    wp_mail( 'you@example.com', 'Reminder', 'You have a meeting' );

}

function boj_cron_single_settings() {

    //verify event has not been scheduled
    if ( !wp_next_scheduled( 'boj_single_cron_hook' ) ) {

        //schedule the event to in one hour
```

```
            wp_schedule_single_event( time()+3600,
                'boj_single_cron_hook' );

        }

    }
    ?>
```

Code snippet boj-single-event.php

 When scheduling a single cron event, you do not need to unschedule it. The cron event runs once and unschedules itself when complete.

Unscheduling an Event

When a cron job is scheduled in WordPress, it is stored in the wp_options table. This means the scheduled job will not be removed, or unscheduled, by simply deactivating the plugin that scheduled it. If the plugin is deactivated without properly unscheduling the cron job. WordPress can't execute the scheduled job because the plugin code will no longer be available. However, the cron job scheduled will still be stored and WordPress will try to execute it on the schedule set.

To properly unschedule a cron event, use the wp_unschedule_event() function.

```
<?php wp_unschedule_event( timestamp, hook, args ); ?>
```

The function accepts the following parameters:

➤   timestamp — Time of the next occurrence to run

➤   hook — The action hook to unschedule

➤   args — Arguments to pass to the hook's callback function

Now unschedule the cron job you scheduled earlier.

```
<?php
//get time of next scheduled run
$timestamp = wp_next_scheduled( 'boj_cron_hook' );

//unschedule custom action hook
wp_unschedule_event( $timestamp, 'boj_cron_hook' );
?>
```

First, use the wp_next_scheduled() function to determine the exact time of the next occurrence for your scheduled hook. After the next scheduled time has been determined, unschedule the cron job using wp_unschedule_event(). The only two parameters required are the time and custom hook associated with the scheduled job. After this function has been executed, the cron scheduled job will be unscheduled in WordPress and will no longer execute.

Specifying Your Own Cron Intervals

As discussed, WordPress has three recurrence values by default: Hourly, Twice Daily, and Daily. WordPress makes it easy to create a custom recurrence setting to use when scheduling cron jobs. To create a custom recurrence, use the cron_schedules filter hook. Now create a recurrence option for a weekly scheduled job.

```php
<?php
add_filter( 'cron_schedules', 'boj_cron_add_weekly' );

function boj_cron_add_weekly( $schedules ) {

    //create a 'weekly' recurrence schedule option
    $schedules['weekly'] = array(
        'interval' => 604800,
        'display' => 'Once Weekly'
    );

    return $schedules;
}
?>
```

The first step is to call the add_filter() function to execute the cron_schedules filter hook. The filter executes your custom function boj_cron_add_weekly(). Notice how the variable $schedules is passed as a parameter to your custom function. This variable stores all recurrence schedules as an array in WordPress. To create your new schedule, you add a value to this array.

You first define the name of your recurrence to weekly by setting $schedules['weekly'] = array(). Next, set the two values for your new schedule: interval and display. The interval value is the number of seconds when the cron job should run. In this example, use 604800, which is how many seconds exist in a week. The display value is the friendly display name of the new recurrence.

The final step to your custom schedule is to return the $schedules value from the function. Now you have a custom recurrence value defined in cron. You can easily use this new recurrence value when scheduling a cron event:

```php
<?php wp_schedule_event( time(), 'weekly', 'boj_cron_hook' ); ?>
```

Viewing Cron Events Scheduled

When working with cron jobs, it can be useful to see exactly what jobs are scheduled in WordPress. There is no built-in way to view these events, so create a plugin to view all cron jobs scheduled in WordPress.

First, create a new menu for your plugin page.

```php
<?php
add_action( 'admin_menu', 'boj_view_cron_menu' );

function boj_view_cron_menu() {

    //create view cron jobs settings page
```

```php
    add_options_page( 'View Cron Jobs', 'View Cron Jobs',
        'manage_options', 'boj-view-cron', 'boj_view_cron_settings' );

}
?>
```

Next, create the `boj_view_cron_settings()` function to display the cron jobs scheduled:

```php
<?php
function boj_view_cron_settings() {

    $cron = _get_cron_array();
    $schedules = wp_get_schedules();
    $date_format = 'M j, Y @ G:i';
```

First, set the variable `$cron` to the value of `_get_cron_array()`. This function stores all scheduled cron jobs in an array. Next, set `$schedules` to the value of the `wp_get_schedules()` function. This function stores all registered cron recurrence options available. The final variable set is the `$date_format`, which you use to format the cron run date and time later.

Now it's time to create the table to display the cron jobs scheduled in a nice, familiar format.

```html
<div class="wrap" id="cron-gui">
<h2>Cron Events Scheduled</h2>

<table class="widefat fixed">
    <thead>
    <tr>
        <th scope="col">Next Run (GMT/UTC)</th>
        <th scope="col">Schedule</th>
        <th scope="col">Hook Name</th>
    </tr>
    </thead>
    <tbody>
```

The table features three columns of data: Next Run, Schedule, and the Hook Name. Now for the fun part: it's time to loop through the scheduled cron jobs and display them in your table.

```php
        <?php foreach ( $cron as $timestamp => $cronhooks ) { ?>
            <?php foreach ( (array) $cronhooks as $hook => $events )
                { ?>
                <?php foreach ( (array) $events as $event ) { ?>
                <tr>
                    <td>
                        <?php echo date_i18n( $date_format,
                            wp_next_scheduled( $hook ) ); ?>
                    </td>
                    <td>
                    <?php
                    if ( $event[ 'schedule' ] ) {
                        echo $schedules[ $event[ 'schedule' ] ]
                            [ 'display' ];
                    } else {
                        ?>One-time<?php
```

```
                }
                ?>
                </td>
                <td><?php echo $hook; ?></td>
            </tr>
                <?php } ?>
            <?php } ?>
        <?php } ?>
        </tbody>
    </table>
    </div>
<?
}
?>
```

This can look a little overwhelming, but it's actually quite straightforward. The code loops through the `$cron` variable, which stores the array value from `_get_cron_array()`, extracting the data needed from each array element.

To display the next scheduled run time, use the WordPress function `date_i18n()`. This function converts a date into a localized format based on the timestamp set. The timestamp in this example was set in the `$date_format` set earlier to display the date in a format such as Month Day, Year @ Time. To get the time that you want to format, use the `wp_next_scheduled()` function.

Next, the schedule is displayed from the `$schedules` variable. If the event is recurring, the recurrence value is displayed. If the event does not have a recurrence set, then "One-time" is displayed. The final piece of information displayed is the hook name scheduled to execute.

Now when viewing your plugin settings page, all scheduled cron jobs in WordPress will be displayed with their next scheduled run time, recurrence, and hook being executed, as shown in Figure 13-1.

FIGURE 13-1

Now look at the full plugin source code:

```php
<?php
/*
Plugin Name: View Cron Jobs Plugin
Plugin URI: http://example.com/wordpress-plugins/my-plugin
Description: A plugin demonstrating Cron in WordPress
Version: 1.0
Author: Brad Williams
Author URI: http://wrox.com
License: GPLv2
*/

add_action( 'admin_menu', 'boj_view_cron_menu' );

function boj_view_cron_menu() {

    //create view cron jobs settings page
```

```php
    add_options_page( 'View Cron Jobs', 'View Cron Jobs',
        'manage_options', 'boj-view-cron', 'boj_view_cron_settings' );

}

function boj_view_cron_settings() {

    $cron = _get_cron_array();
    $schedules = wp_get_schedules();
    $date_format = 'M j, Y @ G:i';
    ?>
    <div class="wrap" id="cron-gui">
    <h2>Cron Events Scheduled</h2>

    <table class="widefat fixed">
        <thead>
            <tr>
                <th scope="col">Next Run (GMT/UTC)</th>
                <th scope="col">Schedule</th>
                <th scope="col">Hook Name</th>
            </tr>
        </thead>
        <tbody>
            <?php foreach ( $cron as $timestamp => $cronhooks ) { ?>
                <?php foreach ( (array) $cronhooks as
                    $hook => $events ) { ?>
                    <?php foreach ( (array) $events as $event ) { ?>
                        <tr>
                            <td>
                                <?php echo date_i18n( $date_format,
                                    wp_next_scheduled( $hook ) ); ?>
                            </td>
                            <td>
                                <?php
                                if ( $event[ 'schedule' ] ) {
                                    echo $schedules[
                                        $event[ 'schedule' ] ][ 'display' ];
                                } else {
                                    ?>One-time<?php
                                }
                                ?>
                            </td>
                            <td><?php echo $hook; ?></td>
                        </tr>
                    <?php } ?>
                <?php } ?>
            <?php } ?>
        </tbody>
    </table>
    </div>
<?
}
?>
```

Code snippet boj-view-cron-jobs.php

TRUE CRON

As mentioned earlier, a WordPress cron is not a "true" cron, in that it runs based on page requests and not a true timed interval. However, you can set up a true cron and disable the WordPress page request cron.

The first step to set up a true cron is to disable cron in WordPress by adding the following line of code to your `wp-config.php` file.

```
define('DISABLE_WP_CRON', true);
```

This disables WordPress from loading `wp-cron.php` to look for cron jobs to execute. Now that you've disabled cron in WordPress, you need to set up some other method to execute cron.

A common method is using `wget` to load `wp-cron.php` on a schedule. If your server is Linux-based, cron will already exist and can be scheduled using the `crontab` command. If your server is Windows-based, you can install `wget` and create a scheduled task to execute it. The `wget` command would work like this:

```
wget http://www.example.com/wp-cron.php
```

When `wget` requests `wp-cron.php` **WordPress** looks for all scheduled cron jobs and executes as needed. Setting up true cron **on your server** will guarantee your cron jobs will run perfectly on schedule without missing a beat.

PRACTICAL USE

Now that you understand how cron works, look at some more advanced cron example plugins.

Deleting Post Revisions Weekly

A post revision is saved in the database each time you save a post or page. This can grow the size of your database quickly, and it should be purged on occasion. In this example, you create a plugin that schedules a weekly cron job to delete all post revisions from the database that are older than 30 days.

First, create the custom action hook that the cron job will run every week.

```php
<?php
//create the custom hook for cron scheduling
add_action( 'boj_del_rev_cron_hook', 'boj_cron_rev_delete' );

function boj_cron_rev_delete() {
    global $wpdb;

    $sql = " DELETE a,b,c
        FROM $wpdb->posts a
        LEFT JOIN $wpdb->term_relationships b ON (a.ID = b.object_id)
        LEFT JOIN $wpdb->postmeta c ON (a.ID = c.post_id)
        WHERE a.post_type = 'revision'
```

```
                AND DATEDIFF( now(), a.post_modified ) > 30 ";

        //execute query to delete all post revisions and meta data
        $wpdb->query( $wpdb->prepare( $sql ) );

    }
    ?>
```

The action hook `boj_del_rev_cron_hook` triggers the custom function `boj_cron_rev_delete()`. First, you must define `$wpdb` as a global variable, so the `wpdb` class will be available for use in interacting with the WordPress database. Next, generate the query to delete post revisions older than 30 days.

The `$sql` variable stores the query to execute. As you can see, the query joins the `posts` table with the `term_relationships` and `postmeta` tables. This ensures that not only is the post revision deleted but also any post meta data stored for that revision.

Finally, execute the query using the `wpdb` `query()` and `prepare()` functions. The prepare function is one of the most important functions in the `wpdb` class. This function is used for escaping variables passed to your SQL queries. Even though the query in this plugin has no user defined variables, it's a best practice to always use the `prepare()` function when running database queries.

Now that the delete post revision function has been constructed, it's time to add a setting to enable the scheduled job. This plugin will use the Settings API, as covered in Chapter 7, "Plugin Settings," to add a single check box option to the General settings page in WordPress.

```php
<?php
add_action( 'admin_init', 'boj_cron_rev_admin_init' );

function boj_cron_rev_admin_init(){

    //register the options in the Settings API
    register_setting(
        'general',
        'boj_cron_rev_options'
    );

    //register the field in the Settings API
    add_settings_field(
        'boj_cron_rev_field',
        'Delete post revisions weekly?',
        'boj_cron_rev_setting_input',
        'general',
        'default'
    );

    //load the option value
    $options = get_option( 'boj_cron_rev_options' );
    $boj_del_rev = $options['boj_del_rev'];

    // if the option is enabled and not already
    // scheduled lets schedule it
    if ( $boj_del_rev == 'on' &&
```

```
            !wp_next_scheduled( 'boj_del_rev_cron_hook' ) ) {

            //schedule the event to run hourly
            wp_schedule_event( time(), 'weekly',
                'boj_del_rev_cron_hook' );

        // if the option is NOT enabled and scheduled lets unschedule it
        } elseif ( $boj_del_rev != 'on' &&
            wp_next_scheduled( 'boj_del_rev_cron_hook' ) ) {

            //get time of next scheduled run
            $timestamp = wp_next_scheduled( 'boj_del_rev_cron_hook' );

            //unschedule custom action hook
            wp_unschedule_event( $timestamp, 'boj_del_rev_cron_hook' );

        }

    }
?>
```

Use the `admin_init` action hook to execute the custom `boj_cron_rev_admin_init()` function. To register the plugin option, use the `register_setting()` and `add_settings_field()` Settings API functions. The code registers a `boj_cron_rev_options` option. This option is where the plugin will store its only option value, whether the scheduled job is enabled. The callback function is set to `boj_cron_rev_setting_input()` when adding the settings field.

The second part of the code determines whether the option is enabled for the plugin. The option value is loaded using `get_option()` and stored in the `$boj_del_rev` variable. If the option is enabled, it checks if the job has been scheduled, and if not schedules it. If the option is disabled, it checks if the job has been unscheduled, and if not unschedules it.

Next, create the `boj_cron_rev_setting_input()` function to display the option check box.

```php
<?php
function boj_cron_rev_setting_input() {

    // load the 'boj_del_rev' option from the database
    $options = get_option( 'boj_cron_rev_options' );
    $boj_del_rev = $options['boj_del_rev'];

    //display the option checkbox
    echo "<input id='boj_del_rev'
        name='boj_cron_rev_options[boj_del_rev]'
type='checkbox' ". checked( $boj_del_rev, 'on', false ). " />";

}
?>
```

As before, you load the option value using `get_option()`. This will be used to determine if the check box is checked. The HTML check box field is then displayed. Use the checked function to compare the $boj_del_dev variable and 'on'. If they match, the option is enabled and should be checked. The check box option will now be displayed on the General settings page, as shown in Figure 13-2.

The final piece to the plugin is to create a weekly recurrence filter for cron. This enables the plugin to delete post revisions once a week.

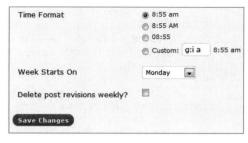

```php
<?php
//register a weekly recurrence
add_filter( 'cron_schedules', 'boj_cron_add_weekly' );

function boj_cron_add_weekly( $schedules ) {

    //create a 'weekly' recurrence schedule
    $schedules['weekly'] = array(
        'interval' => 604800,
        'display' => 'Once Weekly'
    );

    return $schedules;
}
?>
```

FIGURE 13-2

Your cron job can use weekly as the recurrence setting. That's it! You now have a fully functional plugin that can automatically delete all post revisions older than 30 days once a week. Now review the full plugin code:

```php
<?php
/*
Plugin Name: Delete Post Revisions Weekly
Plugin URI: http://example.com/wordpress-plugins/my-plugin
Description: Deletes post revisions older than 30 days once a week
Version: 1.0
Author: Brad Williams
Author URI: http://wrox.com
License: GPLv2
*/

//create the custom hook for cron scheduling
add_action( 'boj_del_rev_cron_hook', 'boj_cron_rev_delete' );

function boj_cron_rev_delete() {
    global $wpdb;

        $sql = " DELETE a,b,c
            FROM $wpdb->posts a
            LEFT JOIN $wpdb->term_relationships b
                ON (a.ID = b.object_id)
            LEFT JOIN $wpdb->postmeta c
                ON (a.ID = c.post_id)
            WHERE a.post_type = 'revision'
```

```
            AND DATEDIFF( now(), a.post_modified ) > 30 ";

    //execute query to delete all post revisions and meta data
    $wpdb->query( $wpdb->prepare( $sql ) );

}

add_action( 'admin_init', 'boj_cron_rev_admin_init' );

function boj_cron_rev_admin_init(){

    //register the options in the Settings API
    register_setting(
        'general',
        'boj_cron_rev_options'
    );

    //register the field in the Settings API
    add_settings_field(
        'boj_cron_rev_field',
        'Delete post revisions weekly?',
        'boj_cron_rev_setting_input',
        'general',
        'default'
    );

    //load the option value
    $options = get_option( 'boj_cron_rev_options' );
    $boj_del_rev = $options['boj_del_rev'];

    // if the option is enabled and
    // not already scheduled lets schedule it
    if ( $boj_del_rev == 'on' &&
        !wp_next_scheduled( 'boj_del_rev_cron_hook' ) ) {

        //schedule the event to run hourly
        wp_schedule_event( time(), 'weekly',
            'boj_del_rev_cron_hook' );

    // if the option is NOT enabled and scheduled lets unschedule it
    } elseif ( $boj_del_rev != 'on' &&
        wp_next_scheduled( 'boj_del_rev_cron_hook' ) ) {

        //get time of next scheduled run
        $timestamp = wp_next_scheduled( 'boj_del_rev_cron_hook' );

        //unschedule custom action hook
        wp_unschedule_event( $timestamp, 'boj_del_rev_cron_hook' );

    }

}

function boj_cron_rev_setting_input() {

    // load the 'boj_del_rev' option from the database
```

```php
    $options = get_option( 'boj_cron_rev_options' );
    $boj_del_rev = $options['boj_del_rev'];

    //display the option checkbox
    echo "<input id='boj_del_rev'
        name='boj_cron_rev_options[boj_del_rev]'
        type='checkbox' ". checked( $boj_del_rev, 'on', false ). " />";

}

//register a weekly recurrence
add_filter( 'cron_schedules', 'boj_cron_add_weekly' );

function boj_cron_add_weekly( $schedules ) {

    //create a 'weekly' recurrence schedule
    $schedules['weekly'] = array(
        'interval' => 604800,
        'display' => 'Once Weekly'
    );

    return $schedules;
}

?>
```

Code snippet boj-delete-rev-cron.php

The Blog Pester Plugin

Now create a plugin to send an email automatically when no new posts have been published in the last three days. This can be a handy reminder to create a new post.

First, start by creating the custom action hook and function:

```php
<?php
//create the custom hook for cron scheduling
add_action( 'boj_pester_cron_hook', 'boj_cron_pester_check' );

function boj_cron_pester_check() {
    global $wpdb;

    //retrieve latest published post date
    $sql = " SELECT post_date FROM $wpdb->posts
        WHERE post_status = 'publish' AND post_type = 'post'
        ORDER BY post_date DESC LIMIT 1 ";
    $latest_post_date = $wpdb->get_var( $wpdb->prepare( $sql ) );

    if ( strtotime( $latest_post_date ) <= strtotime('-3 day') ) {
        //post is older than 3 days

        //populate email values
        $email_to = 'you@example.com';
```

```
    $email_subject = 'Blog Reminder';
    $email_msg = 'Water your blog!
        Its been three days or more since your last post';

    //send scheduled email
    wp_mail( $email_to, $email_subject, $email_msg );

    }

}
?>
```

The `boj_cron_pester_check()` function is executed by cron and can check when the last post was published. Use the `get_var()` and `prepare()` functions of the `wpdb` class to execute the custom query and return the single value of the last published post date.

To compare the dates, use the PHP `strtotime()` function. This function takes a date, or any English textual date time, and returns a UNIX timestamp. This makes it easy to compare two dates because they are now in the same format. In the previous code, you are comparing the variable `$latest_post_date` to the UNIX timestamp for 3 days ago, or `'-3 day'` in this case. If the latest post date is less than or equal to the value of `'-3 day'` then the post is older than 3 days. The final step is to populate the email variables and use `wp_mail()` to send the reminder email.

Now create the `admin_init` function to register the plugin option and schedule the cron job.

```
<?php
add_action( 'admin_init', 'boj_cron_pester_init' );

function boj_cron_pester_init(){

    //register the options in the Settings API
    register_setting(
        'writing',
        'boj_cron_pester_options'
    );

    //register the field in the Settings API
    add_settings_field(
        'boj_cron_pester_field',
        'Enable Blog Pester?',
        'boj_cron_pester_setting',
        'writing',
        'default'
    );

    //load the option value
    $options = get_option( 'boj_cron_pester_options' );
    $boj_pester = $options['boj_pester'];

    // if the option is enabled and
    // not already scheduled lets schedule it
```

```php
    if ( $boj_pester == 'on' &&
        !wp_next_scheduled( 'boj_pester_cron_hook' ) ) {

        //schedule the event to run hourly
        wp_schedule_event( time(), 'daily', 'boj_pester_cron_hook' );

    // if the option is NOT enabled and scheduled lets unschedule it
    } elseif ( $boj_pester != 'on' &&
        wp_next_scheduled( 'boj_pester_cron_hook' ) ) {

        //get time of next scheduled run
        $timestamp = wp_next_scheduled( 'boj_pester_cron_hook' );

        //unschedule custom action hook
        wp_unschedule_event( $timestamp, 'boj_pester_cron_hook' );

    }

}
?>
```

The plugin adds an option to the Writing Settings page using the Settings API, as shown in Figure 13-3. Enabling the blog pester option schedules the cron job to run daily. This means if no new blog post has been published in the last 3 days, an email will be sent once a day until a new blog post is published.

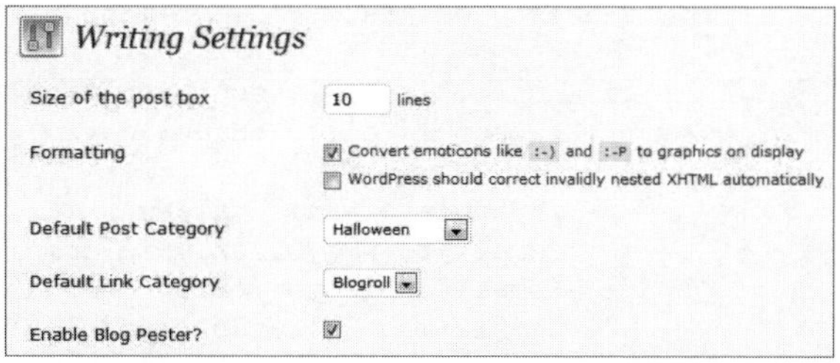

The final step to the plugin is creating the check box form field to enable or disable the pester email.

FIGURE 13-3

```php
<?php
function boj_cron_pester_setting() {

    // load the 'boj_pester' option from the database
    $options = get_option( 'boj_cron_pester_options' );
    $boj_pester = $options['boj_pester'];

    //display the option checkbox
    echo "<input id='boj_pester'
        name='boj_cron_pester_options[boj_pester]'
        type='checkbox' ". checked( $boj_pester, 'on', false ). " />";

}
?>
```

As before use the `get_option()` function to retrieve the pester setting value. Also use the checked function to determine if the option is enabled.

Now review the full blog pester plugin source.

```php
<?php
/*
Plugin Name: Blog Pester Plugin
Plugin URI: http://example.com/wordpress-plugins/my-plugin
Description: Sends an email after 3 days with no new posts
Version: 1.0
Author: Brad Williams
Author URI: http://wrox.com
License: GPLv2
*/

//create the custom hook for cron scheduling
add_action( 'boj_pester_cron_hook', 'boj_cron_pester_check' );

function boj_cron_pester_check() {
    global $wpdb;

    //retrieve latest published post date
    $sql = " SELECT post_date FROM $wpdb->posts
        WHERE post_status = 'publish' AND post_type = 'post'
        ORDER BY post_date DESC LIMIT 1 ";
    $latest_post_date = $wpdb->get_var( $wpdb->prepare( $sql ) );

    if ( strtotime( $latest_post_date ) <= strtotime('-3 day') ) {
        //post is older than 3 days

        //populate email values
        $email_to = 'you@example.com';
        $email_subject = 'Blog Reminder';
        $email_msg = 'Water your blog!
            Its been three days or more since your last post';

        //send scheduled email
        wp_mail( $email_to, $email_subject, $email_msg );

    }

}

add_action( 'admin_init', 'boj_cron_pester_init' );

function boj_cron_pester_init(){

    //register the options in the Settings API
    register_setting(
        'writing',
        'boj_cron_pester_options'
    );

    //register the field in the Settings API
    add_settings_field(
        'boj_cron_pester_field',
        'Enable Blog Pester?',
        'boj_cron_pester_setting',
```

```
        'writing',
        'default'
    );

    //load the option value
    $options = get_option( 'boj_cron_pester_options' );
    $boj_pester = $options['boj_pester'];

    // if the option is enabled and
    // not already scheduled lets schedule it
    if ( $boj_pester == 'on' &&
        !wp_next_scheduled( 'boj_pester_cron_hook' ) ) {

        //schedule the event to run hourly
        wp_schedule_event( time(), 'daily', 'boj_pester_cron_hook' );

    // if the option is NOT enabled and scheduled lets unschedule it
    } elseif ( $boj_pester != 'on' &&
        wp_next_scheduled( 'boj_pester_cron_hook' ) ) {

        //get time of next scheduled run
        $timestamp = wp_next_scheduled( 'boj_pester_cron_hook' );

        //unschedule custom action hook
        wp_unschedule_event( $timestamp, 'boj_pester_cron_hook' );

    }

}

function boj_cron_pester_setting() {

    // load the 'boj_pester' option from the database
    $options = get_option( 'boj_cron_pester_options' );
    $boj_pester = $options['boj_pester'];

    //display the option checkbox
    echo "<input id='boj_pester'
        name='boj_cron_pester_options[boj_pester]'
        type='checkbox' ". checked( $boj_pester, 'on', false ). " />";

}

?>
```

Code snippet boj-blog-pester.php

The Delete Comments Plugin

As a final example, create a cron plugin with multiple options. This plugin can delete spam and moderated comments older than the number of days set. For example, you can delete all spam comments older than 15 days.

To start, create the `admin_init` function to register your plugin settings and schedule the cron job.

```php
<?php
add_action( 'admin_init', 'boj_cron_comment_init' );

function boj_cron_comment_init(){

    //register the options in the Settings API
    register_setting(
        'discussion',
        'boj_cron_comment_options'
    );

    //register the select field in the Settings API
    add_settings_field(
        'boj_cron_comment_type_field',
        'Select Comments to Delete',
        'boj_cron_comment_type',
        'discussion',
        'default'
    );

    //register the text field in the Settings API
    add_settings_field(
        'boj_cron_days_old_field',
        'Delete Comments Older Than',
        'boj_cron_days_old',
        'discussion',
        'default'
    );

    //load the option value
    $options = get_option( 'boj_cron_comment_options' );
    $boj_comments = $options['boj_comments'];

    // if the option is enabled and
    // not already scheduled lets schedule it
    if ( $boj_comments &&
        !wp_next_scheduled( 'boj_comment_cron_hook' ) ) {

        //schedule the event to run daily
        wp_schedule_event( time(), 'daily',
            'boj_comment_cron_hook' );

    // if the option is NOT enabled and scheduled lets unschedule it
    } elseif ( !$boj_comments &&
        wp_next_scheduled( 'boj_comment_cron_hook' ) ) {

        //get time of next scheduled run
        $timestamp = wp_next_scheduled( 'boj_comment_cron_hook' );

        //unschedule custom action hook
```

```
                wp_unschedule_event( $timestamp, 'boj_comment_cron_hook' );

    }

}
?>
```

This plugin adds two setting fields to the Discussion settings page in WordPress, as shown in Figure 13-4. One field is a select form field to set what type of comments to delete. The second field is a text form field to set how old a comment should be before it is deleted.

FIGURE 13-4

Now create the two form fields you registered in the previous function.

```php
<?php
function boj_cron_comment_type() {

    // load the 'boj_comments' option from the database
    $options = get_option( 'boj_cron_comment_options' );
    $boj_comments = $options['boj_comments'];

    //display the option select field
    echo '<select name="boj_cron_comment_options[boj_comments]">';
        echo '<option value="" '.
            selected( $boj_comments, '', false ) .'>None</option>';
        echo '<option value="spam" '.
            selected( $boj_comments, 'spam', false ) .
            '>Spam Comments</option>';
        echo '<option value="moderated" '.
            selected( $boj_comments, 'moderated', false ) .
            '>Moderated Comments</option>';
        echo '<option value="both" '.
            selected( $boj_comments, 'both', false ) .'>Both</option>';
    echo '</select>';

}
?>
```

The first form field is a select field. Use the `selected()` function to compare the option value saved in WordPress to the option value, and if identical, set the option value to selected. The next field is the text form field.

```php
<?php
function boj_cron_days_old() {

    // load the 'boj_days_old' option from the database
    $options = get_option( 'boj_cron_comment_options' );
    $boj_days_old = ( $options['boj_days_old'] ) ?
        absint( $options['boj_days_old'] ) : 30;

    //display the option text field
```

```
      echo '<input type="text"
          name="boj_cron_comment_options[boj_days_old]"
          value="' .esc_attr( $boj_days_old ). '" size="3" /> Days';

}
?>
```

To set the $boj_days_old variable, use a PHP ternary operator. If the value exists, it will be used, and if no value exists (that is, the plugin was just installed) the default value of 30 will be used.

Now that the setting fields are in place, you need to create the custom action hook and function to delete the comments.

```
<?php
//create the custom hook for cron scheduling
add_action( 'boj_comment_cron_hook', 'boj_cron_delete_comments' );

function boj_cron_delete_comments() {
    global $wpdb;

    $options = get_option( 'boj_cron_comment_options' );
    $boj_comments = $options['boj_comments'];
    $boj_days_old = ( $options['boj_days_old'] ) ?
        $options['boj_days_old'] : 30;

    //verify option is enabled
    if ( $boj_comments ) {

        if ( $boj_comments == "spam" ) {
            $boj_comment_status = 'spam';
        } elseif ( $boj_comments == "moderated" ) {
            $boj_comment_status = '0';
        }

        $sql = " DELETE FROM $wpdb->comments
            WHERE ( comment_approved = '$boj_comment_status' )
            AND DATEDIFF( now(), comment_date ) > %d";

        if ( $boj_comments == "both" ) {
            $sql = " DELETE FROM $wpdb->comments
                WHERE ( comment_approved = 'spam'
                    OR comment_approved = '0'  )
                AND DATEDIFF( now(), comment_date ) > %d";
        }

        $wpdb->query( $wpdb->prepare( $sql, $boj_days_old ) );

    }

}
?>
```

First, the plugin loads both option values into the two variables: `$boj_comments` and `$boj_days_old`. If the variable `$boj_comments` has a value, you know the plugin settings have been enabled by the user. Next, you need to build the query that will delete the comments based on the settings saved the by user. The query also uses the DATEDIFF MySQL function to verify the comment is older than the number of days set by the user. After the query has been generated, it is executed using the `query()` and `prepare()` functions of the `wpdb` class.

When configured you can easily set which comments to delete and how old they must be before they are deleted. The cron job is scheduled to run daily to check for comments to delete.

Now review the full plugin code.

Available for download on Wrox.com

```php
<?php
/*
Plugin Name: Delete Comments on a Schedule
Plugin URI: http://example.com/wordpress-plugins/my-plugin
Description: Deletes spam and moderated comments older than days set
Version: 1.0
Author: Brad Williams
Author URI: http://wrox.com
License: GPLv2
*/

//create the custom hook for cron scheduling
add_action( 'boj_comment_cron_hook', 'boj_cron_delete_comments' );

function boj_cron_delete_comments() {
    global $wpdb;

    $options = get_option( 'boj_cron_comment_options' );
    $boj_comments = $options['boj_comments'];
    $boj_days_old = ( $options['boj_days_old'] ) ?
        absint( $options['boj_days_old'] ) : 30;

    //verify option is enabled
    if ( $boj_comments ) {

        if ( $boj_comments == "spam" ) {
            $boj_comment_status = 'spam';
        } elseif ( $boj_comments == "moderated" ) {
            $boj_comment_status = '0';
        }

        $sql = " DELETE FROM $wpdb->comments
            WHERE ( comment_approved = '$boj_comment_status' )
            AND DATEDIFF( now(), comment_date ) > %d ";

        if ( $boj_comments == "both" ) {
            $sql = " DELETE FROM $wpdb->comments
                WHERE ( comment_approved = 'spam'
                    OR comment_approved = '0'  )
                AND DATEDIFF( now(), comment_date ) > %d ";
```

```php
        }

        $wpdb->query( $wpdb->prepare( $sql, $boj_days_old ) );

    }

}

add_action( 'admin_init', 'boj_cron_comment_init' );

function boj_cron_comment_init(){

    //register the options in the Settings API
    register_setting(
        'discussion',
        'boj_cron_comment_options'
    );

    //register the select field in the Settings API
    add_settings_field(
        'boj_cron_comment_type_field',
        'Select Comments to Delete',
        'boj_cron_comment_type',
        'discussion',
        'default'
    );

    //register the text field in the Settings API
    add_settings_field(
        'boj_cron_days_old_field',
        'Delete Comments Older Than',
        'boj_cron_days_old',
        'discussion',
        'default'
    );

    //load the option value
    $options = get_option( 'boj_cron_comment_options' );
    $boj_comments = $options['boj_comments'];

    // if the option is enabled and
    // not already scheduled lets schedule it
    if ( $boj_comments &&
        !wp_next_scheduled( 'boj_comment_cron_hook' ) ) {

        //schedule the event to run daily
        wp_schedule_event( time(), 'daily', 'boj_comment_cron_hook' );

    // if the option is NOT enabled and scheduled lets unschedule it
    } elseif ( !$boj_comments &&
        wp_next_scheduled( 'boj_comment_cron_hook' ) ) {

        //get time of next scheduled run
        $timestamp = wp_next_scheduled( 'boj_comment_cron_hook' );

        //unschedule custom action hook
```

```
            wp_unschedule_event( $timestamp, 'boj_comment_cron_hook' );

    }

}

function boj_cron_comment_type() {

    // load the 'boj_comments' option from the database
    $options = get_option( 'boj_cron_comment_options' );
    $boj_comments = $options['boj_comments'];

    //display the option select field
    echo '<select name="boj_cron_comment_options[boj_comments]">';
        echo '<option value="" '.
            selected( $boj_comments, '', false ) .'>None</option>';
        echo '<option value="spam" '.
            selected( $boj_comments, 'spam', false ) .
            '>Spam Comments</option>';
        echo '<option value="moderated" '.
            selected( $boj_comments, 'moderated', false ) .
            '>Moderated Comments</option>';
        echo '<option value="both" '.
            selected( $boj_comments, 'both', false ) .'>Both</option>';
    echo '</select>';

}

function boj_cron_days_old() {

    // load the 'boj_days_old' option from the database
    $options = get_option( 'boj_cron_comment_options' );
    $boj_days_old = ( $options['boj_days_old'] ) ?
        absint( $options['boj_days_old'] ) : 30;

    //display the option text field
    echo '<input type="text"
        name="boj_cron_comment_options[boj_days_old]"
        value="' .esc_attr( $boj_days_old ). '" size="3" /> Days';

}
?>
```

Code snippet boj-delete-comments.php

SUMMARY

Cron is a powerful tool that opens up a lot of interesting possibilities for plugin developers. Understanding how cron works, and optimizing cron to work properly, can give your plugins a more advanced feature set and help take your plugin to the next level!

14

The Rewrite API

WHAT'S IN THIS CHAPTER?

➤ Understanding the concepts of URL rewriting

➤ Creating Rewrite rules in plugins

➤ Making a complete, new permalink structure

➤ Integrating a non-WordPress page with the same URL layout

➤ Generating a custom feed

The Rewrite API is often considered as one of the trickiest areas in WordPress and is certainly one of the least documented on the Web. This chapter first gives you some background information on why URLs are rewritten, then explains how to do this in WordPress, and finally shows you real-life client situations in which you can leverage the Rewrite API.

WHY REWRITE URLS

Dynamic sites use URLs that generate content from query string parameters. These URLs are often rewritten to resemble URLs for static pages on a site with a subdirectory hierarchy. For example, the URL to a wiki page might be `http://example.com/index .php?title=Rewrite_URL` and be actually rewritten to `http://example.com/Rewrite_URL`. A request to this latter, prettier URL will be transparently rewritten by the web server to the former URL.

This introductory section familiarizes you with the concept of "pretty permalinks" (sometimes called "fancy URLs" in web applications) and URL rewriting, in general and specifically in WordPress.

Permalink Principles

Web applications and sites can have two completely different audiences: human readers and search engines. Online resources should be both search engine and user friendly.

Search Engine Friendly

Suppose you have coded a complete online store for a client, with various products and categories. From a programmer's perspective, each URL of the site would be similar to `http://example.com/shop.php?action=display&category=12&subcat=4`. This URL easily maps to variables that can then typically fetch information from a database or perform actions.

The problem with that URL is that search engines may index it or just index `http://example.com/shop.php`, which may not even return something intelligible.

User Friendly

As a human user, you want a URL to be easy to understand and, if possible, memorable. For instance, consider the two URLs that would actually display the same product page:

➤   `example.com/shop.php?action=display&category=123&subcat=7&product_id=43`

➤   `example.com/shop/liquor/whisky/lagavulin/`

The first URL is long and cryptic, whereas the second one is shorter and self-explanatory.

Even when URLs are not obscure like the first one, having a directory-like structure makes it much more understandable. The following two URLs would, for instance, point to the same page on a WordPress powered site:

➤   `http://example.com/index.php?year=2011&paged=6`

➤   `http://example.com/2011/page/6/`

Apache's mod_rewrite

Web server developers have imagined ways to rewrite URLs, from something programmatically convenient (`shop.php?product=43`) to something user and search engine friendly (`/buy/ardbeg/`). This section highlights how this is done with the Apache web server, but other web server software (Lighttpd, Nginx, IIS, and so on) all have similar techniques.

The key module for permalinks in Apache is `mod_rewrite`, a module that enables defining rewrite rules typically found in the `.htaccess` file. A classic rewrite rule consists in the following code block:

```
<IfModule mod_rewrite.c>
RewriteEngine on
RewriteRule [ pattern] [ substitution ] [ optional flag(s) ]
</IfModule>
```

The pattern and substitution parameters can use regular expressions. Consider for instance the following rewrite rule:

```
RewriteRule /buy/([^/]+)/ /shop.php?product=$1 [L]
```

Now, when a client requests a URL that starts with /buy/ followed several times by a character that is not a slash ([^/]+) and then a slash, the web server internally redirects the request to /shop.php and passes the parameter product with the value caught inside the parentheses of the pattern.

If you want to learn more about mod_rewrite and URL rewriting in a non-WordPress environment, you can read a thorough guide at http://articles.sitepoint.com/article/guide-url-rewriting.

URL Rewriting in WordPress

A typical WordPress URL such as /2011/03/hello-world/ doesn't match an actual physical path on the web server. (No "hello-world" directory is in a "03" directory, which is in a "2011" folder.) At some point, the URL was therefore rewritten.

 If your WordPress setup runs on a capable server (usually Apache with mod_rewrite), you can enable "Pretty Permalinks" to benefit from the user and search engine-friendly URLs, such as example.com/2011/03/hello-world/ *instead of* example.com/index.php?p=1. *Read more about this beginner feature on the Codex at* http://codex.wordpress.org/Using_Permalinks.

When installed, WordPress creates an .htaccess file in its root directory that contains the following block:

```
<IfModule mod_rewrite.c>
RewriteEngine On
RewriteBase /
RewriteRule ^index\.php$ - [L]
RewriteCond %{REQUEST_FILENAME} !-f
RewriteCond %{REQUEST_FILENAME} !-d
RewriteRule . /index.php [L]
</IfModule>
```

This mod_rewrite directive contains a conditional rewrite rule, which tells the following to the web server:

1. If the request is index.php, redirect to this file and don't try to match any other rewrite rule. (The [L] flag stands for Last.)

2. If the request is not a file (%{REQUEST_FILENAME} !-f)...

3. ... and if the request is not a directory (%{REQUEST_FILENAME} !-d)...

4. ... then rewrite the URL to index.php and don't try to apply another rewrite rule.

This .htaccess directive redirects requests such as /2011/page/6/ to /index.php. This means that practically all requests in the frontend area of a WordPress site are internally redirected to index.php, which then has to guess how to interpret the request. Enter the Rewrite API.

HOW WORDPRESS HANDLES QUERIES

You now know that when a visitor loads a WordPress powered page, the file actually loaded is
`index.php`. For instance if you request `http://example.com/2011/03/hello-world/`, WordPress
internally redirects this URL into `http://example.com/index.php?p=1` and eventually fetches from
the database data for the post with ID 1. How is the translation from a URL to a MySQL query done?

The following section explains what magic happens when the web server displays a WordPress
powered page and how plugins can interfere with this process.

Overview of the Query Process

You need to understand how and when events occur within WordPress because this can highlight
the parts where your plugin can interfere with the process. You can now dissect the flow of events
when a page is requested and determine which files are included and which functions are called:

1. The root `index.php` file is loaded, as per the `.htaccess` rewrite rule, and loads the file
   `wp-blog-header.php`.

2. This file loads `wp-load.php`, which searches and includes `wp-config.php`, which will
   in turn load `wp-settings.php` that includes the function files, active plugins, and then
   pluggable functions.

3. Two new objects are instantiated: `$wp_query` and `$wp_rewrite`. You learn about these later.

4. A few other files are loaded, such as translation files and the theme's functions file.

 If you have not done it already, read the source of `wp-settings.php`: *This file
explains the flow of initial events, of which you've read an overview in Chapter 1,
"An Introduction to Plugins."*

WordPress is now fully loaded and plugins can start interacting, but it doesn't know yet
what to display and what page has been requested. Back to `wp-blog-header.php`: After
everything is loaded, this file calls the function `wp()`, which starts the magic — the function
`WP::parse_request()`.

The function `parse_request()` from the `WP` class (found in `wp-includes/classes.php`) prepares
everything WordPress needs to know to understand the page request:

5. This function fetches the list of all the registered rewrite rules. Just as previously explained
   with `mod_rewrite`, it consists in a list of pattern => replacement pairs, to tell WordPress
   that `/category/tutorials/page/2/` actually means `/index.php?category_name
   =tutorials&paged=2`.

6. The function goes through each rewrite rule, compares it to the requested URL, and tries to
   find a match. If no match is eventually found, this is a 404 error.

At this point, if the page is not a 404 error, WordPress now has a permalink translation pattern
with query variable placeholders, such as `index.php?category_name=<string>&paged=<number>`.
It now needs to get the values of these query variables.

7. The function `parse_request()` now obtains the list of the registered query variables, and for each variable checks if a value has been set by the permalink pattern, by POST, or by GET submission.

8. Now, WordPress knows everything it needs to convert the initial URL request into a proper MySQL database query, get post data, load the required theme template, and display the requested page.

Two expressions may have caught your attention in the preceding flow description: "registered rewrite rules" and "registered query variables." If at some point these are registered, maybe there's a way for plugins to modify them? Of course there is!

The rewrite Object

The `$wp_rewrite` object, previously introduced, is the first object you mess with when playing with the Rewrite API. Have a look at its content: Using a simple `print_r( $wp_rewrite )` displays the following information:

```
WP_Rewrite Object (
...
[permalink_structure] => /%year%/%postname%/
[use_trailing_slashes] => 1
...
[rules] => Array (
  [category/(.+?)/?$] => index.php?category_name=$matches[1]
  [tag/([^/]+)/page/?([0-9]{1,})/?$] => index.php?tag=$matches[1]&paged=$matches[2]
  [tag/([^/]+)/?$] => index.php?tag=$matches[1]
  [(.+?)/trackback/?$] => index.php?pagename=$matches[1]&tb=1
  ...
  )
[endpoints] => Array ()
...
)
```

Some of the preceding properties should already be familiar to you: The rules array contains the list of all registered rewrite rules. The `$rewrite` object contains all the information related to the permalink structure of your site, such as the complete set of rewrite rules that were fetched at the previous flow or the list of registered feeds and their URL structure (`/feed/rss2/` for instance).

The query Object

Similarly and before you learn how to alter it, have an inner look at the `$wp_query` object, with a `print_r()` call when requesting the page `/2011/hello-world/` on a WordPress powered site:

```
WP_Query Object (
  [query_vars] => Array (
    [page] => 0
    [year] => 2011
    [month] => 03
    [pagename] =>
    [category_name] =>
```

```
    [name] => hello-world
    ...
  )
  ...
  [is_single] => 1
  [is_preview] =>
  [is_page] =>
  ...
  [query] => Array (
    [year] => 2011
    [name] => hello-world
  )
  ...
)
```

The $wp_query object defines the list of authorized query variables that can be matched by the rewrite rules and collects all the information needed to translate the initial page request into a MySQL query.

What Plugins Can Do

Using functions of the Rewrite API, plugins can interfere with the $wp_rewrite and $wp_query objects, for instance to perform the following actions as you will learn in the next section, "Practical Uses":

➤ Create your own rewrite rules, and define how WordPress will interpret them.

➤ Integrate a WordPress site with non-WordPress pages and keep a consistent URL pattern and site layout.

➤ Create a custom feed with a custom feed permalink.

Now that you know the underlying concepts of the Rewrite API, it's time for you to write actual code.

PRACTICAL USES

You will now dive into practical examples of use and code for real life situations. You will learn to:

➤ Leverage the Rewrite API to easily generate an arbitrary number of sub pages under the hierarchy of one parent page.

➤ Define a custom permalink structure to easily integrate non-WordPress content into a WordPress powered site.

➤ Register new services with URL endpoints, for instance to display QR codes.

➤ Generate feeds for any custom content, such as the last uploaded images.

Rewriting a URL to Create a List of Shops

You've just redesigned the site of your latest client, a big retail company with dozens of stores across the country. You now have to list these stores within their web site. How can you do this?

➤ Option 1: Manually create a page for each store. Ewww. No fun.

➤ Option 2: Create one page at `http://example.com/shops/` and automatically make WordPress understand that `http://example.com/shops/somecity/` needs to display the information page for that store located in that particular city. Much more fun!

Creating the rewrite Rule

The function that creates a new rewrite rule is `add_rewrite_rule()`, which needs two arguments, similar to how `mod_rewrite` works: a string defining the URL pattern to be matched and another string for the URL replacement. In your Rewrite Rules Shop plugin, write the following:

```php
<?php
// Add rules
add_action( 'init', 'boj_rrs_add_rules' );
function boj_rrs_add_rules() {
    add_rewrite_rule( 'stores/?([^/]*)',
        'index.php?pagename=stores&store_id=$matches[1]', 'top' );
}
?>
```

This internally redirects all requests to the URL `stores/something/` to the page Stores with an additional parameter, that is, `index.php?pagename=stores&store_id=something`.

Note that you passed a third parameter to `add_rewrite_rule()`,`'top'`, to specify that this list will be added before all rewrite rules, to make sure it is matched early and before built-in rules.

Registering the query Variable

Now you need to add this additional parameter `store_id` to the list of registered query variables:

```php
<?php
// Add the store_id var so that WP recognizes it
add_filter( 'query_vars', 'boj_rrs_add_query_var' );
function boj_rrs_add_query_var( $vars ) {
    $vars[] = 'store_id';
    return $vars;
}
?>
```

So far, you have modified the list of defined rewrite rules held in the `$wp_rewrite` object and the list of authorized query variables, kept in the `$wp_query` object. You're almost done!

Flushing the Rewrite Rules

The trick with rewrite rules is that when they are modified (if you add, modify, or delete one), you need to tell WordPress to refresh and rebuild the list. To do so, you can either visit the Permalink

Options page in the admin area or use the function `flush_rewrite_rules()`. You can do this on plugin activation and plugin deactivation:

```php
<?php

// Add the rewrite rule and flush on plugin activation
register_activation_hook( __FILE__, 'boj_rrs_activate' );
function boj_rrs_activate() {
    boj_rrs_add_rules();
    flush_rewrite_rules();
}

// Flush when deactivated
register_deactivation_hook( __FILE__, 'boj_rrs_deactivate' );
function boj_rrs_deactivate() {
    flush_rewrite_rules();
}
?>
```

Note the best practices when adding new rewrite rules:

➤ On plugin activation, add the rule and flush.

➤ On `init`, also add the rule, in case another plugin flushes the rules.

➤ Don't flush rules on every page request (for example hooking in `init`); that would cause unnecessary overhead.

➤ On plugin deactivation, flush the rules again to clear the list.

The Functional Plugin

You can now review the whole plugin.

```php
<?php
/*
Plugin Name: List Stores
Plugin URI: http://example.com/
Description: A rewrite rule to list stores as children of the Stores page
Version: 1.0
Author: Ozh
Author URI: http://wrox.com
*/

// Add the rewrite rule and flush on plugin activation
register_activation_hook( __FILE__, 'boj_rrs_activate' );
function boj_rrs_activate() {
    boj_rrs_add_rules();
    flush_rewrite_rules();
}

// Flush when deactivated
register_deactivation_hook( __FILE__, 'boj_rrs_deactivate' );
```

```
function boj_rrs_deactivate() {
    flush_rewrite_rules();
}

// Add the rewrite rule
add_action( 'init', 'boj_rrs_add_rules' );
function boj_rrs_add_rules() {
    add_rewrite_rule( 'stores/?([^/]*)',
        'index.php?pagename=stores&store_id=$matches[1]', 'top' );
}

// Add the store_id var so that WP recognizes it
add_filter( 'query_vars', 'boj_rrs_add_query_var' );
function boj_rrs_add_query_var( $vars ) {
    $vars[] = 'store_id';
    return $vars;
}
?>
```

Code snippet boj_rewrite_shops/plugin.php

That's it for the plugin part: Now http://example.com/stores/denver/ redirects to the Stores WordPress parent page with the additional internal parameter store_id. You can now create that page and do a simple theme modification.

Creating the Shops Page that Can Generate Its Children

The additional internal parameter store_id is a query variable, which value can be read using the function get_query_var(), as following:

```
<?php
// Get store id
$store = get_query_var( 'store_id' );
?>
```

You can now create a regular WordPress page using the Add New Page admin page, but there is a twist: This page uses a page template.

When WordPress displays a Page (as opposed to a Post), it looks for the template file page.php within the current theme directory. You can set individual pages to use a more specific template file stores.php, simply by creating a new file within the theme directory and starting it as follows:

```
<?php
/*
Template Name: Store
*/
?>
```

Now in the Page write interface, within the Page Attribute meta box, you will be given the option to select this page template in the drop-down, as shown in Figure 14-1.

The page template code and layout depend on how your theme is coded, for instance how <div> elements are used and named. In this example you can assume the client's site is running WordPress' default theme, TwentyTen, so your store.php page template will have the same structure as the original page.php:

FIGURE 14-1

```php
<?php
/*
Template Name: Store
*/
?>

<?php get_header(); ?>

<div id="container">
    <div id="content" role="main">

    </div><!-- #content -->
</div><!-- #container -->

<?php get_sidebar(); ?>
<?php get_footer(); ?>
```

Within the <div id="content"> now resides the code that either lists all stores (if http://example .com/stores/ is requested) or displays a specific store information (when the requested page is for instance http://example.com/stores/miami/). To do so, you can simply do the following:

➤ Define an array of store data: store name, manager name, address, and phone number for every existing store.

➤ Check the value of get_query_var('store_id') and if it matches the ID of an existing store, display data for that given store.

➤ If get_query_var('store_id') doesn't match an existing store or is empty, list all stores.

The complete page template store.php you can save into the theme directory follows:

```php
<?php
/*
Template Name: Store
*/
?>

<?php get_header(); ?>

<div id="container">
    <div id="content" role="main">
    <?php

    // define all stores
    $stores = array(
```

```php
        'milwaukee' => array(
            'name'    => "Milwaukee Store",
            'manager' => 'Richie Cunningham',
            'address' => '565 N Clinton Drive, Milwaukee',
            'phone'   => '555-31337-1337'
        ),
        'springfield' => array(
            'name'    => "Springfield Store",
            'manager' => 'Bart Simpson',
            'address' => 'Evergreen Terrace, Springfield',
            'phone'   => '555-666-696969'
        ),
        'fairview' => array(
            'name'    => "Fairview Store",
            'manager' => 'Susan Mayer',
            'address' => '4353 Wisteria Lane, Fairview',
            'phone'   => '4-8-15-16-23-42'
        )
    );

    // Get store id
    $store = get_query_var( 'store_id' );

    // if store exists, display info
    if( array_key_exists( $store, $stores ) ) {

        extract( $stores[$store] );
        echo "<p>Store: $name</p>";
        echo "<p>Manager: $manager</p>";
        echo "<p>Location: $address</p>";
        echo "<p>Contact us: $phone</p>";

    // if store does not exist, list them all
    } else {

        // Get current page URL
        global $post;
        $page = untrailingslashit( get_permalink( $post->ID ) );

        echo '<p>Our stores:</p>';
        echo '<ul>';
        foreach( $stores as $store => $info ) {
            $name = $info['name'];
            echo "<li><a href='$page/$store/'>$name</a></li>\n";
        }
        echo '</ul>';
    }

    ?>
    </div><!-- #content -->
</div><!-- #container -->

<?php get_sidebar(); ?>
<?php get_footer(); ?>
```

Code snippet boj_rewrite_shops/store.php

You can now create a regular page within WordPress, using this page template, as shown in Figure 14-2.

FIGURE 14-2

On the front side of the site, you can now access the main Stores page, located at `http://example .com/stores/`, which lists all stores and links to each individual store page, for instance `http:// example.com/stores/fairview/` as shown in Figure 14-3:

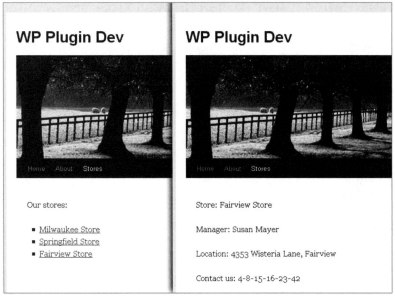

FIGURE 14-3

Creating a New Permalink Structure and Integrating Non-WordPress Pages

In the previous plugin, you created a WordPress page to handle URLs rewritten to it. You can now create other rewrite rules using a different approach.

The client you're now working with already has a product listing script and wants you to integrate it in its new web site you created for them. You can make WordPress handle all requests to `http://example.com/shop/something/` and use the existing listing script.

Creating a rewrite Tag

In the Permalink Options settings page, you can define custom permalinks using tags such as `%year%` or `%monthnum%`. You can now define a new tag `%product%` and use it in the permalink structure of the site:

```php
<?php
// Create new tag %product% and handle /shop/%product% URLs
add_action('init', 'boj_products_rewrite');
function boj_products_rewrite() {
    add_rewrite_tag( '%product%', '([^/]+)' );
    add_permastruct( 'product', 'shop' . '/%product%' );
}
?>
```

The first function call, `add_rewrite_tag()`, defines the tag and what can match it. Here, the tag `%product%` matches one or more characters that are not a forward slash, using the regular expression `([^/]+)`. This function call also registers a new query variable with the same name `product`.

The tag defined, the function `add_permastruct()`, describes a new permalink structure, with two parameters: an arbitrary name for the structure and how URLs and tags should be formed.

Now look at the rewrite rules that have been added to the `$wp_rewrite` object and its `rules` property:

```
[shop/([^/]+)/feed/(feed|rdf|rss|rss2|atom)/?$]
    => index.php?product=$matches[1]&feed=$matches[2]
[shop/([^/]+)/(feed|rdf|rss|rss2|atom)/?$]
    => index.php?product=$matches[1]&feed=$matches[2]
[shop/([^/]+)/page/?([0-9]{1,})/?$]
    => index.php?product=$matches[1]&paged=$matches[2]
[shop/([^/]+)/?$]
    => index.php?product=$matches[1]
```

Example URLs matching these rewrite rules could be the following:

- ➤   `http://example.com/shop/something/feed/rss2/`
- ➤   `http://example.com/shop/stuff/atom/`
- ➤   `http://example.com/shop/thing/page/3/`
- ➤   `http://example.com/shop/item/`

These URLs can internally redirect to the following:

➤ http://example.com/index.php?product=something&feed=rss2

➤ http://example.com/index.php?product=stuff&feed=atom

➤ http://example.com/index.php?product=thing&paged=3

➤ http://example.com/index.php?product=item

Congratulations: Using just two function calls, you created a complete, new permalink structure that can handle pagination and feed generation!

Displaying the Shop Products

Now that requests to /shop/something/ successfully redirect to /index.php?product=something, you can integrate the existing product listing script. Here the actual script integration is commented and replaced with a simple output:

```php
<?php
// If query var product as a value, include product listing
add_action( 'template_redirect', 'boj_products_display' );
function boj_products_display() {
    if ( $product = get_query_var( 'product' ) ) {
        // include( 'display_product.php' );
        echo "Here goes information for product <strong>$product</strong>";
        exit;
    }
}
?>
```

By hooking into the early action 'template_redirect', you can hijack the normal page display and, if the query variable product (registered by the previous add_rewrite_tag() function call) has a value, include the shop listing script. Don't forget to use exit() so that WordPress does not try to further handle the page display and, unable to find a post, output a 404 error.

To test for pagination or feed generation, you can also check the values of get_query_var('paged') and get_query_var('feed').

Flush the rewrite rules when they're created the first time, and your plugin is now complete and functional.

The Functional Plugin

You can now review the whole plugin.

Available for download on Wrox.com

```php
<?php
/*
Plugin Name: Products Permalink Structure
Plugin URI: http://example.com/
Description: Create a whole permalink structure
Version: 1.0
Author: Ozh
```

```
Author URI: http://wrox.com
*/

// Add permalink structure and flush on plugin activation
register_activation_hook( __FILE__, 'boj_products_activate' );
function boj_products_activate() {
    boj_products_rewrite();
    flush_rewrite_rules();
}

// Flush on plugin deactivation
register_deactivation_hook( __FILE__, 'boj_products_deactivate' );
function boj_products_deactivate() {
    flush_rewrite_rules();
}

// Create new tag %product% and handle /shop/%product% URLs
add_action('init', 'boj_products_rewrite');
function boj_products_rewrite() {
    add_rewrite_tag( '%product%', '([^/]+)' );
    add_permastruct( 'product', 'shop' . '/%product%' );
}

// If query var product as a value, include product listing
add_action( 'template_redirect', 'boj_products_display' );
function boj_products_display() {
    if ( $product = get_query_var( 'product' ) ) {
        // include( 'display_product.php' );
        echo "searching for product $product ?";
        exit;
    }
}
```

Code snippet boj_rewrite_products/plugin.php

Adding an Endpoint and Altering Output Format

A URL endpoint defines a new service, like /trackback/ on WordPress singular URLs. You can code a plugin that adds a "format" endpoint, so the user will add /format/XXX/ to any URL and turn your site into a fun API:

➤ Appending /format/qr/ to URLs displays the QR code of the current URL.

➤ /format/json/ on a singular URL (a post, a page) returns the post data as a JSON encoded string.

A QR Code, also sometimes called flash code in a mobile application, is a black-and-white square pattern readable by QR scanners, mobile phones, and smartphones with a camera. It contains encoded information, which can be text, URL, or other data such as a phone number. Common in Japan, QR Codes are being adopted by more and more mainstream brands.

Defining the Endpoint

To define the endpoint for your service, you can use the function `add_rewrite_endpoint()`, which needs two parameters: a string for the syntax of the endpoint (here `format`) and a number to identify on which "places," that is types of URLs, the endpoint will be added.

The file `wp-includes/rewrite.php` defines several constants to match "places" where endpoint will be added. For example with `EP_CATEGORIES` (which has a value of 512), you can match only URLs under the `/category/` permalink, such as `http://example.com/category/tshirts/format/qr/`.

Following is a complete list of constants.

CONSTANT	VALUE, FOR INFORMATION	PLACES
EP_NONE	0	None
EP_PERMALINK	1	Permalinks
EP_ATTACHMENT	2	Attachment pages
EP_DATE	4	Date pages
EP_YEAR	8	Year pages
EP_MONTH	16	Month pages
EP_DAY	32	Day pages
EP_ROOT	64	Root page
EP_COMMENTS	128	Comment pages
EP_SEARCH	256	Search pages
EP_CATEGORIES	512	Category pages
EP_TAGS	1024	Tag pages
EP_AUTHORS	2048	Author pages
EP_PAGES	4096	"Pages" pages
EP_ALL	8191	Everything

For instance, if you want to add an endpoint to author pages, you can write `add_rewrite_endpoint('something', 2048)` or `add_rewrite_endpoint('something', EP_AUTHORS)`.

If you want to append an endpoint to both author pages and search pages, add the two place values: `add_rewrite_endpoint('something', EP_AUTHORS + EP_SEARCH)`.

In your plugin add the endpoint to all URLs:

```php
<?php
// Add the endpoint rewrite rules
add_filter( 'init', 'boj_ep_add_rules' );
function boj_ep_add_rules() {
    add_rewrite_endpoint( 'format', EP_ALL );
}
?>
```

This single function call registers /format/ as a valid endpoint to all URLs, and registers a new query variable, also named format. This enables URLs such as /tag/tshirt/format/qr/ to be internally rewritten to /index.php?tag=tshirt&format=qr.

You can now check the value of the query var format and modify the page output:

```php
<?php
// Handle the custom format display if needed
add_filter( 'template_redirect', 'boj_ep_template_redirect' );
function boj_ep_template_redirect() {
    switch( get_query_var( 'format' ) ) {
        case 'qr':
            boj_ep_display_qr();
            exit;
        case 'json':
            if( is_singular() ) {
                boj_ep_display_json();
                exit;
            }
    }
}
?>
```

To finalize your plugin, you now need to add the following functions or features:

➤ boj_ep_display_json() encodes the global variable $post using json_encode() and displays it.

➤ boj_ep_display_qr() determines the current URL being visited, fetches an image from Google's QR Code API using functions covered in the HTTP API chapter, and then displays it.

➤ Activation and deactivation hooks add the endpoint and flush the rewrite rules.

The Functional Plugin

You can now review the whole plugin.

Available for
download on
Wrox.com

```php
<?php
/*
Plugin Name: Format endpoint
Plugin URI: http://example.com/
Description: Add a /format/ endpoint to all URLs
Version: 1.0
Author: Ozh
```

```php
Author URI: http://wrox.com
*/


// Add permalink structure and flush on plugin activation
register_activation_hook( __FILE__, 'boj_ep_activate' );
function boj_ep_activate() {
    boj_ep_add_rules();
    flush_rewrite_rules();
}

// Flush on plugin deactivation
register_deactivation_hook( __FILE__, 'boj_ep_deactivate' );
function boj_ep_deactivate(){
    flush_rewrite_rules();
}


// Add the endpoint rewrite rules
add_filter( 'init', 'boj_ep_add_rules' );
function boj_ep_add_rules() {
    add_rewrite_endpoint( 'format', EP_ALL );
}

// Handle the custom format display if needed
add_filter( 'template_redirect', 'boj_ep_template_redirect' );
function boj_ep_template_redirect() {
    switch( get_query_var( 'format' ) ) {
        case 'qr':
            boj_ep_display_qr();
            exit;
        case 'json':
            if( is_singular() ) {
                boj_ep_display_json();
                exit;
            }
    }
}

// Display JSON information about the post
function boj_ep_display_json() {
    global $post;
    // Tell the browser this is a JSON file
    header('Content-type: application/json');
    echo json_encode( $post );
    exit;
}

// Display a QR code
function boj_ep_display_qr() {
    // get current location and strip /format/qr/ from the URL
    $url = ( is_ssl() ? 'https://' : 'http://' )
        . $_SERVER['HTTP_HOST']
        . preg_replace( '!/format/qr/$!', '/', $_SERVER['REQUEST_URI'] );
```

```php
    // encode URL so it can be used for the QR code query
    $url = urlencode( $url );

    // Google QR code URL:
    $qr = "http://chart.apis.google.com/chart?chs=150x150&cht=qr&chl="
        . $url . "&chld=L|0";

    // Get the image generated by Google
    $image = wp_remote_retrieve_body( wp_remote_get( $qr ) );

    // Display QR code image
    header( 'Content-Type: image/png' );
    echo $image;
    exit;
}
?>
```

Code snippet boj_endpoints_format/plugin.php

Adding a Custom Feed for the Latest Uploaded Images

By default WordPress generates several feed formats (RSS, RSS2, and ATOM) and their permalink structure is defined in the `$wp_rewrite` object. For example, out-of-the-box, you can display the following:

➤ An Atom feed of all the posts: `http://example.com/feed/atom/`

➤ An RSS feed of posts tagged "beer": `http://example.com/tag/beer/feed/rss/`

➤ An RDF feed of the comments to a given post: `http://example.com/2011/hello-world/feed/rdf/`

With a plugin you can define your own feeds and what they output, for instance a feed of the latest images uploaded within WordPress, available at `http://example.com/feed/img/`.

Registering the New Feed

The Rewrite API function you use to register a new feed is `add_feed()`, which needs two arguments: the feed name such as "atom" or, here, `img`, and the callback function that can output content.

```php
<?php

// Register the feed
add_filter( 'init', 'boj_addfeed_add_feed' );
function boj_addfeed_add_feed() {
    add_feed( 'img', 'boj_addfeed_do_feed' );
}
?>
```

From now on, the URL `http://example.com/feed/img/` will be handled by the callback function `boj_addfeed_do_feed()`. Because images in WordPress are actually the custom post type "attachment" as covered in Chapter 11, "Extending Posts," you can easily build your own `$post` and Loop to display the latest images in an XML ATOM manner. As usual flush the rules on activation and deactivation, and the plugin is complete.

The Functional Plugin

You can now review the whole plugin.

```php
<?php
/*
Plugin Name: Image feed
Plugin URI: http://example.com/
Description: Add a feed for latest uploaded images
Version: 1.0
Author: Ozh
Author URI: http://wrox.com
*/

// Add permalink structure and flush on plugin activation
register_activation_hook( __FILE__, 'boj_addfeed_activate' );
function boj_addfeed_activate() {
    boj_addfeed_add_feed();
    flush_rewrite_rules();
}

// Flush on plugin deactivation
register_deactivation_hook( __FILE__, 'boj_addfeed_deactivate' );
function boj_addfeed_deactivate() {
    flush_rewrite_rules();
}

// Register the feed
add_filter( 'init', 'boj_addfeed_add_feed' );
function boj_addfeed_add_feed() {
    add_feed( 'img', 'boj_addfeed_do_feed' );
}

// Callback function: echo the feed
function boj_addfeed_do_feed( $in ) {

    // Make custom query to get latest attachments
    query_posts(array( 'post_type' => 'attachment', 'post_status' => 'inherit' ));

    // Send content header and start ATOM output
    header('Content-Type: application/atom+xml');
    echo '<?xml version="1.0" encoding="'.get_option('blog_charset').'"?'.'>';
    ?>

<feed xmlns="http://www.w3.org/2005/Atom">
    <title type="text">Latest images on <?php bloginfo_rss('name'); ?></title>
    <?php
    // Start the Loop
    while (have_posts()) : the_post();
    ?>
    <entry>
```

```
    <title><![CDATA[<?php the_title_rss() ?>]]></title>
    <link href="<?php the_permalink_rss() ?>" />
    <published><?php echo get_post_time('Y-m-d\TH:i:s\Z'); ?></published>
    <content type="html"><![CDATA[<?php the_content() ?>]]></content>
  </entry>
  <?php
  // End of the Loop
  endwhile ;
  ?>
</feed>

  <?php
}
?>
```

Code snippet boj_addfeed/plugin.php

SUMMARY

The goal of this chapter was to demystify the area of URL rewriting in WordPress, frequently considered to be a complicated subject. With the concrete plugin examples crafted here, you can now make your own way in this field. The Rewrite API will be invaluable, especially when you will have to integrate into WordPress existing content and existing scripts, which can happen frequently with clients who already have a presence on the web.

The Rewrite API is often deemed hard to understand because it's less used and known than most other APIs, and indeed it's not the API you will employ on a daily basis. Knowing what it can do and mastering it can definitely be a plus over your competitors!

15

Multisite

WHAT'S IN THIS CHAPTER?

➤ Using Multisite versus standard WordPress

➤ Understanding Multisite terminology

➤ Exploring common Multisite functions

➤ Switching between sites in a network

➤ Managing how to aggregate content across sites

➤ Working with network and site options

➤ Understanding users and site roles

➤ Determining database schema differences

➤ Installing and configuring Multisite

WordPress Multisite, formerly WordPress MU or Multiuser, is a powerful feature included in WordPress. Multisite enables you to create multiple sites with a single install of WordPress. This makes it easy for anyone running WordPress to create and administer a network of sites. This network can enable open user and site registration, or be a closed network where only administrators can create new sites and users.

Each site in your Multisite network can also run separate plugins, offer different themes, store unique content, and have a completely separate user base. It doesn't take much to realize how powerful Multisite is in WordPress. Because of this, as a plugin developer you need to understand what features are available when working with Multisite in WordPress.

DIFFERENCES

WordPress Multisite is included in every install of WordPress since version 3.0. Multisite, however, is not enabled by default. There are some key differences between standard WordPress and Multisite, so you need to understand those differences when developing plugins for WordPress.

WordPress Versus Multisite Network

By default when you install WordPress you install a single site. Since WordPress 3.0, Multisite (sometimes shortened to WPMS) has been included in WordPress. WordPress Multisite enables you to run multiple sites in a single installation of WordPress. When enabling Multisite you have a choice on how sites will be viewed in WordPress: either as subdomains (site1.example.com) or subdirectories (example.com/site1). You can even map domain names to each site (example .com) so that visitors to your sites would have no idea they are all powered by a single install of WordPress.

As you can imagine this is an extremely powerful feature in WordPress. There is no limit to the number of sites WordPress can run; the only restriction is the resources available on your hosting server. WordPress.com is actually a Multisite install of WordPress and powers millions of sites on the Internet. For example, WordPress.com hosts sites ranging from a single blogger to TechCrunch.com.

Understanding Multisite Terminology

You need to understand the terminology used in WordPress Multisite. Two important terms in Multisite are network and site. A network is the entire Multisite installation, or the network. A site is a single site inside the network. Therefore WordPress Multisite is a network of sites.

When developing plugins for Multisite, you need to determine whether you want to work across the network or in a single site. For example, you may want to retrieve posts from a single site in the network. Alternatively, you may want to create a networkwide option for your plugin.

All sites in your Multisite network have a status. The status is important and can determine whether the site is viewable by the public. Following is a list of the available site statuses in Multisite:

- ➤ `Public` — Site is public if privacy is set to enable search engines.
- ➤ `Archived` — Site has been archived and is not available to the public.
- ➤ `Mature` — Site is flagged as mature.
- ➤ `Spam` — Site is considered spam and is not available to the public.
- ➤ `Deleted` — Site is flagged for deletion and is not available to the public.

The only two statuses that don't remove the site from public viewing are `Public` and `Mature`. `Mature` can be used if you want to allow mature sites in your network, but need a way to warn users prior to them viewing the content. `Public` is based on the privacy settings and whether search engines are allowed to index the site.

Advantages of Multisite

Running Multisite for your websites offers many advantages. The most obvious advantage is you have only a single install of WordPress to administer. This makes life much easier when updating WordPress, plugins, and themes. If you have a WordPress Multisite network of 50 sites, and a plugin update is released, you need to update only that plugin once, and it will affect all sites in your network. If each site were a separate install of WordPress, you would have to update the plugin 50 times.

Another advantage to Multisite is the ease with which you can aggregate content across your network. For example, if you have 50 sites in your network, you could easily aggregate all those posts to your main blog to showcase your network of sites. If the sites were separate installs of WordPress, it would take quite a bit more work to aggregate that content.

Administering a network of sites in Multisite is also versatile. You can easily limit disk space usage on each site. You can also dictate what file type extensions are allowed for uploading along with file size limits. You can even lock down plugins and themes from being administered, or even used, by the users in your network.

ENABLING MULTISITE IN WORDPRESS

Installing WordPress Multisite is actually quite straightforward. One of the great features of Multisite is that it can be enabled prior to installing WordPress, or anytime thereafter. So if you decide to convert your WordPress site into Multisite a year down the road, you can certainly do that.

The first step to enabling Multisite is to modify your `wp-config.php` file. This file contains your database connection settings and other important configuration options. To enable Multisite you need to add the following line above where it says `/* That's all, stop editing! Happy blogging. */`:

```
define( 'WP_ALLOW_MULTISITE', true );
```

Adding this line to your `wp-config.php` file enables the Tools ➪ Network menu options, as shown in Figure 15-1.

Visiting this new menu option takes you to the Create a Network of WordPress Sites admin page. If you have not done so already, you will be required to disable all plugins prior to enabling Multisite. Here you can find detailed instructions on the necessary steps to complete the Multisite installation. In this tutorial you configure Multisite to work with subdirectories, so if you plan to use subdomains, be sure to follow the installation instructions closely as the code may differ slightly.

FIGURE 15-1

The next step is to create a `blogs.dir` directory inside your `wp-content` folder. Multisite handles image permalinks differently than standard WordPress. All images are uploaded to `wp-content/blogs.dir/BLOG_ID/files/YEAR/MONTH`. Permalinks for files look like `http://example.com/files/2011/10/image.png`.

After you create the blogs.dir directory, you need to add the following code to your wp-config.php file. Note that this is example code and the DOMAIN_CURRENT_SITE constant would contain your Web site's domain in place of example.com:

```
define( 'MULTISITE', true );
define( 'SUBDOMAIN_INSTALL', false );
$base = '/';
define( 'DOMAIN_CURRENT_SITE', 'example.com' );
define( 'PATH_CURRENT_SITE', '/' );
define( 'SITE_ID_CURRENT_SITE', 1 );
define( 'BLOG_ID_CURRENT_SITE', 1 );
```

The final step is to modify your .htaccess file in the root directory of your WordPress installation. Replace the existing WordPress rules with the following code:

```
RewriteEngine On
RewriteBase /
RewriteRule ^index\.php$ - [L]

# uploaded files
RewriteRule ^([_0-9a-zA-Z-]+/)?files/(.+) wp-includes/ms-files.php?file=$2 [L]

# add a trailing slash to /wp-admin
RewriteRule ^([_0-9a-zA-Z-]+/)?wp-admin$ $1wp-admin/ [R=301,L]

RewriteCond %{REQUEST_FILENAME} -f [OR]
RewriteCond %{REQUEST_FILENAME} -d
RewriteRule ^ - [L]
RewriteRule ^([_0-9a-zA-Z-]+/)?(wp-(content|admin|includes).*) $2 [L]
RewriteRule ^([_0-9a-zA-Z-]+/)?(.*\.php)$ $2 [L]
RewriteRule . index.php [L]
```

After making the required changes, you may be required to log back in to WordPress. WordPress Multisite is now enabled and installed and ready to use!

MULTISITE FUNCTIONS

When Multisite is enabled an entire new set of features and functions become available for plugin developers to take advantage of. Understanding what functions are available can help you include Multisite-specific functionality in the plugins you create. It can also help to understand how you can make your plugins Multisite-compatible from the start.

The Power of Blog ID

Each site in your WordPress Multisite network has a unique ID, or blog ID. This blog ID will be used in just about every Multisite-specific function you use. This is how WordPress determines what site you want to work with. The blog ID is also used in the prefix of the database tables for your site.

For example, if you enable Multisite and create a second site in your network, WordPress creates several database tables prefixed like `wp_2_posts` where `wp_` is the table prefix you defined when installing WordPress, and `2_` is the blog ID of the new site. As you create additional sites, WordPress creates additional database tables in the same manner.

The blog ID is stored in the global variable `$blog_id` as shown here:

```php
<?php
global $blog_id;
echo 'Current blog ID: ' .$blog_id;
?>
```

The `$blog_ID` global variable does exist in standard WordPress but will always be 1. In Multisite mode the blog ID will be the ID of the blog the current user is viewing.

Common Functions

When working with WordPress Multisite you can take advantage of some common functions. The first function is called `is_multisite()` and determines whether Multisite support is enabled. Look at an example:

```php
<?php
if ( is_multisite() ) {
    echo 'Multisite is enabled';
}
?>
```

As you can see this function doesn't accept any parameters. It simply checks if Multisite is enabled in WordPress and if so returns `True`. Anytime you plan on using Multisite-specific functions in WordPress, it's imperative that you use this function to verify Multisite is running. If Multisite is not running, the default Multisite functions will not be available for use in WordPress, and you will get errors in your plugin.

Another useful function for retrieving network site posts is `get_blog_post()`. This function retrieves a post from any site in the network.

```php
<?php get_blog_post( $blog_id, $post_id ); ?>
```

The function accepts two parameters: `$blog_id` and `$post_id`. Look at an example:

```php
<?php
//set blog and post ID
$multisite_blog_id = 3;
$multisite_post_id = 4;

//load the post data
$post_details = get_blog_post(
    $multisite_blog_id, $multisite_post_id );

//display the post title and content
```

```
echo 'Post Title: ' .$post_details->post_title .'<br />';
echo 'Post Content: ' .$post_details->post_content .'<br />';
?>
```

This example assumes you have a site with an ID of 3 and you want to retrieve post ID 4. This is a quick-and-easy way to retrieve a post from any site in your network.

It can also be useful to retrieve specific information about a site you are working with. To retrieve site information you can use the get_blog_details() function.

```
<?php get_blog_details( $fields, $getall ); ?>
```

The function accepts two parameters:

➤ $fields — Blog ID, a blog name, or an array of fields to query against

➤ $getall — Whether to retrieve all details

This function returns an object containing all public variables stored in the wp_blogs table. You can also retrieve a single, specific variable.

```
<?php
$blog_details = get_blog_details( 1 );
print_r( $blog_details );
?>
```

Running the preceding code would produce the following object output:

```
stdClass Object
(
    [blog_id] => 1
    [site_id] => 1
    [domain] => example.com
    [path] => /
    [registered] => 2010-10-31 19:14:59
    [last_updated] => 2010-11-11 14:19:34
    [public] => 1
    [archived] => 0
    [mature] => 0
    [spam] => 0
    [deleted] => 0
    [lang_id] => 0
    [blogname] => Example Website
    [siteurl] => http://example.com
    [post_count] => 420
)
```

As you can see there is a lot of valuable data returned about the site specified. You can also retrieve a single option value by stating the name to return:

```
<?php
echo 'Total post count: ' .get_blog_details( 1 )->post_count;
?>
```

Switching and Restoring Sites

One major advantage to using WordPress Multisite is how easy it is to aggregate content, and other data, between different sites in your network.

You can use two primary functions to pull data from sites in your network. The first of these functions is `switch_to_blog()`. This function enables you to switch to any site in your network.

```php
<?php switch_to_blog( $blog_id, $validate ); ?>
```

The function accepts two parameters:

➤ `$blog_id` — The ID of the site you want to switch to

➤ `$validate` — Whether to check if the site exists before proceeding

The second function is `restore_current_blog()`. This function restores the user back to the current site. You should always execute this function after calling `switch_to_blog()`. If not, everything that processes after the switch will pull from the site you switched to, and not the current site. This can mess up your widgets, site settings, and more.

Now look at an example. In this example, you create a custom settings page and display posts from the blog ID 3.

```php
<?php
add_action( 'admin_menu', 'boj_multisite_switch_menu' );

function boj_multisite_switch_menu() {

    //create custom top-level menu
    add_menu_page( 'Multisite Switch', 'Multisite Switch',
        'manage_options', 'boj-network-switch', 'boj_multisite_switch_page' );

}
?>
```

First create a custom top-level menu. This will point to the `boj_multisite_switch_page()` function, which will be the display page for the posts from site 3.

```php
<?php
function boj_multisite_switch_page() {

    if ( is_multisite() ) {

        //switch to blog ID 3
        switch_to_blog( 3 );

        //create a custom Loop
        $recentPosts = new WP_Query();
        $recentPosts->query( 'posts_per_page=5' );

        //start the custom Loop
        while ( $recentPosts->have_posts() ) :
```

```
        $recentPosts->the_post();

        //store the recent posts in a variable
        echo '<p><a href="' .get_permalink(). '">' .
            get_the_title() .'</a></p>';

    endwhile;

    //restore the current site
    restore_current_blog();

    }


}
?>
```

As always you need to verify Multisite is enabled using the `is_multisite()` function check. If Multisite is not enabled, the `switch_to_blog()` and `restore_current_blog()` functions will not be available to use in your plugin. Next, use the `switch_to_blog()` function to switch to blog ID 3. In this case you hardcoded the blog ID, but this could always be a dynamic variable set by a user. Now that you've switched to the site you want to pull content from, you need to create a custom Loop to retrieve the content.

To create the custom Loop, you define a variable named `$recentPosts` and instantiate an instance of `WP_Query`. Next set the query parameters; in this case you set `posts_per_page` to 5. This returns the five latest posts found. Now that `WP_Query` has been defined, it's time to execute the Loop and retrieve the results. You do this with the `have_posts()` and `the_post()` functions. The custom loop will then echo out the posts found from the query.

The final step is to execute `restore_current_blog()`. If you did not run this function, WordPress would stay on the site you switched to. If you execute additional loops below this, they would all pull from blog ID 3, and not from the current site you are viewing.

Now when you visit the plugin settings page the latest five posts from blog ID 3 display. Review the entire plugin:

```
<?php
/*
Plugin Name: Multisite Switch Example Plugin
Plugin URI: http://example.com/wordpress-plugins/my-plugin
Description: A plugin to demonstrate Multisite site switching
Version: 1.0
Author: Brad Williams
Author URI: http://wrox.com
License: GPLv2
*/

add_action( 'admin_menu', 'boj_multisite_switch_menu' );

function boj_multisite_switch_menu() {

    //create custom top-level menu
```

```
        add_menu_page( 'Multisite Switch', 'Multisite Switch',
            'manage_options',
            'boj-network-switch', 'boj_multisite_switch_page' );

}

function boj_multisite_switch_page() {

    if ( is_multisite() ) {

        //switch to blog ID 3
        switch_to_blog( 3 );

        //create a custom Loop
        $recentPosts = new WP_Query();
        $recentPosts->query( 'posts_per_page=5' );

        //start the custom Loop
        while ( $recentPosts->have_posts() ) :
            $recentPosts->the_post();

            //store the recent posts in a variable
            echo '<p><a href="' .get_permalink(). '">' .
                get_the_title() .'</a></p>';

        endwhile;

        //restore the current site
        restore_current_blog();

    }

}
?>
```

Code snippet boj-multisite-switch.php

This is a basic example that demonstrates the power of the switch_to_blog() functionality in Multisite.

The switch_to_blog() function is not just limited to site content. You can also retrieve other WordPress data including widgets, sidebars, menus, and more. Basically any data stored in the content database tables (wp_ID_tablename) is available when using the switch_to_blog() function. Now look at a few examples. In the following example, you can assume you have a site with an ID of 3 and you want to retrieve a navigation menu from the site.

```
<?php
//switch to blog ID 3
switch_to_blog( 3 );

//display the nav menu Main Menu
```

```php
wp_nav_menu( 'Main Menu' );

//restore the current site
restore_current_blog();
?>
```

First run `switch_to_blog()` to switch to blog ID 3. Next use the `wp_nav_menu()` function to display a menu named Main Menu from the site. Finally run the `restore_current_blog()` function to reset back to the blog you are viewing. The end result displays the nav menu Main Menu created on site 3 anywhere you run this code in your network.

As another example you can also easily load a sites sidebar using the same method.

```php
<?php
//switch to blog ID 34
switch_to_blog( 34 );

//load the primary sidebar
get_sidebar();

//restore the current site
restore_current_blog();
?>
```

It's important to note that `switch_to_blog()` is database-only. This means a site's plugins are not included in a switch. So if site 2 has the Halloween Revenge plugin running, and you switch to site 2, Halloween Revenge will not be available for use unless it is also activated on the site performing the switch.

Network Content Shortcode Examples

Now take the switch example and integrate shortcode support. This plugin enables you to add a shortcode to a post, define what blog ID you want posts from, and display on your post or page.

First create a new shortcode using the `add_shortcode()` function, introduced in Chapter 10, "The Shortcode API."

```php
<?php
add_shortcode( 'network_posts', 'boj_multisite_network_posts' );
?>
```

The new shortcode will be [network_posts]. Next create the function to generate the network posts to display when the shortcode is used in a post or page.

```php
<?php
function boj_multisite_network_posts( $attr ) {
    extract( shortcode_atts( array(
            "blogid"      =>    '1',
            "num"         =>    '5'
```

```
            ), $attr ) );

      if ( is_multisite() ) {

          $return_posts = '';

          //switch to site set in the shortcode
          switch_to_blog( absint( $blogid ) );

          //create a custom Loop
          $recentPosts = new WP_Query();
          $recentPosts->query( 'posts_per_page=' .absint( $num ) );

          //start the custom Loop
          while ( $recentPosts->have_posts() ) :
              $recentPosts->the_post();

              //store the recent posts in a variable
              $return_posts .= '<p><a href="' .get_permalink() '">' .get_the_title()
.'</a></p>';

          endwhile;

          //restore the current site
          restore_current_blog();

          //return the results to display
          return $return_posts;

      }
  }
?>
```

The shortcode can accept two parameters: blogid and num. This enables the user to set which site in the network to pull the posts from and how many to display. As always check to verify Multisite is enabled on the site before proceeding.

$return_posts is the variable that stores all the posts to return to the shortcode for display, so start by setting that variable to nothing to flush it out. Next use the switch_to_blog() function to switch to the site specified in the shortcode. If the user did not set a specific blog ID, it will default to 1.

Now it's time to create a custom loop to retrieve the posts to display. You can see the posts_ per_page parameter is set to $num, which is set in the shortcode. If the user does not set the number of posts to display, it defaults to 5. Next loop through the posts loaded and store them in $return_posts.

After the custom loop finishes running, you need to execute restore_current_blog(). This resets the site back to the site you are viewing, and not the site you switched to earlier. The final step is to return $return_posts. This replaces the shortcode in a post or page with the custom loop results.

Now you can easily retrieve posts from any site in your network using the shortcode such as
`[network_posts blogid="3" num="10"]`. Review the full plugin:

```php
<?php
/*
Plugin Name: Multisite Switch Shortcode Plugin
Plugin URI: http://example.com/wordpress-plugins/my-plugin
Description: A plugin to aggregating content using a shortcode
Version: 1.0
Author: Brad Williams
Author URI: http://wrox.com
License: GPLv2
*/

add_shortcode( 'network_posts', 'boj_multisite_network_posts' );

function boj_multisite_network_posts( $attr ) {
    extract( shortcode_atts( array(
            "blogid"     =>     '1',
            "num"        =>     '5'
            ), $attr ) );

    if ( is_multisite() ) {

        $return_posts = '';

        //switch to site set in the shortcode
        switch_to_blog( absint( $blogid ) );

        //create a custom Loop
        $recentPosts = new WP_Query();
        $recentPosts->query( 'posts_per_page=' .absint( $num ) );

        //start the custom Loop
        while ( $recentPosts->have_posts() ) :
            $recentPosts->the_post();

            //store the recent posts in a variable
            $return_posts .= '<p><a href="' .get_permalink().
                '">' .get_the_title() .'</a></p>';

        endwhile;

        //restore the current site
        restore_current_blog();

        //return the results to display
        return $return_posts;

    }
}
?>
```

Now take the switch shortcode example to the next level and retrieve posts from multiple sites in the network and display based on the latest post date. As in the previous example, use the add_shortcode() function to register the shortcode in your plugin:

```php
<?php
add_shortcode( 'latest_network_posts',
    'boj_multisite_latest_network_posts' );
?>
```

Next create your custom boj_multisite_latest_network_posts() function:

```php
<?php
function boj_multisite_latest_network_posts() {

    if ( is_multisite() ) {

        $return_posts = '';
```

As always check to verify Multisite is enabled using the is_multisite() function. You can also set $return_posts to nothing to flush it out. Now it's time to retrieve the posts:

```php
//get posts from current site
$local_posts = get_posts( 'numberposts=5' );

//switch to blog ID 3
switch_to_blog( 3 );

//get posts from another site
$network_posts = get_posts( 'numberposts=5' );

//restore the current site
restore_current_blog();
```

Use the get_posts() function to retrieve the latest five posts from the current site. Next switch to blog ID 3 and run the same get_posts() function to retrieve the five latest posts from that site. Notice you are storing the returned array values in separate variables: $local_posts and $network_posts. Finally call restore_current_blog() to reset back to the current site you are on.

Now that you have five posts from each site stored in separate arrays, you need to merge them into a single array.

```php
//merge the two arrays
$posts = array_merge( $local_posts, $network_posts );
```

Now that you have a single array of posts, you need to sort the posts based on post date so that they are in proper reverse chronological order with the latest post first. Use the PHP usort() function to sort the array based on a custom comparison function you will create later on.

```php
//sort the post results by date
usort( $posts, 'boj_multisite_sort_posts_array' );
```

Now that the posts are in the proper order in the array, you need to loop through the results and assign them to the `$return_posts` variable.

```php
foreach ( $posts as $post ) {

    //store latest posts in a variable
    $return_posts .= $post->post_title .' - posted on '
        .$post->post_date .'<br />';

}
```

Use a standard `foreach` PHP loop to loop through the results. Finally return the results for display by the shortcode.

```php
    //return the results to display
    return $return_posts;

    }
}
```

The final step is to create the custom function `boj_multisite_sort_posts_array()` to sort the post array by the date that was called earlier from the `usort` function.

```php
//sort the array by date
function boj_multisite_sort_posts_array( $a, $b ) {

    //if dates are the same return 0
    if ($a->post_date == $b->post_date)
        return 0;

    //ternary operator to determine which date is newer
    return $a->post_date < $b->post_date ? 1 : -1;

}
```

This function simply compares two values and returns either a 1 or –1 based on which is greater. The `usort()` function sorts based on the number assigned.

Review the entire plugin code:

```php
<?php
/*
Plugin Name: Multisite Latest Network Posts Plugin
Plugin URI: http://example.com/wordpress-plugins/my-plugin
Description: Displays the latest posts from multiple sites
Version: 1.0
Author: Brad Williams
Author URI: http://wrox.com
License: GPLv2
*/

add_shortcode( 'latest_network_posts',
```

```php
    'boj_multisite_latest_network_posts' );

function boj_multisite_latest_network_posts() {

    if ( is_multisite() ) {

        $return_posts = '';

        //get posts from current site
        $local_posts = get_posts( 'numberposts=5' );

        //switch to blog ID 3
        switch_to_blog( 3 );

        //get posts from another site
        $network_posts = get_posts( 'numberposts=5' );

        //restore the current site
        restore_current_blog();

        //merge the two arrays
        $posts = array_merge( $local_posts, $network_posts );

        //sort the post results by date
        usort( $posts, 'boj_multisite_sort_posts_array' );

        foreach ( $posts as $post ) {

            //store latest posts in a variable
            $return_posts .= $post->post_title .' - posted on '
                .$post->post_date .'<br />';

        }

        //return the results to display
        return $return_posts;

    }

}

//sort the array by date
function boj_multisite_sort_posts_array( $a, $b ) {

    //if dates are the same return 0
    if ($a->post_date == $b->post_date)
        return 0;

    //ternary operator to determine which date is newer
    return $a->post_date < $b->post_date ? 1 : -1;

}
?>
```

Code snippet boj-multisite-latest-network-posts.php

One thing to consider when using `switch_to_blog()` is performance. This function can cause a heavy performance hit on your server depending on the size of your network. Whenever you use this function, it's always best to cache the results, if possible, rather than retrieve in real-time. This can greatly reduce the server load when retrieving content and other data across sites in your network. Caching is covered in detail in Chapter 16, "Debugging and Optimizing."

A Network Content Widget Example

Another common task when working in a Multisite environment is a widget to display recent posts from sites in the network. You can create a plugin with a widget to display the recent posts from any site in the network.

```php
<?php
//widgets_init action hook to execute custom function
add_action( 'widgets_init', 'boj_multisite_register_widget' );

//register our widget
function boj_multisite_register_widget() {
    register_widget( 'boj_multisite_widget' );
}
?>
```

First use the `widgets_init` action hook to run the custom function to register your new widget. In this example the new widget will be registered as `boj_multisite_widget`. Next create a new class using the registered widget name and extending the `WP_Widget`.

```php
<?php
//boj_multisite_widget class
class boj_multisite_widget extends WP_Widget {

    //process our new widget
    function boj_multisite_widget() {

        $widget_ops = array( 'classname' => 'boj_multisite_widget',
            'description' => 'Display recent posts
                from a network site.' );
        $this->WP_Widget( 'boj_multisite_widget_posts',
            'Multisite Recent Posts',
            $widget_ops );

    }
```

You also define the widget settings. You set the widget name to Multisite Recent Posts, the description of what the widget does, and the custom class name that will be used when displaying the widget.

Now it's time to create the widget settings form. This widget contains three settings: Title, the site to load recent posts from, and the number of posts to display.

```php
        //build our widget settings form
        function form( $instance ) {
```

```
global $wpdb;

$defaults = array( 'title' => 'Recent Posts',
    'disp_number' => '5' );
$instance = wp_parse_args( (array) $instance, $defaults );
$title = $instance['title'];
$siteid = $instance['siteid'];
$disp_number = $instance['disp_number'];
```

You will be making a custom database query to retrieve the network blog IDs, so you need to define $wpdb as a global variable. The widget defaults are set in the $defaults variable; in this case you set the default title to Recent Posts and the default number of posts to display to 5. Next the instance values are loaded, which are your widget setting values.

Now that you have loaded the widget values, you need to add the form field settings for the widget. The first field is a text field to store the widget title that will be displayed:

```
//title textfield widget option
echo '<p>Title: <input class="widefat" name="'
    .$this->get_field_name( 'title' )
    .'" type="text" value="'
    .esc_attr( $title ). '" /></p>';
```

As always you want to use the proper escaping function when displaying data entered in by a user, in this case esc_attr() to display the $title value.

The next field to add is a select form to set which site in the network to display recent posts from. To create this form field, you need to retrieve a list of all public blog IDs in your network. Create a custom query to retrieve the IDs.

```
//get a list of all public blog IDs
$sql = "SELECT blog_id FROM $wpdb->blogs
    WHERE public = '1' AND archived = '0' AND mature = '0'
    AND spam = '0' AND deleted = '0' ";

$blogs = $wpdb->get_col( $wpdb->prepare( $sql ) );
```

The query retrieves all public blog IDs in your Multisite network and returns them in an array stored in the $blogs variable. Now that you have the blog IDs, you need to loop through the results to build the select list.

```
if ( is_array( $blogs ) ) {

    echo '<p>';
    echo 'Site to display recent posts';
    echo '<select name="' .$this->get_field_name('siteid')
        .'" class="widefat" >';

    //loop through the blog IDs
    foreach ($blogs as $blog) {

        //display each site as an option
```

```
                echo '<option value="' .$blog. '" '
                    .selected( $blog, $siteid )
                    .'>' .get_blog_details( $blog )->blogname
                    .'</option>';

        }

        echo '</select>';
        echo '</p>';
    }
```

Before working with an array, it's a good practice to verify it is actually an array. You can do so using the PHP function `is_array()`. After you confirm that `$blogs` is an array, you can display the option text and `select` field. To display each site as an `option`, loop through the array values. Use the `get_blog_details()` function to display the site name in the option field. The `$blog` variable, which stores the blog ID, is set to the value of the option field.

The final form field to display is the number of posts option.

```
                //number to display textfield widget option
                echo '<p>Number to display: <input class="widefat" name="'
                    .$this->get_field_name( 'disp_number' ). '" type="text"
                    value="' .esc_attr( $disp_number ). '" /></p>';

    }
```

FIGURE 15-2

Just as the title option before, this is a standard text form field to store the number of posts to display. That's the final widget form field, so be sure to close out the function with }. Now your widget settings form has been created and looks like Figure 15-2.

Next you need to save your widget settings using the `update` widget class function.

```
        //save the widget settings
        function update( $new_instance, $old_instance ) {

            $instance = $old_instance;
            $instance['title'] = strip_tags( $new_instance['title'] );
            $instance['siteid'] = absint( $new_instance['siteid'] );
            $instance['disp_number'] =
                absint( $new_instance['disp_number'] );

            return $instance;
        }
```

The widget class will handle saving the options for you. Be sure to sanitize the widget settings. Both `siteid` and `disp_number` should always be a number, so use the `absint()` function to verify the setting is a positive integer.

The final step is to display the widget.

```
//display the widget
function widget( $args, $instance ) {
    extract( $args );

    echo $before_widget;

    //load the widget options
    $title = apply_filters( 'widget_title', $instance['title'] );
    $siteid = empty( $instance['siteid'] ) ? 1 :
        $instance['siteid'];
    $disp_number = empty( $instance['disp_number'] ) ? 5 :
        $instance['disp_number'];

    //display the widget title
    if ( !empty( $title ) ) { echo $before_title . $title .
        $after_title; };

    echo '<ul>';
```

First, extract the $args variable to gain access to the global theme values like $before_widget and $after_widget. Next load the widget settings. The $siteid and $disp_number variables are both using a ternary operator to set their values. This means if the option value is empty it will be set to a default value. $siteid would default to 1, and $disp_number would default to 5.

Now display the $title, surrounded by the $before_title and $after_title global theme values. Now it's time to display the recent posts from the site saved in the widget.

```
//switch to site saved
switch_to_blog( absint( $siteid ) );

//create a custom loop
$recentPosts = new WP_Query();
$recentPosts->query( 'posts_per_page='
    .absint( $disp_number ) );

//start the custom Loop
while ( $recentPosts->have_posts() ) :
    $recentPosts->the_post();

    //display the recent post title with link
    echo '<li><a href="' .get_permalink(). '">'
        .get_the_title() .'</a></li>';

endwhile;

//restore the current site
restore_current_blog();

echo '</ul>';
echo $after_widget;

}

}
```

Using the `switch_to_blog()` function, the widget switches to the site saved in the widget settings. After the site has been loaded, create a custom loop using the `WP_Query` class. The `posts_per_page` query parameter is defined by the `$disp_number` widget setting. The recent posts display in an unordered list using a `while` loop. After the loop completes, you need to restore the current site using `restore_current_blog()`.

You now have a Multisite widget to easily display posts from any site in your network! This simple example shows the power of aggregating content throughout a Multisite network in WordPress and how easy it is to accomplish that.

```php
<?php
/*
Plugin Name: Multisite Recent Posts Widget
Plugin URI:  http://example.com
Description: Retrieves the most recent posts in a Multisite network
Author: Brad Williams
Version: 1.0
Author URI: http://wrox.com
*/

//widgets_init action hook to execute custom function
add_action( 'widgets_init', 'boj_multisite_register_widget' );

//register our widget
function boj_multisite_register_widget() {
    register_widget( 'boj_multisite_widget' );
}

//boj_multisite_widget class
class boj_multisite_widget extends WP_Widget {

    //process our new widget
    function boj_multisite_widget() {

        $widget_ops = array( 'classname' => 'boj_multisite_widget',
            'description' =>
                'Display recent posts from a network site.' );
        $this->WP_Widget( 'boj_multisite_widget_posts',
            'Multisite Recent Posts', $widget_ops );

    }

     //build our widget settings form
    function form( $instance ) {
        global $wpdb;

        $defaults = array( 'title' => 'Recent Posts',
            'disp_number' => '5' );
        $instance = wp_parse_args( (array) $instance, $defaults );
        $title = $instance['title'];
        $siteid = $instance['siteid'];
        $disp_number = $instance['disp_number'];

        //title textfield widget option
```

```php
echo '<p>Title: <input class="widefat" name="'
    .$this->get_field_name( 'title' )
    . '" type="text" value="' .esc_attr( $title )
    . '" /></p>';

//get a list of all public blog IDs
$sql = "SELECT blog_id FROM $wpdb->blogs
    WHERE public = '1' AND archived = '0' AND mature = '0'
    AND spam = '0' AND deleted = '0' ";
$blogs = $wpdb->get_col( $wpdb->prepare( $sql ) );

if ( is_array( $blogs ) ) {

    echo '<p>';
    echo 'Site to display recent posts';
    echo '<select name="' .$this->get_field_name('siteid')
        .'" class="widefat" >';

    //loop through the blog IDs
    foreach ($blogs as $blog) {

        //display each site as an option
        echo '<option value="' .$blog. '" '
            .selected( $blog, $siteid )
            . '>' .get_blog_details( $blog )->blogname
            . '</option>';

    }

    echo '</select>';
    echo '</p>';
}

//number to display textfield widget option
echo '<p>Number to display: <input class="widefat" name="'
    .$this->get_field_name( 'disp_number' ). '" type="text"
    value="' .esc_attr( $disp_number ). '" /></p>';

}

  //save the widget settings
function update( $new_instance, $old_instance ) {

    $instance = $old_instance;
    $instance['title'] = strip_tags( $new_instance['title'] );
    $instance['siteid'] = absint( $new_instance['siteid'] );
    $instance['disp_number'] =
        absint( $new_instance['disp_number'] );

    return $instance;
}

 //display the widget
function widget( $args, $instance ) {
```

```php
        extract( $args );

        echo $before_widget;

        //load the widget options
        $title = apply_filters( 'widget_title', $instance['title'] );
        $siteid = empty( $instance['siteid'] ) ? 1 :
            $instance['siteid'];
        $disp_number = empty( $instance['disp_number'] ) ? 5 :
            $instance['disp_number'];

        //display the widget title
        if ( !empty( $title ) ) { echo $before_title . $title
            . $after_title; };

        echo '<ul>';

        //switch to site saved
        switch_to_blog( absint( $siteid ) );

        //create a custom loop
        $recentPosts = new WP_Query();
        $recentPosts->query( 'posts_per_page='
            .absint( $disp_number ) );

        //start the custom Loop
        while ( $recentPosts->have_posts() ) :
            $recentPosts->the_post();

            //display the recent post title with link
            echo '<li><a href="' .get_permalink(). '">'
                .get_the_title() .'</a></li>';

        endwhile;

        //restore the current site
        restore_current_blog();

        echo '</ul>';
        echo $after_widget;

    }

}
?>
```

Code snippet boj-multisite-widget.php

Creating a New Site

You can easily create new sites in your Multisite network in the admin dashboard of WordPress. But what if you want to create a new site in your plugin? As always there's a function for that, and it's called `wpmu_create_blog()`.

```php
<?php wpmu_create_blog( $domain, $path, $title,
    $user_id, $meta, $blog_id ); ?>
```

This function accepts six parameters:

➤ `$domain` — The domain of the new site.

➤ `$path` — The path of the new site. This is the subdirectory or subdomain name depending on which setup you use.

➤ `$title` — The title of the new site.

➤ `$user_id` — The user ID of the user account who will be the site admin.

➤ `$meta` — Additional meta information.

➤ `$blog_id` — The blog ID of the site to be created.

The only required parameters are the first four; the last two are optional. If the new site is created successfully, the function returns the newly created blog ID.

As you noticed, the function begins with `wpmu_`. Many of the Multisite functions were once a part of WordPress MU, prior to the merging of the two code bases. These function names can contain `wpmu`, or `blog`, to support backward compatibility.

As an example create a plugin that enables users to create sites in WordPress Multisite. First, create a custom top-level menu for the plugin page.

```php
<?php
add_action( 'admin_menu', 'boj_multisite_create_menu' );

function boj_multisite_create_menu() {

    //create custom top-level menu
    add_menu_page( 'Multisite Create Site Page',
        'Multisite Create Site',
        'manage_options', 'boj-network-create',
            'boj_multisite_create_sites_page' );

}
?>
```

Now create the function to display a form for creating a new site.

```php
<?php
function boj_multisite_create_sites_page() {

    //check if multisite is enabled
    if ( is_multisite() ) {
```

As always you need to verify Multisite is enabled before using any Multisite-specific functions. Next add the code to retrieve the form fields submitted and create a new site in the network with the values:

```php
<?php
//if the form was submitted lets process it
```

```
if ( isset( $_POST['create_site'] ) ) {

    //populate the variables based on form values
    $domain = esc_html( $_POST['domain'] );
    $path = esc_html( $_POST['path'] );
    $title = esc_html( $_POST['title'] );
    $user_id = absint( $_POST['user_id'] );

    //verify the required values are set
    if ( $domain && $path && $title && $user_id ) {

        //create the new site in WordPress
        $new_site = wpmu_create_blog( $domain, $path,
            $title, $user_id );

        //if successfully display a message
        if ( $new_site ) {

            echo '<div class="updated">New site '
                .$new_site. ' created successfully!</div>';


        }

    //if required values are not set display an error
    } else {

        echo '<div class="error">
            New site could not be created.
            Required fields are missing</div>';

    }

}
?>
```

First check if `$_POST['create_site']` is set. This will be set only if the form has been submitted. Next populate the variables based on the form entries. Notice you'll be using the proper escaping functions to verify the data submitted from the form is escaped properly.

Next verify that `$domain`, `$path`, `$title`, and `$user_id` all have values because they are the required fields when creating sites using `wpmu_create_blog()`. If the values are not filled out, an error message displays. After you verify all values exist, it's time to execute the `wpmu_create_blog()` function to create the new site. If the site is created successfully, the variable `$new_site` will contain the ID of the newly created site and a success message will be displayed.

The final piece is to create the form for the new site fields.

```
<div class="wrap">
    <h2>Create New Site</h2>
    <form method="post">
    <table class="form-table">
    <tr valign="top">
```

```html
                    <th scope="row">
                        <label for="fname">Domain</label>
                    </th>
                    <td><input maxlength="45" size="25" name="domain"
                        value="<?php echo DOMAIN_CURRENT_SITE; ?>" />
                    </td>
                </tr>
                <tr valign="top">
                    <th scope="row"><label for="fname">Path</label></th>
                    <td>
                        <input maxlength="45" size="10" name="path" />
                    </td>
                </tr>
                <tr valign="top">
                    <th scope="row">
                        <label for="fname">Title</label>
                    </th>
                    <td>
                        <input maxlength="45" size="25" name="title" />
                    </td>
                </tr>
                <tr valign="top">
                    <th scope="row">
                        <label for="fname">User ID</label>
                    </th>
                    <td>
                        <input maxlength="45" size="3" name="user_id" />
                    </td>
                </tr>
                <tr valign="top">
                    <td>
                    <input type="submit" name="create_site"
                        value="Create Site" class="button-primary" />

                    <input type="submit" name="reset"
                        value="Reset" class="button-secondary" />
                    </td>
                </tr>
                </table>
                </form>
            </div>
```

This is a fairly basic form that accepts the parameters required to create a new site.

Now review the entire plugin code:

```php
<?php
/*
Plugin Name: Multisite Create Site Example Plugin
Plugin URI: http://example.com/wordpress-plugins/my-plugin
Description: A plugin to demonstrate creating sites in Multisite
Version: 1.0
Author: Brad Williams
Author URI: http://wrox.com
```

```
License: GPLv2
*/

add_action( 'admin_menu', 'boj_multisite_create_menu' );

function boj_multisite_create_menu() {

    //create custom top-level menu
    add_menu_page( 'Multisite Create Site Page',
        'Multisite Create Site',
        'manage_options', 'boj-network-create',
        'boj_multisite_create_site_settings' );

}

function boj_multisite_create_site_settings() {

    //check if multisite is enabled
    if ( is_multisite() ) {

        //if the form was submitted lets process it
        if ( isset( $_POST['create_site'] ) ) {

            //populate the variables based on form values
            $domain = esc_html( $_POST['domain'] );
            $path = esc_html( $_POST['path'] );
            $title = esc_html( $_POST['title'] );
            $user_id = absint( $_POST['user_id'] );

            //verify the required values are set
            if ( $domain && $path && $title && $user_id ) {

                //create the new site in WordPress
                $new_site = wpmu_create_blog( $domain, $path,
                    $title, $user_id );

                //if successfully display a message
                if ( $new_site ) {

                    echo '<div class="updated">New site '
                        .$new_site. ' created successfully!</div>';


                }

            //if required values are not set display an error
            } else {

                echo '<div class="error">
                    New site could not be created.
                    Required fields are missing</div>';

            }

        }
```

```php
        ?>
        <div class="wrap">
            <h2>Create New Site</h2>
            <form method="post">
            <table class="form-table">
            <tr valign="top">
                <th scope="row">
                    <label for="fname">Domain</label>
                </th>
                <td><input maxlength="45" size="25" name="domain"
                        value="<?php echo DOMAIN_CURRENT_SITE; ?>" />
                </td>
            </tr>
            <tr valign="top">
                <th scope="row"><label for="fname">Path</label></th>
                <td>
                    <input maxlength="45" size="10" name="path" />
                </td>
            </tr>
            <tr valign="top">
                <th scope="row"><label for="fname">Title</label></th>
                <td>
                    <input maxlength="45" size="25" name="title" />
                </td>
            </tr>
            <tr valign="top">
                <th scope="row">
                    <label for="fname">User ID</label>
                </th>
                <td>
                    <input maxlength="45" size="3" name="user_id" />
                </td>
            </tr>
            <tr valign="top">
                <td>
                <input type="submit" name="create_site"
                    value="Create Site" class="button-primary" />
                <input type="submit" name="reset" value="Reset"
                    class="button-secondary" />
                </td>
            </tr>
            </table>
            </form>
        </div>
        <?php
    } else {

        echo '<p>Multisite is not enabled</p>';

    }


}
?>
```

Code snippet boj-multisite-create-site.php

There is also an easy method to update a site's status. This is useful if you want to dynamically archive a site, or flag a site as spam. To do so use the `update_blog_status()` function.

```php
<?php update_blog_status( $blog_id, $pref, $value, $refresh ); ?>
```

The function accepts four parameters:

➤ `$blog_id` — The blog ID of the site to update

➤ `$pref` — The status type to update

➤ `$value` — The new value of the status

➤ `$refresh` — Whether to refresh the site details cache

The first three parameters are required. The `$pref` parameter is the status to update, which accepts `site_id`, `domain`, `path`, `registered`, `last_updated`, `public`, `archived`, `mature`, `spam`, `deleted`, and `lang_id`. In this example you update a site in your network to be archived.

```php
<?php
update_blog_status( $blog_id, 'archived', 1 );
?>
```

Multisite Site Options

Options in Multisite are stored similar to standard WordPress but use a different set of functions:

➤ `add_blog_option()` — Creates a new option

➤ `update_blog_option()` — Updates an option and creates it if it doesn't exist

➤ `get_blog_option()` — Loads a site option that already exists

➤ `delete_blog_option()` — Deletes a site option

The major difference between this set of functions and the standard option functions is you have to pass a blog ID parameter to each function. The function will then switch to the site specified, handle the option task, and then switch back to the current site.

```php
<?php add_blog_option( $blog_id, $key, $value ); ?>
```

The `$blog_id` is the ID of the site you want to add an option to. The `$key` is the name of the option to add, and the `$value` is the value of the new option.

Loading site options is just as easy. Using the `get_blog_option()` function, you can load any site-specific option required.

```php
<?php
$blog_id = 3;
echo '<p>Site ID: '.$blog_id .'</p>';
echo '<p>Site Name: ' .get_blog_option( $blog_id, 'blogname' )
    .'</p>';
echo '<p>Site URL: ' .get_blog_option( $blog_id, 'siteurl' ) .'</p>';
?>
```

Users in a Network

Users in a Multisite network work slightly different than in standard WordPress. If Allow New Registrations is enabled under Network Settings, visitors to your site can register new accounts in WordPress. The major difference is each site in your network can feature a different set of users. Users can also have different roles on different sites throughout the network. Users are not automatically members of every site in your network, but rather the main (first) site in your network. For example if your network features two sites, a Halo Blog and a Tekken Blog, any user who registers would be a member of the Halo Blog but not the Tekken Blog.

Before executing any code that is site-specific, you should verify the user logged in is a member of that site. Multisite features multiple functions for working with users. To verify a user is a member of the site, use the `is_blog_user()` function:

```php
<?php is_blog_user( $blog_id ) ?>
```

The function accepts one parameter, `$blog_id`, which is optional. If the parameter isn't specified, it defaults to the current blog you are on.

```php
<?php
if ( is_blog_user() ) {
    //user is a member of this site
}
?>
```

You can also specify a blog ID if you want to verify the user is a member of a different site in the network:

```php
<?php
if ( is_blog_user( 3 ) ) {
    //user is a member of blog ID 3
}
?>
```

Now that you understand how to check if a user is a member of a site, look at adding members to a site. In Multisite you use the `add_user_to_blog()` function to add any user in WordPress to a specific site in your network.

```php
<?php add_user_to_blog( $blog_id, $user_id, $role ); ?>
```

This function accepts three parameters:

➤ `$blog_id` — The ID of the site you want to add the user to

➤ `$user_id` — The ID of the user to add

➤ `$role` — The user role the user will have on the site

Look at a working example:

```php
<?php
$blog_id = 18;
```

```php
$user_id = 4;
$role = 'editor';

add_user_to_blog( $blog_id, $user_id, $role );
?>
```

Now build a real-world example plugin. This plugin auto-adds logged-in users to any site they visit in your network. This is useful if you want users to become members on every site in your network without manually adding them to each one.

Start off by using the `init` action hook to execute your custom function to add users to a site:

```php
<?php
add_action( 'init', 'boj_multisite_add_user_to_site' );
?>
```

Next create the `boj_multisite_add_user_to_site()` function to add the users.

```php
<?php
function boj_multisite_add_user_to_site() {

    //verify user is logged in before proceeding
    if( !is_user_logged_in() )
        return false;

    //load current blog ID and user data
    global $current_user, $blog_id;

    //verify user is not a member of this site
    if( !is_blog_user() ) {

        //add user to this site as a subscriber
        add_user_to_blog( $blog_id, $current_user->ID, 'subscriber' );

    }

}
?>
```

The first step is to verify the users are logged in, and if not return `false` and exit the function. After you have verified the users are logged in, call the global `$current_user` and `$blog_id` variables. These variables store the data of the current logged-in users and the blog ID the users are currently viewing. Next confirm if the users are already members of the site they are viewing. If the users are already members, there is no reason to add them again.

The final step is to add the users to the site using the `add_user_to_blog()` function. You'll pass in the blog ID, current user ID, and the role the users are assigned on the site, in this case subscriber. That's it! For this plugin to work across your entire network you'll either need to upload to the /mu-plugins directory or Network Activate the plugin in the Network Admin ⇨ Plugins page. That forces the plugin the run across all sites in your network.

Review the entire plugin:

```php
<?php
/*
Plugin Name: Multisite Auto-Add User to Site
Plugin URI: http://example.com/wordpress-plugins/my-plugin
Description: Plugin automatically adds the user to any site they visit
Version: 1.0
Author: Brad Williams
Author URI: http://wrox.com
License: GPLv2
*/

add_action( 'init', 'boj_multisite_add_user_to_site' );

function boj_multisite_add_user_to_site() {

    //verify user is logged in before proceeding
    if( !is_user_logged_in() )
        return false;

    //load current blog ID and user data
    global $current_user,$blog_id;

    //verify user is not a member of this site
    if( !is_blog_user() ) {

        //add user to this site as a subscriber
        add_user_to_blog( $blog_id, $current_user->ID, 'subscriber' );

    }

}

?>
```

Code snippet boj-multisite-add-users.php

As easily as you can add users, you can also remove users from a site using the remove_user_from_blog() function.

```php
<?php remove_user_from_blog( $user_id, $blog_id, $reassign ); ?>
```

This function accepts three parameters:

➤ $user_id — The user ID you want to remove

➤ $blog_id — The blog ID to remove the user from

➤ $reassign — The user ID to reassign posts to

Look at a working example:

```php
<?php
$user_id = 4;
$blog_id = 18;
$reassign = 1;

remove_user_from_blog( $user_id, $blog_id, $reassign );
?>
```

 Remember adding and removing users from a site in Multisite is not actually creating or deleting the user in WordPress, but instead adding or removing them as a member of that site.

Another useful function when working with Multisite users is `get_blogs_of_user()`. This function retrieves site info for all sites the specified users are a member of.

```php
<?php
$user_id = 1;
$user_sites = get_blogs_of_user( $user_id );
print_r( $user_sites );
?>
```

Running this code example would result in an object array being returned:

```
Array
(
    [1] => stdClass Object
        (
            [userblog_id] => 1
            [blogname] => Main Site
            [domain] => example.com
            [path] => /
            [site_id] => 1
            [siteurl] => http://example.com
        )

    [2] => stdClass Object
        (
            [userblog_id] => 2
            [blogname] => Halloween Revenge
            [domain] => example.com
            [path] => /myers/
            [site_id] => 1
            [siteurl] => http://example.com/myers
        )

    [8] => stdClass Object
        (
```

```
                    [userblog_id] => 8
                    [blogname] => Freddy Lives
                    [domain] => example.com
                    [path] => /kruger/
                    [site_id] => 1
                    [siteurl] => http://example.com/kruger
            )

    )
```

You can also do a `foreach` loop to display specific data from the array:

```php
<?php
$user_id = 1;
$user_sites = get_blogs_of_user( $user_id );

foreach ( $user_sites AS $user_site ) {

    echo '<p>'.$user_site->siteurl .'</p>';

}
?>
```

Multisite Super Admin

Multisite also introduces a new user role: Super admin. Super admin users have access to the Network Admin section of WordPress. This is where all network settings, themes, plugins, and so on are managed. Super admins also have full control over every site in the network, whereas a normal admin can administer only their specific sites.

In Multisite you can easily assign an existing user to the super admin role by using the `grant_super_admin()` function. This function accepts only one parameter, which is the user ID to which you want to grant super admin privileges.

```php
<?php
$user_id = 4;
grant_super_admin( $user_id );
?>
```

As quickly as you can grant super admin privileges, you can just as easily revoke them using the `revoke_super_admin()` function. This function also accepts only one parameter, which is the user ID to revoke as super admin.

```php
<?php
$user_id = 4;
revoke_super_admin( $user_id );
?>
```

Both of these functions are located in `wp-admin/includes/ms.php`. This means these functions by default are not available on the public side of your site and can be used only on the admin side.

For example, if you tried calling either of these functions with a shortcode, you would get a Call to Undefined Function PHP error.

To list all super admins in Multisite, use the `get_super_admins()` function. This function returns an array of all super admin usernames in your network.

```php
<?php
$all_admins = get_super_admins();
print_r( $all_admins );
?>
```

This would return the following array of super admins:

```
Array
(
    [0] => admin
    [1] => brad
)
```

You can also easily check specific users' IDs to determine if they are a super admin in your network. To do so use the `is_super_admin()` function.

```php
<?php
$user_id = 1;

if ( is_super_admin( $user_id ) ) {
    echo 'User is Super admin';
}
?>
```

Checking the Site Owner

Every site in your Multisite network has a site owner. This owner is defined by the admin email address stored in the site options and is set when a new site is created in your network. If you allow open site registration, the user who created the site will be set as the site owner. If you created the site in the dashboard, you can set the owner's email at time of creation.

In some cases you may want to retrieve a site owner and corresponding user data. Following is an example of how you can so.

```php
<?php
$blog_id = 3;
$admin_email = get_blog_option( $blog_id, 'admin_email' );
$user_info = get_user_by( 'email', $admin_email );
print_r( $user_info );
?>
```

First, use the `get_blog_option()` function to retrieve the `admin_email` value for blog ID 3. Next use the `get_user_by()` function to retrieve the user data based off the admin email. This function enables you to retrieve user data by either user ID, slug, email, or login. In this case use the admin email to load the user data. The results are shown here:

```
stdClass Object
(
    [ID] => 3
    [user_login] => freddy
    [user_pass] => $P$B0VRNh0UbN/4YqMFB8fl3OZM2FGKfg1
    [user_nicename] => Freddy Krueger
    [user_email] => freddy@example.com
    [user_url] =>
    [user_registered] => 2011-10-31 19:00:00
    [user_activation_key] =>
    [user_status] => 0
    [display_name] => Freddy
    [spam] => 0
    [deleted] => 0
    [first_name] => Freddy
    [last_name] => Krueger
    [nickname] => fredster
    [description] =>
    [rich_editing] => true
    [comment_shortcuts] => false
    [admin_color] => fresh
    [use_ssl] => 0
    [aim] =>
    [yim] =>
    [jabber] =>
    [source_domain] => example.com
    [primary_blog] => 3
    [wp_3_capabilities] => Array
        (
            [administrator] => 1
        )

    [wp_3_user_level] => 10
    [user_firstname] => Freddy
    [user_lastname] => Krueger
    [user_description] =>
)
```

As you can see a lot of useful user information is returned for the site admin account.

Network Stats

Multisite features a few functions to generate stats about your network. The get_user_count() function returns the total number of users registered in WordPress. The get_blog_count() function returns the total number of sites in your network. You can also use the get_sitestats() function to retrieve both values at once in an array.

```php
<?php
$user_count = get_user_count();
```

```
echo '<p>Total users: ' .$user_count .'</p>';

$blog_count = get_blog_count();
echo '<p>Total sites: ' .$blog_count .'</p>';

$network_stats = get_sitestats();
print_r( $network_stats );
?>
```

MULTISITE DATABASE SCHEMA

WordPress Multisite features a different database schema from standard WordPress. When updating or enabling Multisite, WordPress creates the necessary tables in your database to support Multisite functionality.

Multisite-Specific Tables

WordPress stores global Multisite settings in centralized tables. These tables are installed only when Multisite is activated and installed, excluding wp_users and wp_usermeta.

➤ wp_blogs — Stores each site created in Multisite.

➤ wp_blog_versions — Stores the current database version of each site in the network.

➤ wp_registration_log — Keeps a log of all users registered and activated in WordPress.

➤ wp_signups — Stores users and sites registered using the WordPress registration process.

➤ wp_site — Stores the primary site's address information.

➤ wp_sitecategories — If global terms are enabled, they are stored in this table.

➤ wp_sitemeta — Stores various option data for the primary site including super admin accounts.

➤ wp_users — Stores all users registered in WordPress.

➤ wp_usermeta — Stores all meta data for user accounts in WordPress.

You'll probably notice we're missing some important WordPress tables in this list. The rest of the tables created for Multisite are site-specific tables.

Site-Specific Tables

Each site in your network features site-specific database tables. These tables hold the content and setting specific to that individual site. Remember these tables are prefixed with the $table_prefix defined in wp-config.php, followed by $blog_id and then the table name.

➤ wp_1_commentmeta

➤ wp_1_comments

➤ wp_1_links

- ➤ `wp_1_options`

- ➤ `wp_1_postmeta`

- ➤ `wp_1_posts`

- ➤ `wp_1_terms`

- ➤ `wp_1_term_relationships`

- ➤ `wp_1_term_taxonomy`

As you can see these tables can make your database quickly grow in size. That's why the only limitation to WordPress Multisite is the server resources available to power your network of sites. If your network contains 1,000 sites, your database would have more than 9,000 tables. Obviously this wouldn't be ideal to host on a small shared hosting account.

SUMMARY

WordPress Multisite features limitless possibilities. Enabling Multisite opens the door to creating an amazing network of sites. This also opens up new doors for your plugins with the additional Multisite features and functions.

When developing plugins for WordPress, you need to test your plugins in a Multisite setup to verify they are compatible. Now that Multisite is included in every WordPress download by default, more and more users are converting their standard site to Multisite to take advantage of the rapid site deployment features and network capabilities.

16

Debugging and Optimizing

WHAT'S IN THIS CHAPTER?

➤ Keeping updated with WordPress

➤ Debugging your plugins

➤ Logging debug errors

➤ Caching data for optimal speed

You can debug and optimize code in many ways. WordPress provides several simple-to-use tools that make plugin developers' lives easier. One of the largest problems in the community is that many plugin developers simply don't use these basic techniques, leaving loads of room for improvement.

Throughout this chapter, you learn how to deal with outdated versions of WordPress, debug issues with your plugins, and cache (store) data for later use. The topics presented in this chapter are all simple features that you can use to make a better plugin.

SUPPORTING OLD VERSIONS (NOT)

As a developer, it's easy to think that you should maintain backward compatibility with older versions of software. It usually makes sense to do this to capture the largest possible audience and please users.

However, the WordPress philosophy on maintaining compatibility with old versions is quite different. In the WordPress development community, backward compatibility may sometimes even be looked down upon. Users are expected to stay updated with the latest version of the software. This philosophy comes down to a few key points.

➤ Users are given an "update nag" at the top of their WordPress admin screens, which prompts them to update.

➤ There is a multitude of ways to update. Users can even do this with a couple of mouse clicks from their WordPress admin.

➤ WordPress core release cycles are frequent, usually every three to four months.

➤ WordPress doesn't maintain security updates for older versions. Using the latest version is the only way to be sure you use the most secure version of WordPress.

For those reasons, a developer should expect users to be as updated as possible when developing publicly available plugins.

Being too far ahead of users can also be a bad thing. Some backward compatibility to give users time to transition between new WordPress versions is good practice. A good rule of thumb is to maintain backward compatibility for one major release cycle. This way, you stay current with new WordPress functionality and allow a three-to-four-month window for users to update.

Some plugins will simply be backward compatible because they use no new functions. However, if your plugin takes advantage of a function in a new release, you can use the PHP function `function_exists()` to check if the user is using the latest version before executing the specific function.

Suppose you want to use the WordPress 3.1 function `get_users()` but also wanted to maintain compatibility with users still using WordPress 3.0. Your code would look like this.

```php
<?php

/* If the get_users() function is available. */
if ( function_exists( 'get_users' ) ) {

    /* Use the get_users() function. */
    $users = get_users();
}

/* If the get_users() function is not available. */
else {

    /* Perform alternate functionality. */
}

?>
```

The code snippet uses `function_exists()` to check if the `get_users()` function exists. If it does exist, this means the user is using WordPress 3.1 or a newer version and the plugin can use the `get_users()` function. If the function does not exist, the plugin can fall back to an alternative way to handle the functionality.

Keeping Current with WordPress Development

To be a great plugin developer for the WordPress platform, it's paramount that you keep up with WordPress development. WordPress is constantly being developed. Not a day will go by without a core code committer or contributor thinking about or coding solutions for old problems, new features, or proposing different ideas about the direction of WordPress. It's a large community with many moving parts and avenues of information.

At minimum, you need to keep up with the development of the core WordPress code. Some benefits for plugin developers follow:

➤ Keeping up with new features and functions for use

➤ Finding out when old functions are deprecated or removed

➤ Knowing when there's a WordPress bug that affects your plugins

Staying current with WordPress development is crucial for developing the best plugins. You can sometimes cut out many lines of code when new features or functions are introduced. You can clean out old functionality and replace it with new functionality when functions are deprecated. And you can make your own life easier by not putting in workarounds for WordPress bugs that have been holding back development of your plugin.

You should also know how releases are handled within WordPress. Understanding this simple concept can enable you to know when you need to do an overview of your plugins to see if an update is needed. The two types of releases are major releases and point (or minor) releases.

➤ **Major releases** come in the form of 3.0, 3.1, and 3.2. These releases are made available every few months with new features, new functions, and bug fixes. Many code changes are made between major releases.

➤ **Point releases** are minor releases between major releases. Between the version 3.1 and version 3.2 major releases, you might have versions 3.1.1, 3.1.2, and so on. These releases are generally bug fixes and security releases. New functions are rarely added.

Being involved in the WordPress community can help your plugin development. Many sites and blogs keep up with development and trends in WordPress. However, the most important place to keep track of development is the WordPress issue and development tracker: `http://core.trac .wordpress.org`. This is where the latest development takes place.

It may take a little time to understand how the system works, but when you do, you'll probably even find yourself getting involved in WordPress development. The best way to start learning the system is to simply start reading each ticket placed on the site and follow the development flow.

 It'll be tough to find better ways of becoming a good plugin developer than getting involved in core WordPress development. It helps you stay on top of new functionality and gives you an intimate understanding of the core code.

Deprecated Functions

A *deprecated function* is a function being phased out of WordPress. It has been explicitly marked as something that developers should no longer use in their plugins. Typically, deprecated functions have a replacement function. PHP functions aren't the only things deprecated in WordPress. Sometimes files and function parameters or arguments are deprecated.

You can usually find deprecated functions within one of several files WordPress uses to house these functions.

➤ `wp-includes/deprecated.php` — General deprecated functions

➤ `wp-includes/ms-deprecated.php` — Deprecated multisite functions

➤ `wp-includes/pluggable-deprecated.php` — Deprecated pluggable functions

➤ `wp-admin/includes/deprecated.php` — Deprecated admin functions

Browsing through the core code for deprecated functions can be tedious at times. It's a good method for viewing all the deprecated functions. However, you'll most likely deal with deprecated functions when debugging, which is described later in this chapter.

Dealing with Obsolete Client Installs

When you release publicly available plugins, you have no control over whether the users keep their WordPress installation up to date. When you deal directly with clients, you can communicate directly with the clients and sometimes have access to their WordPress install.

If you work with clients who use an outdated version of WordPress, you should consider it your responsibility to make sure they use the latest and most secure version of WordPress. If the clients don't want to update, it's always nice to have a handy list of reasons why they should update.

Some benefits to keeping your clients' installs updated include the following:

➤ It makes developing clients' plugins easier. It can cut back on development time and cost.

➤ Your clients use the most secure version, so there's less of a chance of their site being hacked.

➤ Clients may want you to update the site for them and keep it updated, which can be great for repeat business.

If you deal with clients that don't want to update for whatever reason, the biggest thing you can stress is security. Clients tend to listen when you let them know the horrors of getting their site hacked.

If upgrading clients' sites, the most important thing you can do is keep multiple backups. The WordPress update process is simple, but the moment you get lazy with backups is usually the moment you need one.

DEBUGGING

One of the biggest problems that plagues WordPress plugins today is that most plugins haven't been properly debugged. This could be from a lack of understanding of what debugging is, knowledge about the subject, or motivation to fix the issues. By following the steps outlined in this section, you can be a few steps ahead of the competition by simply cleaning up your code.

Debugging is the act of finding "bugs" in software. Bugs are errors found within the code. In PHP, major issues can crash an entire Web page and display an error message on the page. However, some issues are hidden in many cases. WordPress has a method for exposing these issues.

As a plugin developer, you should always develop plugins with debugging enabled. Some benefits of debugging include the following:

➤ Knowing exactly where a bug is in your code

➤ Fixing minor issues that don't necessarily affect the functionality of your plugin but could potentially expose larger, unseen issues

➤ Correcting major issues that affect functionality of the plugin but are tough to find by browsing the code

➤ Getting notices when WordPress has deprecated a function, parameter, argument, or file

Don't let the idea of debugging scare you away from doing it. Most debugging issues are minor problems that take only minutes to correct. Plus, debugging can help you become a better developer by pointing out common mistakes you might make.

Enabling Debugging

In this section, you enable debugging for your WordPress install. You need to enable debugging whenever developing plugins. It can make your plugin better by letting you know what issues arise during the development phase.

In your WordPress install, open the `wp-config.php` file, which is at the root of the install by default. The `wp-config.php` file will have a line that looks like this:

```
define('WP_DEBUG', false);
```

What this line does is tell WordPress that debug mode should be disabled, so no debug messages should be shown. You don't want debugging disabled on your development install. You need to enable it.

To turn debugging on, change `false` to `true`. The debugging line in your `wp-config.php` file should now look like the following.

```
define('WP_DEBUG', true);
```

Enabling debugging makes two important things possible for debugging your plugins:

➤ Displays debug messages directly on the screen as they happen. This is the default behavior when `WP_DEBUG` is set to `true`.

➤ Enables you to use the error logging feature of WordPress, which is covered in the "Error Logging" section of this chapter.

Displaying Debug Messages

After you enable debugging, view your WordPress install. If you're running any other plugins, you'll most likely see numerous error messages displayed in various places on the page. This is because most plugins aren't coded to the standards they should be. You have the advantage of this chapter, so there's no excuse for any of your plugins to be displaying debug errors.

Now take a look at what a deprecated function looks like when used with debugging enabled. Suppose you wanted to check if a specific taxonomy exists. Prior to WordPress 3.0, the function you would use for this would be the `is_taxonomy()` function. However, this function was deprecated in WordPress 3.0 and a new function was introduced. If you wanted to display a message that the "category" taxonomy exists pre-3.0, your code would look like this.

```php
<?php

if ( is_taxonomy( 'category' ) )
    echo 'The category taxonomy exists.';

?>
```

Using this code can produce the debug message shown in Figure 16-1.

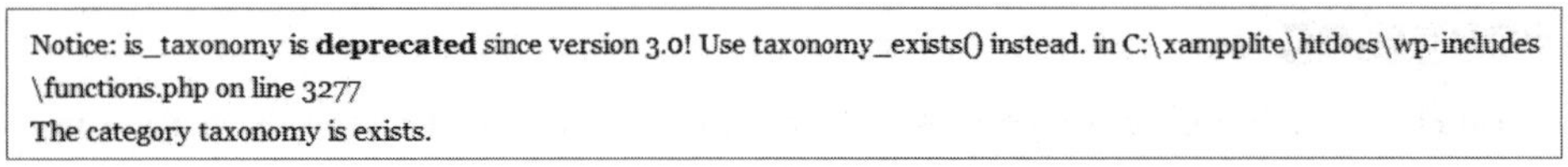

> Notice: is_taxonomy is **deprecated** since version 3.0! Use taxonomy_exists() instead. in C:\xampplite\htdocs\wp-includes
> \functions.php on line 3277
> The category taxonomy is exists.

FIGURE 16-1

The debug message tells you several things about using the `is_taxonomy()` function.

➤ The deprecated function is `is_taxonomy()`.

➤ The version the function was deprecated is 3.0.

➤ The replacement function is `taxonomy_exists()`.

This is usually all you need to know to update your plugin's code. To update the code you just used, you would replace the deprecated function with the given replacement function. In some instances, no replacement function will be displayed. You'll have to deal with those scenarios on a case-by-case basis because each might have a different solution.

To update the use of the `is_taxonomy()` function with its replacement function, change `is_taxonomy` to `taxonomy_exists`.

```php
<?php

if ( taxonomy_exists( 'category' ) )
    echo 'The category taxonomy is exists.';

?>
```

Making this simple change can bring your code up to date and remove any debug messages relating to it from the site.

Correcting Debug Messages

Most debug messages are created by PHP notices. Some developers may even laugh off notices as "harmless" issues because they're not crashing the site. Although this may be true to some degree, some cases actually reveal larger problems with the code. You should consider it your responsibility to always clear out all debug issues within your plugins.

In this section, you see three of the most common debug messages and how to fix each within your plugins.

➤ Deprecated WordPress functions

➤ Undefined variable/property notice

➤ Trying to get property of a nonobject notice

To see debug messages in action, you must write a bad plugin. This will be the only time in this book that you'll be prompted to create such horrible code, but you're allowed to do it this time because it's a learning exercise.

For this example, keep it simple. Your plugin will attempt to add a post author information box at the end of posts that shows the author name and description. Create a new plugin file called `boj-error-plugin.php` in your WordPress plugins directory and add the following code to the file.

Available for download on Wrox.com

```php
<?php
/*
Plugin Name: Error Plugin
Plugin URI: http://example.com
Description: Plugin that creates debug errors.
Version: 0.1
Author: WROX
Author URI: http://wrox.com
*/

/* Filter 'the_content'. */
add_filter( 'the_content', 'boj_error_plugin_author_box' );

/* Appends an author box to the end of posts. */
function boj_error_plugin_author_box( $content ) {

    /* If viewing a post with the 'post' post type. */
    if ( 'post' == $post->post_type ) {

        /* Open the author box <div>. */
        $author_box = '<div class="author-box">';

        /* Display the author name. */
        $author_box .= '<h3>' . get_the_author_meta( 'display_name' ) . '</h3>';

        /* Display the author description. */
        $author_box .= '<p>' . get_the_author_description() . '</p>';

        /* Close the author box. */
        $author_box .= '</div>';
    }
```

```
        /* Append the author box to the content. */
        $content = $content . $author_box;

        /* Return the content. */
        return $content;
    }

?>
```

There are several issues with this plugin. Because you enabled debugging on your WordPress install, you're probably looking at a screen with three debug messages, as shown in Figure 16-2. There are actually four issues, but one issue isn't revealed because the rest of the code is so bad it never has a chance to execute.

Notice: Undefined variable: post in C:\xampplite\htdocs\wp-content\plugins
\boj-error-plugin.php on line 18

Notice: Trying to get property of non-object in C:\xampplite\htdocs\wp-content
\plugins\boj-error-plugin.php on line 18

Notice: Undefined variable: author_box in C:\xampplite\htdocs\wp-content\plugins
\boj-error-plugin.php on line 34

FIGURE 16-2

The biggest issue with the code is this line.

```
    if ( 'post' == $post->post_type ) {
```

It's trying to check if it's viewing a post with the post type of post. The first issue is an "undefined variable" issue. The $post variable isn't defined anywhere. Because it's not defined, it definitely isn't an object. You get a Trying to Get Property of Nonobject error in this case. Both of the first two issues can be fixed by getting the global $post variable, which is done by adding a single line before the preceding line.

```
    global $post;
```

After fixing these issues, the third debug message disappears when viewing blog posts but reappears for other post types such as pages. This message is caused by the next line of the plugin, resulting in an Undefined Variable notice.

```
    $content = $content . $author_box;
```

The problem with this line is that the $author_box variable will not always be set. This notice is one of the issues you'll run into the most and is one the easiest issues to fix. It is good practice to either explicitly set your variables early in the function or check if they've been set before trying to use them in other parts of your code. In this instance, you use the PHP `isset()` function to check if the `$author_box` variable has been set before appending it to the `$content` variable.

```
if ( isset( $author_box ) )
    $content = $content . $author_box;
```

After fixing the first three issues, you'll notice a fourth issue appear. The debug message lets you know that you used a deprecated function: `get_the_author_description()`. The message also tells you that it has been replaced by `get_the_author_meta('description')`. This debug message is caused by this line of the plugin:

```
$author_box .= '<p>' . get_the_author_description() . '</p>';
```

Again, this is a simple change. You need to replace only the deprecated function with the new function. Your new code would look like the following.

```
$author_box .= '<p>' . get_the_author_meta( 'description' ) . '</p>';
```

Making these small changes clears the plugin of debug messages completely. It can also make the intended functionality of the plugin work. After completing each change, your code appears as shown in the following plugin.

Available for download on Wrox.com

```php
<?php
/*
Plugin Name: Error Plugin Fixed
Plugin URI: http://example.com
Description: Errors fixed in the "Error Plugin."
Version: 0.1
Author: WROX
Author URI: http://wrox.com
*/

/* Filter 'the_content'. */
add_filter( 'the_content', 'boj_error_plugin_author_box' );

/* Appends an author box to the end of posts. */
function boj_error_plugin_author_box( $content ) {
    global $post;

    /* If viewing a post with the 'post' post type. */
    if ( 'post' == $post->post_type ) {

        /* Open the author box <div>. */
        $author_box = '<div class="author-box">';

        /* Display the author name. */
        $author_box .= '<h3>' . get_the_author_meta( 'display_name' ) . '</h3>';

        /* Display the author description. */
        $author_box .= '<p>' . get_the_author_meta( 'description' ) . '</p>';
```

```
            /* Close the author box. */
            $author_box .= '</div>';
    }

    /* Append the author box to the content. */
    if ( isset( $author_box ) )
        $content = $content . $author_box;

    /* Return the content. */
    return $content;
}

?>
```

Code snippet boj-error-plugin-fixed.php

ERROR LOGGING

WordPress offers another useful tool for debugging your site: error logging. This feature is an extension of the debugging process previously described. It creates an error log file that keeps track of issues as they happen on your WordPress installation.

This feature is useful for debugging issues with plugins because it logs each error into a specific file, which enables you to easily read through all issues at once. However, perhaps more important, this is useful for live sites. Generally, you wouldn't display debug messages on a live site, but you might want to keep track of them in a file that's hidden from the eyes of site visitors.

Enabling Logging

By enabling error logging, you gain an easy way to keep track of all debug messages on your site. This can give you an exact debug message and the date/time the error occurred. Error log messages are saved in a `debug.log` file within the WordPress install's `wp-content` directory by default.

To enable error logging, you need to edit your WordPress install's `wp-config.php` file as you did in the debugging section. You turned `WP_DEBUG` mode on in that section. Now, you need to turn on `WP_DEBUG_LOG` by adding the following code to the file.

```
define( 'WP_DEBUG_LOG', true );
```

The debugging section of your `wp-config.php` file would now look like this:

```
define( 'WP_DEBUG', true );
define( 'WP_DEBUG_LOG', true );
```

What these two lines do is tell WordPress that you want to enable debugging and that debug messages should be saved in an error log file.

You can also optionally disable the display of debug messages on the site and save them only in the debug file. This is a useful technique if you want to keep track of debug messages on a live site rather than a development install. To do this, you need to add two new lines to your `wp-config.php` file.

```
define( 'WP_DEBUG_DISPLAY', false );
ini_set( 'display_errors', 0 );
```

Setting Log File Location

When error logging is enabled, WordPress creates a `debug.log` error log file in the `wp-content` folder. In most situations, this location and filename will work fine. However, if you want to change it to something else, you have the option to do so.

After enabling error logging, you may optionally add the following line to change the path and filename.

```
ini_set( 'error_log', '/example/example.com/wp-content/logs/debug.log' );
```

This tells WordPress that you want your debug log to be in a logs folder. One important thing to note is that you need to use the correct directory path here rather than a URI path.

Understanding the Log File

The `debug.log` file created by enabling error logging can be read with any basic text editor, so you shouldn't have any trouble opening it and reading its contents.

In the "Debugging" section, you created an error plugin. You also learned how to correct debug messages displayed on the screen. The error log file is another way to view those debug messages, and the messages saved in the log file will look much the same as what you saw onscreen. Following is a view of a log file that the error plugin you created would produce when first using it.

```
[27-Oct-2010 16:07:37] PHP Notice:  Undefined variable: post in
    C:\xampplite\htdocs\wp-content\plugins\boj-error-plugin.php on line 18

[27-Oct-2010 16:07:37] PHP Notice:  Trying to get property of non-object in
    C:\xampplite\htdocs\wp-content\plugins\boj-error-plugin.php on line 18

[27-Oct-2010 16:07:37] PHP Notice:  Undefined variable: author_box in
    C:\xampplite\htdocs\wp-content\plugins\boj-error-plugin.php on line 34
```

As you can see, each message creates a new line (or entry) within the file. The message looks nearly the same as what you looked at in the "Debugging" section. The only exception here is that you have an exact time and date of when the issue occurred.

After reading through your error log messages, you need to revisit the "Debugging" section to work through the issues. One thing about the error log is that messages aren't cleared from the file after you've fixed the issue on the site. Notice the timestamp as you clear away issues so that you're not looking for issues you've already fixed.

CACHING

Caching is a way to store data for later use. People use many different types of caching and different methods to cache data on their sites. You would typically save data that's expensive to generate so that it can be loaded quickly whenever it's needed. It's a way to optimize page load times.

Rather than focusing on building in caching within individual plugins, WordPress provides a method for plugins to handle caching. WordPress has the WordPress Object Cache feature, which is a PHP class that plugins can use for storing data. WordPress doesn't store this data on its own. It provides a way for caching plugins to cache the data. This method allows for different caching solutions based on user needs.

Two great benefits exist for using WordPress' built-in method for caching.

➤ There's a single set of functions that all plugins can use without conflicting with other plugins.

➤ Caching plugins can be created to handle persistent caching, which saves data across multiple page views.

Using the WordPress Object Cache will not speed up your plugins directly. By default, cached data is saved only for the web page view it is executed on. For example, you could store data once and use it multiple times on a single page without having to execute the same code. When using a persistent-caching plugin, this data can be stored and accessed across multiple page views.

The biggest reason to use this system is that it enables your plugin users to choose the caching method that benefits them the most or works with their server setup the best. WordPress simply provides the needed functions as an all-encompassing API that multiple plugins can use.

 In Chapter 7, "Plugin Settings," you learned how transients work. Transients are a way to ensure that data is cached for a specific amount of time. However, if a user has installed a persistent-caching plugin, transients will be served using the WordPress Object Cache.

Saving, Loading, and Deleting Cached Data

WordPress provides several easy-to-use PHP functions for working within the caching system. Each function enables you to save, update, load, or delete cached data. There are other cache-related functions than what's provided in this chapter; however, the functions you'll learn are the functions you'll use the most often.

Each function uses at least one of the following parameters.

➤ $key — A unique ID to store and retrieve data by. The cache key doesn't need to be unique across multiple cache groups, but it must be unique within an individual group.

➤ $data — The data your plugin wants to save and retrieve.

➤ $group — A way to group multiple pieces of cached data. For example, multiple cache keys can be grouped together. This parameter is optional.

➤ $expire — How long the data should be stored in seconds. This parameter is optional and defaults to 0, allowing the data to be stored indefinitely.

wp_cache_add()

The `wp_cache_add()` function should be used when your plugin needs to store data to a cache key that doesn't already exist. If the cache key does exist, no data will be added.

```php
<?php
wp_cache_add( $key, $data, $group, $expire );
?>
```

wp_cache_replace()

The `wp_cache_replace()` function enables plugins to overwrite previously saved data for the cache key.

```php
<?php
wp_cache_replace( $key, $data, $group, $expire );
?>
```

wp_cache_set()

The `wp_cache_set()` function is a combination of the `wp_cache_add()` and `wp_cache_replace()` function. If the data for the cache key is not already saved, it will create it. If it does exist, it will overwrite the preexisting data.

```php
<?php
wp_cache_set( $key, $data, $group, $expire );
?>
```

wp_cache_get()

The `wp_cache_get()` function provides a way for plugins to load cached data by cache key and group. It returns `false` if no data is found. It returns the cached data if it exists.

```php
<?php
wp_cache_get( $key, $group );
?>
```

wp_cache_delete()

The `wp_cache_delete()` function clears cached data for the specified cache key and group. It returns `true` if the data was successfully removed and `false` if not.

```php
<?php
wp_cache_delete( $key, $group );
?>
```

Caching Data Within a Plugin

In this section, you create a simple plugin that caches a list of related posts to append to the content of single post views. Each blog post on the site stores its data with a unique cache key based on the post ID in a `boj_related_posts` cache group.

Use two of the caching functions for this simple exercise. Use the `wp_cache_set()` function to cache the related posts list and the `wp_cache_get()` function to get the cached posts.

Your new Cache Related Posts plugin has a filename of `boj-cache-related-posts.php`.

```php
<?php
/*
Plugin Name: Cache Related Posts
Plugin URI: http://example.com
Description: A related posts plugin that uses the object cache.
Version: 0.1
Author: WROX
Author URI: http://wrox.com
*/

/* Add related posts to the content. */
add_filter( 'the_content', 'boj_cache_related_posts' );

/* Appends a list of related posts on single post pages. */
function boj_cache_related_posts( $content ) {

    /* If not viewing a single post, return the content. */
    if ( !is_singular( 'post' ) )
        return $content;

    /* Get the current post ID. */
    $post_id = get_the_ID();

    /* Get cached data for the specific post. */
    $cache = wp_cache_get( $post_id, 'boj_related_posts' );

    /* If no data has been cached. */
    if ( empty( $cache ) ) {

        /* Get the post categories. */
        $categories = get_the_category();

        /* Get related posts by category. */
        $posts = get_posts(
            array(
                'category' => absint( $categories[0]->term_id ),
                'post__not_in' => array( $post_id ),
                'numberposts' => 5
            )
        );

        /* If posts are found. */
        if ( !empty( $posts ) ) {

            /* Create header and open unordered list. */
            $cache = '<h3>Related Posts</h3>';
            $cache .= '<ul>';

            /* Loop through each post, getting a link to its single post page. */
```

```
        foreach ( $posts as $post ) {
            $cache .= '<li><a href="' . get_permalink( $post->ID ) . '">' .
                get_the_title( $post->ID ) . '</a></li>';
        }

        /* Close the unordered list. */
        $cache .= '</ul>';

        /* Cache the related post list for 12 hours. */
        wp_cache_set( $post_id, $cache, 'boj_related_posts', 60 * 60 * 12 );
    }
}

/* If there's cached data, append it to the content. */
if ( !empty( $cache ) )
    $content .= $cache;

/* Return the content. */
return $content;
}

?>
```

Code snippet boj-cache-related-posts.php

The first cache function used in the plugin was `wp_cache_get()`. It checks if a list of related posts has been cached using the key of the current post's ID, `$post_id`. It also checks if this data has been stored in the `boj_related_posts` group. If the related posts are saved with that specific key and group, this list is appended to the content. It bypasses the need to regenerate the related posts list.

The `wp_cache_set()` function caches the related posts list for later. This enables the posts list to be retrieved with the `wp_cache_get()` function. It is used after the related posts list was created. The list was then saved based on the post's ID and the `boj_related_posts` group. You also set a 12-hour time limit on the cached data.

Basic caching functionality usually requires only two things, which this plugin does:

➤ Check if there's any cached data. If so, use that data and skip over the functionality required to generate it.

➤ If no cached data exists, generate and cache it. It can then be used later.

SUMMARY

Entire books could be written on debugging and optimization alone. The purpose of this chapter was not to cover every possible avenue you may take. The goal was to present you with a starting point to work from and to give you a look into the features that WordPress provides.

Some of the most important things you can do are keep updated, debug your plugins, and use the built-in cache system. Your plugins can use the most up-to-date functionality, be less prone to issues, and make users happy by working with their preferred caching solution. All these things require little time and can make your plugins better.

17

Marketing Your Plugin

WHAT'S IN THIS CHAPTER?

➤ Choosing a license for your plugin

➤ Submitting your plugin to the plugin repository

➤ Promoting your plugins

➤ Getting involved in the WordPress community

Some of the most popular WordPress plugins aren't necessarily the best-coded or most useful plugins. Sometimes they're simply more popular because the developer has a knack for great marketing. You may have the most solidly coded, optimized, and useful plugin in the world, but without a little marketing or some luck, no one will know your plugin exists. Having others recognize your work and put it to use is the ultimate goal.

Developers aren't known for their marketing skills. They're known for their ability to code useful things for sites, if they're known at all. Because the average user doesn't know the difference between a PHP variable and function, you're not going to wow them with how great your code is. Unfortunately, it's not that easy to promote a plugin. If it were, all great coders would be marketing experts.

As a plugin developer in the WordPress community, you need to play the role of developer and marketer. Don't worry. You don't need a marketing or communications degree to promote your plugin. Sure, it'll take some work, but the goal is to get people to use your plugins. The methods discussed in this chapter are simple things anyone passionate about their work can do.

Whatever your motivation for developing plugins is, whether it be money, popularity, or a desire to share something useful with others, this chapter can help put you on the path to making your plugins visible to the larger WordPress community.

CHOOSING A LICENSE FOR YOUR PLUGIN

WordPress isn't without its own licensing issues and debates. It's rare that a week goes by without a heated argument about licensing cropping up. The biggest issue has been about how plugins and themes should be licensed. Some clear lines have been drawn, and some not-so-clear lines, and developers are always looking for loopholes and workarounds to the license WordPress is under. You won't be presented with too much ideology here, though. This section is about choosing a license that benefits your plugin from a marketing angle.

WordPress is licensed under the GNU General Public License (GPL), which is an open source software license. This license is preserved and protected by the Free Software Foundation (FSF). WordPress is licensed under the GPL because its predecessor, b2/cafelog, was licensed under the GPL. WordPress is a fork of this software and must retain the software's original license.

The GPL is a license that protects users' freedoms. It grants users the power to copy, modify, and share the software so long as they pass along the same freedoms they've been granted by including the GPL in copies that they share with others. This is essentially the basis for any open source software. The idea is to protect the users' freedoms to take these actions.

Different Options

Most plugins will be licensed under the GPL. It's the easiest licensing choice and offers no conflicts with WordPress because WordPress is licensed under the GPL.

Although the GPL is the license generally used by most developers in the community, alternative options are available to you that do not conflict with the GPL or the ideals of open source software. These licenses are GPL-compatible licenses. If you choose to do so, you may license your plugin under one of these licenses.

The GNU site keeps a list of GPL-compatible licenses that you may use for your plugins: `http://www.gnu.org/licenses/license-list.html`. Some of the more popular licenses include:

➤ LGPL

➤ Apache

➤ MIT (X11)

➤ BSD

Although these are popular open-source licenses, you won't find many WordPress plugins licensed under them. Most will be licensed under a version of the GPL. However, you do have alternatives available to you that are non-GPL but compatible. You should also choose a license that best represents your plugin.

Plugins may also be dual- or split-licensed.

➤ **Dual** — Releasing the plugin under two licenses. Each of these licenses must be compatible and all the code in the plugin would fall under both licenses.

➤ **Split** — Separating different parts of the plugin under different licenses. Certain parts may be licensed differently than other parts. This is sometimes an option when including

JavaScript, CSS, or image files that don't require WordPress to be used. The FSF has stated that these files don't always require a GPL-compatible license.

All plugins submitted to the WordPress.org plugin repository (described later in this chapter) must be licensed completely under a GPL-compatible license. You cannot use any license that is not compatible with the GPL, even if it's legal to do so. This is simply the WordPress.org site's policy on plugin submission.

Why It Matters

WordPress has always been a piece of software that's representative of user freedom. WordPress wouldn't exist if the original software weren't licensed under the GPL, which enabled it to be forked into the software that it is today. The goal is to not restrict what users can do with the software when they receive it. It's about granting users freedom. They should be able to modify, copy, and share the software with others without restriction.

If you plan to create a plugin for WordPress and want to place additional restrictions on how your plugin or its code can be used, WordPress is likely not the best platform to develop on top of. The GPL license WordPress is placed under is meant to remove restrictions on how the user can use the software.

None of the authors of this book are legal professionals, so the purpose of this book is not to give you legal advice about licensing your plugin. However, if you decide to use a GPL-incompatible license, you may be setting yourself up for legal issues.

Aside from any legal implications, licensing your work under a GPL-incompatible license is one of the worst things you can do for good publicity for your work in the WordPress community. At best, your plugin won't be allowed within official channels. At worst, you and your work might be looked upon as outcasts within the community. Neither of these things is desirable when trying to market your plugin.

The biggest benefits of licensing your plugins under the GPL or a GPL-compatible license follow:

➤ **Protect users' freedoms** — Enables your users to edit, copy, and share changes with others without restrictions other than passing along those same freedoms.

➤ **Help developers learn** — Other developers can learn from your code if you allow it to be open, which allows them to improve upon and release more plugins to the community.

➤ **Improvement** — Keeping your code open means that others may use it for other purposes, which may allow them to find bugs or distribute improvements under the same license. You can then use this code to improve your own work.

➤ **Use others' code** — You're free to take, modify, and distribute other GPL-licensed code within your work. This enables you to build upon the work of others rather than coding everything from scratch.

➤ **Avoid legal issues** — Because WordPress is licensed under the GPL, you won't have any issues with the copyright holders.

➤ **Community acceptance** — GPL-licensed plugins enable your work to be accepted into the community.

Perhaps most important for marketing is the last point. To get your plugin work out there, it's best to be accepted by the community. If you want your work to be known, arguing licensing issues with the people who work on and improve WordPress every day is probably not the best route to take.

Even if you don't agree with the opinions of others, the WordPress philosophy, or the license, you should respect it. It's important that you not alienate yourself by not respecting the people who have contributed code to WordPress (the copyright holders).

Making Money While Using the GPL

WordPress and any work licensed under a GPL-compatible license are referred to as free software. The term "free" here refers to user *free*dom. It does not mean that your plugins cannot cost money. You can charge a fee for transferring the plugin to others or charge money for client work. You can even build an entire business around open source, free, code if you choose to go that route with your plugin work. You are not restricted from building a business on top of WordPress. Many developers have extremely successful businesses that align perfectly with the GPL license.

The license WordPress uses is about the distribution of code. One of the largest misconceptions about the GPL is that it's not good for client or private work. Many potential clients and businesses don't understand that this is not an issue. Because the license comes into effect only at the moment of distribution, the license of the work isn't relevant because you're not distributing it. You're not required to release work you do for clients under a GPL-compatible license. You can assure your clients that any work you do for them won't be released elsewhere.

 If you decide to publish your work under a GPL-incompatible license, it is your responsibility to seek professional legal advice rather than relying on the opinions of others or this book.

SUBMITTING TO WORDPRESS.ORG

WordPress.org is the central Web site for the WordPress software. This site hosts a plugin repository where thousands of plugins are available for download by millions of WordPress users. This is the place where most users download plugins, so having plugins on this repository opens up numerous possibilities for getting your work known by others.

All WordPress plugins on the repository are hosted at `http://wordpress.org/extend/plugins` as shown in Figure 17-1. This repository page lets WordPress users search for plugins; check out featured plugins; and browse through lists of the most popular, newest, and recently updated plugins.

FIGURE 17-1

The plugin repository handles many of the things you'd have to develop and maintain if you weren't using the plugin repository. If you're developing a publicly available plugin, there aren't many reasons to not use the official plugin repository.

Some of the benefits of hosting your plugin on the WordPress.org plugin repository include the following:

➤ **User trust** — Your work is on the "official" repository, so there's a level of trust from users that you'll earn just by hosting the plugin there. This is something that's harder to build by hosting your plugin on your own site or elsewhere.

➤ **Easy updates** — You don't have to build an update script within your plugins or force your users to manually update them. Users can update plugins with a few clicks from their admin panel.

➤ **Version control** — Plugins are placed in a Subversion repository, which makes updating your plugin easy. The plugin repository is updated every 15 minutes, so plugin updates go live quickly.

➤ **Stats** — You can view the number of times your plugin has been downloaded throughout its history and the percentage of users currently using each version.

➤ **Compatibility** — The repository enables users to click a Works/Doesn't Work button to let you know if each version of the plugin works with specific versions of WordPress.

➤ **Ratings** — Users can rate your plugins on a star-based rating system, which enables you to get a feel for how well your plugin is received by users.

➤ **Plugin information** — You can share all relevant information about your plugin for users directly on its page in the repository, which makes including instructions easy.

➤ **Forum integration** — All plugins on the repository are integrated with the support forums, so you can keep track of and answer support questions directly on the WordPress site.

➤ **Donation link** — You can provide a link so that users can donate money to you if they want.

Imagine having to handle all those things yourself. It would be a lot of extra work just to publish a plugin. Of course, you don't have to use the official repository to host your plugins. It's simply a great tool for plugin developers to get their work out to the public easily.

Your goals may not include releasing plugins for public use. Perhaps you're more interested in developing plugins for clients. You may be thinking that submitting work to the WordPress.org repository doesn't apply to you. To a degree, this is true. However, you should look at this as an opportunity to promote yourself or your company. One of the easiest ways to let others see the level of work you'll provide professionally is to release some work back to the public for free. It gets some examples of your work out there, which lets you start a portfolio and may result in future client work.

Creating an Account

Anyone with a user account at WordPress.org can submit plugins and use many other features of the Web site. Even if not hosting your plugins on the site, you'll want to have an account there. This can provide you with many useful tools.

Registering a new account is easy and takes only a few simple steps. After you set up a new account, you can submit plugins to the official repository.

1. Visit `http://wordpress.org/support/register.php`.

2. Enter your information into the required fields.

3. Check your email inbox for a confirmation email and password.

4. Follow any additional instructions provided in the email.

Submitting a Plugin

Before being allowed to host your plugin on the plugin repository, you must submit your plugin idea for approval. This process is painless, and plugins are typically approved within a few days, sometimes even within a few hours of submission.

As shown in Figure 17-2, you must submit a plugin name, description, and URL (optional) to `http://wordpress.org/extend/plugins/add`.

After you submit your plugin, your plugin gets a new page specifically for it on the repository at `http://wordpress.org/extend/plugins/plugin-name` where `plugin-name` is the plugin's folder name. This is the permanent link to your plugin on the repository, which is where users can read about and download the plugin.

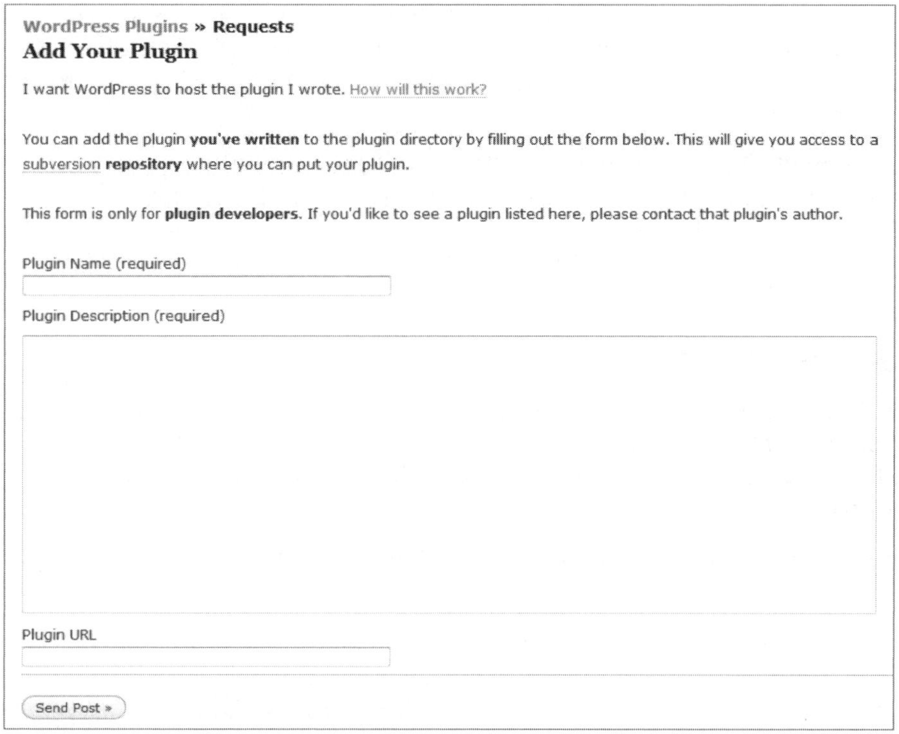

WordPress Plugins » **Requests**
Add Your Plugin

I want WordPress to host the plugin I wrote. How will this work?

You can add the plugin **you've written** to the plugin directory by filling out the form below. This will give you access to a subversion **repository** where you can put your plugin.

This form is only for **plugin developers**. If you'd like to see a plugin listed here, please contact that plugin's author.

Plugin Name (required)

Plugin Description (required)

Plugin URL

(Send Post »)

FIGURE 17-2

Setting Up SVN

All plugins on the WordPress plugin repository are hosted on a Subversion repository, which is a version control system. You need to learn how to use Subversion to add and update your plugin files on the plugin repository.

You can find a brief introduction to using Subversion on the site at http://wordpress.org/extend/plugins/about/svn, which should give you enough of an understanding of using Subversion for the repository. However, it's all done via the command line. Most plugin developers use a Subversion client to check out (get plugin files) or commit (add or update plugin files). Subversion clients provide easy-to-use interfaces for using Subversion.

Numerous Subversion clients are available for different operating systems. Two of the most popular Subversion clients for Windows and Mac are listed here, but you can experiment with other clients and find the tool that suits you best.

➤ **TortoiseSVN** (Windows) — http://tortoisesvn.net

➤ **Versions** (Mac) — http://www.versionsapp.com

The purpose of this section isn't to teach you how to use Subversion. There's a freely available Subversion book available online for learning how to use it at `http://svnbook.red-bean.com/nightly/en/index.html`. Learning at least the basics of Subversion is something you need to do to host your plugin on the repository.

All plugins on the repository are given a unique Subversion URL: `http://plugins.svn.wordpress.org/plugin-name`, where `plugin-name` is the name of the plugin folder. You will have access to that specific directory in the repository. To add and update files and folders with your preferred Subversion client, you need to use your WordPress.org username and password for authentication.

Creating a readme.txt File

Plugins on the WordPress plugin repository are required to have a `readme.txt` file included in the plugin's top-level directory. The repository loads information from this file to build the plugin's page in the repository. This is the information provided to the public, so you want it to be informative and useful for potential users.

The `readme.txt` file creates the sections for the plugin, as shown in Figure 17-3.

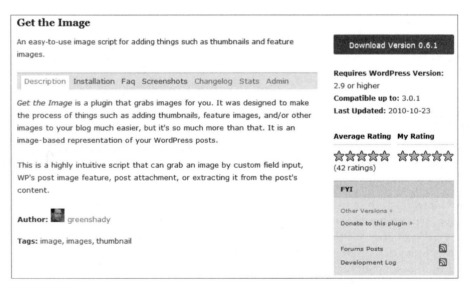

FIGURE 17-3

Your plugin's `readme.txt` file needs to be submitted using Markdown syntax. Markdown is a tool for converting text to HTML on the Web and uses specific markup. You can learn how to use the syntax on the Markdown project page at `http://daringfireball.net/projects/markdown/syntax`.

Following is an example `readme.txt` file for plugins, which you can modify for your plugins.

Available for download on Wrox.com

```
=== Example Plugin Name ===
Contributors: username
Donate link: http://example.com
Tags: example, example-2, example-3
Requires at least: 3.0
Tested up to: 3.1
Stable tag: 1.0

Write a short plugin description no longer than 150 characters.

== Description ==

Write a long description of the plugin. Shown on the main plugin page.

== Installation ==

Provide installation instructions for the plugin.

== Frequently Asked Questions ==

= Example question? =

An answer to the example question.

== Screenshots ==

1. Screenshot caption for screenshot-1.png.
2. Screenshot caption for screenshot-2.png.

== Changelog ==

= Version 1.0 =

* Change since previous version.
* Another change since previous version.
* One more change since previous version.

== Extra ==

Provide an extra section(s) if needed for your plugin.
```

Code snippet readme.txt

The most important section of the `readme.txt` file is the first section of the file, which is where you add your plugin information.

```
=== Example Plugin Name ===
Contributors: username
Donate link: http://example.com
Tags: example, example-2, example-3
```

```
Requires at least: 3.0
Tested up to: 3.1
Stable tag: 1.0
```

The first line should be your plugin's name. Each of the following lines have specific meanings that you need to make sure are correct.

➤ **Contributors** — Comma-separated list of WordPress.org usernames that should have access to update the plugin. If you're the only developer, only add your username. If you're working with others, each person needs a WordPress.org account to add their username.

➤ **Donate link** — A custom link you can provide for users to send you donations for your hard work on the plugin.

➤ **Tags** — Comma-separated list of tags that cover the functionality of your plugin. You can find a list of popular tags at `http://wordpress.org/extend/plugins/tags`.

➤ **Requires at least** — The minimum version of WordPress a user must have installed to use the plugin.

➤ **Tested up to** — The latest version of WordPress your plugin has been tested against.

➤ **Stable tag** — The version number for the most up-to-date and stable version of your plugin.

Other sections of the `readme.txt` file are less important than the first section but are vital to creating a great page for your plugin on the repository and getting users to download and use your plugin. These sections are also much more open to what you'd like to write and aren't as specific as the first section.

➤ **Description** — Perhaps the most useful section of the `readme.txt` file, the description section represents what's shown on the main page for your plugin. This is the section that you should use to grab a user's attention by describing your plugin, listing its features, and including any vital notes that a user must see.

➤ **Installation** — This section enables you to provide detailed installation instructions. Most users know how to install plugins, but documentation on any extra steps about setup (or even upgrading) can be provided here.

➤ **Frequently Asked Questions** — Whenever you start noticing the same questions asked about using the plugin, you can begin documenting those questions and the answers to them here. This can help cut back on potential support issues.

➤ **Screenshots** — Not all plugins have screenshots. However, if possible, it's always nice to give users something to look at to garner their interest. Screenshots must be included in the top-level directory of the plugin and numbered like this: `screenshot-1.png`, `screenshot-2.png`, and so on. (You can use `png`, `jpg`, `jpeg`, or `gif` images.)

➤ **Changelog** — This is a section to document what changes have been made to the plugin from version to version. Providing this information gives you and your users a clear history of version changes.

➤ **Extra** — You may also optionally include extra, arbitrary sections to your `readme.txt` file if your plugin requires any additional information.

GETTING YOUR PLUGIN RENOWNED

The difference between good developers and great developers sometimes comes down to one thing: passion. If you develop plugins or do work that you're not passionate about, that lack of passion will show through with your work and the promotion of your work. It's easy to be involved in the community and market your work if you're passionate about that work.

Sometimes passion isn't quite enough when starting. You can do certain things to promote your work. By reading through this section of the chapter, you can gain a base set of tools and methods for getting your plugins renowned. But, you need to *want* to promote your work.

You won't find quick fixes, tricks, or false promises in this section of the chapter. Everything presented here are methods and techniques that great plugin developers focus on almost every day — the things anyone can do by simply putting in the time.

Naming Your Plugin

Naming your plugin can be one of the toughest parts of the process to create a plugin. There are no definite rules to naming a plugin, but you can follow some general guidelines to choose a name.

A great plugin name can help your plugin in many ways when you start with developing plugins. If you, your company, or your work is not widely known, use this opportunity to create a great name to help put your work on the map.

Tips on Creating a Plugin Name

You should be mindful of four things when creating a solid plugin name. Your plugin name should be the following:

➤ **Relevant** — Be sure your plugin name is actually descriptive of what your plugin does.

➤ **Catchy** — Having a unique plugin name might catch users' eyes simply because it's unusual. Be careful when being catchy, though; relevancy is more important.

➤ **Simple** — Keep your plugin name short, simple, and easy to pronounce. You want your work to be shared. Don't make it too tough to spell.

➤ **Memorable** — The plugin name should be easy to remember. Don't put complicated words or phrases in the title.

The most important thing you can do is have a descriptive name. If you name your plugin something that's completely unrelated to the functionality of the plugin, users might not give it a second look, even if they're searching for the exact functionality your plugin provides.

Suppose you've built a plugin that integrates Twitter features into the comments field on a blog. Which of the following plugin names will more likely catch a user's attention and describe your plugin?

➤ Comment Form Tools

➤ Twitter Comments

➤ Awesome, Super-Cool Twitter Comments

Believe it or not, each of these plugin names has merit. It's up to you to decide which best fits your plugin and how you want to market it.

➤ **Comment Form Tools** — If you plan to extend the plugin in the future to include non-Twitter features, you might consider a more general name for the plugin.

➤ **Twitter Comments** — This name is short and descriptive. It's most likely the best choice of the three. You cannot go wrong with this choice.

➤ **Awesome, Super-Cool Twitter Comments** — This breaks the rule of keeping the name short, but it's catchy. Users might download this plugin for its unusual name alone.

How to Not Name Your Plugin

One of the worst things you can do when naming your plugin is to confuse potential users. Tons of WordPress plugins are out there, so you don't want your plugin's name to be too similar to another plugin's name. Before releasing your plugin, you should research similar plugins to make sure there are no potential naming conflicts.

You shouldn't use some words in your plugin name:

➤ **WordPress** — It's already a WordPress plugin, so there's no need to use "WordPress" in the name. You should probably avoid using "WP" as well.

➤ **Plugin** — There's no need to repeat that your plugin is a plugin, so this isn't helpful at all when naming a plugin.

➤ **Version** — You shouldn't add the plugin version information to the name. WordPress has a place for version numbers as described in Chapter 2, "Plugin Foundation."

➤ **Offensive Words** — This should seem like a no-brainer, but it's worth noting here. Don't alienate users by using potentially offensive words in your plugin name.

What words not to use in a plugin name usually just comes down to using a little forethought. Don't include things the user will already know or anything that might offend a user.

Branding Your Plugin

Generally, you wouldn't add your name or company name within the plugin title. As described in Chapter 2, there are relevant places to add this information to your plugin. However, it can be a useful branding technique that enables users to easily identify plugins made by you or your company. You can never underestimate the power of branding your plugins in this way. If your work is good (and it should be because you're reading this book), your company name can add an extra "gold label" to the plugin that's recognizable as quality work.

Suppose your company's name is Radioactive. A good way to brand your plugins is to prefix your plugin name with your company name. Following is a list of fictional plugin names that could be used to your advantage in terms of marketing.

➤ Radioactive Twitter Comments

➤ Radioactive Related Posts

➤ Radioactive Music Collection

➤ Radioactive Profile Widget

This technique also removes the possibility of user confusion when browsing plugins with similar names. It's doubtful that other developers will use "Radioactive" in their plugin names.

Building a Web Site

If you do not have a personal blog or Web site, you're missing out on one the easiest promotional methods available. Your site should also be running on WordPress. Yes, there are sites that provide WordPress work while running a different content management system. Running your site on something other than WordPress does little to help the legitimacy of your work. You can't expect users to trust that you're creating quality WordPress plugins if you're not using WordPress for your own site.

Creating a Page or Site for All Your Plugins

With your own site, you can create a page that showcases all your plugins. You'll be in control of how they're presented to the world from one central location. Some things you can do to present plugins on your plugins page include the following:

➤ Listing plugin names and descriptions with links to their individual plugin pages.

➤ Showing thumbnail images or screenshots from your plugins.

➤ Creating a catchy welcome/intro message on why using one of your plugins would be beneficial.

You can also set up an entire site dedicated to a single plugin or all your plugins. One of the best Web site examples you'll see dedicated to a plugin is the Gravity Forms site (`http://www.gravityforms.com`) as shown in Figure 17-4. The front page features eye-catching screenshots while providing useful information to the visitor.

FIGURE 17-4

Having a Great Design

Unfortunately, not all developers are great designers, but design plays an important role in marketing. You don't need to have a flashy design or the most creative design on the Web. Sometimes a simple design with relevant information can be better than anything flashy. Great designs never get in the way and enable the site's content to stand on its own.

If you don't have a single design bone in your body, you may consider hiring a professional designer to design your Web site and plugin pages. You may trade some development work for design work. Hiring a designer within the WordPress community may even earn you a friend within the community who can help promote your work. You should always look for ways to form relationships with others within the community.

Blogging About WordPress

You don't need to build a site just for promoting your plugins. A great way to make your work more popular is by blogging about WordPress. There's no doubt that you'll come up with nifty code snippets and ideas while developing plugins. Sharing these things on your blog can help grow your user base. If you produce quality work on your blog, people will notice. This makes getting a foothold in the plugin world much easier. You're indirectly promoting your work by being helpful to others.

Even if you just want a break from code, you can run a WordPress-specific blog that doesn't share code tutorials. You can blog about current WordPress events and news, and hold thought-provoking discussions. The purpose of blogging about WordPress is to be involved in the community by sharing your ideas and knowledge. The WordPress community loves reading great blogs about WordPress. Creating your own WordPress blog can help promote your work.

Creating a Page for Your Plugin

You've covered how to set up a page for your plugin on the WordPress.org plugin repository. This is something useful for promoting your work. However, you're competing with thousands of other plugins on the repository. Your plugin can quickly become hidden in the sheer mass of available options, which can make it tough for users to find your plugin.

A dedicated page on your Web site for individual plugins can work wonders for your plugin marketing. The most important thing you can do when building a page on your Web site for a plugin is to keep the information presented relevant and descriptive of what functionality your plugin provides. This information needs to be easily accessible.

➤ Provide an accessible download link for your plugin. You'd be surprised how many developers create great plugin pages but forget the most important thing.

➤ Write a clear description of what your plugin does.

➤ Offer documentation and tutorials.

➤ Link to related WordPress documentation if helpful.

➤ Keep a dedicated changelog of the history of your plugin.

> ➤ Display screenshots of the plugin in action if possible.

> ➤ Link to the plugin's page on the WordPress.org plugin repository if your plugin is hosted there.

Announcing Your Plugin

Announcing your plugin is also one of the most important things you can do to let others know that you've built a new WordPress plugin. If you don't have a blog or Web site, you should. This should be the first place you announce your plugin. The people most likely to freely promote your work are your blog readers. Some of them will have their own blogs and will write a post to announce it. Others will post links to your plugin on social networking sites.

The first step to promoting a new plugin should always be announcing it on your blog. When announcing your plugin, you should stick to writing about the plugin. Throwing it in as an afterthought to a blog post about other things won't get it much attention. The post should be entirely dedicated to the plugin. This provides an opportunity for you to give readers a great description of what the plugin does and why they should use it.

Some other things you can do when announcing a plugin include the following:

> ➤ Get other WordPress blog writers to perform a review of the plugin.

> ➤ Announce its release on social networking sites, such as Twitter.

> ➤ Post its release on WordPress-specific forums and message boards.

 Announcing a new plugin on your blog is also a bit of an unspoken tradition in the WordPress community. Developers just do it because everyone else does, so it's an expectation for new plugins.

Supporting Your Plugins

Ideally, if your plugin is well coded and easy to use, you won't have to offer much support. However, there will always be users who can't quite get it to work, don't understand specific instructions, or want to customize something. Offering support for your plugins creates an opportunity for you to become more popular among users.

If you're building plugins professionally, you need to consider creating a dedicated support channel on your Web site. This can be a ticket system, support forums, or some other type of support system. You may even opt to offer commercial support. Email may work as a support system when you're just starting out, but after your work becomes more popular, emails can quickly become tough to manage.

If you're just releasing plugins for fun or noncommercially, running support from your own site may seem like overkill. All plugins added to the WordPress.org repository (described earlier in this chapter) are tied into the WordPress support forums (http://wordpress.org/support). You can use these forums to offer support for your plugins and not worry about running support from your site.

Following are several benefits to offering support for your plugins:

➤ Build a relationship with your users. These users might tell their friends or blog about your plugin.

➤ Find bugs with your plugins. No plugin will ever be perfect. Investigating user issues can help you find bugs.

➤ If building your own support system, you have control over the rules and can run support in a manner that fits best with how you want to run things.

Getting Feedback

Feedback from users and other developers is essential to creating great plugins. You're the developer of the plugin, so you probably know the code inside out and can use the plugin with no problems. Not everyone is looking at the plugin from your point of view, though. Feedback is a great way to see how others use your plugin.

Many support questions you encounter come down to a user not understanding how something works rather than a code issue. Listening to user feedback enables you to fix user experience issues that aren't easily seen by plugin developers.

Feedback is a large component in making WordPress a better platform. Following is a list of avenues users may take to give feedback to WordPress, which serve as great examples of how to handle feedback.

➤ **Ideas** (http://wordpress.org/extend/ideas) — A forum to present, discuss, and rate ideas for the core WordPress code.

➤ **Kvetch!** (http://wordpress.org/extend/kvetch) — Anonymous feedback system for users to praise or complain about WordPress.

➤ **Requests and Feedback** (http://wordpress.org/support/forum/requests-and-feed-back) — A forum dedicated to asking for feature requests and offering feedback.

➤ **Polls** — Public surveys and polls are sometimes published to enable users to vote on new ideas or features.

WordPress has a multimillion user base, so having an organized way to get feedback is crucial. Individual plugins don't generally have that many users, but a popular plugin can easily have thousands of users. If you build plugins on your own, feedback can become overwhelming without a dedicated system for keeping track of it.

You can receive feedback on your plugins in many ways.

➤ **Email** — Set up a contact form on your Web site so that users can directly email you with feedback.

➤ **Blog comments** — Allow users to post comments on your plugin announcement posts.

> ➤ **Ideas forum** — If you run your own support forums, create an extra forum just for new ideas and feedback.

> ➤ **Polls** — Periodically publish polls or surveys to gain user feedback. PollDaddy is a great service for setting up polls and tracking results: `http://polldaddy.com`.

> ➤ **Support** — As described in the section "Supporting Your Plugins," supporting your plugins can be beneficial. You should consider all support questions as feedback on how to improve your plugins.

Getting feedback is only part of the process. To improve your plugin and grow your user base, you need to act upon that feedback. Not all feedback and feature requests from users will be great ideas. You're still the developer and need to make that decision. Even if you don't use an idea presented by a user, you should still treat the idea and the user seriously. If necessary, explain why you decided not to go with a certain idea.

The biggest benefit of listening to and using feedback outside of improving your plugins is building a community. Building relationships with your users can benefit your work because your users are the people who will be promoting your plugins.

Getting Out of the Basement

Developers are stereotyped as guys living and working from their parents' basement or garage. Of course, you know not all code-savvy people are recluses. On the Web, shying away into the basement won't help getting your plugin renowned. Fortunately, the Web offers opportunities for anyone to be a social butterfly.

To be great at marketing your plugins, yourself, and your company, you need to be socially active in the WordPress community. This means getting involved in the development of WordPress, introducing yourself to other developers, chatting in community forums, commenting on other people's blogs, and just being active in any way you can find.

One of the worst things you can do is leave comments on other blogs such as, "Hey, check out my new plugin!!! It's the best plugin ever!!!" That's seen as the equivalent of spamming. Let your work be known by allowing people to get to know you and keeping your comments relevant. Most blogs have a comment form field where you can leave a link back to your Web site. Many blog owners will visit the sites of people who leave useful and relevant comments. This opens an opportunity for someone new to recognize your work and possibly even promote it.

Being socially active isn't just about self-promotion. You should enjoy being involved in the community. Find those sites and blogs that you feel comfortable being a part of. If you're not enjoying yourself, it won't take long for you to give up on the process.

Other Promotion Methods

As you can probably see at this point, promoting your work is less about promoting specific plugins and more about promoting yourself or your company. If you're creating a company, you need to focus on building that brand's image within the WordPress community. If you're a solo act, you are the brand, so your focus should be on letting other people get to know you.

Following is a list of additional routes you may take to promote your work.

➤ Write for other blogs about WordPress. If you're not well known within the community, ask WordPress-related sites if you can write some guest articles. Usually, these sites have an About the Author section at the end of the post with a link back to your site.

➤ Get involved with others via social networking sites such as Twitter and Facebook. Because you're likely to be a member of a social networking site anyway, don't let this opportunity go to waste. Befriend others within the WordPress community on these sites.

➤ Post on WordPress-related forums and message boards. Get to know other members at these places. A great message board for developers is WP Tavern: `http://wptavern.com/forum`.

➤ Spend some time offering your services for free to new WordPress users via the WordPress support forums: `http://wordpress.org/support`. This can enable you to take on new issues and gain some appreciation from users who are having trouble.

➤ Write patches and submit tickets for the core WordPress code at `http://core.trac.wordpress.org`. You'll become a better developer, and others will notice your work if it's good.

➤ Go to a WordCamp. WordCamps are one- or two-day local events held all over the world where people simply talk about WordPress, eat great food, and listen to presentations. You can find WordCamps on the WordCamp Web site: `http://wordcamp.org`.

Everything on that list is something simple you can do to make yourself both a better developer and enable you to get more involved in the community. These are things you'll likely do not just as a marketing tactic but as something you enjoy doing.

You don't have to do everything on the list. However, the more ways you can get yourself involved, the more opportunities you have for promoting your plugins.

SUMMARY

Although it would be nice if you could hire a marketing expert to help market your work, it's unnecessary. You don't need to be an expert in the field to promote your work. If you enjoy the work you're doing and think others might find the work useful, it's easy to promote it.

The most important thing you should learn from this chapter is that you need to be socially active within the WordPress community to promote your plugins. The WordPress community is a large and diverse group of people, so you have a massive audience to promote your plugins to. Remember that you shouldn't be involved only to promote your plugins. You should be involved because you enjoy being a part of the community. By doing this, your work can promote itself.

18

The Developer Toolbox

WHAT'S IN THIS CHAPTER?

➤ Using the WordPress core as a reference

➤ Understanding inline documentation

➤ Exploring popular core files and functions

➤ Using community resources and Web sites

➤ Learning about external tool Web sites

➤ Creating a developer toolbox

When developing plugins for WordPress, you must have a good list of resources to help guide you in the right direction. This list of resources is the developer's toolbox. In this chapter you cover the most popular and helpful resources available for plugin development. You also review tools that every developer should use to help optimize the process of plugin development.

CORE AS REFERENCE

The best reference when developing plugins for WordPress is the core WordPress code. What better way to learn functions, and discover new functions, than to explore the code that powers every plugin you develop. Understanding how to navigate through the core WordPress code is a valuable resource when developing professional plugins. Also, contrary to online resources and the Codex, the core is always up to date.

Inline Documentation

Many of the core WordPress files feature inline documentation. This documentation, in the form of a code comment, gives specific details on how functions and code work. All inline documentation is formatted using the PHPDoc standard for PHP commenting. The following comment sample is the standard PHPDoc template for documenting a WordPress function:

```
/**
 * Short Description
 *
 * Long Description
 *
 * @package WordPress
 * @since version
 *
 * @param    type    $varname    Description
 * @return   type                Description
 */
```

Inline documentation is an invaluable resource when exploring functions in WordPress. The comment includes a short and long description, detailing the purpose of a specific function. It also features the WordPress version in which it was added. This helps determine what new functions are added in each release of WordPress.

Parameters are also listed, along with the data type of the parameter and a description of what the parameter should be. The return type and description are also listed. This helps you understand what value a specific function will return. For example, when creating a new post in WordPress, the newly created post ID would be returned if successful.

Now look at real inline documentation for the delete_option() function.

```
/**
 * Removes option by name. Prevents removal of protected WordPress options.
 *
 * @package WordPress
 * @subpackage Option
 * @since 1.2.0
 *
 * @uses do_action() Calls 'delete_option' hook before option is deleted.
 * @uses do_action() Calls 'deleted_option' and 'delete_option_$option' hooks on
 *     success.
 *
 * @param string $option Name of option to remove. Expected to not be SQL-escaped.
 * @return bool True, if option is successfully deleted. False on failure.
 */
function delete_option( $option ) {
```

The inline documentation features a clear description of the purpose of this function. You can see the function is part of the WordPress package and was added in version 1.2.0. The comment also lists any action hooks executed when calling this function, in this case the delete_option, deleted_option, and delete_option_$option action hooks.

The only parameter required for this function is $option, which is described as the option name. Finally, the return value is boolean; True if successful and False on failure.

Inline documentation is an ongoing process. All new functions added to WordPress are documented using this process. Helping to document existing functions is a great way to dive into core contributing to WordPress.

Finding Functions

Now that you understand how to use inline documentation to learn functions in WordPress, you need to know how to find those functions. To start make sure you have downloaded the latest version of WordPress to your local computer. You will be searching through these code files for functions.

Every core file, excluding images, can be viewed in a text editor program. When choosing a text editor to use, make sure it supports searching within files. You can find an extensive list of text editors on the Codex at http://codex.wordpress.org/Glossary#Text_editor.

When searching through the core WordPress files for a specific function, you need to make sure calls to that function are filtered out, or you may get hundreds of results. The easiest way to do this is include the word "function" at the start of your search. For example, to find wp_insert_post() simply search for "**function wp_insert_post.**"

Remember not everything in WordPress is a function. If you don't get any results, remove the word "function" from your search. Also remember to search all files (*.*) and not just .txt files, which many text editors default to.

Common Core Files

Many of the functions you use in your plugins are located in specific core files. Exploring these files is a great way to find new and exciting functions to use in your plugins.

The wp-includes folder features many of the files used for public side functions — that is, functions used on the public side of your Web site.

Formatting.php

The formatting.php file contains all WordPress API formatting functions, such as the following:

➤ esc_*() — Includes all escaping functions in this file

➤ is_email() — Verifies an email address is valid

➤ wp_strip_all_tags() — Strips all HTML tags, including script and style, from a string

Functions.php

The functions.php file contains the main WordPress API functions. Plugins, themes, and the WordPress core use these functions, for example:

➤ *_option() — Adds, updates, deletes, and retrieves options

➤ current_time() — Retrieves the current time based on the time zone set in WordPress

➤ `wp_nonce_*()` — Creates nonce values for forms and URLs

➤ `wp_upload_dir()` — Retrieves array containing the current upload directory's path and URL

Pluggable.php

The `pluggable.php` file contains core functions that you can redefine in a plugin. This file is full of useful functions for your plugins, for example:

➤ `get_userdata()` — Retrieves all user data from the specified user ID

➤ `get_currentuserinfo()` — Retrieves user data for the currently logged in user

➤ `get_avatar()` — Retrieves a user's avatar

➤ `wp_mail:` — Is the main function for sending email in WordPress

➤ `wp_redirect()` — Redirects to another page

➤ `wp_rand()` — Generates a random number

Plugin.php

The `plugin.php` file contains the WordPress Plugin API functions, such as the following:

➤ `add_action()` — Executes this hook at a defined point in the execution of WordPress

➤ `add_filter()` — Uses this hook to filter prior to saving in the database or displaying on the screen

➤ `plugin_dir_*()` — Functions to determine a plugin's path and URL

➤ `register_activation_hook()` — Is called when a plugin is activated

➤ `register_deactivation_hook()` — Is called when a plugin is deactivated

➤ `register_uninstall_hook()` — Is called when a plugin is uninstalled and `uninstall.php` does not exist in the plugin directory

Post.php

The `post.php` file contains the functions used for posts in WordPress, as follows:

➤ `wp_*_post()` — Functions for creating, updating, and deleting posts

➤ `get_posts()` — Returns a list of posts based on parameters specified

➤ `get_pages()` — Returns a list of pages based on parameters specified

➤ `*_post_meta()` — Functions to create, update, delete, and retrieve post meta data

➤ `register_post_type()` — Registers custom post types in WordPress

➤ `get_post_types()` — Retrieves a list of all registered post types

This is just a list of the more popular functions and their locations. Many more functions are available to use when developing your plugins. When a new version of WordPress is released, it's always fun to explore these files to see what functions have been added and are available for use in your plugins.

CODEX

One of the most important online resources for plugin development is the WordPress Codex. The Codex is an online wiki for WordPress documentation and is located at `http://codex.wordpress.org`.

The Codex is packed full of information about the use of, and developing with, WordPress. It includes an extensive function reference with some helpful tutorials and examples demonstrating the more common functions in WordPress.

Searching the Codex

You can search the Codex in a few different ways. The most common way is to use the Codex search located at `http://wordpress .org/search/` or by entering your search terms in the search box located in the header of WordPress.org. The default search for the Codex is documentation, but you can also search the Support Forums, WP.org Blogs, and the Bug Database, as shown in Figure 18-1.

FIGURE 18-1

The Codex also features an extensive glossary. This can help you become familiar with terms used in the Codex, as well as in WordPress. You can access the glossary at `http://codex.wordpress .org/Glossary`

The Codex home page also features an index of articles organized by topic. The articles are ordered by level of difficulty, with an article specific to the latest version of WordPress near the top. This article details new features, functions, changes, and so on in the latest version of WordPress. It's always helpful to read this article to become familiarized with any changes to functions and methods for developing plugins in WordPress.

Function Reference

As a plugin developer, the biggest benefit of the Codex is the function reference section located at `http://codex.wordpress.org/Function_Reference`. This section lists all functions in the Codex for the more popular WordPress API functions. This page is a must-bookmark for any WordPress plugin developer.

Each individual function reference page contains a description of the function, basic usage example, parameters required for the function, and also the return values. Think of these function reference pages as quick-and-easily-readable inline documentation on a function. Most function pages also feature an example, or more, demonstrating practical uses of that particular function.

The Codex is a great resource, but by no means is guaranteed to be accurate or up to date. Remember the WordPress core is the only resource that is always 100% up to date.

TOOL WEB SITES

Many different Web sites are available to help in researching and understanding specific functionality in WordPress. These sites can help as new versions of WordPress are released with new functionality that can be used in your plugins.

PHPXref

PHPXref is a cross-referencing documentation generator. Quite simply it is a developer tool that can scan a project directory and translate the files processed into readable cross-referenced HTML files. It automatically processes PHPDoc commenting to produce documentation for the functions included.

An online hosted version of PHPXref is also available, which is more specifically for WordPress. The online version is located at `http://phpxref.ftwr.co.uk/wordpress/`.

Visiting the WordPress PHPXref site, you'll be confronted with what looks like a Windows Explorer layout, as shown in Figure 18-2.

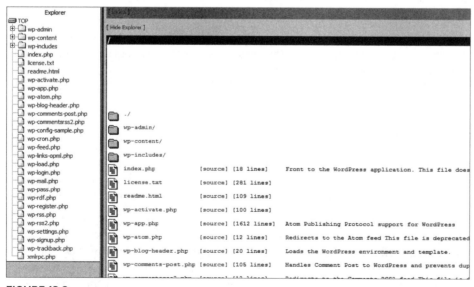

FIGURE 18-2

As you can see, the standard WordPress folder displays on the left with the core subdirectories and root files listed. As an example, click into the wp-includes directory and click the plugin.php file. Clicking this link brings up a summary view of the current file selected, in this case plugin.php. This summary view has useful information including a list of every function in the file, as shown in Figure 18-3.

Seeing a top-level glance of all functions in a WordPress core file is a great way to find new functions, and even locate existing functions for reference. Clicking any listed function takes you to the section of the page detailing the usage of the function. This information is extracted from the inline documentation saved in the WordPress core file. If the function is not documented in WordPress, this section will be empty. You can also easily view the source of any file by clicking the Source View link near the header of the page.

It's easy to see how useful the WordPress PHPXref site is for a developer. This is another required tool to add to your resource arsenal.

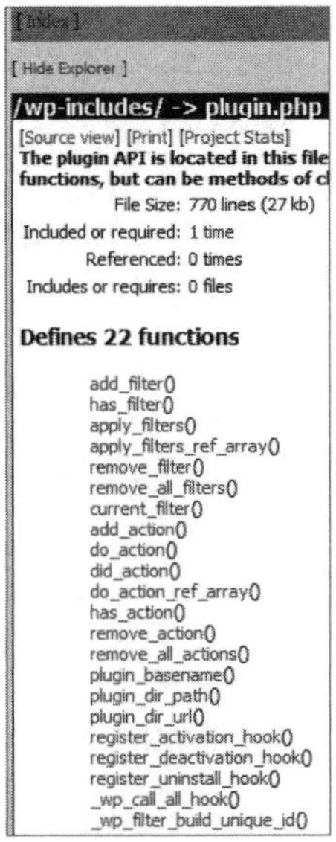

FIGURE 18-3

Hooks Database

The WordPress hooks database, which was created and is supported by Adam Brown, is the essential resource for discovering hooks in WordPress. Adam built a system that digs through all WordPress core files and extracts every action and filter hook that exists in WordPress. He has been indexing these values since WordPress 1.2.1 and updates the hooks database with each new major version of WordPress.

One of the best features of the hooks database is you can view all new hooks added in each version of WordPress. As a plugin developer, hooks are one of the most powerful features that you can use when creating plugins in WordPress. Clicking any hook name produces a hook detail screen showing where the hook is defined in the WordPress core code.

To visit the hooks database visit http://adambrown.info/p/wp_hooks.

COMMUNITY RESOURCES

There are also many different community resources available to help with WordPress development. These resources can help you expand your knowledge on plugin development, troubleshoot plugin issues, and work with new features in WordPress.

Support Forums

WordPress.org features a large support forum for topics ranging from using WordPress to plugin development. You can visit the support forums at http://wordpress.org/support/.

As a plugin developer, multiple forum sections can help expand your knowledge on plugin development, and support any public plugins you have released. Following are the forum sections specific to plugins:

➤ `http://wordpress.org/support/forum/hacks` — Discussing plugin development, coding, and hacks.

➤ `http://wordpress.org/support/forum/wp-advanced` — Discussions are more advanced and complex than usual.

➤ `http://wordpress.org/support/forum/multisite` — Anything and everything regarding the Multisite feature.

➤ `http://wordpress.org/support/forum/plugins-and-hacks` — Plugin support questions. If you released a plugin to the Plugin Directory, users can submit support issues specific to your plugin.

Mailing Lists

The WordPress project has multiple mailing lists set up for discussions on various topics. These mailing lists can be a quick-and-easy way to get some feedback and advice from other developers in the community. The mailing list works as a two-way conversation. You would send a problem or question to the list, and a member of the list responds with the answer. All emails sent to the list are also archived for later reading.

The mailing list geared toward plugin developers is the Hackers mailing list. This list is a place for advanced discussions about extending WordPress.

➤ **Email:** `wp-hackers@lists.automattic.com`

➤ **Join:** `http://lists.automattic.com/mailman/listinfo/wp-hackers`

➤ **Archive:** `http://lists.automattic.com/pipermail/wp-hackers/`

Another potentially useful mailing list is the Trac list. Trac is the open source bug tracking software used to track development of the WordPress core. This can be useful to see what new features are implemented in the latest version of WordPress. This is a high-traffic email list.

➤ **Email:** `wp-trac@lists.automattic.com`

➤ **Join:** `http://lists.automattic.com/mailman/listinfo/wp-trac`

➤ **Archive:** `http://lists.automattic.com/pipermail/wp-trac/`

WordPress Chat

Often it's nice to have a live conversation when seeking help for plugins or about WordPress development. WordPress uses IRC for live chat and has a few active chat rooms. To join the WordPress chat, you need an IRC client (`http://codex.wordpress.org/IRC#IRC_Client_Applications`) installed on your computer. All WordPress chat channels are located on the Freenode server at `irc.freenode.net`.

➤ **#wordpress** — The main room for WordPress. Room conversations can vary from basic WordPress usage to advanced plugin development. Many of the core WordPress developers and contributors are in this room and willing to help you.

➤ **#wordpress-dev** — This chat room is dedicated to the discussion of WordPress core development. This room is not for general WordPress discussions, but rather specific to core development or bugs and issues found within the core.

These chat rooms are an awesome resource for real-time help when developing plugins in WordPress. Many WordPress experts hang out in these rooms and enjoy helping others learn WordPress.

For more information on WordPress chat, including how to download an IRC client and connect to Freenode, visit `http://codex.wordpress.org/IRC`.

WordPress Development Updates

When developing plugins, and releasing to the public, you need to stay current on new features and functionality coming in the new version of WordPress. This can help you verify not only if your plugin is compatible with the latest version, but also what new features your plugins can take advantage of. One of the best ways to track WordPress development is through the WordPress Development Updates site located at `http://wpdevel.wordpress.com/`.

The development updates site uses the popular P2 theme, which is a Twitter-like theme for WordPress. You can also find out about the weekly developer chats that take place in the IRC channel #wordpress-dev. These chats discuss the current status of the upcoming WordPress version, feature debates and discussions, and much more.

WordPress Ideas

WordPress.org features an ideas section for creating and rating ideas for future versions of WordPress. This is actually a great resource for gathering ideas for plugins. Many of the ideas submitted could be created using a plugin. The more popular an idea is, the more popular the plugin would most likely be.

The WordPress Ideas area is located at `http://wordpress.org/extend/ideas/`.

Community News Sites

There are some great Web sites that focus on WordPress developer related news and articles. Many of these sites feature development-focused tutorials and tips that can be used when creating your plugins. The following sections explore useful community news sites that are available.

WordPress Planet

WordPress Planet is a blog post aggregator located on WordPress.org. This includes posts from WordPress core contributors and active community members. This news feed is also featured on the dashboard of every WordPress-powered site by default.

WordPress Planet is located at `http://planet.wordpress.org/`.

Planet WordPress

Not to be confused with WordPress Planet, Planet WordPress is a news aggregator site run by our own Ozh Richard. This Web site aggregates blog posts from plugin and core developers and provides them in a single feed. This makes it easy to track WordPress news and topics in a single source.

Planet WordPress is located at `http://planetwordpress.planetozh.com/`.

WPEngineer.com

WPEngineer is a great resource for plugin developers. The site features in-depth tutorials, tips and tricks, news, and more. Many of the articles dive into code examples demonstrating how to achieve a specific result in WordPress. Plugin developers will enjoy the more technical nature of this Web site.

You can visit the Web site at `http://wpengineer.com/`.

WeblogToolsCollection.com

WebLog Tools Collection (WLTC) is a news site focusing on blogging topics, although it generally leans toward WordPress-specific articles. WLTC features a weekly new Plugin and Theme release post, which is a great way to gain instant exposure for your new plugin. WLTC has also hosted the annual WordPress Plugin Competition, giving away cash and prizes to the winning plugins as decided by a panel of expert judges (including Ozh!).

You can visit WLTC at `http://weblogtoolscollection.com/`.

Twitter

Twitter is also a great resource for following WordPress developers, contributors, and the entire community. More specifically the Twitter account @wpdevel tracks every SVN commit made to the WordPress core files. This is a quick and easy way to follow new developments with the latest version of WordPress.

Local Events

Another great resource are local WordPress events. When learning to create plugins in WordPress, it can help to find other enthusiastic developers near you to learn from and work with.

WordCamps are locally organized conferences covering anything and everything WordPress. Many WordCamps feature plugin-development-specific presentations given by some of the top plugin developers in the community. These presentations are a great way to learn new and advanced techniques to use in your plugins. To find a WordCamp near you, visit `http://central .wordcamp.org/`.

WordPress Meetups are also a great way to meet local developers in your area. Meetups generally happen more often, typically on a monthly basis, and are a local gathering of WordPress enthusiasts. Meetups are also generally smaller, more focused groups allowing for more in-depth and personal conversations to take place. To find a local WordPress Meetup, visit `http://wordpress .meetup.com/`

TOOLS

When developing plugins for WordPress, you want to use specific tools to make your life much easier.

Browser

WordPress is web software; therefore, you will spend much of your time debugging plugins in your browser. Some browsers stand above the rest when it comes to developer features. The two more popular development browsers are Firefox and Google Chrome. Both of these browsers feature development tools, and can be expanded with additional tools, to make debugging and troubleshooting much easier.

Firefox features probably the most popular development add-on: FireBug, which adds advanced development tools to Firefox enabling you to easily edit, debug, and monitor HTML, CSS, and even JavaScript. FireBug also supports add-ons enabling you to extend the features in FireBug. One popular FireBug add-on is YSlow, which analyses your Web site to determine why you might have slow load times. You can download FireBug for Firefox at `http://getfirebug.com/`.

Google Chrome is also a great development browser. Chrome features a built-in set of Developer Tools. These tools can enable you to edit and debug HTML, CSS, and JavaScript in real-time. You can also install extensions in Chrome that add additional functionality to the browser. You can download Google Chrome at `http://www.google.com/chrome`.

Editor

Creating plugins for WordPress is as simple as creating a PHP file. PHP files are actually text files with a .php extension. Because of this you can develop PHP files using any basic text editor. Although text editors can certainly get the job done, they won't offer the more advanced features such as syntax highlighting, function lookup, spell check, and so on.

NetBeans IDE

NetBeans IDE is a popular editor that is an open-source development environment that runs on Java. Because of this, it can run on any platform that supports the Java Virtual Machine including Windows, Mac OS, Linux, and Solaris. NetBeans supports PHP with syntax highlighting, PHP debugging using Xdebug, remote and local project development, and many more features. For more information and to download NetBeans, visit `http://netbeans.org/`.

Notepad++

Notepad++ is a popular open-source text editor that runs on Windows, Mac OS, and Linux. The editor is a lightweight text editor, similar to standard Notepad, but offers many features including syntax highlighting, macros and plugins, auto-completion, regular expression find and replace, and more. To download Notepad++, visit `http://notepad-plus-plus.org/`.

TextMate

TextMate is a GUI text editor for Mac OS X. It's a popular editor among developers because it features some programming-centric features. Some of these features include nested scopes, bundles (snippet, macro, and command groupings), project management and more. You can download TextMate at http://macromates.com/.

Coda

Coda is another Mac editor with a focus on web development features. This is not only an editor, but also features file transfer and SVN support. Coda's goal is to be the only program you need when doing web development. You can visit Coda's official site at http://www.panic.com/coda/.

Deploying Files with FTP, SFTP, and SSH

When developing plugins you need to decide whether you plan to run a local instance of WordPress on your computer or use an external web server. If using an external server, you need to use some method to push your files to your server. The most popular method is using FTP.

FTP, or File Transfer Protocol, is a standard network protocol used to copy files from your computer to another computer, or a web server in this case. For FTP, FileZilla is a free, open-source FTP client that works on Windows, Mac, and Linux. You can learn more about FileZilla and can download the client at http://filezilla-project.org/.

SFTP, or Secure File Transfer Protocol, is also a popular method for deploying files to a server. The major different between FTP and SFTP is that SFTP is encrypted. This means any account info, usernames, passwords, and files you transfer are sent over an encrypted transport. Many popular FTP clients, including FileZilla, also support SFTP.

SSH, or Secure Shell, is a third option for transferring files to a web server. SSH is more than just a way to transfer files. For example, you can interact with MySQL using SSH. A popular SSH client is PuTTY, which runs on Windows and UNIX platforms and can be found at http://www.putty .org/. Mac users can use the built-in shell called Terminal when working with SSH.

phpMyAdmin

On occasion you may need to directly work with the WordPress database. The most common method to do this is by using phpMyAdmin, which is a free tool, written in PHP, which provides a simple web interface to view and manage a MySQL database. Most web hosts have this tool installed by default.

Using phpMyAdmin you can easily view what data your plugin adds to WordPress tables. This can significantly help speed up the debug process. You can also run phpMyAdmin on your computer by downloading the software package at http://www.phpmyadmin.net/home_page/downloads.php.

 MySQL can also be administered through SSH; however, SSH is a command-line interface and a bit more advanced than using the web interface of phpMyAdmin.

SUMMARY

As a plugin developer you need a solid set of tools in your developer toolbox. Every developer's toolbox is unique and customized to your tastes and server setup. Becoming comfortable with your developer tools can help you be comfortable when creating professional plugins in WordPress. If you don't have a set of preferred tools, you should ask around and see what other developers use. It's always fun to talk with other programmers to see what tools they use and recommend.

When developing, news and community Web sites are just as important as your tools. These sites can help you expand your knowledge on plugin development, learn about new features and proper usage of those features, and become a part of the greatest community on the web: The WordPress Community. Code on!

INDEX